Striking a Balance

Addendum

The jacket photograph of
New York City Ballet principal dancers
Heather Watts and Bart Cook
is by Steven Caras.

Striking a Balance

Dancers Talk About Dancing

Barbara Newman

Houghton Mifflin Company   Boston   1982

Library of Congress Cataloging in Publication Data
Main entry under title:

Striking a balance.

  Includes index.
  1. Ballet dancers—Biography—Addresses, essays,
lectures. 2. Ballet dancing—Addresses, essays, lectures.
I. Newman, Barbara.
GV1785.A1S72   792.8'2'0922 [B]   81-13184
ISBN 0-395-31325-2   AACR2
ISBN 0-395-32194-8 pbk.

Printed in the United States of America

V 10 9 8 7 6 5 4 3 2 1

Acknowledgments

First and last, I am indebted to the dancers who so generously shared their time and thoughts with me. As no expression of my gratitude would be adequate, I simply offer them my thanks. For cheerful and patient assistance, I am grateful as well to the staff of the Dance Collection of the Library and Museum of the Performing Arts, Lincoln Center; Mary Clarke, *The Dancing Times*; Sarah C. Woodcock, Theatre Museum, Victoria and Albert Museum; Sue Merrett and Janet Judd, Press Office, Royal Opera House, Covent Garden; Boris Skidelsky and Francesca Franchi, Archives, Royal Opera House, Covent Garden; Ulf Esser, Press Office, Stuttgart Ballet; Helen Atlas, *Dance News*. I must also extend my appreciation to Keith Money, Leslie Spatt, and the many photographers who granted me access to their work and per-mission to reproduce it, and to Lord and Lady Crathorne for their gracious hospitality in London.

I could never have completed this book without the support of Jonathan Galassi, John Russell, and Robert Cornfield; the continued efforts of my transcribers, Dennis Pearlstein and Liza Altman; and the advice, guidance, and constant encouragement of Frank Haynes, Carol Inouye, Don McDonagh, and Nancy Reynolds. I thank them all.

For Stephen

Contents

Interviews appear in the chronological sequence of the dancers' births.

Illustrations

Introduction

In the classroom, the kingdom of discipline, every dancer is the same: an anonymous instrument that wills itself to function on command in order to function ever more exactly. On the stage, however, every dancer is unique, and what most clearly distinguishes one from another is far more subtle and mysterious than the relative precision of their physical instruments. The essential distinctions lie beyond ability, in a dancer's personal history, professional education, age, repertory, teachers and mentors, models and idols and goals. Individual artistry flows from innumerable influences and an infinity of choices. It's surprisingly difficult to discover how any dancer makes those choices.

Trying to find out in libraries and performances, I found instead images of dancers, theories about them, opinions and speculation. Photographs show you what someone else saw. Reviews tell you what someone else thought of what he saw. Even sitting in the theatre, at no remove at all from the dancing, you only know what you can actually see. I wanted to know what each dancer intended me to see.

The execution of technique, whether in classroom combinations or formal choreography, is the only aspect of ballet that can be measured objectively — a dancer either is or is not in fifth position. But there is no measure or science, no absolute approach, to the process by which an instrument of accuracy transforms itself into a dancer and learns to transform steps into dance. That process differs subjectively from artist to artist. If you want to know anything about it, or anything about the choices any given dancer has made and why, you must go straight to that dancer and ask. No one else can tell you, because no one else knows.

Of course, a subject like 'a dancer's choices' is so unwieldy in its breadth as to be virtually ridiculous. To avoid wasting the dancers' valuable time and my own exceptional opportunity, I focused each interview on a detailed discussion of a single role, hoping the role might serve as a channel for the dancer's thoughts. Although every Giselle dances the same steps in the same sequence to the same music, no two Giselles look the same or affect an audience the same way. What had shaped your approach to dancing when you arrived at *Giselle?* I could ask, and How did you choose to approach that ballet? What determined your identity as a dancer? How did you determine Giselle's? As the role would be the pivot of each discussion, I selected it myself, matching dancer to role according to the logic of history or my own experience.

Several of the dancers here had stopped performing before I ever saw a ballet, which made their choices about themselves and their art — and the interplay between the two — all the more intriguing to me. The fact that they survive and can, in their own words, fix those choices in their proper historical contexts, is precisely why I asked them to do so.

But I did see most of these dancers perform, often, and many of them molded my taste and established my standards. Others did too, and I eagerly invited them all to speak. Unfortunately, some declined, some never responded, several expressed genuine interest but could not find the time, and a few offered to dance for me, claiming they could only explore their dancing by doing it. I regret their absence and the loss of their discrete artistic insights, all of which I would happily have included.

I have intentionally chosen dancers whose combined careers span this century, and have tried to edit the interviews to preserve the substance and inflection of their speech. Time kills dance and memory and history. Words link the generations and bind the past to the present and the present to the future. Here's what the dancers said.

B.N.
New York
February 1981

Striking a Balance

Felia Doubrovska

Felia Doubrovska (b. St. Petersburg, Russia, 1896–d. New York, 1981) entered the Imperial Ballet School at the age of ten, graduated into the Imperial Ballet at the Maryinsky Theatre in 1913, and danced there for seven years before leaving Russia. Engaged by Serge Diaghilev in Paris for his Ballet Russe, she danced the Fairy of the Pine Woods in the company's 1921 pro-duction of The Sleeping Princess, *which was the first* Sleeping Beauty *staged outside Russia since the ballet's première in 1890. At the opening of the 1921 production, Doubrovska's husband of less than a year, Pierre Vla-dimiroff, danced Prince Charming to Olga Spessivtseva's Aurora. Doubrovska created leading roles in Bronislava Nijinska's* Les Noces *(1923),* Leonide Massine's *Ode (1928), and George Balanchine's* La Pastorale *(1925),* The Gods Go a-Begging *(1928), and* Apollon Musagète *(1928). She created the Siren in his* Prodigal Son *in 1929, during what proved to be the last season of the Ballet Russe. Ten years later, she retired from dancing following a season with the Metropolitan Opera Ballet; ten years after that, in 1949, she joined the faculty of Balanchine's School of American Ballet, where she taught for the next thirty years.*

The first time I saw Madame Doubrovska, she was sitting on a Broadway bus at eleven at night, chattering to her neighbor in Russian and brandishing a New York City Ballet program. I had no idea who she was. The next time I saw her, she was crossing the promenade at the New York State Theater with the slow, stately tread of royalty and the same undeclared confidence that a path would open before her, which it did.

"Who is that woman?" I asked a friend.

"Doubrovska."

"Who is it?" I asked again, amazed.

"It's Madame Doubrovska," she repeated. "Don't you recognize her?"

Impossible, I thought. Doubrovska lives in black-and-white photographs, in books, in history; she doesn't walk around on her own two feet — in sensible shoes — during intermissions. How wrong I was. Les Noces, Apollo, *and*

The Prodigal Son *are still danced today. And Doubrovska, the original Bride, the original Polyhymnia, the original Siren, lives a short walk from my home, a spirited survivor of a precious past.*

[Sadly, Madame Doubrovska died only weeks before these pages went to press.]

W hen I was seven, [Samuil] Andrianov — that's the husband of [Elizaveta] Gerdt, and a first dancer — saw me dancing around the Christmas tree and playing and said, "She will be a wonderful ballerina."

You know that in 1920 I went on skis out of Russia, with my mother, to Finland. And then I got very lucky. Our friend Maria Kouznetsova was in Paris. She was a very fine singer, and her husband, [George] Pozemkovsky, was a tenor from the Maryinsky. She had always come to the Maryinsky to see us dance. So she arranged that we do a little concert in Paris, at the Grand Théâtre des Champs-Elysées. She and Pozemkovsky would sing, Pierre and [Lubov] Egorova would dance together — *Spectre [de la Rose]*, and something I think from *Carnaval* — and I also would dance. I thought it would be nice to do the *Valse Bluette* of Drigo. I had seen it at the Maryinsky but had never danced it myself. I thought I probably knew it well enough to dance it. So we wrote to Drigo in Italy for the music, and he very kindly sent it to us. It was a lovely dance, very pretty. I remember that I danced with flowers in my hands, and then I threw them into the audience. Very pretty.

At first my name was only in the program, not up on the theatre anywhere. But then after a few days it was outside too, on the theatre. I don't know why this concert was such a success. We only gave a few performances, and then it was over. The newspaper reviews compared my dancing to Madame [Anna] Pavlova, very nice reviews. Well, somehow these newspapers got from Paris to Spain, where Mr. Diaghilev was then. And he read them and said, "Who is this youngest dancer in the company with such a success?" I was twenty-two, you see. So he asked Pierre, my husband, who had already danced in his company, to bring me to the Champs-Elysées for an audition.

I had never seen him before that day. Before I danced for him, he looked at me and said, "You will do for character parts." I said, "No. I am a classical dancer, not a character dancer. At the Maryinsky, I was soloist in classical parts." It didn't seem brave or not brave to answer him back. At home, in our country, you're sure about yourself; my family had position — I don't mean they were millionaires — but

2

a nice position, a normal life. And it was the truth about my dancing. My graduation performance, I danced Black Swan with [Anatole] Oboukhoff, and the last part I had done in Russia before leaving was Lilac Fairy.

But I never used to work hard. At school I was very lazy, and when the teacher didn't look, I didn't work hard at all. But once I had a role, then I worked very hard, for two or three weeks sometimes, on making that role just right. And when I was angry, I always danced hard, as if to say, 'Well, I'll show you what I can do.'

So then I danced for him. The first time was not so good; I was very nervous. He said not to worry, I should dance again, and the second time was much better. And he said, "I engage you for *Sleeping Beauty*." I remember watching his mustache move when he spoke. First I danced a fairy in the Prologue, and then later Bluebird.

Massine had left the Diaghilev company when I came there. After Massine was [Anton] Dolin, and [Serge] Lifar was not yet on the horizon. Dolin was very handsome then, when he was young, and he is also very handsome now with his white hair. He danced Bluebird with all of us, five ladies. Here is a picture of him with all the Bluebird ladies — [Alice] Nikitina, [Ludmilla] Schollar, [Vera] Savina, [Alexandra] Danilova, and me. Now, look. Savina was short, Schollar was fat, Danilova was fat — oh yes, then she was much heavier than I, much more legs. Sometimes she didn't stay on pointe because she was too fat. But you see that I was very small, my bones were very light, and so it was easy for Dolin to partner me. One day he said to Diaghilev, "Give me one girl, just one. I cannot dance with all these different people." So first it was Schollar, and then it was me.

Diaghilev was nice, very nice. I adored him. But he liked to tease. After Massine and Savina left the company and he divorced her, Diaghilev invited her back. That's why she was there as one of the Bluebirds then. It wasn't cruel; it was just him teasing. Then he invited Massine back too. That was when Massine made *Zéphire et Flore*. And Diaghilev said to Massine, "You can dance Bluebird with Savina." Now, on Saturday night, I had danced Bluebird with Dolin, and the next day was my day off. But when Savina was dancing with Massine, she cut herself on the jewels on his tunic when he was setting her down, and so I danced it that next day with Massine instead of her. On my day off! That was the only time I danced with him.

Diaghilev heard that Balanchine knew music very well and had come from our wonderful Conservatory in Russia. So he said to Balanchine, "I have in the cellar the score for [*Le Chant du*] *Rossignol*, by Stravinsky." And Balanchine said, "O.K. I'll try it." Diaghilev was amazed. He said, "You're not afraid to try Stravinsky?" He knew it was very difficult music, very strange. But Balanchine said, "I'll do it. No big deal." So that was the first ballet he did for Diaghilev. For that he used [Alicia] Markova as the little bird, the Rossignol, in a great big cage. She was just a tiny child. And I played Death, coming to the cage for the bird. I remember my make-up was done by a very great painter, Henri Matisse, who did also the costumes.

It was a wonderful ballet, very Oriental. Balanchine did so well that Nijinska, who was already choreographer, started to become jealous. Diaghilev was most astonished at the way Balanchine accepted the music. So he said to him, "Do another ballet, this one for Doubrovska and Lifar." That was *Pastorale*. Maybe it did not have such a big success because of the Auric music, but it was very amusing. I had to flirt with the little boy — this was Lifar — who has a wife. One day it was [Tamara] Geva and the next day Danilova, but I am playing the Star, like a movie star, who is much more interesting to him than his wife.

That was the first ballet Balanchine ever made for me. Look, here I have a photograph. That is Serge kneeling there, and you see what he is doing? Turning me en promenade arabesque and holding only my straight knee. It is exactly the same thing in *Serenade*, this arabesque and being turned at the knee, only you see that in this I am wearing a short skirt. I had to hold my back very carefully to do this. It was very hard, and everyone could see me very clearly because there was no long skirt to hide in.

Before the Revolution, Diaghilev had borrowed dancers from the Maryinsky, which was always closed for the summer months. When the company came together after the war, [Vera] Nemtchinova was the first ballerina, and Nikitina was there later. She was not very strong technically and not very pretty, but she had a small head, nice neck, and lovely arms and legs; and when she danced, she had personality and elegance. Diaghilev had Balanchine make *La Chatte* for her, first for Spessivtseva and then for her when Olga was injured.

Everyone says that Nemtchinova taught her role in *Boutique* [*Fantasque*] to Danilova. It's not true; she had already left the company when Danilova began to dance it. In fact, Danilova began to dance that part *because* she was gone. *Boutique* was always opening the season, either with Massine or [Leon] Woizikowsky, and Danilova learned it from Woizikowsky. She was not a pure classical dancer anyway, more a demi-caractère dancer. When she danced *Boutique*, it was like a glass of champagne. Diaghilev was so happy that he said we didn't need Nemtchinova. Later she asked to come back, but he said, "Never."

4

Much earlier, I remember, one night there was a party *chez* Chanel, at her palace. Only the first artists were there, not the entire company as at many other parties. Diaghilev said to me, "Listen to this music very carefully." So I listened to some of it, and I said, "Why? I don't like this music. Why should I have to listen?" Diaghilev would only answer, "I suggest you listen." And do you know? It was Stravinsky, playing *Les Noces* on the piano. Diaghilev wanted me to pay attention because I was going to be the Bride.

It was so hard, the music, so complicated. For the first dance, where I'm wearing the long braids and the girls are all dancing around me, we had a little song that we used to sing to ourselves in our heads, over and over, just to keep the beat, to stay with the music: "*Che su, po che su / Natas'i nukosu.*" Yes, the same as the chorus sings then, but we had no chorus in rehearsals, and we sang to ourselves to stay on the right count.

After *Les Noces*, Nijinska did *Les Biches*. Spessivtseva was supposed to dance the Adagietto, but Diaghilev gave the role to Nemtchinova. It was her best, best, best role. Nijinska was older than the rest of us, but still she danced; she was the Hostess of the house. She wore a lot of pearls and was very grand, offering one hand and then the other.

Then Diaghilev gave me Nijinska's role. "She is not elegant enough. She doesn't like dancing it. You do it. You will be more elegant," he said. "Go to Coco Chanel. Ask all the models to pass, and choose the dress in which you will be able to dance." There was lots of dancing in that role, on pointe, cabrioles, bourrées. "All right," I said, "I will go. And who is going with me? Serge? Boris [Kochno]?" "Nobody. I trust you. But take a piece of color. It must be the same color."

So I went alone to Chanel, and when I got there, they said, "The models have already passed." "I'm from Diaghilev," I said. "Oh, he sent you. We'll have them pass again." So I chose a dress and took it back to the theatre. Diaghilev told me to put it on, to model it for him. I was slim then, the size of the mannequins. When I wore the dress in front of him, he said, "Not bad. You have good taste," and after that, I always wore that dress. [Lydia] Sokolova used to dance the role too, but not in my dress or in Nijinska's. I was the only one who wore the dress I had chosen. And Nijinska herself taught me that role. She used to like me as a dancer.

Apollo we rehearsed in England while we were traveling all over the country. I danced the role of the Muse of Silence [Polyhymnia]. You know the pose with the one knee bent to the side, the toe here, resting on pointe, and one hand on the knee? That was my pose, exactly for me, like when you put your name at the end of a letter. My signature.

The solo was very pleasant, very easy. I did it all with my finger at my lips until the very end, when there is a little outburst and then the finger is right away up again. Diaghilev generally didn't like too much emotion from a woman onstage, and if Diaghilev decided something, there was no discussion. One day, Boris called me to Diaghilev, who said to me, "Where do you dance?" "Here, for Diaghilev." "Do we agree that this is not a music-hall? Why do you do so much with your face, your eyes? You have to have more dignity." I always danced too much with my eyes. Many critics talked about my eyes generally. Maybe I didn't show very much emotion, but my eyes always spoke.

Danilova and I rotated in *Firebird* with Lifar. When Diaghilev asked me first to do it, I said, "No. I've seen pictures of [Tamara] Karsavina doing it, and now it's all different." I had two rehearsals with Karsavina herself. Others had either seen her do it or learned from [Serge] Grigoriev, who didn't know. He was *butaphor* — that is a person onstage who never danced, who fanned people or carried a tray.

Once in Paris, after Monte Carlo, Boris told me I was to dance this role. That was in 1928. Karsavina was a guest for this performance, in *Petrouchka*. We had three days of rehearsal, during which Karsavina and I shared a dressing room. I asked her, "Why are you not dancing *Firebird*? I never saw you do it. I would so like to see that." She answered, "I'm not in shape. I've had my baby and all." It's not so hard technically, but for eleven, twelve minutes it's nothing but jump, jump, reaching for the apple. She said it was too hard now and that even before, when she was in shape, it was hard. I understood that — it was hard for me too. That's why I didn't like to dance it except for the Berceuse; that was very beautiful and you got a rest. After the first solo and the adagio, it is all pleasure.

So this day, this program was *Firebird* first with Doubrovska, *Apollo* second, and then *Petrouchka,* put third because Karsavina was the guest. And Lifar was to dance the Blackamoor for the first time. It was an important day because Diaghilev had invited [Vaslav] Nijinsky to come to the theatre. We were all onstage before *Petrouchka* with Diaghilev and Nijinsky. Karsavina kissed Nijinsky and said, "I'm so glad to see you. Do you remember me? I'm Tamara. Do you remember this dress? We used to dance together." But there was no expression on his face. They picked me out in the Firebird costume and pushed me forward, but he gave no reaction. That was the last time I saw him, and I never saw him dance.

6

Except I do remember, when I was in school, we performed *Pavillon d'Armide*. Pavlova was lying on a couch, and six of us, little Negroes, came up from under the stage to fan her, like her slaves. Suddenly, in front of me, I saw a man jump from here, one side of the stage, to *here,* all the way on the other side. And then jump the same again! I was so amazed I dropped my fan on Pavlova's face. Of course it was Nijinsky. I had only heard his name then; I was maybe ten, maybe eleven.

Balanchine too had wonderful elevation, enormous, but he was not interested in being a dancer.

But here is something different. When the *maître de ballet* does something especially for you, he tries it this way, that way. Your body inspires him. Balanchine never prepared before the rehearsal except to listen to the music. It gave him all the ideas of what he was going to do. He showed the movement, then looked and . . . all right, that was all right. Then the next step he might change. But if it's made for you, you can do it — you can do anything. It fits you and so you're more confident. When you're a child, you are nervous, but it's a different nervosity from later. You think, 'They amuse themselves with watching me. I will show them.' When you're older, you're more serious with yourself, more exigent. You want to do your best. Sometimes I would move this way or another way, and Balanchine would say, "That's good. Keep it in."

Kochno wrote the story of *Prodigal Son* and had great influence on Diaghilev. Diaghilev generally didn't decide the dancers for a ballet himself. Of course he was the boss, but always he would call the composer, the choreographer, and the designers together, and they would discuss and he would listen to everybody's opinion. Then he would decide: "Yes, this I like. You are right. You are not right."

In this ballet, *Prodigal Son,* everything was new for me. All that acrobatic movement — all new. As for Lifar, oh yes, he did his part all right, but my role was to try to please him, to conquer him — but not the regular way. When a woman does a little coquetry with a man, she smiles, she turns, she does different things to attract him. I tried to do the Siren that way to begin with, teasing, flirting. But Diaghilev and Balanchine said, "No. Something is wrong. When you go to bed tonight, think to yourself about it. Think more seriously."

And then Balanchine said just the right thing, just the perfect word to make me understand. "You have to be a snake. A snake. You hypnotize him. You don't kill him, but . . ." Everything was in my eyes and in showing myself. Not one smile. You have to conquer him and bring him to his knees.

My opinion is that in *Prodigal Son* the legs are talking — Diana

7

Adams was very good at that, at making the legs talk — and because at that time I had lovely legs, Balanchine used that. One day in rehearsal, he asked me to lie down on the floor on my back, just flat, and to bend my knees and then slowly kick, one leg straight, then the other. Like this. And the next day, he said to hold myself up with my hands and make the kicking into slow walking, with my body very flat. You see? The end of the solo. He started me that way, on the floor, because he didn't want to scare me. Now he's changed, he wants everyone to learn very fast, but then he was very patient. He explained the music and one hundred things.

When we began, I was not frightened or embarrassed. I just enjoyed it. One day there was going to be a big party, but Balanchine said, "No, we stay and rehearse." Diaghilev came to watch with some artists of the ballet, and they laughed between themselves because I was so cute. I didn't yet understand the part. I did it twice, with the others laughing like that, and then I said, "I'm sorry. I'm not feeling well. I cannot continue the rehearsal." I took my coat and went home. "Mama," I said, "I'm out of the company." Because no one ever walked out like that on rehearsal. But this is very important, what happened. A letter came from the régisseur, Mr. Grigoriev, that said, "Come apologize to Mr. Balanchine." So I went to another rehearsal and said, "I did not mean to cut your rehearsal. I am very sorry to interrupt our work." And that was the end of it; no one ever mentioned it again.

One thing I remember, very difficult, was in the pas de deux. Lifar would pick me up under my arms and walk with me, while my arms were twisting out in front, not holding on to him at all. Now the Siren is kneeling on the stage for that.

It was all very serious, and I had a rather Oriental make-up that Balanchine did on me himself. He put it on me for every performance. The costume was velvet, wine red, but panels on the sides were painted even darker to make me look thinner. It never gave me any trouble, neither the cape or the headdress. All along, all through rehearsals, he said, "Try it" — this or that — and we did and it worked. Sometimes it seemed very amusing, almost silly. And we had an enormous success in Paris. It was very pleasant for me to dance this *Prodigal Son*. This ballet, and also *Apollo, Symphony in C,* and *Serenade,* will be here always.

The music? Well, in school of course we had studied music, but nothing as difficult as Stravinsky. But we must have learned something because this score, Prokofiev, seemed very easy.

Prodigal Son was made very fast. It was the last new ballet. After we performed it at Covent Garden, we had a great party. I was wearing a beautiful dress that Chanel gave me. People said to me, "How can you be so elegant after all that *acrobatisme?*" And that is how dancers are: dancers have to change all the time, one thing to another thing.

I remember that party because Diaghilev seemed so tired. Igor Markevitch was around him then, and I heard that Diaghilev wanted to make a little company for little experiments, and to keep the other, big one to make money. It was very sad that he was so tired. I remember him saying at the party, "I would like to go home."

Then, after that, Anna Pavlova was in Monte Carlo when we arrived there. My husband, Pierre, was there too; he had been dancing with her, and her company had just come from Egypt. Just as we were going up the stairs to the Hôtel de Paris, where Pavlova was giving a big party, someone called up to us and said, "Have you heard the news? Serge Diaghilev has passed away." Of course there was no party then. And here is something I thought was terrible. On the posters at the theatre in Monte Carlo it said, "Famous Dancer Diaghilev Passed Away." They called him a dancer.

I was not from the ballet family. I didn't know how you had to manage. I was in good, good shape, I had some good critiques, and I was starting to be known. And the year after Diaghilev died, we were supposed to have come to America; if that had happened, I would have begun to be known here. So I have some remorse. I went to Pavlova's company after Diaghilev died. Then, in America, I did *Orfeo* at the Metropolitan Opera Ballet with choreography by Boris Romanov, but I didn't do any publicity about it. I had no name, only the school behind me.

Now I love to teach, not only to be correct but to show what my teachers gave me. [Enrico] Cecchetti, [Michel] Fokine, [Eugenia] Sokolova, [Vera] Trefilova, [Nicolas] Legat — he gave wonderful combinations. [Olga] Preobrajenska and Egorova in Paris, [Klavdia] Kulichevska at the Maryinsky. From each of them I learned something different, and I want to give them to my students.

Cecchetti, for instance. His style was wrong; he taught everything posed, artificial, and we were all *allongé* dancers. But during the winter, everyone — Karsavina, Pavlova, and I too — went for two months to Italy to study with him because he gave us *la force,* strength. We had to start and finish every combination, no stopping in the middle. Whatever he gave in class, we had to do. We died, but we did. "Monsieur Cecchetti," we would say, "I'm tired." "I'm not tired," he would say back.

And Fokine. He was only one season teaching the girls in school, and then they put him with the boys' class. One day he came to me at the barre — I was standing in développé *à la seconde.* He took off my shoe and said, "Why are your toes so pointed, so curled together like that? They must be free, relaxed, so you can stand on pointe and still be able to jump." You see, if they are all curled tight, you cannot push to jump.

Sometimes the rule is always the same: when you do développé, you always turn your heel up. But everyone has different preparation for pirouette. Do it the way that is convenient for you, that is comfortable. We can correct children, but not ballerinas. I always say to the students, "Don't copy or imitate the teacher. Some have little mannerisms, and you will be learning those as well." You can learn something from every teacher, but you have to move naturally, not exaggerated, not artificial.

Here's a lesson: before you go onstage, never talk, never look at anybody. Think only of yourself, how you have to enter the stage and leave the stage graciously, without too much 'Thank you, thank you.' But especially don't talk to anyone. When you're young, you learn just to walk after you've finished dancing. Learn it when you're young, so it comes inside of you. When you're old, you don't have to think of it. If someone teaches you well to speak English or French, then you do it naturally.

When I teach, I tell the girls, "Here you have to do everything correctly. When you're onstage, you have to forget those class things. Know them already and just dance. Dance and enjoy it."

April 1979
New York

Anatole Vilzak

Anatole Vilzak (b. St. Petersburg, Russia, 1896) graduated from the Imperial Ballet School into the Maryinsky Theatre in 1915. He was awarded the rank of premier danseur three years later and performed the mainstays of the traditional, classical repertory — Swan Lake, Giselle, Sleeping Beauty, Le Corsaire *— often partnering such illustrious ballerinas as Olga Spessivtseva, Mathilde Kchessinska, and Ludmilla Schollar. He and Schollar were married and left Russia in 1921. Engaged by Serge Diaghilev the same year, he danced as premier danseur for the Ballet Russe until 1925 and, with his wife, also staged an abbreviated version of* Swan Lake *for that company. After the 1936–37 season at the Metropolitan Opera House, where he appeared as premier danseur with the resident company, the American Ballet Ensemble, Vilzak stopped dancing and devoted himself to teaching. This second distinguished career began in 1935 at the School of American Ballet. Between 1940 and 1946, he and Madame Schollar directed their own school in Steinway Hall; since 1965, he has taught at the San Francisco Ballet School.*

Certain questions expire with time. I wanted to talk to someone who, before joining Diaghilev's Ballet Russe, had already established a reputation in the classical repertory that is still danced today. The facts about the Ballet Russe are well known and often cited. What's less often remembered is that the three great Tchaikovsky ballets — Swan Lake, Sleeping Beauty, *and* Nutcracker *— were together the cornerstone of that repertory before Diaghilev ever arrived in Paris. I was lucky to find anyone at all whose knowledge and experience matched my curiosity point for point. I was privileged to find Anatole Vilzak, a premier danseur of tsarist Russia.*

I did Siegfried many times at the Maryinsky Theatre, with Spessivtseva and many other Maryinsky ballerinas. You know, I'm eighty-three, and the Maryinsky Theatre was a long time ago.

All my family was in the circus. In Petrograd, before even they changed that to Petersburg, there was a big circus, tremendous, the Ciselli circus. I was a small boy and I did everything. I did tumbling tricks and bounced the big ball on my head. And I played the violin a little and danced all the time. It was very easy. I did tap dancing too, but my brothers and sisters said, "You can't do that." I said, "Why? It's like America." But my brothers said, "You can't because you're white, and that's Negro dancing." "Oh," I told them, "that's no problem." And I immediately put something black on my face, and then I danced.

My whole family together was an act in the circus, three brothers and two sisters, and my other sister was on the horse. But my mother wanted to take me and put me in the *chaltrani*, the ballet school. For my brothers it was a tragedy, because it made everything change. We had done everything together, like teamwork. I liked the circus and I got a success there; when I did something, they would yell, "Bravo, bravo" and applaud. It was all her idea, my mother's. I understood nothing. She said, "Good-bye. Now you're going to school."

I was in the last class under the Tsar. I was fast in school because I wanted to do something. For fencing, for *maquillage* — that is make-up — for dance, for violin, for gymnastics, I was perfect number. Six was passing number; five and you stayed behind. I was twelve, the highest mark you could be. But in arithmetic, history, I wasn't so good. I didn't like them. In fact, I should have graduated two years before I did, but I stayed behind because of these subjects.

We all studied music at the school. Two times a week someone from the orchestra would come to teach us, either piano or violin, and I studied violin. It was very good because, later, Madame Schollar played piano and I the violin. And in school, Balanchine played piano very well and I played my violin. We did it together; it was teamwork. Balanchine was younger — he graduated after me, after the Revolution — but I stayed behind my class, so we met by luck. Much later, when I saw Balanchine in Washington, I said to him, "George, why didn't we make a record? Maybe you don't need the money, but I need the money. We would be rich. We'd ask five dollars and everyone would buy it." But we didn't, because there was no machine.

I was only nineteen when we finished school. And I have to say I was lucky, because Mikhail Mikhailovitch Fokine liked me. And I liked him. Mikhail Mikhailovitch had a company in the Maryinsky Theatre. It was very special. Sometimes he would sit down in rehearsal and look to see who was all right, who was not — in some ballets, some of the girls and boys were not so good. For special ballets, small ballets like *Eros* or *Les Sylphides,* he would always pick the dancers from looking in the classroom, and then that little group would perform. There was a rank in the classes, and he couldn't always take who he wanted. "I want this girl because she's good." "No. You can't take her. Impossible." And then he couldn't. But he always liked me.

I do remember *Eros,* in which I was fiancé to this girl. The girl was Mathilde Krassinskaya [Kchessinska]. Behind us there was beautiful décor, French style — window, big door, window. And when I would say good-bye to her, I would kiss her hands and give her a very small angel, like a doll. Mikhail Mikhailovitch picked me, just for that.

The first year after I graduated from the school, I was in the corps de ballet, in *Swan Lake* and other things too. So I began to see them from the stage and learn them a little bit. And then step by step, I was premier. You had to be two years, three, in the company. But I studied, studied, studied, looking at every ballet from behind, from the wings. There were ballets with many students from the school, and always we would be looking from the wings. Afterwards, we'd discuss — "That's good. That's not good. She did something wrong." — and sometimes we'd fight about it. That's very important, to look.

That way I saw [Samuil] Andrianov, a very nice man, as Siegfried. And [Pierre] Vladimiroff did it very well; I liked him in it very much. And of course I took from them for myself, my own performance. That's like a chain.

Who taught it to me was [Alexander] Monakhov. That was my teacher. In school, we had special lessons with Monakhov three times a week. We studied how to make action, mime, how to say 'I like you.' And he would always say, "Please, don't do too much. If you say, 'I like you,' that's enough. Don't do all this, rocking back and forth with the hands somewhere over the heart. It's too much. And you must put up your shoulders, like you're holding her to you, so it's real. First 'I like you' with the hands coming together, and then 'I like you better,' the shoulders up."

Monakhov made the Prince natural for me. Monakhov did so many things for us, for me especially. He liked me. He taught us how to walk when you are a prince, when you have a sword hanging on your side — you cannot walk any way you want with a sword. He would bring things from the theatre and from the *butaphoria,* the props, everything that belongs to the ballets, so you could practice using them, the chair or sword or hat. Like in *Three Musketeers,* with the big hat, it's very important how you take it off your head and bow.

You have to curve your hand around the brim of a big hat. You can't just snatch at it, like a cap — that's for country boys. This is a big hat, with plumes. You must be perfect in everything.

You know, I saw an English company on television, and their mime is not so good at all. He would say, 'You are so beautiful' and would go this way, with the back of his hand wiping around the face. That's nothing. It looks like you've got something wrong with your tooth. It's no good. It should be the palm of your hand, just gliding over the surface of your face. Not open and flat, but relaxed. Not touching it; just all around the face, and then your fingers touch your lips like a kiss, like a sigh coming from you, to say, 'So beautiful.' It's all changed now from what we used to do. What I saw on TV, I turned my head away. It was impossible. Sometimes they put their hands together here on the chest, on the right, on the left, in the middle, up, down. They look for the heart; where is the heart?

And there should be more expression, because mime is very important for ballet. Like in *Giselle*, first act, Albrecht must say to Hilarion three times, 'Please go away. Go somewhere else.' Now, he should start with the finger, just pointing, very small. And the second time, more insistent; and then angry, impatient, bigger. You stamp your foot into the ground; it's like saying, 'That's an order.' More each time, not three times pointing the same weak finger.

So Monakhov rehearsed us, taught the mime. And for the steps was another teacher, Andrianov, who had done the role before. Always there's a more experienced dancer to show you. And always — for example, when you finish dancing pas de deux for a moment — Monakhov would come, together with Andrianov, and they would say, "No, that's not good. You must not be too far from each other." Both together. Teamwork.

Spessivtseva was my partner all the time, for *Swan Lake* and other ballets too. And again I was very happy, because I liked her. She was perfect, so beautiful and delicate. If you had pas de deux with her, you had to hold her very carefully. You couldn't ignore something like that.

Now, once in the school ... Behind the big school we had a little theatre, and the students, both boys and girls, would give performances there. [Klavdia] Kulichevska was always there. She was ballerina from Maryinsky Theatre, and she would come and watch. At one rehearsal, we were so nervous and so excited because it was the first time we could meet the girls. If you like someone, some girl, always you want to do something. But we had no permission. We were always separated from them, always. In the building, the boys were upstairs on the third floor and the girls downstairs below us, on the second floor. We never took any classes with the girls except ballroom dancing, only that, once a week. That's not enough. We had no adagio class with them, no partnering, never, in the school.

So at this performance, with the girls for the first time, we would run behind the scenery — we were so nervous — and there I met Spessivtseva. Every boy from our school, every boy, liked her because she was so beautiful. Beautiful like blue heavens. So behind the scenery is not the first time I ever met her, but the first time nobody saw us. We were not allowed to speak anywhere, not allowed to touch — impossible — because the discipline was very severe. And now, Spessivtseva came to me and said, "Tola?" I am Anatole, so she said, "Tola," like a nickname. I said, "What, Olga?" And she didn't say anything else, but kissed me, on the forehead, and immediately ran away. It was the first time a girl had kissed me. I looked quickly around to make sure that nobody saw, and then I didn't know what to do. I wanted to find a mirror because maybe I was all red in the face, or pale, and my breath was stopped. I couldn't speak. I couldn't move. Then I was only dancing very little things with her, but when I began to do Siegfried, I did it always with her.

I didn't decide that she would be my partner. There was a ballet master, like Andrianov, and there was [Nicholas] Sergeyev, our régisseur. But Sergeyev was very strange because when he watched the rehearsal, he would always stay on the bench, snapping his fingers and saying, "Do it. Do it. You don't know it." He would ask me, "Why don't you know it?" and I would say, "Nobody showed me." "But you don't know it," he would repeat. He would call someone and say, "Would you please show this boy what to do." Always somebody else to show, but not himself.

Before Olga and I ever performed *Swan Lake,* we had many rehearsals. Olga and I together. We rehearsed with the full company after — when you are ready, yes, general rehearsal — but first with her. Private rehearsals for a long time, with Andrianov, Sergeyev — but he was not so important — and Monakhov, and Vladimiroff came also. Vladimiroff finished school four years before me, so he could come and make suggestions.

Like me, Olga had never danced this ballet before. She graduated in the same class with me, and we went along together very quickly. We had many tiny details to learn over and over. One of them watching would say, "No, that's not right. You must go there. You must have more expression. That's no good. Again from beginning. Again. Again." And we go again and again. "And now, relax."

And I always think twice before I even relax, because I don't want to do a mistake. I want to dance it right. So even when I'm relaxing, I'm thinking about it. That's not really relaxing for me. And then we start again.

After we were ready and we'd asked all our questions, then there was general rehearsal, on the stage. And then you had to put on the costumes. The ballerina — Madame Schollar, Spessivtseva, [Yelena] Lukom — always had tutus to rehearse, because when you wear a tunic, it's completely different. Different for the girl to dance in and also for me, for the partner. It should be like in performance, so you can learn the choreography, the different positions.

So we rehearsed finally on the stage but without orchestra. Orchestra had played it maybe a thousand times, or maybe it was money. I don't know why. We had piano and violin, and also we had *chef d'orchestre.* The stage is, of course, very big, but the space for us is not different from rehearsals. In the school, there is a tremendous big studio, the same size as for the ballet on the stage, because it's important to learn the amount of space you will have. When you jump, you must know.

That was the first time I danced a full-length ballet at Maryinsky. I had been onstage with a partner before, but in little things in the ballets; no one wanted to do them — they were silly. You were behind everyone, maybe with four pair of others. There was nothing — you did maybe jump, jump, entrechat, tour.

Listen to me. When you are in the Maryinsky Theatre and you want to dance a very important role, you must do everything, you must learn everything. You must turn, you must do perfect battu, you must jump, you must know how to support, how to do adagio, how to act, how to walk — you must do everything. Because you've got many, many rehearsals behind you, and then you are it. And after performance, Monakhov has been standing in the wings taking notes, and he says, "I will see you tomorrow." That means 'tomorrow, just privately.' He will say then, "You did something wrong." "No, that's impossible." "Yes, you did. I showed you to turn your back, and you just did this instead. That's no good. You did mistake, mistake, mistake. Don't forget next time." And then he watches again the next time, and takes down more notes, more mistakes. All the time they're watching.

The character of the Prince in *Swan Lake* is all in the choreography. But we learned that too from Andrianov, from Vladimiroff. Vladimiroff was more like my character. Andrianov was more quiet, not so much expression; Vladimiroff played the character bigger, more expressive, and I liked that. So I did it like he did, not quiet or calm like Andrianov. Sometimes the Prince should be quiet, but sometimes he is someone with more drama, more tragedy. You must become involved with that. Yet all the time, Monakhov controls everything, stops you, "No, that's too much. Just do enough, not too much." You go along with your own feelings, and he watches and controls.

When I learned *Swan Lake*, I also started to learn the other roles, the rest of the classical repertory. But we had only Wednesday night for ballet and Sunday, and the rest were all opera, changing all the time. Vladimiroff was dancing the role of Siegfried, and sometimes Andrianov, and I did exactly what they did, exactly the same. I made no changes of my own because I had no permission. Impossible. I did exactly what [Marius] Petipa and [Lev] Ivanov made together.

But here is one tiny change I did. I like *Corsaire* very much, but not the pas de deux. That is just all right, but *Corsaire* is big, big, full-length ballet, a beautiful ballet. And there are high jumps, all very big. I loved to do that. I did the role of Conrad, with Lukom. There are many scenes where you must show that you like Medora, Lukom's character, and you must kiss her, pretend to kiss her. I really *did* kiss her. Maybe I was cuckoo, maybe I ate too much, maybe it was because I liked her, Helen Lukom, that I kissed her. And after that, I had not such a good time with my wife. Because, you know, now make-up is made so you can kiss a thousand times and there will be no mark. But in my time, in Maryinsky, it was just all right, so when I kissed her, she was all covered with my make-up. My wife didn't like it; she said I kissed too much.

Lukom, Madame Schollar, and Lydia Lopokova were the same size. I am not so tall, and they were a good size for me, especially when you turn. On pointe, they were just perfect. Now, with Diaghilev company I did *Sleeping Beauty* with Lopokova, with Spessivtseva, and with Egorova, but Egorova was taller. I liked Lopokova very much, and she was a nice size. Here is a funny thing with Lopokova. This was in London, in *Sleeping Beauty,* where there are the supported pirouettes. Mostly we did two pirouettes — that was all right. And then sometimes, pushing her, helping her around, we did three. And Lopokova always said thank you to me. During performance, she would turn her head over her shoulder and whisper, "Thank you." And once I did with her four pirouettes, I helped her around in four, and I wondered to myself, 'What will be the result?' And she turned and said, "Thank you, thank you" — two times, for the two extra turns. And once we did five, and she said again, "Thank you, thank you," twice but no more. So after we finished, I said to her, "Lydia, you forgot to thank me. We did three extra and you said only two." So in a little voice, she said, "Thank you" again, for the third pirouette.

When Madame Schollar and I put on *Swan Lake* for Diaghilev, the company was not as big as in Petersburg but we put on exactly what we had danced there, the same, but only Act II and III. With Diaghilev, I danced it with Trefilova; she was also very good to dance with. Her size was good and she weighed only about one hundred pounds, so she was very fine.

Maryinsky company and private company, there's a big difference. Some of it was money. Sometimes M. Diaghilev asked Pierre, the father of Princess Grace's husband now, or other people, for money. Always he asked for money; without it, we could not do our big productions.

The original *Sleeping Beauty*, our Maryinsky production, was very big and very good, but now I see many changes. [Frederick] Ashton did very good changes with his *Sleeping Beauty*, but Ashton had seen it himself on the Diaghilev company. I know him very well, Ashton, because there was a little company, the company of Ida Rubinstein, and we were dancing there together at the same time. Then he was in the corps de ballet, and now he is a very good boy. What he did very well was the Turgenev, *A Month in the Country*. You know why it is very good? Because there is not too much movement but you understand every moment. The public will understand, and that's very important. That's the way I was taught to dance: you don't need big, melodramatic things, but you focus everything so it is clear.

Swan Lake is now very different all over. I don't like it so much. And *Giselle* . . . I did *Giselle* with Spessivtseva at the Maryinsky Theatre. At the end, she is lying on the stage. I pick her up, and I know where her grave is, so I carry her and I put her back in the grave, there again. And I feel so much frustration because she is gone; when I look, she is disappeared and only one flower is left. I run to the grave, but nobody's there. It was like that at Maryinsky. Now that's all gone. They change everything now. It's impossible.

Erik Bruhn did a *Swan Lake* himself in Canada. And in that production, did you see a swan? Did you see a lake? No. It's gone. Why? In Maryinsky production, you could see the swans and the lake before anybody comes out, and then Odette appears with the crown. That should be. That's so romantic, so beautiful. Why change that?

But here's what I want to tell you. Sometimes Bruhn and [Rudolf] Nureyev were in my class at the Chase company, yes, American Ballet Theatre. And it's a funny thing to say, but I don't like to have celebrities in my class. Because in my class I do everything as I wish, and I try to do very difficult movements. And they don't like it. They don't want to learn what they've learned too much already. They want everything slower, so I must hold myself. I do very simple — glissade, assemblé — very straightforward. For them, of course, in a rehearsal it's different, but in a class, one hour with the music, they don't want to do quite so much.

About Nureyev. He's a very, very good boy. I saw him twelve, fifteen years ago — he was perfect. Perfect jump. But at the end of Act I *Swan Lake*, I had no solo variation. The hunters are there, maybe we all go hunting together, and it should be in boots. Nureyev changed it there to like *Sylphides*: tights and slippers, not boots. In the first act, I didn't dance. Just the mime and the story, with my mother there and all my friends. I see the girls, the fiancées, and then in Act III I dance with them, each one a little bit. And my friend Benno was in Act II with me, but adagio I do alone with ballerina. But step by step, now everything changes.

I have taught this role to no one. Nobody asked me. They don't want to do the same thing. You know, when Svetlana [Beriosova] was in the Metropolitan Ballet company, she studied with us. Madame Schollar and I had a school in Steinway Hall. Svetlana was already a ballerina, and she always came to our class. And one day she said, "Mr. Vilzak, people from my company want to ask you how to mime. What to do. How to make the *gestes*. If you don't mind, would you show?" I said, "Yes, I will be glad to." And one day they came, three or four girls and some boys, and I gave a lesson. "When you hunt," I said, "you shouldn't do it very sharp, but more timid." And I said, "When you like someone, don't say too much, like a gypsy dancer shaking all over. It's important that the shoulders go up, like a breath." It was maybe three lessons, maybe a month, that's all.

I try even now to teach my students this kind of involvement. I try, but it's difficult. But I say, "Could you imagine that you like something a lot?" For a boyfriend it's too early, so I say, "Do you like ice cream?" And they say, "Yes, yes," and clap their hands. It's harder for them now because you have to think, you need imagination, you must reflect on what you're doing. Like, when you're afraid of something, it's a very important gesture to put your hands in front of you. You must push that thing away and pull yourself back from it. You can't just shrug and say, 'I'm afraid' without showing what's real. The way people really act, they stay back, they say, 'Don't touch me.'

You must go to the library, read, study, look even at pictures. They are very good for learning. You must know what you are going to represent in every ballet, know before you ever do it, maybe one year, maybe five or six months before. To dance, you must learn, you must think, you must have your opinion about something, your own opinion. And after, you ask, "Am I right?"

May 1979
San Francisco

Serge Lifar

Serge Lifar (b. Kiev, Russia, 1905) was sixteen years old when he began his ballet training with Bronislava Nijinska in Kiev. At eighteen he traveled to Paris to join Diaghilev's Ballet Russe where, in only two years, he advanced from the corps de ballet to the rank of premier danseur. He then created many roles for Leonide Massine and George Balanchine, most notably the title roles in the latter's Apollon Musagète *(1928) and* Le Fils Prodigue *(1929), and choreographed his first ballet,* Le Renard, *which received its première at the same performance as* Le Fils Prodigue. *Following Diaghilev's death and the disbanding of the Ballet Russe later in 1929, Lifar joined the Paris Opéra Ballet. Except for the years 1944–47, he remained there for the balance of his career, serving variously as premier danseur,* maître de ballet, *and company choreographer until 1958. He has also written volumes of memoirs, choreographic theory, ballet history, and biography.*

Once Madame Doubrovska had agreed to discuss her role in The Prodigal Son *with me, I couldn't resist the symmetry of asking Serge Lifar for his thoughts about his own dancing, particularly in that ballet. I remembered reading, in his colorful biography of Serge Diaghilev, of the intimate personal identification Lifar discovered between himself and the Prodigal Son just hours before he danced the role for the first time. I also remembered reading that Balanchine admired Lifar enormously in the role but had dismissed his emotion-laden identification with the character by saying "His performance would have been just as good, whether he ever discovered or not that the Prodigal Son was really him in disguise, because he had been given interesting steps to perform and had been rehearsed very carefully." How much of dancing is inspiration and how much is preparation seems always to be a matter of personal opinion. Lifar offered his to me in French. My thanks to Nancy Reynolds without whose superior fluency I could not have completed the interview.*

Nijinska accepted me at the dance academy of the Kiev Opera Conservatory on January 2, 1921. Until then, I knew nothing, either of dance or of the existence of such an art or of the glory of Anna Pavlova. I was from a bourgeois family. When I was eight years old, I began to study the piano and also the violin, which I hated. I felt imprisoned at the Conservatory.

When I was demobbed from the Red Army, I had youth but no religion, no training, no education. I don't know how I discovered dance, at eighteen, but I fell in love with it. I entered the studio exactly like one embarking on a first love affair, with shivers. I was struck by the order of it, which corresponded to the order in music. It was order amid the disorder of life — the barre, the neatness of petits battements to Chopin, thirty girls all together.

I studied for only one month with Nijinska, and I idolized her, loved her, and admired her. When she escaped to Vienna, I was abandoned. For two years I worked alone, on my own, and with the coaching of my friends, the better pupils; the students themselves became my teachers. I spent those two years before the mirror, where I found my own double. It was the birth of my self-discovery. I was in love with myself and yet distant; what I loved was not myself but that image in the mirror. The miracle of each artist is to see himself without seeing himself. The barre and the mirror are a whole world, both happiness and sadness. In the mirror was not a person like myself, but something that existed wholly in imagination. Because I had never experienced it before, I believed that I had discovered an artistic discipline that had never existed before.

Thus I discovered art, and I learned about it from books. By reading, I learned who Diaghilev was and that Nijinska was the sister of the great Nijinsky. Paul Valéry became my philosophical master with the words: *Chez moi, il est jamais la spéculation d'esprit* (For me, no spiritual speculation exists). I was entirely for myself, *moi pour moi.*

The telegram Nijinska sent to Kiev in 1922, asking for her students, was read to all of us — [Serge] Unger, [Jan] Hoyer, [Czestaw] Hoyer, and [Serge] Lapitsky. We all knew about Diaghilev by then. When we arrived in Paris, my friends told her that the fifth student she had requested couldn't come and that I had come instead. Why did she send for us? It's a long story, going back to *The Sleeping Princess* in London in 1921 — and incidentally, I now own Stravinsky's orchestration of Tchaikovsky's music, which was used for that production. Although history records it as a failure, *Sleeping Princess* was a great triumph. It ran for months without an empty seat, but then closed abruptly. Why? Well, after three months of the London engagement, one of the backers, [Calouste] Gulbenkian, arrived and fell madly in love with Olga Spessivtseva. He paid court to her lavishly and offered her any gift she wanted, anything. If she had asked for the crown jewels of Russia, he would have bought them for her from the King of England. And what did she ask for? A tutu. Just that. A tutu. He sent her a truckload, a whole truck full of tarlatan. But then he took a suite of rooms at the Savoy Hotel and asked Diaghilev to arrange a rendezvous. When Diaghilev refused, the money Gulbenkian had been providing for the company stopped immediately, and *The Sleeping Princess* had to close. Because of his debts, Diaghilev fled to Paris, but because many of the dancers remained in London, he needed more dancers. So Nijinska sent for her students.

So, on January 23, 1923, after hair-raising adventures, there arrived in Paris Lifar and four idiots. What we saw when we arrived was Dolin. Diaghilev was always looking for grace, and in addition to thinking Dolin beautiful, he also thought he was *sportif.*

I was the last person in the corps of *Noces.* And then, in 1924, I was sent to Turin for two months to study with Cecchetti in secret. When I returned, I was able to do triple tours en l'air and twelve pirouettes, which astonished everyone. I was criticized by the company because my fifth position on landing was not perfect, but I challenged them to do better, and no one else could do triple tours at all except [Stanislas] Idzikowsky.

Diaghilev had discovered me. One day he took me, like a little dog, to the home of Misia Sert, where I was introduced to Balanchine, Geva, Danilova, and [Nicholas] Efimov. Later I recommended to Diaghilev that they all be taken into the company. Meanwhile, Nijinska was furious with him for sending me, *her* pupil, to Cecchetti without her knowledge. It was a secret only because Diaghilev wanted to make my progress a surprise. And then, when he said to her that I would be another Nijinsky, she became still angrier. But in fact, I *did* replace Nijinsky. The masculine history of dancing is Nijinsky, Lifar, Nureyev, Baryshnikov.

Zéphire et Flore was my first big role and also my first important choreographic idea. I invented my role myself. Then I recomposed the role of the little boy in *Boutique Fantasque.* It was my first triumph and Massine loved me in it. And precisely as I had recommended Massine as a choreographer to Diaghilev, I now recommended my chum Balanchine as a choreographer. With *Barabau,* Balanchine became *my* choreographer. Diaghilev educated us both, taking us to museums, showing us sculpture and painting, all those Christs.

In 1927, Diaghilev was offered a contract to go to America that demanded both his presence and mine. But he was afraid of traveling on water and wouldn't go; he turned the contract down rather than go on water.

Also in 1927 was *La Chatte,* a greater triumph than *Spectre de la Rose.* In it, Spessivtseva was the greatest marvel since Pavlova. The ballet revolutionized stage décor with its mica settings. Balanchine created a new style of choreography because in Spessivtseva and me he had flexible instruments. He looked for certain qualities in the dancers, and we gave them to him. The instrument is the co-author of the ballet.

I danced with my legs and with my head. It was a very athletic role, full of poses and *plastique,* not at all classical. That ballet offered the first modern virtuosity; there was a corps of six men who moved like horses, and at the end of my variation, I lay on the stage like a mummy, stretched out stiff on my side and holding my head off the ground. Stravinsky saw *La Chatte* in a studio in Albemarle Street, and then he made *Apollo* for me.

Apollo was a divine success, the best and most artistic of the Ballets Russes creations and Diaghilev's favorite. He thought the score was pure musical expression, like Mozart, and the 'chariot' sequence was his idea. I found my first variation the most difficult, but Balanchine thinks I was the best Apollo ever. Today the ballet is all changed, but why modernize a masterpiece?

Creating that role was an absolute collaboration between Balanchine, myself, and Stravinsky, who was at the piano for our rehearsals. When Massine choreographed, he demonstrated, and you were obliged to copy him exactly. But Balanchine touched the dancers and worked things out with them — it was very easy.

I accepted the task of choreographing *Renard* without love, but Diaghilev wanted me to do it. The rehearsals for *Prodigal Son* were going very badly. Everyone was fighting with everyone else. There was a lawsuit between Kochno and Prokofiev about the authorship of the libretto. There was no collaboration between Diaghilev and Balanchine. Diaghilev selected the collaborators on his own, and no one had anything to say about his choices.

Diaghilev was having a very bad year. Many things were troubling him. He was irritated with his third 'Russian composer son,' Igor Markevitch. The first was Stravinsky, the second Prokofiev, and now he wanted to 'adopt' the third, Markevitch. Dolin had returned to the company, but had no success in *Le Bal,* which was an insignificant ballet anyway. Diaghilev was quarreling with Kochno, who had dared to sue Prokofiev. He even quarreled with me — I don't know why. I put acrobats in my ballet, *Renard,* but it wasn't going well at all.

Also, Diaghilev was not happy either with Balanchine, who wanted to make things for Pavlova, or with *Prodigal Son*. He thought it was too realistic — he didn't like the table being turned upright — and he was against realism. With Diaghilev, the choreographer followed orders, and now he even ordered changes in the steps. At this point he wanted to entrust the entire company to me, but I refused. The whole atmosphere was morbid and lugubrious. Diaghilev was in a macabre humor and occupied himself with lighting the stage.

I got drunk at the luncheon before the final dress rehearsal — Balanchine didn't attend the luncheon at all — and I was still drunk at the rehearsal. I only sketched the ballet with Doubrovska. It was the first time I had ever come to the theatre drunk, but I had a presentiment of drama.

Opening night, the choreography of my own ballet, *Renard,* expressed nothing to me. I was too troubled to take a bow, so I gave the bow to Stravinsky. But *Prodigal Son* was an expression of my soul. I played all the drama, and when the curtain fell, there was no applause, only crying. There was an interior force working when I danced the dramatic finale, something very special in my life.

That night, true dramatic ballet, realistic ballet, was born, and after Balanchine, choreographers were born. Although Diaghilev was against realism, at the end of the ballet he said to me, "You have taught me something."

In the Siren, Doubrovska had her greatest creation. At first I found my character very cold — certainly erotic, but not like it is today. The great duet is now pornographic, like [Maurice] Béjart; the legs are now much more entwined. The tendency today is to pornographize choreography, to make it vulgar, to invent sensual geometry. Then the ballet was pure but erotic, erotic not in the actual movements but in the line. In fact, there was not really very much choreography, just movement indicated by Balanchine but not yet wholly discovered. I did the steps and I added the drama, the soul, the atmosphere. When the Prodigal is left alone and must crawl back to his home, there is so much music and so little to do. To give the impression that you are always moving, and to fill up the music, I staggered my movements, a little forward, then a little backward over the same ground, then a little more forward.

Balanchine found the ballet while making it. He married himself to us. It was creation in improvisation. I interpreted it as I was, and I created it. After that, I abdicated the Ballet Russe for a new liberty and to begin life again, my life and the life of the dance.

May 1979
New York

Lew Christensen

Lew Christensen (b. Brigham City, Utah, 1908) received his ballet training in Utah from his uncle, Lars Christensen, and Stefano Mascagno; he studied in New York with Michel Fokine and at the School of American Ballet. In 1935, he abandoned both vaudeville and Broadway, where he had been dancing with his brother Harold, to join George Balanchine's American Ballet Ensemble, then the resident company at the Metropolitan Opera House. Having created principal roles in Balanchine's The Bat *(1936) and his* Orpheus and Eurydice *(1936), Christensen danced the title role in the first American production of* Apollon Musagète *(1937). He appeared as a principal dancer with Ballet Caravan, repeating his Apollo on its 1941 South American tour, and with Ballet Society, where he was also ballet master from the first performance in 1946 until 1948, when the company became the New York City Ballet. Although no longer dancing, he remained with the New York City Ballet as ballet master until 1952. That year he assumed his present position as director of the San Francisco Ballet, succeeding his brother Willam who had founded the company in 1937. Since 1936, when he choreographed* Encounter *for Ballet Caravan, Lew Christensen has written more than ninety works for the ballet, opera, and musical theatre, of which the ballets* Filling Station *(1938) and* Con Amore *(1953) may be the most widely known.*

In 1928, four Russians made history with a ballet about a Greek god. When the impresario Diaghilev united Balanchine and Stravinsky for the first time — their friendship and collaboration would last more than forty years and yield some twenty-six works — they created Apollon Musagète, *whose title role was first danced by Serge Lifar. Nine years later, a young American dancer in an even younger American ballet company inherited the role. He hadn't come from Russia via the fabled theatres of Paris, London, and Monte Carlo, but from Utah via vaudeville and musical comedy. A month before* Apollon Musagète *opened at the Metropolitan Opera House, Balanchine's steadfast American impresario, Lincoln Kirstein, described the dancer as "a young man who could be credited as a potential divinity." Balanchine simply told him, "You are a woodcutter, a swimmer, a football player, a god." The young man was Lew Christensen, who had set out to become a ballet dancer in America when American ballet barely existed. In the process of fulfilling his private goals, he accidentally became one of its pioneers.*

*A*pollo. That's quite a long time ago. 1937. You probably weren't even born then, I don't believe.

Actually, Harold and I always wanted to get into a ballet company. First we had to get into the business of vaudeville. It was hard to get into, and the Berkoffs got us in. Through their friends, we played all the circuits, all the towns you can think of. I remember one time we ended up in Moose Jaw, Canada, or someplace like that. And then we finally worked our way to New York, where we played the subway circuits. You know what they are? Well, there used to be theatres up and down Broadway, and up into the Bronx — you could make them all by subway — called the subway circuits: Fox, Loew's, RKO. We lived six months in New York and just played those, or we'd go over to New Jersey or anyplace the subway would go.

We were in my brother's ballet company at different times for well over eight years without making the break. We tried to get into the Opera at Chicago, but we didn't fool around with the Metropolitan. We just kept on doing vaudeville. Then we finally were picked for *The Great Waltz*. That left most of our mornings and afternoons free. So we could study. We studied with Fokine, Balanchine, whoever was at the schools in town, and there were damn good teachers. Balanchine was starting up, but at that time he hadn't gotten a formal company and he didn't have any money. But he became ballet master at the Metropolitan, and that's when we were invited, Harold and I, to join, about 1935.

For a while, we were rehearsing there and still dancing in *The Great Waltz*, which we despised, but it at least kept us in food and paid our rent. See, we couldn't leave until we had a job at American Ballet that could pay us — that's the shift. So we held on. We quit a bit before the company was organized to do a little vaudeville — nothing much — to keep going until finally the rehearsals at the Met started. Then we dropped vaudeville entirely. As a matter of fact, we burned the costumes and burned the music so we could never go back to it. We were going to do that or never do anything else. I remember going down to the basement, opening up the old furnace, and just saying, "Here they go! You can't go back! Whew!" Threw 'em in. That was the end of that. That's the only way to do it because, you know, you can always say, "Well, the company's not doing so well now. I can always go back and do vaudeville, set up some tours."

Forming a company, Balanchine actually had the hardest time with boys, so it was quite an opportunity for us. It's true you weren't paid much, but if you could just eat and keep the rent paid . . . The company was made up of the dancers who were around; a good many of them came from the [Catherine] Littlefield company. He got some pretty good trained boys, like Bill Dollar, and the rest were fairly well trained for what was demanded of them at that time. Harold and I were at least cultivated along that route. You see, in vaudeville you do all tricks. All the tricks you can think of, we'd put on the stage in about fifteen minutes, just cram them down their throats. But they were ballet, nothing else, just plain ballet steps, ballet movements. The Berkoffs tried to change that around with a little Russian dancing, but I was too tall — it hurt my knees — so we cut that out.

See, I started dancing when I was seventeen, and eight years after that was when I joined the American Ballet. I never really had any formal schooling; I wish I'd been ten or fifteen years younger and gotten into that. I'd learned technique and I'd worked with Fokine, who was quite a bit like Balanchine. I learned all the variations for all Fokine's ballets — not *all* his ballets, but as many as I could. I remember doing the male variations in *Les Sylphides* and also the girls' variations. You learned them all, coda, everything. He had a first-class way of teaching, and you could be an authority for carrying on his choreography by learning that way. Many dancers that I knew at that time knew all the parts, men's and female parts, just in the technique, so you knew how to reproduce them if you had to.

When you begin to learn Balanchine, for an outsider it's a very difficult technique, I don't know why. I just sort of fell into it. I did everything he wanted, and we did it and we did it and we did it so we got to what you'd call the Balanchine style. An outsider who was trained for many years in another school would have had a hard time, but I didn't know any other style. It became an easy style in the sense that you understood him. You understood the choreographer and you knew how he worked, rather than just saying, 'Well, I'll do this and do that' and coming out to do *Don Quixote* pas de deux. When you've been doing *Don Quixote* ballets and things like that, and then try to walk over and do *Symphony in C,* it won't work. You find you've got more feet and legs than you care to take care of. Balanchine's nothing like that at all. It's complete dancing.

What happened was . . . We were at the Met. That's where *The Bat* was put on to replace a lot of small operas. You worked there for six months and then you had six months off. Well, that six months off naturally disturbed a lot of people. So my brother Harold and I and a few of the dancers put together a little company which Kirstein sponsored — that was the Ballet Caravan — that was to take the place of the bad part of the year at the Met when we were off. There was no place else to dance, for one thing. If you wanted to dance, there was only one place you could go where you had a consistent company. Fokine put together a company for Lewisohn Stadium every summer; that took care of a couple of weeks, but what else was there to do? The following year we went back to the Met to dance, and that following summer we did some more Ballet Caravan. The third year we didn't go back to the Met; we stayed with Ballet Caravan. That kept another company going, you see. That went on until 1941 when we were invited to cover South America. So we put the repertoire of American Ballet and Ballet Caravan together, toured South America in 1941, and got home just in time for Pearl Harbor, about one month ahead of time.

I did *The Bat* at the Met, and Gluck's *Orpheus* in 1936. There were lots of movements in that, naturally, because it goes on — it's such a long opera — and we danced through all the different scenes. But that was just one ballet. We did many, many ballets, the opera ballets and our own performances that we would do part of and the opera would do part of. Sunday afternoons we'd have short operas and short ballets. *Orpheus* was one of the longer things. In place of doing the opera with the singers on the stage, which can be quite boring, we put the whole thing into production and the singers in the pit. We even had the Furies flying on wires. It was too much for the Metropolitan Opera public and the Metropolitan Opera critics. It got bawled out. The public liked it, but the critics thought it was awful. Of course, they thought everything Balanchine did was awful. Anything he did was old or old-fashioned or didn't make sense. Now his *Apollo* is a classic. They didn't think of it that way then. He had a hard time, a very hard time.

The dancers liked doing any of his works, but they didn't like dancing at the Met. The Met was a European way of doing things; the dancers didn't count much. We dressed in the ballet room, yes, the rehearsal studio. We used to do *Aida* with black paint on our bodies, and we had to use washtubs to wash ourselves off. Since the opera chorus got to the water first on the floor below and it never got up to the top floor until they were through, you could go home in your black paint. I remember one time we took the fire hose off the wall and washed down. All the water ran down on the costume room, and there was more trouble than you can handle at one time. We weren't the least bit trained to become a European ballet company. We were ballet dancers, we liked to work, we were sociable, and we liked to be in the theatre. But we were Americans; we weren't accustomed to being regimented: "Now, ballet come on down. Ballet down! Ballet outta here!" See, we were kept out of the wings until we had to go on.

I found out that the first wing in the Opera House was reserved for the stars. I made an exit there once, and that was a big mistake. I was doing *Carmen* with Rosa Ponselle — there were some little dances there — and when I'd finished, I made my get-off in the first wing and the stage director grabbed me by the collar and threw me across the backstage. I didn't know why he'd hit me, but then I knew what it was all about. So none of the dancers were very cooperative with the opera company, and I guess that's the reason we only lasted about three years. It was a very bad situation, but it was dancing and we got fed.

We also had to do super jobs; we used to stand for hours. Sometimes you'd be twelve hours in the theatre without a stop, depending on the director, and I guess that's when the union moved in. You had to do the supering, but you didn't get paid additional for it. Then eventually you didn't have to do it; they got somebody else, which was a good change. That meant the ballet organization, the people themselves, became dancers of identity rather than just people shoved onstage to fill in the scenes or keep things hot whenever they got kind of dull.

During that period, they did the Stravinsky festival. That was one of the biggest things as far as ballet's concerned, especially American ballet, that ever happened for many, many years. There could have been something startling before that time — at the old Hippodrome Theater and places like that, European stars, English stars — but it would have been long before I was born. I don't know what it was like. I imagine it would have been very interesting to see them, but I imagine it was pretty corny too. For the festival, we had a special work composed by Stravinsky, *Jeu de Cartes* — that was the first production ever done of that ballet. *Baiser de la Fée* was already composed, and so was *Apollo*; the story of *Baiser* had been done by other choreographers, and *Apollo* had been done by Balanchine for Lifar in Paris.

And this being the big front for the company, the first big push, we had several months to train. Which was marvelous, very fortunate, because we trained every day on the same role, over and over and over. That's the only way we could do it, because he had three huge ballets to do and it takes time to do them. We started them all about the same time, and we were continually working on the Stravinsky festival every day, all day long, for what seems like months. And it was good because it molded every dancer for his part. They picked up the style, picked up an idea of the production, and it worked out fine. And surprisingly enough, in my career up to that time I never really knew how to dance. I knew all the steps, but I didn't know how to put them together into a long movement with a feeling for the idea. That kind of training taught you how to dance: what happens between steps, how things work, how the mood works, how you interpret.

You were taught everything, every move, by Balanchine. He demonstrated it, and then he changed it and remolded it and made it work. He would start something and then he'd put a little change here, a little change there, and it finally became something quite different and quite beautiful. You learned everything, even your finger movements and your head movements — he's that careful a choreographer. After you'd learned the ballet and worked it awhile, you would have the privilege of softening or hardening parts of it to make the thing a whole emotional unit. And then he would watch; even in performance, he would always stand in the wings and watch how it was done and give suggestions. But at the beginning, he taught everything — there was nothing left to you. He always attended his own rehearsals, never had anybody else step in. And you really didn't work by yourself; he wanted to make sure everything was done exactly the way he wanted it. You always go over the hard parts by yourself to get them smoothed out. Then you go to rehearsal like it's a performance, and if it works, it works. If it doesn't work, you go back over it again.

At least in my experience, he tells you what you're supposed to be and what you're supposed to look like, but he doesn't give you the background or anything like that. That's one thing he never does — he never tells you. If you want to look it up, you can look it up and think about it, but you just follow *exactly* what he said. I didn't go into the background because there was nothing existing that I knew of about Diaghilev or Lifar, not even pictures. I don't remember seeing anything, which in a way is good because you don't then go back and say, 'Oh, so-and-so used to do this.' And you're not getting the clichés working for you, so it's always fresh. You're creating it right from scratch.

Apollo's a very difficult ballet because the man is on the stage and the only time he rests is when the Muses do their variations. At

34

that time you're not huffing and puffing and leaving perspiration all over the rocks, but then the finale is so damned hard. It's like you're driving a team of horses, but you're in a plié with them dragging you back. I remember we used to get through it, but by that time your legs are tired and aching. And when finally the horses arrive at the rock, and you have to climb this cliff to get on the chariot to ride away, it's such a relief that it's like going to Heaven. God! You're hurting so, and you walk as calmly as you can to get up there.

It was hard; it required power, you had to push all the time. There are difficult steps, difficult movements. It's not the glissade, jeté, that's hard, but the Balanchine way of doing it, where you force yourself through it. You couldn't say it had any classroom steps; you got off an entrechat cinq, but it was done a little differently. You had to stop quickly or move fast. You had to be strong to do it. If you were the least bit soft kind of dancer, you could just forget it, because you'd never make it. I used to do the pirouettes and stop so abruptly that you would figure somebody would fall down and crash. I'd just stop cold, without balancing around — pirouette, BANG, pirouette, BANG — just to get the contrast in the ballet. That doesn't happen so much any more, I don't believe. They pass through that in a soft way. I found it very demanding, but I liked those kind of things and I could do them. I found out that to do it right really was tiring. For example, three inward pirouettes, change feet, three outward, finish on the ground with your leg to the side — *that* was difficult. That was the most difficult thing for me to do.

The lifting's not so hard. You seldom had to lift with your arms, just a brute lift. I hardly remember the adagio now, but it was quite simple. There's a swing to it, and you do it on one knee with the girl on your back doing that swimming movement. It wasn't so difficult, actually. It's not like picking up a girl . . . like in [*Concerto*] *Barocco*, where they go back and forth and back with you lifting them each time. That's hard. In vaudeville, we had tricks of throwing the girl and catching her, but not quite the same style as you do in the ballet company.

Partnering just came by doing ballets. Oh, we had classes, sure. I used to hate them because we always used to get big fat girls, and they always wore Celanese practice costumes, so when you'd pick them up, they'd slide through their costumes. You'd try to grab hold of them and — nothing there. It wasn't ideal, but at least it taught you to handle people, the kind of people you probably never would dance with. It would be stupid to try. But when we had a nice dancer who was light and thin and knew how to move, it was easy.

In *Apollo,* there is also the demand on your body to respond with accents, full out, full steam, rather than just to pass it over. Those are tiring, but after you got to learn them, they felt good because you were going with the music. The music was just rattling along, and you were going right along with it. You can't ignore it; there's no way you can do the ballet if you ignore the music. Stravinsky has the more pastoral feelings, and the adagio moves very smoothly. The variations and the coda particularly were very demanding musically, and if we didn't respond to them, we'd just ruin it.

The score did seem hard at first, but after a while it's just as easy to listen to *Apollo* as to listen to *The Blue Danube*. You just automatically work; you can understand Stravinsky, and you know where the rhythms are and where they change — it's quite simple after a while. I used to study cello and piano, but my career never allowed me to pursue them to any great degree because we were always touring. I remember I used to have to sleep in the upper berth with my cello, because you couldn't put it in a seat. So you could say I've been in touch with quite a lot of music.

At the beginning of *Apollo*, they bring you out, make you rock, then they begin to dance the prologue and you spin. They teach you how to dance because you're a little awkward, and little by little you become mature. Then you do your variation; we had actually a little harp, like a lute, and you strum it. I believe they had a broken-down column, and you sit there and rest while the Muses' variations are going on, but you never leave the stage. Oh yes, I was watching; you're part of it because they're doing their variations to you. Then there's the second boy's variation and the pas de deux. Then you start to involve the other Muses, get into the coda, drive the horses and up the mountain, and that was that.

It's just a young god that's born, taught how to dance, and then taught music. He's trying his wings. He feels phrases, feels the softness of them, the rigidity of them, and then he goes off and becomes a god. He does his variation, works with the Muses, and then they go off to the Elysian Fields — I guess that's where they go. The way Balanchine set it expresses the character: he begins to expand, he does more, he does more, he does more, he expands it until he gets to that pirouette with the changing feet — at which time you begin to perspire and hope you make it.

The character came out as the choreography developed, and a lot happened between the steps. You begin to learn that probably more important things than the steps themselves happen between steps, and that's when you begin to learn to dance. We had other good teachers there; we had Vladimiroff at the same time, who was a very fine classic teacher. He also taught me what happened between the steps. You don't just do a couple of pirouettes and walk off and spit on your hands. You work your way into it and work your way out of it. That was, as I say, the first time I ever learned how to dance, although I had all the tours and the jumps and the beats. I had to do those in vaudeville, two and three times a day, so I learned them fast.

I never posed it as a problem, adapting to learn how to dance and particularly to learn the style of Balanchine. I always posed it as the natural thing to do, so it was no problem at all. I just did it, and I think that's the only way you can approach it. If you try to approach it with a reference to another way of doing that step, you have trouble, because Balanchine doesn't want that. Forget what you've learned, and just use the muscular controls you've already got to do other things. You just forget everything else and do exactly what he says and it will work out well, which I think is part of his genius. Otherwise, you'd take your class and then go into the rehearsal hall and do exactly the same steps, which would be terribly uninteresting.

I was the only one who did *Apollo* for the American Ballet, and when we put the repertory together and went to South America, I danced it through South America. I don't remember anyone else trying to do it. Of course, after the war [André] Eglevsky and [Jacques] d'Amboise, people like that, did it, and I think it changed quite a bit. Balanchine does that when he revives something: he shifts it around so you don't recognize it. I watched a rehearsal once and wanted to suggest, 'This is what we did,' but I know better than to do that to Balanchine. If he wants to change it, you leave it alone. But I did it exactly the same way all the way through. I felt better in it, because the more you danced it, the better it got. Some of the Muses changed; I did it first with Elise Reiman and later on with Marie-Jeanne. But those dancers were pretty well trained by that time and they could step right in. A little pushing and they got it done.

At first, they had a wig on me, but that didn't work — it was too heavy. It was kind of a gold-thread wig and it weighed a ton. So they disposed of that and just curled my hair and powdered gold dust on it. The costume was gold leather, with ballet slippers, laced. I was very comfortable in it, no trouble at all. I think when you first come out, you only have a pair of trunks on and you're swathed in the cloths. How I got the costume on later, I don't know; they could have put it on onstage.

For me, all these ballets helped each other and related — there's no doubt about it — because there had to be a very strong style. There was an awful lot of acting for me to do in *Orpheus*, playing the lute and suffering because Eurydice was not there. At the end he turns and looks at her, and that's the end of that. And there were long strains of music while they were building the effigy of Eurydice where you had a lot of acting. But in *Apollo* there is no room for acting. You dance every bit of the thing all the way through, never once a personal emotion or a grimace. You just go there and there, and you go on to the next, go on to the next. The story was carried very beautifully that way; it was all built in. You bring nothing personal to it, just your own feeling for the music, your response to the music, which grows as you do it. Otherwise it's exactly the way the choreographer set it. The critics were all there for the New York performances. And we danced it in Buenos Aires on the tour, but because I don't read Spanish or other languages, I don't know what the heck was going on with the critics. Evidently it was taken very well. If anybody said anything, nobody paid any attention to it. Balanchine was the boss.

With Balanchine, you don't take the reins in your own hands; you try to follow as faithfully as you can. You should know what he has in his mind, exactly what he wants, how it's going to begin and finish and what it's going to look like. He doesn't tell you stories and try to build you up; you just do it. And I think that's fine, because you become a very good instrument of his. Otherwise, you've got people fussing about this, fussing about that, the tempo here and the tempo there, which I think destroys a lot of choreography as it's intended. When they get their fingers in it and their temperaments in it, then you're in trouble. It's like piano: if the piano doesn't want to respond and says, "I want to respond *this* way," then you've got something else. Even when I worked with [Eugene] Loring, I learned to do exactly what he asked me to do. As for Mac in *Filling Station*, I did that for myself, and I could trust myself with it because nobody else knew it.

Until the tour in 1941, I had other things to dance, but I don't remember dancing *Apollo* anyplace other than the Metropolitan for those two performances. There was actually no place to dance — that was the trouble. You danced at the Met or you didn't dance. No theatres. Where could you go? Ballet at that time was not supported publicly. The Met at least had an audience, but ballet in general had no audience at all, unlike today when you go to a theatre and the people are crowding in. You had to join in with the opera and the opera crowd would come, and if you were in the ballet, you were sort of building a balletic audience. But there were hardly any theatres big enough to dance in or any money to do the ballets correctly. That's always been the hard part. I guess today they've got it licked; they can do darn near anything they want to, and that's the way it should have been at that time.

But I've got to admit that the struggle we went through, being in that company and fighting for a repertoire and places to dance, was a great adventure, even up to the time after the war when Ballet Society was organized. Then we would choreograph and perform in dark theatres. Like, a Monday the Ziegfeld would be dark, so you could play there. That's the only way you could get a theatre until City Center. It's funny — we used to play there on Tuesdays, and the committee that ran the theatre happened to see the ballet and like it, so they incorporated it into City Center, and then it changed to the New York City Ballet. That was a long process of just struggle and development, but not the kind of struggle where you cry and tear your hair and beat your chest. It was fun and a challenge for everybody. I used to teach in the School, help rehearse some ballets with Balanchine, choreograph, dance ... that's about all you can do, I guess. It was very tiring, but the desire was so much fun that it was a pleasure to work. We just bled, but we worked. And Balanchine was building a repertoire as fast as he could so that if they'd get into a theatre, they would have a repertoire to dance while he built more.

Balanchine had more than he could rehearse — he was doing two or three ballets at a whack — so I'd rehearse for him. After the war we didn't do *Apollo,* and being ballet master came to me naturally. I'd get to class whenever I could, do my own dancing, and rehearse something we'd already done to a point where he could correct it and get it onstage. My relationship with him has been almost like brothers, just great, because we worked on solving problems together. For instance, he revived *Prodigal Son,* and we had to have little wreaths around the skullcaps for the boys, but we ran out of money. So we took the skullcaps to the top of the City Center, way up high, and sat and made them, he and I, without the wardrobe department knowing about it. They were just done on the q.t. No one had any money. It was a fight for existence which to me was a delightful challenge because I loved to do things like that. It was fun to sneak around and do something to get it done. Now that they have the theatre and everything they want, I think some of the drive, some of the freedom for the company is gone.

When I came back after the war — I had spent four years in the army — my technique wasn't what it was supposed to be, and I kept hurting myself all the time. So I was not pushed up to be a star because I couldn't carry it. That's when I gave up, hung up my shoes, and started something else. Anyway, we didn't have stars, not in the sense that they have today, because in Balanchine's company you are all stars and you're all corps de ballet. That's the way he worked. Nobody ever thought of being a star and having the star dressing room and little favors, no. Everybody worked together. To me, it was a nice situation, because everybody was equal and we were all good friends. Everybody was doing the best he could. Nobody was crying; they were having a good time, having a ball, dancing hard. Nobody was out trying to cut somebody else's throat to get that role. You got a role — you'd be a star the next time. Like, in *Baiser* I was corps de ballet, didn't do much, and in *Jeu de Cartes* I was the King of Hearts, a secondary role, and Bill Dollar was the Joker. But it never occurred to me that I was being put down. It just didn't work that way. I felt it was a privilege to do them all.

And I never thought about it as Ballet Caravan becoming something great, or 'We're breaking ground now for a whole new company and for new ideas, and freeing technique to do new works.' I was born innocent, without consciousness of anything of that sort. It was just something we wanted to do. You wanted to dance, you wanted to eat, so let's start doing some ballets. Balanchine was busy, he couldn't do all of them, so we were on our own. Working with as experienced a choreographer as Balanchine was the schooling for my own choreography. In Ballet Caravan we had to do our own ballets, otherwise we'd have had nothing to dance. So that's where I started, out of necessity. I had monkeyed with choreography off and on, but I never did anything serious until I hit the Caravan.

We danced in our own ballets, and we ran the switchboards when we were not on the stage. Everybody did everything; we'd carry the costumes, hang the scenery, put the show on, wrap it up, and go to the next place. I remember walking down the street in Burlington with my brother when we didn't have any money in our pockets to get anything to eat — we hadn't been paid yet. We saw Kirstein coming the other way, and I was just going to go up and say, "Lincoln, can I borrow something?" but he beat me to it. He said, "Could you please lend me a buck?" So nobody had any money to eat. You'd skip that meal.

We managed. We had a lot of fun, though. To skip a meal or do some extra hard work like loading the bus or pushing it up a hill was a lot of fun. At least we were all learning. Today it's much easier for dancers. Their tights are washed for them, their costumes are all brought in, and they have nothing to do with the lights or the music. They just dance. That gives them more time to apply their energies to dancing. Most of the time, we were so exhausted that you walked down the street like you were drunk, but you were really just tired.

And on tour, we played in places that shouldn't have been played in. In the small towns, they showed pictures in the theatres, and the rigging was very primitive. I remember that when Balanchine did that Schubert fantasy [*Errante*], they had what they called Olivettes — lights, a big box with a light in it — and in order to change the color of the scenes or the color of the mood, the dancers had to stand backstage and change the lights according to cues. That's the only way you could do it, because you couldn't carry a large crew, and there were never any crews in these theatres — there were just the people who lived in the towns. And some of the stages were quite slippery. I remember Marie-Jeanne tried to do a variation and kept slipping so much she flew away off the stage on her knees. That never happened to me, but toe shoes are much more difficult to work in than ballet slippers. The men managed; you didn't dance very well, but you usually stood up. But a girl in a toe shoe . . . I still marvel today how they do it. That's a real technique; there's something hard on your toe, you can't feel the floor, but your balance is there and it's accurate. I just don't understand it.

I know more about the theatre than most of the choreographers today because of all that. I know how to hang a show fairly well, how to light it simply, time it with the music, so that at 8:30 when the curtain goes up, it's all put together. Without the help of lighting people and production managers, some choreographers can't even do a thing.

See, my great love was not particularly ballet. It was theatre, the use of theatre and how to make it work. I used to build little stages when I was a kid, build them by the hundreds. And light them and go over to the theatre to see how everything was proportioned, how to rig it, how to put in wings. That was my interest. When I got into vaudeville, I knew exactly what a theatre was like, what had to be done, who you had to talk to to give a cue, and what kind of equipment you had to carry on your own. In Ballet Caravan, I hung the scenery myself, lighted it, crawled on my belly under the theatres to hook up the main switchboard. There was nobody there to do it, but it was easy for me. Consequently, in all my ballets today I use the scenery and lighting in a sense as part of the choreography, because I know how you can do it. A lot of people never figure that out, but it's just automatic for me. You say, "Well, I can't do this particular scene unless something happens." Then you figure out how it can happen before you choreograph it, and then it's done.

I was invited to go and dance with the Ballet Russe, but for some reason I didn't feel much like I wanted to do that. Their new ballet was kind of tired-looking. Massine did some things that were pretty good, but going there didn't particularly interest me, now that we had a company in New York that was going so well and enthusiasm — inspired, I guess, by Balanchine and Kirstein — that kept the thing moving. That's where I wanted to be. There were always gripes, but that's the healthy part of a company. I griped all the time, but I turned down anything that was offered to me. Probably I would have been a big star — or maybe not, I don't know — if I'd gone the other way, but it wasn't attractive to me. I liked where I was and what we were doing; it was fresh and new and I'm glad I did it.

And I learned so much about ballet choreography by staying where I was. On the other hand, I would have been just a boy dancing, maybe Massine works, without knowing how it's put together. Whereas with Balanchine, working with him on brand-new works, you began to learn — just sort of by osmosis — things to do and how to do them. I was learning all the time. I wasn't out particularly to be a great star or make a lot of money. Money never meant a thing to me.

And Apollo was one of my favorite roles. It was demanding, and when you'd got through it, you felt like you'd done something. Maybe you didn't have standing ovations, but who cared? You did have working with Balanchine, a very intelligent man, in a thing like that, which was a great privilege — not just the privilege of knowing him, but of learning from him. Learning was a revelation. I never was conscious of making history. Dancing was just something you had to do, and you'd do everything you could to make it happen.

May 1979
San Francisco

Igor Youskevitch

Igor Youskevitch (b. Piryatin, Russia, 1912) trained and performed as a gymnast before turning to a ballet career at the age of twenty. After intensive study in Paris with Olga Preobrajenska, he danced with Bronislava Nijinska's Théâtre de Danse (1934), with Leon Woizikowsky's company (1935–38), and then as premier danseur of the Massine-Blum Ballet Russe de Monte Carlo (1938–1944; 1955–57). He made his Giselle *debut with the Ballet Russe in 1938 and created roles in Massine's* Gaîté Parisienne *(1938),* Seventh Symphony *(1938), and* Rouge et Noir *(1939). Having emigrated to the United States during World War II, acquired citizenship, and served in the U.S. Navy, he joined (American) Ballet Theatre in 1946 and remained there until 1955. A repertory of* Giselle, Swan Lake *(Act II),* Les Sylphides, *and the great* Nutcracker, Bluebird, *and* Black Swan *pas de deux cemented his reputation as a premier danseur noble, but he also danced leading roles in such modern works as Antony Tudor's* Romeo and Juliet, *George Balanchine's* Apollo, *Michel Fokine's* Helen of Troy, *and Valerie Bettis'* A Streetcar Named Desire. *His historic partnership with Alicia Alonso began in 1946 and blossomed both at Ballet Theatre, where they created the leading roles in Balanchine's* Theme and Variations *(1947), and in Cuba and South America with Ballet Alicia Alonso (1948–1959). Youskevitch retired from dancing in 1962; he opened his own school in New York in 1964 and is currently on the staff at the University of Texas at Austin.*

I can't remember a time when the name Igor Youskevitch wasn't synonymous with the role of Albrecht and with the title danseur noble. *But I never saw him dance, and when you miss someone's career completely — through the misfortune of time or geography — you've missed it, and there are no second chances. Or so I had always thought, until Youskevitch taught a class I had expected to take from his wife. The splendors of his renowned technique have naturally vanished, but the* danseur *has survived and still flourishes in his bearing and manner. Youskevitch radiates more unashamed grandeur and*

unabashed gallantry in the studio than most male dancers today bring to the
stage. What he taught me about dancing that winter evening had little to do
with steps.

I first saw dancing at the age of about six, when I was still in Russia. It was not a ballet but a bumblebee dance that I still remember, in an opera, *Tsar Saltan.* I did not think at all of a dancing career at that age, but I was very interested in gymnastics and very active in it after the age of ten. But that wasn't in Russia. Soon after I was about eight years old, we emigrated and went to Yugoslavia, where I went to high school and university, just like you're supposed to.

Living in Yugoslavia, I had a lot of friends in the theatre, some of them dancers, so I knew something about ballet people and I saw ballet. I liked it, but I still did not feel I had enough talent to start dancing as a profession. The push was provided by an accident: I was offered a dancing job. One of the dancers in the theatre, Xenia Grunt, was planning to present a concert with numbers of her own choreography — mostly acrobatic, which was in fashion at that time. For some reason, she could not find any male dancer to do it with her. Belgrade is not that big, and most of the dancers who were equipped to do the acrobatic type of dancing were under contract to the theatre. So she turned to a gymnastic organization, feeling that if she could find a young man with strong muscles, she could train him to be an adequate partner for her purpose.

She came to one of our public gymnastic concerts, and after it she offered me the job. She felt that I had enough theatrical presence that she could train me very easily. I was very interested. First of all, it was a strict business proposition; I was supposed to get so much money for each concert, and I needed it. That was one of the official reasons that I accepted the job. Unofficially, of course, I was interested in dancing anyway.

After about two months of intensive training, I went on, and the concert went very well. I did everything I was supposed to do, just on the basis of what she taught me. As a matter of fact, I even danced two solos. They were not very technical, because in two months I could not absorb everything, but they were adequate and I felt very comfortable. And of course after the concert I felt completely professional, and I had enough justification to enroll in a ballet school and continue.

I studied first with Elena Poliakova — she was one of the old Imperial ballerinas — and then eventually I went with Grunt to Paris. We presented a couple of concerts, which were not a very good success, but I was encouraged by the critics who said that I had possibilities. So when Grunt went back to Yugoslavia, I stayed in Paris and studied with Olga Preobrajenska, and soon after I got into a leading company.

The only teacher I had from whom I learned was Olga Preobrajenska. I studied or took classes with many teachers after her, but I cannot say that I learned from them. I practiced, but I didn't really learn. Her class was so well rounded that I built up a strong enough technique to be able to endure whatever role I danced. And *Giselle* gave me my first full-length part.

I always asked myself 'Why?' when I was studying. 'Why do I have to do that?' And the answer is in mechanical truths. Movement is purely mechanical. It involves timing and stress and force. You have to put all these together with one effort. Some people say, "Oh, I was shown by Ivan Ivanovich. He was a great dancer." It doesn't make any difference. You have to rely on mechanical truths, not on somebody's say-so, not Ivan Ivanovich or anyone else.

Now, Preobrajenska studied in Russia with Cecchetti, so in her class she used quite a lot of Cecchetti technique, which changed and streamlined everything. I learned that particular method from her, and with that method she taught me how to turn. Basically, there is a certain way to turn which is mechanical — there's nothing wrong with that. If you know this mechanical way, then the approach doesn't matter, and you can turn from various positions.

The Russian school teaches preparation for pirouette with the back leg straight in fourth position. But what do you do after that? When the time comes to pirouette, you must bend both knees, because you can't turn from a straight leg. Cecchetti teaches that you go right away from both bent knees, balanced. Now this, I felt, is the better way to learn pirouette because you push straight up. With the back leg straight it's harder to turn, because when you quickly bend your knee, you are not centered properly.

The basic idea of classical dancing is not to show effort or preparation. The preparation is like a dirty detail that shouldn't be shown to the audience. In old times, the working leg was always opened first for preparation pirouette and held, which is very silly because it doesn't help you to turn whatsoever. Just the opposite. I've seen many dancers do tendu to second and then wobble on the standing leg because they are not balanced. The tendu doesn't help you to keep your balance. It's a handicap.

We jumped in and turned from second right away in order to

prevent the preparation from registering. Our generation of dancers taught that this is an improvement, because the other is showing what you are going to do. In the time of Vestris, everybody would wait: "Ah, now he is going to turn. Let's count how many." I have seen dancers do that in *Giselle,* and I close my eyes. They dance the Act II variation, it's supposed to be emotional, they are dying at the end — supposed to be dying — and suddenly they stop for a big preparation. It's silly, and it disrupts the whole thing.

I first saw *Giselle* at the Opéra in Paris, in about 1936 or '37, before I even joined the Ballet Russe company. The Albrecht was Serge Lifar, and I believe his partner was [Lycette] Darsonval.

Now, in the very beginning of *Giselle*s in our time, the only *Giselle*s were at the Opéra in Paris, at Ballet Russe since 1938, and at Festival Ballet, with which Anton Dolin was connected. There were really two versions, one by Lifar and the other by Dolin, but both versions came from one source, [Nicholas] Sergeyev, who brought from Russia what he had written down in notebooks. So the two *Giselle*s were quite similar, very abbreviated, with the basic accent on the principal roles and the rest cut down to size, and Dolin and Lifar each adjusted the ballet a little to his own liking.

When Lifar staged it for the Ballet Russe, he was to dance a few performances. I was his understudy, and I danced it after he left. It was a sketchy *Giselle,* the story and small characters were kind of neglected, but of course I was concentrating on learning all the steps. At the rehearsals, I was supposed to learn everything that Lifar did, but since he usually did not dance full force, I only had a half-indication of the role, not a complete picture. I had seen *Giselle* before, I knew more or less what was going on, I knew a little bit about the period historically, but I did not have any experience. I don't remember ever having any separate rehearsals or private coaching, not with Lifar.

And when he left, I found myself in a hole. I suddenly realized that I knew all the dancing steps but I really didn't know the role, what to do in between glissades and assemblés. I went to the theatre — it was in Covent Garden — and I was planning to go downstairs to the studio and just try to figure it out in my mind. On the way, I met Boris Kochno, and he asked me what I was doing there so early. I said, "Well, I'm dancing *Giselle,* and I've found that I really don't know the role. I have to think about it." You see, I had not had time to think; I was too busy learning the steps. "Wellll, let's go," he said.

And he went downstairs with me and actually helped me to do a basic role. I can't say that I did the role completely in that rehearsal, but he gave me a certain focus just by talking. "All right," he said.

"What are you supposed to do? Who are you? Where are you going?" While he talked, I was thinking, and inventing for myself what I felt like doing at each moment, and we went through the whole ballet that way. It helped me tremendously, because I felt much more secure; at least I knew basically what I was supposed to do. So I did my first performance — that was with Markova, in 1938, and I was dancing in a blond wig because Lifar did it in a blond wig — and it was fairly successful, but definitely the role was not made yet.

It's very hard, at least for me, to create a complete role while rehearsing. I create only a frame, a skeleton, of the role, and then it grows. Every time I danced it, I would add something. On the spur of the moment, the way the situation came to me, I would do something that I would retain and keep building on. By doing it often enough, eventually I made a role for myself.

Albrecht went through certain stages. Originally, I was doing faithfully what I had been shown by Lifar, which was an Albrecht who is in love with Giselle. That was my understanding: he's in love with Giselle, and what happens is just an accident. But then I departed completely from this first influence. I realized that of course it cannot be that way, because the action of the story indicates deceit of a certain kind. Obviously Albrecht came with a specific goal in mind. He was a nobleman, probably the landlord of everything around, and it's far-fetched that he had really honorable intentions. Eventually I settled on the idea that Albrecht was really a wolf. He fell in love with a little peasant girl, and he was just going about it as any red-blooded male would, without thinking too much of the consequences or about his fiancée. It was a kind of flirtation on the side, which in his mind would not affect his marriage in any way.

So then I was doing my own Albrecht, and I don't remember any specific dancer that influenced me after that. Oh, I saw others, and I evaluated my own performance, comparing it to theirs, but I was not really influenced or tempted to copy any one dancer. At the time I started to dance the role, I only knew one Albrecht, Lifar, and he did well but not completely to my liking. At that time, many people were joking that the ballet should be renamed *Albrecht,* because he was carrying on considerably in many places where I felt the Albrecht should be in the background. Later I saw Dolin dance it too, and he was completely different from Lifar, more restrained. But Dolin wasn't a very romantic dancer; the movement was not really flowing, not lyrical enough for the part. So I looked and pinpointed what I should *not* do.

Even now, although I'm not dancing it any more, I'm still working on the character. Not really changing it, but thinking of certain details that might bring it out a little better. For example, the sword plays an important part because Albrecht is recognized through the sword, it almost kills Hilarion at a certain point, and then Giselle grabs it and almost commits suicide. Albrecht could be mad at the sword. I'm restaging *Giselle* in Pittsfield in January, and I'm planning that when Albrecht grabs the sword from Giselle's hands, he'll break it over his knee. That feels like the right action for a person who is divided; he's not yet really emotionally involved, but he's mad that he's stuck in such a situation.

Many things add to the character like that. During the scene where she's plucking the flower, I tried to pay attention to her physique rather than to the flower. I'm interested in *her*, and I wanted to indicate that it's not an innocent, idealistic love, but that he's really trying to make her. After her death he realizes that he is more emotionally involved than he planned to be, but in the first act he's a wolf. And when the court and his fiancée come in, he's playing his deceit to the end. He's upset, he doesn't know what to do, so he decides just to tell some kind of a story and cover up, hoping Giselle will not react. Right after her death, he kind of has mild hysterics, and then he's led away by his friend. And in the second act, his realization that he loved Giselle much more than he expected is supposed to come through more. There, he shows his remorse.

Of course the hardest variation, the big technical variation, is in the second act. It did not in itself present any technical problem except from the point of view of endurance. Even when you're not actually dancing, any ballet takes away a lot of strength from you. And since this variation is at the end of the ballet, you're already a little tired. It takes many performances to build up the endurance to do it, and you build it up as you go along. That's the only difficulty I had in the beginning, and later on I made it much harder than it was.

Some of the variations in classical ballet became very traditional, like Giselle's variation in the first act, but I don't think that really applies to male variations. Very often, depending on the dancer and what type of technique he has, the male variation can be adjusted or altered.

For the beginning of the Act II variation, I did what was customary: on the diagonal, you do, three times, glissade or a soubresaut, double cabriole, assemblé. I did entrechat huit after the double cabriole, although entrechat six or assemblé was customary. The middle part I also did as customary: tombé, fouetté, jeté en tournant, to both sides. And then the last diagonal is chassé, chassé, assemblé, double tour. This is usually repeated three times, and then you take a preparation, pirouette, double tour, and you fall to the floor. I did that version until Bronislava Nijinska saw me in *Giselle* and suggested something. She said, "You know, Vaslav Nijinsky did this diagonal a little differently." Well, the way I was doing it had always bothered me, because there is a definite musical change after the second double tour but the step doesn't change. It's a logical place for something else to be done, and that's exactly what she told me. She said, "At this point, after the second double tour, Nijinsky would do a big soubresaut, then entrechat cinq de volée, then double tour." That goes with the change in the music, so I started to do it that way.

Only again I added a little more. I did soubresaut, then occasionally entrechat cinq but — just to save strength — not always. But then I did two double tours in a row, with no preparation in between. After the two double tours, I jumped into preparation, *en dehors* one slow pirouette with outstretched arms, and then I would bring the arms up and, without another preparation, do many pirouettes. Then double tour and fall down. I felt it provided a certain urgency and a finish to it, first slow with arms out, then fast, fast, and down. I did that particular variation ever since that time, and I wish somebody would do it now, but they're changing it.

But there's another thing. I never approached Albrecht as a ballet dancer. In a ballet that has a definite plot, I wouldn't approach any role from the dance point of view. If I had to do a gesture or a step, I wouldn't think of how this step would be better danced balletically. I would approach it as a human being first. I'd say, 'I have to do this, which indicates that. How can I do it with a dance step?' so as to emphasize, not the dancing, but more the expression of the step, what it's supposed to convey.

We never thought of dancing as a place to develop technique. We learned a certain basic classical technique, and anything new in a technical sense was learned if it was necessary. If a choreographer is doing a new ballet and he wants you to do a certain step that's not a customary classical step, you learn that step as you rehearse the ballet. And in that sense, you learn another technical trick of some kind. But nobody ever bothered to think of technique itself without the ballet. Why should we? If something is new, fine, but you don't specifically think, 'Ah, let me invent a new technical something.' The entrechat huit I put into Albrecht's variation was a technical elaboration, but it was not really *new*. It was just a little more of the same thing as part of the general characterization.

Watching the younger dancers, I feel that's one of the mistakes they're all making. They're approaching everything as ballet dancers. So in the places where they will receive no applause, where the technical steps are really of no importance, they're elaborating on the dance step and forgetting what the step is for and who the character is.

Many dancers approach a moment in the second act like ballet dancers, and it always bothers me. What they do is this: Albrecht is looking for Giselle; she appears, and then she passes him. He runs and he looks — 'Where are you?' — and then he stops, on demi-pointe, with a big port de bras. And it's always funny. They're not dancing right then. It doesn't matter how you stand — it's a question of the character.

And another thing I saw someplace — Albrecht with the big cape. As he came to Giselle's grave, suddenly he took the edges of the cape in both hands and made a big running circle of the stage, with the cape flying behind. I wanted to say, "It's a plane! It's a bird! It's a Superman. No, it's Albrecht in *Giselle*." Possibly it's from all that music to be used up, but somehow that run . . .

I saw Mischa [Baryshnikov] do *Giselle*. There is no question that he is a wonderful dancer and technically unbelievable, but his technique looks too contemporary. It's not really in style with *Giselle*. When men perform certain steps, you can say, "Oh, that is very old-fashioned. That comes from the nineteenth century." For example, piqué and ballotté are steps that come from way back. The technique that was used in the nineteenth century is of course a little different from what's used today. And the things that Baryshnikov does were never done before in those ballets, and I feel they're out of place in *Giselle*.

Giselle is a Romantic ballet, and the idea of that period was this: for the first time in the ballet, there was an effort to portray emotion in movement. In reality, the steps were still ordinary classical. They didn't know yet, or have enough courage or imagination, to get away from the classical and do something more emotional, but the idea was there of performing them in a way that indicates some kind of emotional involvement. The technique that Baryshnikov is using leaves no room for emotional involvement. It's so technical that you cannot make it expressive.

Within the frame of the classical steps you cannot do a great deal, but there is leeway. Step and character fit up to a certain point. I'll tell you what I did, for example, in the very beginning of the variation — that's soubresaut, double cabriole, assemblé. While I was doing entrechat huit instead of assemblé, I wasn't thinking at all of classical positions for my arms. They went up as they went, not perfectly classical, but as they went. And I would drop my head way back. The feet were doing the classical steps, but the body was reaching for something a little bit.

Of course what I call the emotional part of the step cannot be pinpointed so the audience understands exactly what I mean. But it gives a certain style to it, a little difference. I remember that Lifar showed me very simple mime for Act I, just straight gestures: 'I,' 'You,' 'Love,' 'I swear.' I was just standing plain, without any movement. But I changed that. I added very small details, so I was moving with my whole body while I was doing the mime. It somehow took away the age of these old-fashioned gestures. Some places, that fits. In *Giselle,* many things fit better if they are more realistic.

But in other ballets, they may not fit. I remember in *Swan Lake* . . . It was before the full-length *Swan Lake* was performed — we usually presented only the white act. The dramatic action in that act is very choppy. After the cygnets, while the White Swan is off the stage, the time would come for me to perform my variation. Usually, you came out of the wings, went into fifth position, waited for the music, and started dancing. But I said, 'I have to make some kind of approach to it.' I thought I would come out as if I were looking for the White Swan and couldn't find her. I would be very sad, get into my position, and start to dance right away. And it didn't work. I felt comfortable, but it just wasn't right. The whole act was constructed in a more abstract way, so any realistic type of playing didn't fit. It was too much. It was much better just to come out and dance, much less offensive than to portray anything more realistically.

I danced *Giselle* with Markova, briefly with [Tamara] Toumanova, and most of the time, of course, with Alicia [Alonso]. There is no question that I preferred dancing with Alonso, for a very specific reason. We approached the roles the same way, and we were willing to give and take. If I invented something, I needed a certain response from her, and she was willing to respond and to change herself a little bit. So we could always work out our relationship onstage to our mutual satisfaction, which I could not do with other partners. If your partner is alert and reacts to something you do, you feel comfortable, but if the other person doesn't respond, it falls flat.

Markova was set in her ways of doing things. Of course, she was an excellent Giselle, with a lightness and quality that I cannot say anything against, but I never could be completely comfortable with her. Sometimes I would try new things. When they did not work, I would realize it was not my fault but Alicia's, because she moved in such a way that I had to follow her. Once, in the first-act pantomime, when I said, 'I,' 'Love,' 'You,' and 'I swear,' we wound up almost at the back of the stage. I noticed that somehow, at the end of this pantomime, I had my back to the audience. 'Why is my back to the audience?' I wondered. Then I realized that while I was telling her

I loved her, she was moving backward, so I constantly had to adjust myself. And finally, my back was to the audience and she was facing them. That's called upstaging. In the ballet it's not that drastic, but if you're upstaged in the movies, you're really out of the picture! Well, I *was* aware of it in the next performance, so when she would move back, I would move back too. I was pantomiming going backward with her, and we wound up together, all the way at the backdrop.

Also, it was hard for us to rehearse together because we were fighting constantly — not in words, but in movement. I have definite ideas of how to partner, how to hold and so forth, and as I said, she was set in her ways. I would take her by the hand and she would pull back; I would do one thing and she the other. I remember starting to rehearse an extended pas de deux from Massine's *Seventh Symphony* and immediately getting into trouble. I would turn her and she would not move. So we rehearsed separately, though of course eventually we had to dance together. What's the solution? Who won? I am stronger than she is, so I would just move her.

She did a very good Giselle, especially in the second act, but because she was so light, she didn't like to jump very much when her partner lifted her. Every partner that danced with her resented that. First of all, lifting even ninety pounds is not that simple. And I always felt that what makes a classical lift exciting is that the result is out of proportion to the effort. If there is no help from the woman, it's just pure strength for the man to lift her. So there must be hidden effort. When the ballerina makes a certain effort, very lightly, then she goes all the way up and she looks light. But if she doesn't make any effort, she still goes up, but she looks heavy no matter what. For some reason, Alicia never could help in that way.

I think dancing Dolin's version, with Dolin, affected her general attitude towards performing *Giselle*. For example, while dancing in Ballet Theatre, with Markova and without Markova, I had changed one of the details at the end of the first act, when Giselle falls down dead. In the old way, in Lifar's version and Dolin's version, Albrecht goes to Giselle and picks her up and hugs her and hugs her and hugs her and all that. And the poor mother is standing alongside and just watching. It always felt kind of funny; after all, he is the villain in a certain way and he is the cause. Naturally, the first person who has to go to Giselle is the mother. So I made the mother pick up Giselle and carry on, and Albrecht would come and drop down at her feet.

So I was rehearsing with Alicia one day, and we came to that point. She drops dead and the mother picks her up, and suddenly Alicia stops and says, "Wait a minute. What's this?" I said, "We have changed that. It's more logical." But she didn't want to change it; she kept saying, "Albrecht always picked me up." We argued for some time about what was best to do, and finally I told her that who picks her up shouldn't make any difference to her because she's dead anyway.

As I say, I was always critical of the versions I had seen, even the one I was dancing in Ballet Russe. But I was a dancer, not a choreographer, not a reviver of ballets, so I really had no right to change anything. But I had certain ideas. When I started to dance it with Alonso, which was when I joined Ballet Theatre in 1946, I told her about my ideas and she agreed with me. We discussed and planned, and together we started to adjust Dolin's version a little. Certain things I had brought in right away because I was invited as a leading dancer, and — especially if we had already danced the older, classical ballets and had some experience — the soloists had a leeway. It was a honeymoon. I could say a little more, right off the bat, and adjust certain things, especially with Alicia's cooperation. But we still couldn't do everything because the version was set, and in order to change it drastically, we'd have had to reshape the whole thing and involve the corps de ballet.

The first full adjustment we were able to make — not full, but at least to our liking — was when we did *Giselle* at the Greek Theatre in Los Angeles, apart from Ballet Theatre. The deal was that we would stage it using the scenery and costumes Alicia had in Cuba, and some of the Cuban dancers. The rest would be hired locally; we auditioned them. And we made a large version: there was a mother pantomime in the first act when she describes the Wilis, and everything was opened.

Here is one change I wanted to make. Albrecht coming to Giselle's grave with the flowers has always bothered me, especially because he comes out exactly in front of it but he doesn't see it. There's a lot of music, and he dances around and suffers until finally, 'Here she is.' It was designed as a premier danseur entrance, but who in hell comes to the cemetery with such a balletic approach? There is so much music. The Russians have this music forever, and he goes around and he goes around and he goes around. I felt this is not really music for Albrecht to display his emotions; it's a kind of background music, sad music, that describes his general feeling. So I made him come out and stop at various crosses, through all that music, as if he is looking for something. And then in the last moment, he sees Giselle's grave.

I played mandolin and a little guitar, just chords, but I'm not a musician and I had no musical training. But it's important to relate to the music. I think the music in *Giselle* is damn good. It's old-fashioned, true, but it's written very well, and it really describes the characters.

A musical dancer would be a dancer that could hear the music and feel the rhythm of it. Depending on the music, a dancer without musical training takes a certain time to hear all the rhythmical changes, to count it out, or to remember the melody, whatever the method. The more musical a dancer is, the quicker he absorbs that musical rhythm.

You see, there are different ways of operating. In the old ballets like *Giselle,* the music is already written with a kind of melodic description, a feel of what you're supposed to do. Sometimes conductors like to modernize the playing or conducting, and they try to smooth things. Sometimes they don't bring all those qualities out, which I feel is wrong because this music is written specifically so all that schmaltz contributes to the action.

It's very funny. You are conscious when you are dancing of a certain rhythm of the music. If your mind wanders or concentrates on something besides that rhythm, your body still tends to follow the rhythm faithfully. At least it did for me. But on certain occasions, I found I was not able to finish my variation in *Giselle.* I'd realize at the very last moment that I had no momentum. If I didn't concentrate consciously and the music slowed down — for some reason, conductors slow down — I was going with it, and finally I almost stopped. I knew that I had to take force, but I couldn't, because the music was slowed down. Usually you are conscious of what you are doing. So if the music is too slow, you just go ahead, push it along, give some indication to the conductor that he is too slow. But sometimes, unconsciously, you go along with him.

I think the best critic I ever had was my wife [Anna Scarpova]. She was in Ballet Russe with me, but of course she saw my performances with Ballet Theatre as well, and if I did something wrong or she didn't like it, she would tell me about it most definitely. The critics were helpful, but not always specific enough or constructive enough that you could follow their suggestions. They were writing in a more general form — and also, I did not always agree.

Sometimes critics may not understand what the dancer is trying to do. This happened to me, not with *Giselle,* but with *Helen of Troy.* While I was with Ballet Theatre, I danced the role of Paris. Because it's a light, tongue-in-cheek kind of ballet, I decided that I was going to be a dumb football player with big muscles, not quite sure of what's going on. I had fun doing it that way. Then we danced it in some provincial city, and one of the critics said, "Mr. Youskevitch didn't look like Paris. He looked like a football player." Well, that's exactly what I wanted to portray, so he paid me a compliment without knowing it.

The audience reaction is sometimes very misleading. You know that you didn't do certain things, but they feel you were wonderful. Little details that go by very fast are not noticeable in the audience, not everything can be seen, and your feeling onstage is a little exaggerated anyway, so in that sense there's a discrepancy. But the audience reaction gives you confidence and a little more energy.

With *Giselle* this can help you, because it has to be danced and also it has to be balletically acted. Not acted in the dramatic way, but with some kind of emotional involvement that goes across. This makes the part of Albrecht very hard. In the classical repertory, it is usually considered *the* role for a male dancer, as Giselle is *the* role for the female dancer. You have to be quite experienced to dance it; you have to know the stage, you have to be able to act at the moment. Sometimes you want to smile, but you feel it's strained. If I didn't feel strained as I was doing things, I felt I was doing them right.

But sometimes you put a strain on yourself offstage. When I was very young, before the Ballet Russe days, I danced in England with the Woizikowsky company. In such a small company, of course I didn't dance only one ballet. Let's say I danced *Sylphides*, and then after the second ballet I would have *Spectre de la Rose*. We had a long run at the Coliseum theatre in London, and there was a little restaurant called George's very close by. And in between, during the second ballet, George would bring me a big steak with french fries, and I would eat the whole steak before I danced *Spectre de la Rose*. But as I grew older, I changed my ways.

There are two types of role for dancers, now at least; and even before now, there were more abstract ballets. You must approach these a little differently. In the story ballet, you know the character, what you are, and the period. In the abstract type of ballet, sometimes you cannot make up your mind what you are until the last note of the music. The choreographer is not always helpful in such a ballet; most of them do not really explain the idea. So you have to figure out for yourself how to behave.

You take the cue from what type of steps the choreographer gives you. That is a certain indication that you're lyrical or dramatic or whatever. Then of course the music gives you a certain feel. Taking the steps, the feel of the music, and then your relationship to people onstage, what you are supposed to do when, and what they are doing while you are doing it, you can build up your own story. I usually created a story for myself, not necessarily a down-to-earth story, but a story of what kind of spirit I was. Just to make sense of things helped me a lot.

For a man dancer, it's very important to justify the action. If you know why you're doing a certain step, or you make up your own story — 'I'm doing this step in order to reach the sky' or whatever — the step acquires a better importance and a better expression than if you just perform it without a goal. And I feel it's also a more masculine way of performing, because men in general are more rational and less emotional than women. When I know that I have justified everything I do, I know also the feel of how I should do it.

Now, Balanchine made *Theme and Variations* on me. His ballet was abstract but with an idea, that this is a contemporary way to portray the feeling of the grandeur of the Imperial, classical ballet. I approached the role in that way; I felt the abstract movements I was doing were O.K., provided I did them in the spirit of that classical period. So I was imagining 'I am the prince in *Swan Lake*' or 'I am the prince in *Giselle*,' or 'I am the prince in . . .' anyplace, because classical ballet is a noble type of dancing with a noble bearing. And in my relationship with the ballerina, I was also trying to do the same. There is a certain feeling between us that I felt should be the same as in any classical pas de deux. Without very realistic lovemaking, it's still a kind of refined love affair. No matter how abstract, that should go on. If you feel logical, if you feel justified, it gives you confidence.

Balanchine and I had some talks about the ballet, and he didn't quite like my interpretation. He was always telling me that I should do it less romantically and more abstract. I would tell him, "I'm trying, but I cannot." I was going according to my idea of the ballet, and I felt my interpretation was the one that was proper. It worked for me, and . . . well, I had a good success with this part.

Here is something different. For Tudor's *Romeo and Juliet* at Ballet Theatre, I was taught the steps — not by Hugh [Laing]; maybe by Johnny Kriza, who knew the part, but anyway by someone who was the understudy but had never danced it. I rehearsed with Alicia [Markova], and then Tudor came to a rehearsal to check.

My approach to the role was completely different from Hugh's. I felt that what was extremely important was that both Romeo and Juliet are very young and both are in love. Those are the two things that should be brought out. There is no psychology, no rushing around, no anxiety of any kind. Just love and youth — that's why it's a tragedy. They just didn't think. If they were a little bit older, there would be no tragedy whatsoever. Hugh was dancing very emotionally; I would say he danced a neurotic type of Romeo. Being a classical dancer, I was doing it very romantically. And of course Tudor looked at all this, and he said, "Would you like me to coach you all in the proper way of doing my choreography?" And I opened my mouth and said, "No."

January 1979
New York

Alicia Alonso

Alicia Alonso (b. Havana, Cuba, 1921) took her first ballet class at the age of eleven at the Sociedad Pro-Arte Musical in Havana. Arriving in New York four years later, she continued her training with Anatole Vilzak and at the School of American Ballet. She began her dancing career in the musicals Great Lady *and* Stars in Your Eyes *and with Ballet Caravan. Having joined the corps of (American) Ballet Theatre in 1940, she was promoted to ballerina two years later. Although she maintained her affiliation with that company until 1960, she left periodically for guest engagements with the Havana Pro-Arte (1941–43) and the Ballet Russe de Monte Carlo (1955–57) and for regular appearances with the company she founded in 1948, Ballet Alicia Alonso, renamed Ballet Nacional de Cuba in 1955. In 1943, following eye operations that confined her to bed for a year and a half, she made her debut as Giselle, a role with which she would be increasingly identified. As the first American guest artist to dance in Russia, she performed it with the Bolshoi and Kirov companies in 1958; she also staged her own production for the Paris Opéra and the Ballet Nacional de Cuba. Her repertory has included* Swan Lake, Coppélia, La Fille Mal Gardée, *and* Sleeping Beauty, *and such contemporary works as Antony Tudor's* Lilac Garden *and* Undertow, *Agnes de Mille's* Fall River Legend, *and George Balanchine's* Apollo. *In 1947, she and Igor Youskevitch, her constant partner, created the leading roles in Balanchine's* Theme and Variations. *Today, Alonso remains director of the Ballet Nacional de Cuba and its prima ballerina.*

Most dancers die — or at least retire — before they become legendary, but Alicia Alonso dances on, an authentic legend in her own lifetime. Her ties to Giselle *alone span thirty-seven years, longer than most people dance. I had never laid eyes on her before September 29, 1977, when she danced the role in New York for the first time in seventeen years. At first, the fact that she could still execute it seemed extraordinary. By Act II, the depth, detail, and technical brilliance of her performance had surpassed my expectations and justified the extravagance of her legend.*

*T*he first *Giselle* I saw was Markova and Dolin with Ballet Russe de Monte Carlo, here in New York. I had never seen this ballet before that I can remember, or heard about it. It was the most beautiful ballet I had ever seen. It impressed me tremendously. I was sure I would dance it since I liked it so much — there was no doubt about it. That's not confidence, no. It's just that I had an advantage: I had already danced here, as a professional, and when I went back to Cuba, I would always dance with the school there. That was a non-professional school, a private school. Now that I say it in these words, it sounds so easy, but inside of me then, I knew that someday I would dance it. Not because I thought I would be a great dancer or a ballerina, but that — if I worked hard enough — I would be able to do it either in the school or in whatever place it was.

In Ballet Theatre, first I learned corps de ballet. Immediately I was in the Wilis, and they also put me in the friends, right from the beginning. And I saw many Giselles. I saw Markova, Nana Gollner, Lucia Chase, Viola Essen I think it was, and Patricia Bowman — Goodness gracious! — and Toumanova, Tamara Toumanova, doing Giselle, all before I did this role myself.

From every dancer you watch, you learn. I want to explain it to you. It is wrong for a dancer not to watch and learn, because there is always something you can learn from someone. It's not stealing; it's learning. There are no two people who can do the same thing exactly the same, because they are different. And once you think you're doing the same, you're not. You interpret it through you.

While I was in the corps de ballet, as a friend of Giselle and as one of the two Wilis — which I did with Nora Kaye — I was watching other dancers. And when there's a ballet that I like very much, and in this case we're talking about *Giselle,* I try to learn everybody's part, male and female. I could dance that whole ballet in my head, with all the entrances and exits. And I believed in whatever part I was doing; I made a role out of it. I made a story of my own that would fit into the person I was dancing, a complete story.

But also, what is very important . . . I didn't realize in those days that I was, in my mind, filing all that I was looking at. I realized it in later years, when I was lying in bed without being able to dance. Then I began to study this ballet; I went through my file of it. I began to look inside of me and think: 'This part, this person used to do very beautifully. This other part, I like this, this, this.' I started to go through all the richness of what I had seen, and then I started to make it completely my own *Giselle* — from my files of experience and my own taste.

I did not dance the role of Giselle until after I was operated on, and even then I had not danced in that many performances. Only as often as they played it at Ballet Theatre, which was not as much as today. But still I saw people like that dancing before I had to have my eyes operated on.

How did I learn the role on my fingers? How do you learn a song? How do you learn anything that you want to learn? By watching, repeating, looking, and inquiring. I have very good memory, eye memory. I look at something from the front, and it immediately stays right on my retina, on my eyes. When I was lying in bed, I was going through everything that I remembered, and I became an audience: I sat in front, and I was watching the performance. And when I forgot anything, whether someone comes from the left or from the right, then I would do it on my fingers and try to ask, 'Wasn't this person on from the left when Hilarion was coming from here? When he was going out, wasn't the other coming in?' I went through little things, so I wouldn't be able to forget. And when I worked after that with Pat Dolin, it was what I had been doing in my mind that I put into practice.

After I had my eye operations, I came back, and when they proposed to me to dance *Giselle,* I studied with Anton Dolin. And he said to me, "Do it the most that you can like Markova," because the dancer that I used to see most was Alicia Markova — she was a person that I admired in this role. "And the audience . . ." he said. "It will break them to see something so different. They will not accept it. And she's so wonderful. Follow that pattern." He was the one who taught me the role. He had rehearsed and danced with her, and he helped me very much with learning it.

I was performing every night and matinées Saturday and Sunday. I was dancing principal roles and soloist roles, and sometimes I even came in for corps de ballet. So I was dancing no less than two or three ballets a night. And rehearsing during the day. And also rehearsing *Giselle.* So to learn a ballet like *Giselle* in four or five days, at the same time that you're performing — well, what I had done already in my mind was quite close.

I always believed I would go back to dancing, but the doctors, no. They still don't understand how I did. I danced without them knowing. By the time they told me, "Go ahead and try to dance," I said, "Never mind, don't tell me. I've been dancing already, in the studio." I kept on working because I wanted — not only that role — I wanted to dance. Period.

So when I first did it, I tried to do certain things and gestures in certain moments like Markova did, because of the way Pat told me. Certain things came out different a little bit because . . . I couldn't help it. It came out of me. Right in the first performance, already I did some things I didn't know I had done. I was not conscious about it. But immediately I began to be conscious about it, and since then, I've been continually working consciously about finding the more approximate *Giselle,* the one I feel goes with my ideas of it. In our company, in Ballet Nacional de Cuba, we try definitely to understand the Romantic style, definitely to understand in what time was that ballet done, what is the story about, what kind of person each of them was. And then, out of that work, to put their personality into it. This is very important. And that's what I have to decide and try to do with myself.

That role is very special. I think it captures the essence of Romanticism in a very beautiful way. It has a definite style, it has a story that is eternal, and it has a contrast of the first act to the second act — they're so different — that to the audience becomes very beautiful, very entertaining. And also, I think *Giselle* is one of the classics that has the right length as a spectacle, and it combines music, a style of dancing, choreography, pantomime.

Something that every dancer likes is that it's very definite, clear. The expression of a dancer is not just technique. The art is how skillfully the technique is used. It's skill, like a doctor with the operating table, how skillfully he manages those instruments. The dancer has to be that skillful, to have a technique and at the same time to be able to use it in an extremely expressive way.

At the beginning at Ballet Theatre, the Romantic style was new to everyone. Markova had been doing it for a long time, but for the company itself it was new. As a matter of fact, there were certain critics who said Markova's Giselle somehow didn't match the company. It was one style and the company was another one. I learned the style through books, and reading old write-ups. And from then on, from then on, I've been reading everything about the Romantic era, looking at lithographs and critics of the time. I started then, and I have never finished. I'm still doing it. I still read about different dancers of the *Romantisme,* their different styles. Not only because I like that epoch, no. I read about all of ballet. Before I do any ballet in my life, I try to know the most about it that I can. But since we're talking about *Giselle,* I want you to know this: I have read everything, tried to look at every little review that I can get my hands on, from [Carlotta] Grisi to everyone.

I think all the background material gives you richness, richness to understand the part and to take the most advantage of it. I think it's most important when we do any part. When you dance *Giselle,* whether you're a corps de ballet or a soloist or prima ballerina or

64

premier danseur, you should know all about it. You should read and research the most you can about it, so you can portray the style and believe in what you're dancing. Today when you see a company, you notice not that they do it automatically, not that they do it because they have been told what to do, when to do, but that one of the most difficult things for them is to believe in what they're doing when they do it.

In Act I, when she comes out of the door, Giselle is life itself! She's not exactly doomed, but slowly, as you look at this person, you begin to understand that she's not just like all the other women, that there's something different on her, something more fragile. You cannot put your actual finger on it, but there's something about her that doesn't quite let go. It should make the audience hold their breath looking at her, because they don't know what will happen.

There are different versions of *Giselle*. In some versions, the audience gets the feeling that she knows Loys, and everybody around already knows him. In our version, Ballet Nacional de Cuba, we do it that she's introducing him for the first time to her friends, to all the peasants. They don't know him. Because they are there, because they are celebrating this special once-a-year festival of the harvest, and they are going to make Giselle their queen for the festival, they find her for the first time with him. Maybe, in the story, one of them has seen him, another one saw him another time, but not all of them could have seen him. And they analyze that this man is not a peasant. If he were, they would ask the logical question: 'Where does he live? He's not one of us.' All the peasants cannot know him, because they ask instead, 'What work does he do for a living? I don't see him picking the grapes. I don't see him working the earth.' That's why she presents him to the friends and says, 'I will dance for him.'

But that doesn't mean this is the first time *I* see him. Not Alonso — it's Giselle we're talking about. She's known him long enough to love him. There is no time when you know that you love — I mean, a pure love. There is not one moment that you say, "There it is." You cannot talk about time, about counting dates, being very practical, when you're talking about art.

The way she expresses being in love is being innocent. Her love for him is playful because of her pureness. Do you realize that during all *Giselle* he's asking her for a kiss and she never gives it to him? In the first part — this is a very old pantomime — he's asking her, and she plays with him and laughs. And then she gives it to him on the shoulder or on the forehead. That's what makes Hilarion very mad. She touches Loys' forehead with her finger, from her mouth, and she runs, very gay, very happy, like bells. She feels that by touching him she's done something beautiful. That shows you how pure she is in her thoughts. And then she plays again with trying to kiss him; he puts his hands out and she puts the kisses there. It's done, not in a malicious way, but still very pure. She does it in front of everyone, very playful.

Do you realize that the last scene — I mean, the way we do it and it usually is this way — that last scene in the grave, she still goes and puts a kiss on his hands and disappears? She is a ghost and she will go far away. She says good-bye by touching his hands with her kisses. It's sort of like a reminiscence, like 'Remember when there was life,' like a memory.

I'm telling you the way *we* do *Giselle.* When I say that I work on Giselle, I'm not only working on the person of Giselle, on the main role. For me, everything that surrounds Giselle is most important to understand, the why of the existence of Giselle, the problems of Giselle, what happens to Giselle. You cannot do Giselle alone. You have to do it with a frame, with a company, with every detail. That's the way I feel it, and that's the way we do it. What I have tried to do is not just dedicate myself to the ballerina Giselle but to the story of Giselle. I believe that *Giselle* is a masterpiece of *Romantisme,* and when you open the book, you should read all of it. You should not only see the name of Giselle and read this person. You understand?

I have worked this version based on the original. Every person and everything that's part of the story has a place in it and has a why, a reason. Even the Wilis; each Wili has a story in herself. They know why they are dead and why they are here. Each of them! We make it like this because this makes the frame and makes the story, and this goes into the audience. It's like . . . If you see a painting of a great master, but he only started, he only drew one person, and the rest is just a sketch, then you say, "Oh, why didn't he finish it?" That's what I think when you see *Giselle.* You have to see every part finished so you can enjoy the whole thing.

Giselle's own story is right there onstage. If her story is not told onstage, then you cannot believe any of the other Wilis. If you read the poem of the Wilis by Heine, which is where Gautier got the idea of the story, then you realize that the other ones are just an old German legend. But you see her actual story.

But go back to Act I. She feels sorry for Hilarion. If you knew Giselle, she can never feel that anybody would be a nuisance. She doesn't want to hurt him; she doesn't want to hurt anyone. She's incapable of hurting anyone. But she's fragile, and that's why she can be hurt. She loves to dance because she loves life itself. She loves everything that's around her, and when she dances, she portrays everything. She's happy, she's tender, she's gay. A very, very happy person, very alive, and yet she's fragile. But sometimes when people are ill, they are the people who enjoy life the most. Because in every bit of it, they realize the value of it. That's her a little bit too. So, just to say that she likes dancing because of dancing seems to me not to show the real person that we're studying: Giselle, in a Romantic era, surrounded by people who love her and believe in her, and so fragile.

Of course she's ill from the beginning, of course. When you have studied this story as I have studied, deeply, to be able to portray it, you do it in this way, artistically and realistically. Now, you study a person who is sick with a heart, trouble with a heart, who can die like a bird, so quick. It must be a person who must have trouble at certain times; she must be weak. It's not the first time that Giselle had anything wrong with the heart. Because why does the mother not want her to dance? You must follow this story logically, and then you create the artistic surroundings, the atmosphere of it. But you must base yourself in something real of life, with logic, and you have to base the pantomime in reality too. You have to have a logic in your pantomime, a logic in the people you present on the stage, and after that comes your artistry. Then you create. You put on the clothes you should, the make-up you should, the gesture. You study it, and then you melt it together, and that *becomes*.

Because, first of all, you're not dancing for yourself — you're dancing for an audience. You believe the part, but they must believe in it too. Therefore, in a theatre, and especially in our theatre today, you have to use every little bit of theatrical technique to be able to create the atmosphere that you want. You must study: If a person is sick of a heart, how sick could she be? How long has she been having this illness? Why would her mother not want her to dance? You must ask a doctor, "What kind of heart did she have? What kind of feeling? How does she feel physically when, for instance, she dances too much? *What* does she feel?" You ask the doctor, who will say, "You feel the heart beat faster than usual, faster. It loses timing. And then, when you take it easy, it goes back again. She feels well, normal." Well, for me it helps. And I've studied, I've studied. Some other dancers have not, and they're beautiful! But to me, it's like that.

It's about time that all dancers learned theatre. They have to learn it. They have to know what is drama, and they must read the history of art. And when they're going to do any ballet, they must read all about it, in every way.

The Mad Scene has a certain pattern, though you can change, you can do this or that. But the Mad Scene has to go together with reality, how it would be portrayed by this person, how this delicate person will snap. There are many ways of doing it, but you have to choose one and study it very carefully.

First of all, she doesn't want to face the truth. She believes so much in Loys. She has never been deceived, she has never been told lies, and she cannot believe this deception. She's not capable of believing it. Therefore, she hides and refuses to see the truth. Slowly, she begins to face it. When, finally, this all works on her mind, it's the shock of realizing the truth that is too much for her, and her heart fails. And this is scientifically correct for a person who has trouble with the heart. Once she faces it, just when she turns to her mother, she cannot hide any more. She dies.

She does mean to commit suicide. That's when she's mad, completely mad. That's what *shows* that she's mad. How can this person see a sword and blame it for everything? The sword becomes to her the fault of everything. She doesn't want to face that it's not the sword but the man who's to blame. They stop her from committing suicide, but she could have. In those days, you put the sword up and you ran and you fell forward — and in the moment she pulls it up to run forward on it, Albrecht takes it away from her. And in that moment, in our version, Hilarion grabs her. When she sees Hilarion and recognizes him, she comes to reality.

She has nothing to face but reality. There's nothing else — she has to. You see, in real life there are certain moments that insane people come into reality. And it's terrible, because then they realize they've been mad. When they take the sword from her, she realizes that everything that's happened is true: that he doesn't love her, that he is a prince, that she cannot marry him. That he lied — most of all, that he lied. And she runs to the mother for help. She's thinking of him, and she wants to explain to him that she's not mad at him, that she forgives him. She's the kind of person who could never be sore with anyone. That's why when you say does she like Hilarion or despise Hilarion, I say she's not that kind of person. And she dies, right there, in Albrecht's arms, before she can even say anything to him.

In Act II, she protects him even from the Queen of the Wilis. First she plays with him without realizing that she may kill him by dancing so much. In the first entrance, she doesn't know really that by dancing she may harm him. But after she realizes it, then slowly it becomes this pleading to the other ones not to kill him; and she defends him.

In that act, the first part is her being introduced to the new world of the Wilis. She's initiated into the Wilis because she died before she was betrothed, and she was deceived, fooled, by the man who loved her — he didn't really love her. So first there's the initiation, the solo. She enters and she goes, flies away. She's not real then. She's the most unreal of them all because she's the newest. She has not completely become a Wili yet.

At one moment before her initiation, do you realize that what the Wilis form in the center of the stage is the sun? Do you see how a child paints a sun? He paints a round circle and light coming out in lines. That's it — that's the pattern. When they bow, it's a sign that the sun is stronger than they are. This goes back to man: when man cannot understand something, he is frightened of it, he respects it, and he bows to it. And when the sun comes, the Wilis disappear. This is the end of a life for them. But they're going to give birth to another life, into their own. They make the sun, they disappear, and when they come back, they say, 'Now comes someone to our moonshape,' and they run and make a moonshape. Do you realize all those things? Well, I have studied all of them, every bit of it, the why of the pattern, the why of the design. It may come across, it may not come across, but it's there.

Then Albrecht comes looking for her, and she plays with him. She appears one way, another way, but she doesn't realize what she can do to him. She's playing like she did in the first act. It's the same, but this time she's playing with flowers instead of kisses. She dances and she dances and then she hides again, until after the Bacchanale. When the Bacchanale comes, the Wilis kill Hilarion, and when they come in again, they have caught Albrecht. They make a diagonal and he comes running, along the diagonal, looking for her. And then she comes. So far, he's been running in back of her, following her, but this time she runs after him.

From then on, she starts to plead for him, because she realizes. And all that time, from then on, she is dancing because she is commanded by the Queen of the Wilis to keep on dancing: 'Make him dance!' But she's begging for his life to the Queen. Not everybody does it accentuating that, her dancing to the Queen of the Wilis, to the other Wilis, to him. Not everybody does that. They do beautifully, but they dance it without accentuating that as much as we do. That's my particular sense of it.

She does save him. She saves him by maintaining herself with him, by making him dance to keep him alive in the end. She dances with him because they make her dance, but she keeps helping him. Now she's the stronger. One thing that she shows him in the end, with her arm, means 'The sun is coming up. I have saved your life,' and she picks him up. While the Wilis go, covering their faces from it, she shows him that its coming up has saved him.

In the old story, he picks her up when she's going to her grave and doesn't allow her to go there. He puts her on the earth, and then the earth opens and swallows her. In our story, we put it that she just disappears, to rest in her own grave where she started. The idea of the Romanticists is that she will rest until she will not be one of these Wilis, who are mean, who will kill, because she's not that kind. She never could be.

I think every role is difficult to dance. If you are a person like I am that is never satisfied, there's always much more to do, always something you can find, technically and artistically. According to the newspapers, I always had a very strong technique, but I find that I am never happy with the way I dance the whole thing technically. Sometimes I'm happier with the first act, sometimes with the second act; it's very difficult to make them come technically even. Or sometimes I felt one part good in the first act, but the other part not so good. Of course, the audience doesn't always realize it. It's you — that's the worst one — you, yourself. It's the searching, this discipline, that keeps alive a part that you dance.

It depends also how I feel myself. One day I do it more alive in the beginning, sometimes more melancholic. Or I do the movements a little bit faster, a little slower, or softer. I have the line of the character I want to follow, and that has a reality in itself, the way I do in myself.

For me, it keeps alive better with the same partner, the same choreography, and the same everything, because in it I can find even more and more and more. Otherwise, I feel that it could become mechanical. When I dance with the same partner in the version that I have put on *Giselle*, I can search for more new things each time, because I know it so well. And otherwise I'm afraid that you can do it very well, but as a dancer, myself, selfishly, I would feel mechanical. Not that the audience will get it, because I don't think they necessarily will.

Youskevitch and I went so much together, we worked together so long. He was my first partner that I had an opportunity to sit down and talk about the approaching of different parts: "Do you think this is like this in that part?" or "I like it better this way." Sometimes we didn't agree. Or sometimes we'd try it and I'd say, "O.K., let's do it your way today, but the next time we do it different." We talked a lot about it, in the pantomime things, in the atmosphere of it, if he would sit down on the bench, or where he would sit down, or when get up. Little details, but the whole idea of it, the way we'd both portray *Giselle*, and we got to understand each other. He got to understand my way of doing *Giselle*, my feeling, and vice versa, I think I did too.

Every time I get a different partner, we work very hard, and we try to understand each other. I try to get him to understand my version of *Giselle* and to understand his, and then to come together on it, because that's the most important.

I think everything you dance, every style of ballet you dance, contributes to enrich the other ones, each to the other. Because the more different things you dance, the more ballets you learn, the more you read, the more you search, the more you understand.

July 1979
New York

Alexander Grant

Alexander Grant (b. Wellington, New Zealand, 1925) came to London in 1946 to study ballet on a Royal Academy of Dancing scholarship he'd won at the age of fifteen. Five months after his arrival, he joined the Sadler's Wells Ballet, where his portrayal of the Barber in Leonide Massine's Mam'zelle Angot *in 1947 established him for the next thirty years as the company's foremost character and demi-caractère dancer. He had already danced more than fifty roles when he made his debut as Petrouchka in 1957. Perhaps the highlights of his career were the nearly two dozen roles created for him by Frederick Ashton. Between the Jester in* Cinderella *(1948) and Yslaev in* A Month in the Country *(1976) lay such models of choreographic invention and characterization as the Pirate Chief in* Daphnis and Chloë *(1951), Eros in* Sylvia *(1952), Tirrenio in* Ondine *(1958), Alain in* La Fille Mal Gardée *(1960), and Bottom in* The Dream *(1964). Since Grant's retirement from the Royal Ballet in 1976, he has been director of the National Ballet of Canada, where he still occasionally performs.*

Alexander Grant is irreplaceable. A linchpin of the Royal Ballet since its infancy, he is for me indelibly stamped on Alain, on Bottom, on Ashton's whirlwind Neapolitan Dance in Swan Lake, *even on the tiny role of Yslaev which I saw him perform only three times. Although there's no telling to what extent those roles look as they do because he created them, he is nevertheless inextricably bound to them. It is every dancer's privilege to re-invent himself every time he takes on a new role. It was Grant's additional privilege, as an ongoing inspiration to Ashton and one of his ablest instruments, to share continually in the invention of the roles themselves. The longer I thought about him, the more I wondered how he went about stepping into someone else's shoes, into a role that existed long before he gave it his body and sensibility. Alain was made for him: Petrouchka he had to make his own.*

I danced all my life, really, because I started when I was six — although at six, you don't know whether you want to dance or not. It's just part of your life as a little boy. Other people have encouraged you to do it, and you grow up just being a dancer. It wasn't until I was about fifteen that I realized it was really what I wanted to do, but I had very little hope of doing it because New Zealand was at the end of the world. We were very lucky, way back in 1938 and '39, to have the Ballet Russe de Monte Carlo and the Colonel de Basil companies come through. That was the first time I'd seen really professional, mature dancers and ballets of that caliber. I remember *Schéhérazade*, and *Aurora's Wedding* with the Russian dance, the Three Ivans, in it. I thought it was fantastic. So the inspiration came, and I was very much inspired by a particular dancer called Leon Woizikowsky, who was doing most of the Massine roles. It was just the kind of dancing that I probably always felt I could do and would like to do. I don't think I met him, but there were repercussions of that visit.

The first dance I ever learned, as a six-year-old, was a Russian dance — you know, the one where you sit down and kick out your heels, the trepak. I became quite well known in that dance. It was my specialty number. And because the Russians were there, somebody had the idea of showing them that New Zealand had a little of this ethnic kind of dance. So one day after class, they brought me on — I don't know what age I was. I felt very embarrassed — and I rushed about and did my trepak to their polite applause.

Then when I was about fifteen, I got a scholarship from the Royal Academy, but it was held up because the war was on. When I went to London, I arrived on the first of February, 1946, and the company was to start at Covent Garden on the twentieth of February. As the new boy, I was told to go and watch, and learn what I could from what was going on. And as boys were still in some shortage after the war, I was rushed over to Covent Garden at six o'clock one night, and I was on in the Farandole in *Beauty* that same night, replacing somebody who was injured. I had managed to get in the night before, in the gallery, and I had seen the rehearsals because I was sort of at the School, although the School really didn't exist because most of the people from it had been taken to form the new touring company. Anyway, I saw it one night and I was on the next night.

In that production, the Three Ivans used to come just before the pas de deux. The ballet mistress came up to me and said, "Have you ever done that kind of Russian dance?" and I said, "Yes." "Right," she said, "we'll teach it to you and put you on next Saturday matinée." I never understood how she knew, because I'd never danced my trepak dance there, and I never had occasion to tell them that I did that kind

74

of work. But there had been somebody in that Russian company in New Zealand who's a very well known teacher now in London — her name was Anna Severskaya and she's Anna Northcote now — and she was a great friend of our ballet mistress at the time, Joy Newton. She'd seen me do the Farandole and said to Joy, "Is that boy from New Zealand? Ask him if he's the boy I saw in New Zealand who did that Russian dance." So before I knew it, I was doing the principal one in the Ivans, and I was still a student.

When I was taken into the company in September, I had danced as a student in the touring company for two weeks, but I'd also danced at Covent Garden practically every performance, doing this Russian dance. And I actually did it when the company later went to Russia. After doing it to the Russians to begin with, way back in New Zealand, I did it to the Russian public at the Bolshoi. Can you imagine? And I finally met Woizikowsky, too. I had the thrill, years later, of being in Warsaw when we were doing Massine's *Three-Cornered Hat,* and Dame Ninette [de Valois] asked him to coach us in the role of the Miller. Harold Turner and Michael Somes were dancing it, and as I was sort of understudy, I was there, so I was coached by Woizikowsky. I danced the Miller there, and I danced it later in Edinburgh during the first Diaghilev exhibition in August of 1954.

Everything sort of ties up in the ballet world. In 1947, de Valois got Massine down to Covent Garden; maybe she asked him whether he would do some of his ballets. We weren't told very much in those days, unlike people today, who want to know everything, but we did what we were told. And we were told that on such-and-such a Sunday afternoon — we didn't work on Sunday normally — we had to have a class in Sadler's Wells Theatre because Mr. Massine was going to look us over. I can remember, knowing about all these famous men and that *there* was the famous Massine, jumping myself silly in that class. I don't know whether it was very controlled, but I jumped. I used to have a good jump in my youth, and I always felt that elevation was very important for the male dancer. He just sat quietly and watched, just looking at the company, because he was secretly casting. We didn't know what ballets he was going to do — I just jumped. He cast me first as a poodle in *Boutique Fantasque,* and the poodle is a jumper. And then I got a part in *Three-Cornered Hat* as the Dandy, which is a small part, and I jumped in that as much as I could. And from that, he then gave me the Barber in *Mam'zelle Angot,* which was an extraordinary, bizarre role.

And there's a funny story about that. He'd played the Barber himself, in America — never in England — and he was reproducing the ballet, and changing it slightly, from a film that he would show

75

us occasionally. It was taken onstage, and he was very much a dandy in it, with a tail-coat and stick and a hat, terribly smart and debonair. So I rehearsed and learned the ballet with this very chic, smooth, dark-haired person in mind. But when the final dress rehearsal came, I thought, 'This is not like the costume that Massine wore. It's a completely different conception.' He had gotten a new designer called, no less, André Derain, and in this new conception of Derain's — with, I suppose, Massine's collaboration — I was turned suddenly into a much more peasanty kind of character, with a bizarre blond wig with curls all over it. I had worked for months on the role with another idea in my head, and I had to put this Shirley Temple wig on. There it was. I said, "Is this part of the costume?" Nobody had told me, and I wasn't experienced enough to go up and have a look at the design. So I had to change all my ideas overnight about how the character should be played. With this blond wig, it wasn't the chic thing one had learnt from Massine — and we learnt so much from Massine. It was a much more dotty kind of character. But somehow I must have caught it because it was a great success.

It taught me a great lesson in preparing. I found that in working for a role, you work with an idea of what the choreographer wants as far as movement and steps, which should give you a key to the character. But you don't become the character 'til you put it on, sitting in the dressing room making up your face. You become the role when you actually turn into it in costume and make-up. The choreography's given you every key in the movement, but the costume enhanced it — that's where you got your real character. You suddenly became that and were no longer you, although you always shine through. You can't get away from yourself. If it was a bulky costume, you thought of how it was going to affect what you were going to do. If the costume wasn't bulky, it wasn't going to affect that at all, but it affected the way you felt in a role.

In *Ondine*, I knew I was going to have a cape, and I kept asking about it. I said, "I must work with this cape because it needs to be used." I felt the cape was going to enhance certain movements I had to do. We were coming up to dress rehearsal again, and whenever I could, I said to our wonderful designer, Lila de Nobili, "You haven't forgotten my cape, have you?" Well, I didn't get that cape until the dress rehearsal, but it was the most *wonderful* cape. It was silk, all cut with scallops, and enormous. Now, you don't see yourself as a dancer, you only feel yourself, but I knew I could do marvelous things with this cape. And I thought, 'I hope they'll never lose it because they'll never be able to reproduce it like this. It's just perfect.' I knew it was good, but I never saw it until they made the film. Usually, when you see a film of yourself, you're very disappointed, because lots of things that you're doing on the stage don't work as well as they have in your mind. But that cape worked better. It was the one thing where something was actually better when I saw it than I'd hoped it would be.

I suppose *Angot* was my first big role, but I'd had a terrible fright before that. I'd been thrown in at the deep end when I first went to the company — it was a lot of luck as well. In that first year, in 1946, the most marvelous ballet had been created by Ashton called *Symphonic Variations*, which was a real testing piece for the company. What happened was that Brian Shaw, who created one of the roles, had to do his army training. People were still in compulsory training in England for some time after the war, and his number had come up, and he had to go away for two years. I suddenly found myself told to learn *Symphonic Variations*, which was twenty minutes long, and you were onstage when the curtain went up and didn't get off until the curtain came down. I was a little green thing, so frightened, and my main partner was Pamela May, an important ballerina who'd been used to much more experienced and expert partners than poor me, just very green. But she did everything to help, coped and encouraged, and I shall always be grateful to her.

A ballet like that was always a problem with me. If I could get my teeth into something by having, you could say, a character to hide behind, I was really comfortable. Maybe it was something to do with coming from so far away all my life. Maybe it was something to do with the nature of the Commonwealth. I don't know. I was always a very humble dancer, but when I was a character, I didn't have to be humble. When it was just me, I really had trouble. That's why that particular ballet was so terrifying. I'd had a lot of experience on the stage, and I wasn't the kind that died of nerves. But when the curtain went up, when I suddenly found myself on in *Symphonic Variations* — and I danced it for two years solid, in its very early days when it was being performed a lot — suddenly found myself in all-over white tights, sort of naked to the world, and just having to be me, it was one of the most difficult things I've ever done. And apart from trying to think, 'Can I remember this ballet?' — because I had to learn it in a great hurry — and apart from having to partner Pamela May, it was a real baptism of fire in my early days.

I think that Ashton was quite happy with me in *Symphonic* or he would have taken me out of it. I was also in *Patineurs*, a boy in brown, and original cast in *Scènes de Ballet*, which were kind of classical works. I did quite a lot of those. But I made such a success in *Mam'zelle Angot*, which was a characterization, and in that kind of demi-caractère work, that it typed me forever. And as everybody was striving to be the classical dancer and the demi-caractère dancer was more rare, and as Ashton, in his ballets, used that kind of dancer to a great degree as a contrasting part to the more prince-like hero role, it meant that as that kind of a character, I was very often in the performance *with* those people, *with* [Margot] Fonteyn and Somes. I *also* had a role, which didn't do me any harm. In fact, one of the first roles of any consequence that Ashton gave me was the Jester in *Cinderella*, which is what I call a demi-caractère role.

Also, I had my height against me. I'm rather short as a dancer, and if I had risen to another kind of position, my performance would have come after three others; I wouldn't have danced as much. But I was there always in the first performance with them, like in *Ondine*, in *Sylvia*, in *Cinderella*, as a foil, with a characterization. Those were roles in which I obviously felt more comfortable. Ashton has an enormous eye anyway, and he always brought out and extended the potential of a particular person. I was lucky enough for him to do that right to the end of my career, when the old bones were getting a bit stiffer. In the last ballet of his I did, *Month in the Country*, I was just a character with hardly a step.

A demi-caractère dancer has many dance technicalities to challenge him. He has to jump just as high, and possibly higher, than the hero. And the steps are used to portray the role he's playing; the character comes through in the steps. That's why a choreographer like Ashton liked to use those roles, because he could create interesting choreography that he wouldn't give to the prince. Or you might say that a pure character role could have boots or shoes, whereas a demi-caractère one still needs soft ballet shoes. How can I explain it? I would say the role of the Miller was a character role, but the role of the poodle was a demi-caractère role.

There's always this putting into boxes with dancers these days, but you must think of who did Petrouchka first, which was Nijinsky. In one night, in the same program, he would be the rose in *Spectre de la Rose*, which is really demi-caractère — the steps are the perfume of the rose — and then he would do *Petrouchka*. Would you say that *Spectre de la Rose* is demi-caractère or classical? Would you say that *Petrouchka* is character or demi-caractère? What would you say? The impact that Nijinsky must have made in *Petrouchka* was that here he was, this Godlike creature and this exotic whatever-it-was in *Spectre de la Rose*, and then he comes out in *Petrouchka*, which is such a contrast. The contrast, the range, was what was so startling. But he could do it all, and he must have had some kind of charisma to make this terrific imprint.

That was all one thought about when you did *Petrouchka*. The role of Petrouchka is very small; you have very little time to establish yourself. It was always a challenge. The thing opens; the three of you do a very quick dance; then you go straight into your scene, in which the steps are to portray what you're doing in the character and what you're feeling. That has to come through the movement, and it has to come out from inside somewhere. There must be something special in it, and it must have come out so strong with Nijinsky. I was never satisfied with Petrouchka because of the time factor, having so little time to establish the character, and knowing that somebody had made such an impact doing it. I was dissatisfied every performance, and I did it every night for seven weeks once in New Zealand. At the end of that, I was nearly going *up* the wall as well as 'round it.

Well, I started with *Petrouchka* as everybody starts, in the rehearsal room, but from the horse's mouth, because I was taught it by [Lubov] Tchernicheva and [Serge] Grigoriev, who had been in the rehearsal room when Fokine choreographed it on Nijinsky. They came and put the ballet on, and they argued with each other in Russian about whether it was this and whether it was that. They were trying to get it exactly as they remembered Nijinsky doing it. They would confer and decide, and then Tchernicheva would show what it is. So I had the most marvelous people teaching it.

I always had wonderful people to work with. I was very lucky. I had Massine. I had Ashton. And I was fortunate enough to learn right from the beginning that there is no talk in dance. You convey what you've got to say with your body and your movement, and the best possible way to communicate with another artist when you're teaching is with your body and not with your talk. I find now dancers question everything; they want to be told. They'll be shown something, you expect them to do it, and they don't do it. You say, "Why don't you do it?" "Well, because so and so and so, and it's impossible this way." We didn't talk. We saw, and we watched. Ballet is a visual art that's handed down. And when you had wonderful people like that who had also seen, and what they were doing was what they had absorbed from people before them, you saw what was required in the slightest movement that they showed you — even if they weren't capable of doing it properly — without it being explained to you. Then you attempted it. And then you used their eye to guide yourself after you had translated it into your body. You did what you saw they were after without one word passing between you. It was a communication of movement, and that's what ballet is. We all in our time learned to communicate with movement and not with talk.

If you're a true artist, you know it has to be real, and it can't possibly be real if you're a copy. You mustn't copy exactly. A great choreographer or a great coach doesn't expect you to, doesn't want you to. They want you to get the idea from what they're showing you, and then you, from inside yourself, feel it. If you're not feeling it, you'll go on trying it 'til you do feel it. But when you're just doing it mechanically, it never works, because there's no truth in it. It's no good, when you're doing character, laying it on top. It has to come right through your body. You've got to believe it, and you can only believe it if you feel what you're doing. If you're feeling, 'I've got to do this because that's what they say I've got to do,' you're never going to have any kind of truth in your performance. And the magical performances are when you reveal the truth, even if it's only twice in a night. That's a magic night, when suddenly the truth is revealed by the artist to the audience, not through talk, but through feeling, emotion, and coordination of movement and music.

The costume comes into that, too. Well, one was aware in *Petrouchka* that one had to use those gloves — they're mittens, actually; they don't have single fingers — so you kept your hands as they would be in mittens so it wasn't a shock when you actually wore them. And I asked Sir Frederick what he remembered of the make-up; he had never seen Nijinsky, but he saw Massine and various people dance the role. And he said he only remembered very, very red cheeks. Petrouchka's obviously got red cheeks and he's rather badly, roughly, painted.

I'd seen Festival Ballet do *Petrouchka* some years before, and of course I'd seen photographs galore. You look at the photographs of Nijinsky and you see what he's saying — it's a visual thing. A picture's not telling you anything with words, but it speaks volumes. I didn't do a lot of study as far as what was written about the ballet, but that follows on what I'm saying. I think that somebody who theorized and read all those things would be so confused. What's important is not what is said, but what is done and what is conveyed through movement. Tchernicheva would show you a movement with her eyes or her face, and you realized that she had absorbed all that through her eyes. She hadn't talked to Fokine or Nijinsky about it. She had just seen, and that had gone into her, and she was trying to bring it out of you. She and Grigoriev were both getting on, very elderly, but they had these wonderful mental pictures of what had affected them from inside.

A terribly important thing in *Petrouchka*, which one got from Tchernicheva, was that one had to do it with the eyes. The eyes are the mirror of what you're thinking, and they have to be used. Even though there was this wooden creature, this sawdust doll, you could see into the soul through the eyes. She didn't make the point; she just emphasized the eyes when she was showing me the role. She had wonderful, large eyes, just the same as Karsavina and Massine. They could all make you believe their eyes were even bigger, and you saw into their soul through their eyes.

Even though it's a very short role, it's exhausting physically because it's exhausting emotionally. The steps didn't make a problem for me because I wasn't so dyed-in-the-wool. I didn't have that 'you can only do a step one way' attitude. By the time I did Petrouchka, I had worked a long time with Ashton, who was always trying to find another way, something that wasn't the same old thing. But you have to know the purity of classical technique, if that's the purest form you've got, in order to know how to change it. That's how it starts, so it's no good doing all those angles without knowing the discipline of the technique. Certain basic principles are absolutely essential. It's probably like a good painter or even a good musician. To write the best avant-garde music, you have to know all about the fugue.

The music was kind of difficult in that its counts and rhythms are all broken up. But it wasn't a surprise to us; one had heard *Petrouchka* a great deal, and one was used to Stravinsky. It must have been a terrible shock in the beginning for those dancers because they hadn't had to contend with that kind of thing, but it isn't so much of a problem for dancers today.

What you want to do is always in the music. A good choreographer finds it first, and you very often don't realize what he's found until you've been doing a role for a while. When a choreographer isn't experienced, or is purposely going against the music, it's a different matter. But when the choreography is absolutely musical, you can find you're doing a movement that suddenly becomes a discovery to you because you hear it in the music. The music is saying exactly that movement, and if you had to choreograph it, you would find it very difficult to get away from that particular movement. Dancers don't always realize that. They're concentrating so on doing the movement well that, until they're into a role, they don't realize what they can get out of that movement because the music is just perfect for it. And then suddenly the two things can jell, and when they do, you've got a great performance.

I, in some extraordinary way, learnt everything when I was young. The main thing that was important to me was the dancing, but I also had a certain amount of acting and singing — although I couldn't sing a note — and I learnt the piano for nine years. When I came to England, there was no piano where I lived, but when nobody was in the rehearsal room, I would go to the piano to hear sounds and play them. I'd just make up something, hoping nobody would listen. I never could commit a musical piece to memory, but I could play a few chords and muck about. I would like to have a piano one day, so that in those certain moods, I could just bang out the notes.

I was always affected by the music, when I worked with it but also when I saw other dancers work with it and when, as I say, the two things really came together. I had the great good fortune so many times of seeing Dame Margot dance. Standing onstage in *Swan Lake*, I'd watch her, and sometimes she *was* the music. And not only Margot, but other dancers. It was wonderful. I realized just how important the music was. Seeing that was part of my visual, hearing, looking training in putting it all together. One tried to strive for that, and I did also feel it myself. When I'd been given a piece of choreography to do and the music said that choreography, what a joy it was to dance.

I honestly believe you have to feel *Petrouchka* in the music and the movement; they tell you what it's all about. You knew that you were a man trying to get out of a rag doll — nobody explained that to me, but one knew it — and this was the challenge all the time. You had to show that you were a puppet being controlled by somebody else, but fighting for your independence as a man. And of course, isn't everybody trying to do that? Sometimes you should almost be convinced he is a puppet, and then he gives you a quick, truthful glimpse that is so human in feeling that you know that that puppet is more than just a puppet.

At the beginning, when the ballet opens, he's just a puppet doing these things, but when they come down from the armrests, the public should realize that there's a conflict going on inside him. The conflict is that he's madly in love with the Ballerina and what on earth is he going to do to make her know it. He's got no way of trying to prove it to her, and when he gets an opportunity in the next scene, he goes about it all wrong and frightens her to death. She finally comes to see him, gives him a tiny bit of a chance, and he messes it all up. Well, how many times have we done that? Everybody is fighting disadvantages all the time, and sometimes we feel so unattractive. It relates tremendously to human nature. Obviously Nijinsky could convey that, and it was a terrible shock for people to see themselves in Petrouchka. It's the story of Beauty and the Beast. What does Beauty see in the Beast? She sees he has a soul and a heart, and he turns in her eyes beautiful. Ugliness can be transcended by the inside, by the soul.

In his own way, Petrouchka is totally self-pitying, and he is blaming everybody. The movement is very much sorry for yourself and angry against somebody else. He succeeds in beating the Magician in the end only because the soul and the spirit are so strong. And there's a warning to people that if you become too self-pitying, you're not going to succeed. I was able to avoid that self-pity in another role I did because I was part of its creation, I was determined to avoid it, and I didn't feel Ashton wanted it. In *La Fille Mal Gardée*, Alain could feel very sorry for himself. You get a glimpse of it occasionally, but then he comes out of it, breaks through it. Petrouchka feels all the time as though he were badly conceived, and he's blaming somebody else for that, whereas Alain never felt like that. You have to be very careful not to be maudlin as Petrouchka. You can't play him pitiful. It's a yearning of the soul.

Love and anger are human traits; that's what people can relate to in Scene II. And although the anger is conveyed towards the Magician and that picture on the wall, you have to be almost as angry with yourself for not being able to find a way to succeed in spite of him. Very often, when we're angry with someone, we have an awful guilt about it. The ballet's full of emotions. Every time, you're exhausted by the emotions of it, not by the dance's physical content.

I was pretty solid as a dancer — I had a solid body. But Petrouchka is a fairly loose role; you can feel like a piece of jelly inside it. You show some strength, but then you show that you're just jelly, like somebody who's putty in the hands. That's another thing you have to contend with — you're puny. You've been made puny, whereas the Moor has been made with a magnificent body, arrogance, and pride. He's a bit silly, but he's got all the trappings. I was very conscious all the time of the contrast between my body and any role. Once or twice, I had instances I was very pleased about. In *Daphnis and Chloë*, I was the big strong Pirate Chief, trying to rape Margot and throwing her around my neck and jumping all over her. Outside the stage door sometimes, people used to say, "You are Alexander Grant, aren't you?" I said, "Yes." "But you're so small." I liked that. They thought I was bigger on the stage because in that role I was being brawny. That's part of the magic of the theatre, but you have to really believe it and know what you're doing. In something like Alain, they were never disappointed in my size when I came offstage because I was small in the character. I was playing somebody rather small, so I was conveying that.

What one tried for in Petrouchka and so many other roles was to *be* the role. The point was to *be* Petrouchka, hoping that people would feel that was how Petrouchka was and should be. I can tell you a very funny story about a dress rehearsal of *Petrouchka* when it was being revived after some time. There's always a terrible worry after the first scene. There's a drum roll that goes on, and at Covent Garden they had to rope together the inset scene, Petrouchka's cell scene, which stood inside the other set. The black walls are brought in from the sides, and the stage crew has to catch a rope on them and pull the flats together tightly. Then Petrouchka is flung inside through the door. And you have to wait patiently behind a curtain, with your big scene coming up, 'til they rope that set together, because they're not going to take the curtain up or bring the lights on until they get the O.K. that it won't fall down. And they get into a state because they're trying to do it quickly. So I said to the conductor, "Play it as you feel it, but there's just one thing I do ask, that you do not start the cell scene 'til you see me come through that door. And I will not come through that door, even if the curtain's up, until the light is on, because there's no good my coming through the door in the dark. If you start the cell-scene music before the light is on and I'm through the door, I'm going to miss the whole first part musically." I said this because he's getting impatient, the drum roll's going on forever, and they want to jump the gun directly the curtain goes up.

So we get to that point. The light's not on yet so I'm not through the door, and he starts the music. So I just went through the door, and I said, "Oh please, stop, stop, stop." Well, the conductor that night said, "What are you doing, stopping the orchestra?" I said, "Well, this is a dress rehearsal, and it'll put me right out throughout the whole of the scene if we don't get this right. We must do it again." And he said, "You have no right to stop the orchestra like that. Who do you think you are?" I walked forward in my costume, with all the big orchestra at Covent Garden sitting there. "If you don't know who I am," I said, "I'm Petrouchka." The orchestra all applauded and roared with laughter, and some of them to this day remind me of it. They never forgot it.

Everything a dancer learns is useful somewhere and can be brought out. Look how useful the Russian dance was to me, which I learned when I was six. I think the fact that I'd done roles like the Barber in *Mam'zelle Angot*, characterizations like the Jester, led up to Petrouchka. I was lucky enough to be given the opportunity to do that role because I had all that experience. Experience can be stored to be used; the trick is to use it at the right time. In fact, the trick of the whole thing is being in the right place at the right time and being able to do what is required of you. That's life.

I was fortunate enough to have a chance of doing most of the roles in our repertoire, but there was one role, which came a little bit late in my life, that I felt I was also led up to by my characterizations. If I had been chosen, it could have been choreographed for me, and I really felt it was a role I could get my teeth into — and that is Mercutio. I would love to have had one opportunity of being Mercutio.

That's the only role that I regret missing in ballet repertoire. It just happened badly; I was of a certain age when it came along, and David Blair was chosen. If Ashton had done the choreography, I might have got the opportunity. I don't know. It was really the only time my luck failed.

You always had absolute trust in what Ashton was doing. It was his eye. You knew that whatever you did, he was going to make you look good; he wouldn't let you do anything ghastly. So you could do anything. And you always felt that if you tried something and he didn't say anything, it was all right. If he did say something, then it was because he didn't like it, it was wrong, and you were on the wrong track. He was always trying to find a new facet of all the artists he worked with, or extend something that was special about them. And because you had such faith and trust in him, he was able to extend you sometimes even further than you thought was possible.

In lacking a certain amount of confidence in myself, I required the confidence of somebody else. I was not one of those who could go knocking on a door and say, "Why am I not doing this role?" I needed those expert eyes to say to me, "We want you to do it." The fact that *they* saw that I could, not that *I* saw that I could, gave me the confidence to do it, and directly I got from them that they wanted me to do the role, I knew I could. That might be a fault. I don't know. It was a kind of key I needed. And then I got to show them that I could do it even better than they thought I could.

I think you see a lot more in a role as you go on dancing it, definitely. I was always searching for more. I don't feel I found everything that was in Petrouchka by any means. I say Petrouchka because that was a particularly complex character, but I'll say that about any role. What was interesting was that when you did a role first for a season and then came back to it, you often found all kinds of things. I wouldn't say you changed the role — you shouldn't — but you developed it. The role should never stop developing. And when you find that the development is not happening with your body, even though you might be able to do it with your mind, that's the time to stop doing the role. If your body can't do what your mind has found in it, that means you're only going backwards, and you should always be going on. You must fall sometimes, but each time you're topping the wall, and you must never fall below a certain brick. You hope the brick you fall below is getting higher all the time. And when you start falling, when the bricks start falling, then you should say, "Please, I think I can't do this role."

Everything helps you, but you have to really be aware yourself. You can't be swayed and biased. You yourself know when you have danced well; you have to be honest enough with yourself to know that. You're dancing for yourself. You're dancing to achieve the satisfaction that you know you've done it well, and if you do that, the public is going to recognize it anyway. Some dancers that haven't done very well say, "Oh, I gave them a marvelous performance tonight." This, of course, is absolutely death. And that's talk — it's not action. If you're trying to talk yourself into the fact that you've done a good performance, it doesn't work, and you know it's not true. You're trying to convince everybody else with talk, and yourself, and you don't succeed. It's best just to think about your performance, and retain what is good and throw out what is bad, all the time. Sometimes a thing that was good in the last performance doesn't quite happen the same. Every performance is a question of timing, of you being on it, of so many things, and it's maddening when you know it worked so well before. But that's what keeps up your interest and enthusiasm. How boring and mundane if you've reached a level and you're able to stick there.

I wanted each performance to be better. What you're trying to do as a dancer — and this is true of every dancer — is to reach the impossible, which is perfection. You never can, but you can keep getting a little bit nearer. That's what you keep in mind; that is your challenge. And that is your opportunity if you belong to a company; they have those roles and that repertoire so you can do that. You can go back to *Swan Lake* after you've done a new role, and that new role has taught you something else about *Swan Lake*. Each new role can add to your knowledge of the dance, and of the movement, and the truth, and the way to convey it.

Why I talk so much now is because I don't dance, you see, and because I haven't got communication with performance. Once you've been a performer, that's all you ever want to do for your whole life — perform.

July 1979
New York

Moira Shearer

Moira Shearer (b. Dunfermline, Scotland, 1926) began her ballet training in Northern Rhodesia when she was six and continued it in London from the age of ten, first with Nicolas Legat, and following his death in 1937, with his wife. She attended the Sadler's Wells Ballet School briefly in 1940 and performed for a year with the International Ballet before entering the corps of the Sadler's Wells Ballet in 1942. Singled out quickly for solo roles in such ballets as Les Sylphides, Le Spectre de la Rose, Les Patineurs, *and* The Gods Go a-Begging, *she also created roles in Ashton's* The Quest *(1943) and de Valois'* Promenade *(1943) while still a member of the corps. In 1946 she created one of the three female roles in Ashton's landmark ballet* Symphonic Variations *and made successive debuts as Aurora, Swanilda, and Odette-Odile. But for several leaves of absence, to film* The Red Shoes *and* The Tales of Hoffman *and to dance* Carmen *with Roland Petit in Paris, she remained ballerina at Sadler's Wells until 1952, when she resigned to undertake an acting career. She danced her first* Giselle *in 1948 and her last, as a guest artist with the company, in 1953. She presently lives in Edinburgh with her husband and family.*

Everyone knows that Moira Shearer is the gifted, beautiful redhead in a film about the world of ballet called The Red Shoes. *Her name and foot are even imprinted in the cement in front of New York's Bijou Theatre, where* The Red Shoes *opened in 1948. Many people might never have discovered ballet without that film, and many others might never have discovered the dancer in themselves. But despite her cinematic assurance, Moira Shearer was not a starlet who happened to have a knack for flashy toe-dancing. She was a ranking ballerina of the Sadler's Wells Ballet, whose classical reputation would have been secure if she'd never put her feet or face on film. Shearer packed a lifetime of artistic achievement into a decade, and the facts of her career easily eclipse any fiction. By coincidence, she danced five roles that the legendary Tamara Karsavina had originated for Diaghilev's Ballet Russe — the female role in the Bluebird pas de deux, the Waltz in* Les Sylphides, *Columbine in* Le

Carnaval, the Young Girl in Le Spectre de la Rose, and Giselle. Before her debut as Giselle, Shearer sought out Karsavina to talk over the role. Their conversation and Shearer's subsequent performances brought the past to vibrant life in the present and forged a lasting link betweeen generations. I hoped that her conversation with me might forge another.

I've heard endless dancers saying, "When I was five, I was taken to see Pavlova and from that moment I knew." Well, I've never believed that one, ever. Because at five years old, what do you know about what you're going to do? It's crazy. In my case, it was absolutely my mother's idea, and I really did dislike it to begin with. As one hadn't chosen it for oneself, it was dismal to have to go through these tortures daily. Like anything that you try and try to do, the tears pour and you feel you're never getting it; even a perfectly simple thing seems terribly difficult at the beginning. And then you suddenly master that particular thing, and that is such an encouragement that after about six or eight months, despite myself, I began to enjoy it, simply because I realized I was — in a tiny way only — succeeding. Then you go on to all the endless other great difficulties.

That was at Legat's studio in London, and one thing I'm terribly grateful for is to have been taught in that Russian style rather than any other. He had been premier danseur at the Maryinsky before the Revolution, but he was also a good teacher, which is very unusual. Usually, the better the dancer, slightly the less good the teacher. What age he was I can't be sure, but he seemed about a thousand and two to me, with a tremendous shining bald head. He was a heavenly old boy, and one enjoyed his classes immensely. O.K., you have to do exercises, inevitably eight of this, sixteen of something else, but everything, even at the barre, was arranged so that it gave you the impression of doing a little sequence of steps. Not quite a dance, but it was rounded off; you had a little ending. It wasn't just bald, eight of one step and puff and blow, turn around, and eight with the other leg, which was very much the case with British style. I found *those* classes an absolute torture because of it; there was no question of dancing at all, even when you came into the center. Legat caused one to dance, literally dance, in his classes, right from the beginning. Of course I took that just as the normal way anybody would teach, because I'd no point of comparison. But later on, one really appreciated Legat to the full because I saw that nobody else did this at all.

I saw it immediately at Sadler's Wells School. You see, by early 1940, before the bad bombing started, Legat himself was dead, and Madame Legat decided to evacuate the school from London. And typically, being extremely Russian, she chose the tipmost point of the Kent coast, looking across the Channel to the German guns. This was her idea of absolute safety. Well, my father took one look at this and said, "No, not possible." So, simply so I could go on with training, I did go to Sadler's Wells School for about six weeks. But then the bombing really started, so I came back here to Scotland with my mother and rather kicked my heels a bit. Then luckily, at the beginning of 1941, a dancer called Mona Inglesby, whom I'd met at Legat's studio, was just forming a company of her own, and she remembered me and asked me to join it. That was International Ballet.

A series of people were teaching at the School. Ursula Moreton, who'd been in Diaghilev's corps de ballet in the 1920s, gave a lot of classes, including special Cecchetti classes to which I said no firmly. I'd watched one or two of them through the glass door and thought, 'This is terrible. I don't want to do those.' Whether this was correct Cecchetti or what it had become — as it's passed down and down, endless changes creep in without people intending it — it was so totally mechanical. All that happened was from the waist to the tip of the foot, and nobody was bothering at all about what happened from the waist to the top of the head which, funnily enough, was the bit of one's body that Legat was much more interested in. Of course you had to have the technique from the waist downward as second nature, but then he really got to work. He was terribly anxious that your back and the carriage of your head were exactly right, and your arms and *épaulement*. You were expected to be proficient enough in all the leg work that you could concentrate on really dancing. It's the top half of you that gives you style, that makes people really enjoy what you're doing. Someone can do . . . oh, those terrible old fouettés, for instance — and if you do a thing often enough, it's going to look terrific. But there is nothing beautiful about that; it is purely a stunt, a trick. Any dancer with the right build and enough technique can do it. But that's not what dancing's all about.

Sergeyev was also at the School when I was there. He was an enchanting old man, he couldn't have been nicer, but the classes he gave were terrible. I just don't think he had the gift of teaching. He would do the worst things for one's leg muscles. He would give very slow développé at the barre, and then cause you to hold it for a very, very slow count of eight or ten. Then he would go 'round with his stick, hitting under the leg, harder than the dear old duck realized, to keep it up. In the end, the leg would just crash down; people would say, "We can't take any more," and he wouldn't really mind. But then you had to turn around and do it on the other side. And he always gave us thirty-two grands battements to the front, another thirty-two to the side, another thirty-two to the back, another thirty-two to the side, 'round to the other side, back again the same thing. One knew as one was struggling to do it that this was harming one rather than helping. Oh, he was awfully sweet; he called us his zoo and gave us all zoological names because we reminded him of certain animals. We loved him, but as one went into his class, I just felt, 'Here is going to be a totally wasted hour and a quarter.' It was terribly depressing.

But once into the company, we didn't have classes with him, because Ninette de Valois herself used to take class. And that was quite horrific in some ways, because she wasn't a natural teacher either. Everything was very busy and had to be done at twice the speed of light. She was a very fast, neat dancer herself and excelled in little batterie steps, and people always do hone, quite unknowingly I think, to the way they dance themselves. It's inevitable. So her classes were pretty frenetic, one way or another, but not quite so damaging as old Sergeyev's.

I seem to be one of the only ones of my age who saw the de Basil and René Blum companies. I was taken to Covent Garden when I was eight, and I remember the program exactly: it was *Sylphides*, *Boutique Fantasque* with Massine and Danilova, and *Contes Russes*. And when I went down in 1936 to start training properly, when I was ten, I saw quite a lot. The old Alhambra in Leicester Square was still a theatre then; [Vera] Nemtchinova was dancing, and Eglevsky, very young. I remember being most enamoured, crazy about Eglevsky. All the dancers from these companies came to Legat's studio when they were in London and did classes with all of us. So as a small girl, one had the opportunity of watching these, to me, gods, which was a very great help for the future.

So I had been to see all the Russians before I saw the English ballet — I think 1939 was the first time. Isn't it strange? And still it wasn't what I wanted to do. Music was what I wanted to do. I always wished I could have gone in for music as a career, on an instrument, piano probably. Now I have a passion to play the trumpet, but that's something quite else. Of course seeing those performances fired one, because one was seeing the finished article and because I loved the theatre in any form. The excitement of all that, and going to the Royal Opera House, with the big orchestra . . . it's pretty good when you're grown up, but as a small child it was terrific.

International Ballet was my first professional thing, and I enjoyed a lot of it very much though I felt terribly aware of the amount there was to learn. Like driving a car — you do your lessons, take your test, 'L' plates are thrown away, and you are a fully fledged driver. But you really learn about driving in your first year, when you're out there on the road faced with every sort of situation. It's exactly the same with dancing. You can train for however many years, but you get into a company, you go out on the stage, whether it's the back ⁀f the corps de ballet or a small solo, and then you start lear⁀ ⁀ dancing, about how to put it across and how to pla⁀ ⁀k effortless.

b⁀ ⁀ classwork and endless rehearsing
f ⁀hree hours actually per-
⁀ as something one
⁀ved that side of it
⁀t I was always very
⁀e. In any company
⁀ any way helped you
aspects of the theatre
⁀otally missing. I can't
⁀emendously interested
e. All the preoccupation
⁀ly the technical dancing
⁀istory of the ballet, which
⁀ they just didn't talk about
⁀ody to talk to. But if you
⁀dn't done a certain amount
⁀e to dance those big classical

⁀llet for one year, 1941 to '42,
⁀ed quite a lot from Mona In-
g⁀⁀ ⁀ay to place one's dancing. You
never felt ⁀ ⁀nal line from A to B and then
running up to the ⁀ ⁀ used the stage very well, which
is very important, and no ⁀ ⁀ ever taught one anything about this. Perhaps many people don't remember her, but she was a lovely, very fluid, classical dancer, with a great flow of movement. She was a genuine pleasure to watch. But she had totally the wrong appearance for a dancer. She was quite thickly built, not terribly good-looking, and she hadn't height. Her father was a Dutch South African, a Boer, and Mona had that very wide, flat face — from the front it was very much like a dinner plate. It sounds very harsh, that, but I can't describe it otherwise. I just thought it was so wretched; with the great facility that she had, she'd worked to get a really lovely technique, and it was never going to look as it should because of her physical make-up. I

used to play a silly adolescent game with myself, taking bits and pieces from all the people available and thinking, 'If this one had something of that person and something of the other, it would make the absolutely ideal dancer.' And you could see people who had the talent, the looks, everything, and were just lazy as lazy.

I didn't audition for the Sadler's Wells. Ninette de Valois remembered me from those six weeks at the beginning of the war, and I think she had seen some performances of the International when we were in London at the Lyric. She got in touch with my mother, because I was still fifteen years old, and said she would like me in the company. And literally in my first week, I danced the Waltz in *Sylphides*. Then I did the leading part in *Gods Go a-Begging* straightaway, and then Freddie Ashton was writing *The Quest* and I was in that too. But I did dance also in the corps de ballet, for four years. That was very much de Valois' policy, that young dancers would be given solo things from time to time, but then they would be right back in the corps, sometimes in the next ballet.

As it happened, I also did one act of *Swan Lake,* in about 1943 or '44. Poor Pamela [May], who was beset for years with terrible cartilage troubles in her knees, was coming back into the company, and de Valois wanted to get her back into *Swan Lake.* But Pamela wasn't able to do the whole thing — we always did the full ballet, never just the second act — so because I was also roughly fair-haired, I danced the black act for her. I put very blond hairnets on my redder hair and she put rather red hairnets on her blonder hair, and we hoped we were fooling the public. In fact, we couldn't have been less like each other. And when she was able to do the whole role, I just faded out of it completely.

Now, I think this is important to say. Sooner or later, particular people come along who the director particularly likes. It's not absolute favoritism, but it does happen . . . in all companies probably . . . it's only human. There were one or two, of my age or slightly older, who went through a phase of this, or de Valois went through a phase on them so to speak. To my great good luck, she never had any phase on me at all, which I found a very good thing. Too much would be given to the dancer of the moment, and nobody could ever fulfill all that was expected, whereupon they would be dropped. But if you were never in this category, or sometimes used as a last resort when there was nobody else, if one was put on like that and was reasonably successful, it was a much more genuine way of arriving at something. I just am very glad that I was never a particularly favored one.

Mind you, I wasn't necessarily aware at the time that this was happening in the company. It was just very hard work, and one was trying to get through it and not drop down with a broken leg oneself. There was a tremendous boom for the ballet during the war because it was the great escapist entertainment; it was so fantastic and unreal that it completely took people out of themselves. So we worked fifty-two weeks a year, no holiday at all, and we toured terrifically. We did eight shows a week, always, and then for two London seasons we did nine shows each week, with three performances of the same program every Saturday at 1:30, 4:45, and 8:30. You'd dance nine ballets in one day, things like [Robert] Helpmann's *Comus* and his *Hamlet*, *Sylphides* inevitably, and *Patineurs* and *Les Rendezvous* endlessly. And by the most extraordinary chance, there was a roaring heatwave on at the time — I'll never forget it. But we were very lucky; we had full houses every single day of the year. I didn't know what it was to be out of work. In fact, there was too much. One was very cushioned and spoiled in that way, and one thought that was normal.

Of course, any classical dancer is aiming for those big classical roles because there isn't anything like them. It would be crazy if you weren't. I did *Sleeping Beauty* first, and then *Swan Lake* and *Coppélia,* all within a year. But I only did *Swan Lake* for three years before de Valois removed me from it. She said she didn't like me in it, that I was too lightweight in every way, so I didn't ever dance it again. I was sad, really, because it's a marvelous part, but I'm sure I wasn't ideal. One role I never enjoyed at all, and unfortunately was always hideously successful in, was Swanilda. I found it arch and pert, all the things I really don't like, and terribly mock-jokey in the middle act. One was very lucky to be doing it at all, I suppose, but I could well have done without it occasionally.

But I *was* a classical dancer, and I was always a little bit 'fish out of water' when it came to real character things, like the Spanish dance in the third act of *Swan Lake*. I enjoyed doing it, but I felt I probably just looked like a classical dancer doing a Spanish dance, instead of really doing it convincingly. You can't help it if you're like that. Even in the classical roles, to be perfectly honest, I never felt a hundred percent happy technically, but that was probably because I had this ridiculously high standard. I never felt technique was my strong point. It would be false modesty not to know what one's very strong points were, and I knew that speed and lightness were really mine, and what I did with the technique I had. But I remember very well, before I started doing Aurora, standing at the back of the stage or in the wings watching Margot do it, and thinking how marvelous for her to have had a certain number of years of dancing these big, heavy, classical parts and of knowing, absolutely, with rock solidity, that she could do them. She could almost relax on the top of the part, knowing that she'd got all the nerves and initial worry over. And that just showed how little I knew about anything.

When I started to do those roles, I was so nervous before going on that I could hardly put one foot in front of the other. But that, in fact, was the best time, which you only appreciate in retrospect. That was the time I had nothing to lose. I was a new, young one; everyone was with you, absolutely, longing for you to do well, and you had no reputation to make a mess of. You may think you're nervous, but it's nothing to the kind of real nervous you get when you're much older and start to get a little bit of reputation as being good in something. Then people start to come wondering, 'Is she going off a bit?' They're much more critical, and if you have done one very good performance, it's got to be topped. It's got to be better, better, better every single time. But it's such a physical thing. You can't always be better. All that nerve strain is very exhausting, and I think it gets worse. This is why I'm so full of admiration for somebody like Margot who has been able to go on for so many years at that level, with people expecting so much more all the time. If I had wanted to very much, which I didn't, I could have gone easily for another ten years. I'd still have been only thirty-eight, and a great many dancers are that age and whirling away like mad. But people are temperamentally either suited to the ballet or they're not, and I actually don't think I was.

Red Shoes was the last thing I wanted to do. I fought for a year to get away from that film, and I couldn't shake the director off. It was 1946, it was the first season at Covent Garden, and I was trying to cope with all the big, heavy parts. I hoped to settle into them and try to improve them, make something of them, and here was this man on and on and on. Oddly enough, of all people it was Ninette de Valois who finally said, "For goodness' sake, do it. Get it off your chest and ours, because I can't stand this man endlessly 'round bothering us any longer. Why don't you just do it, and then it's done." And I said, "Yes, but then what? Can I come straight back into the company again and go on as if nothing had happened? Maybe you will then not want me back." She said, "Of course you come straight back." Which is what I did; I did all the work for six months, 4:30 in the morning 'til 7:30 at night, Sundays too, and then I was back at Covent Garden again, and I was with them until 1952.

The trouble with the dancing in that film was that it was so cinematically worked out that we were very lucky if we ever danced for as long as one minute. It was usually half a minute and then they would cut. Well, you can't get up any steam at all that way, or any flow — you can't really dance. This is why I'm sad that it's what I'm always remembered for. People can still look at it now and think, 'Oh, that's the way she danced,' but I was just at a stage where I was about to make a big jump forward, technically, artistically, in every way. By the time we did *Tales of Hoffman* in 1950, I was a totally different kind of dancer. And also, Freddie Ashton did the choreography for that, we did longer takes, and one really could dance. I'm not ashamed of my dancing in that at all; at least it was genuine dancing. It gave some idea of the way one could dance, which I never felt *Red Shoes* did at all.

But you do the work, you finish it, and then you get on to your next work, and that takes up all your mind and energies. With a film, there is a time lag of eight or ten months, and when the thing comes out, you have no connection with it at all. It's over, it's done with; maybe everybody else is seeing it for the first time, but it no longer really affects you. I was aware it had come out, and people either liked it or they didn't, but I was so caught up with doing *Giselle* for the first time — which was the one I'd always wanted to do most — that, well, *The Red Shoes* went by.

I had always wanted to do *Giselle*, always. I suppose I saw Margot in it first. I was in the corps de ballet for a long time in it, and I danced one of the two leading Wilis for a long time, mostly to Margot's performance because she danced most of them, and sometimes to Beryl [Grey]. I saw [Yvette] Chauviré once and the others who did it with our company, and this to me was a bit of a problem. I would have liked never to have seen anyone before tackling that particular ballet. Inevitably, it was Margot's performance that was stamped on that production, and you were just put into it. It was very difficult to bring anything of one's own to it, because this almost "set" piece was there in your mind's eye the whole time. Seeing a great many people do a thing is not necessarily a great help.

But let me tell you something I did do, which got me into a certain amount of trouble at the time but paid off in the end, and I was terribly glad about what subsequently happened. When I discovered I was going to dance *Giselle*, I remembered that Karsavina lived in London. And I felt, 'Here is somebody, still alive, who remembers how this was danced at the Maryinsky and who has danced it herself many times. Really, it is madness not to get in touch with this woman and find out some things about the part and what she feels about it.' So I plucked up courage and I wrote to her. What I hadn't realized was that nobody was bothering about Karsavina at all, and she was very hurt by it. I heard afterwards that she had always felt ignored completely. I knew she'd been there for the *Spectre* rehearsals. She came to coach Margot and Alexis Rassine — but the whole thing was shut off. Anybody else who was going to dance it never saw Karsavina at all — and that had just been a little isolated episode and never again. I'd never met her; I just wrote out of the blue and explained the situation. She replied at once and said she'd be delighted to see me and would I come to tea. She had a charming little apartment, a very Russian drawing room with masses of things she'd obviously had with her all her life. When I arrived, I just plunged straight in, and the dear old thing had the rug back and was demonstrating for me.

It was the first act particularly I wanted to ask her about, because — it sounds a little pompous of me — I wasn't happy with the kind of production we had of it. I felt it was terribly two-dimensional, quite honestly, and most unbelievable. After all, in ballet everything is wildly unbelievable, but in *Giselle* the first act has got to be real to some extent so you can then have a totally fantastic and unreal second act. We had a series of odd anomalies in that first act. For instance, the mother of Giselle was played as if she were about ninety-eight. Well, at what age could she have produced this young girl? She would have been well up the seventies if you thought about it. I just felt this was crazy for this particular act where, within the unreal setting of people dancing on pointe and so on, you do want some reality so you can feel for this girl in her situation.

One thing I was very keen about was quite definitely to stab myself with the sword. Whether Giselle intends it or not, she is by this time very out of control. But it must be quite clear, so you can believe she dies as quickly as she does die. And also, there's a great deal of hanging on to the side — well, presumably you have wounded yourself in some way. The strangeness of it was that more often than not the sword would be whipped away before any of this could be done, but then Margot would hold her side. Was this because she was exhausted, or what was it? One wasn't sure.

My problem then was that Karsavina showed me one or two of the mimed sections of that first act the way they had done them, which was quite different, and I realized I couldn't possibly put them in. There were little tiny things I could use, but I had to be terribly careful about not disturbing anybody else, since they were going to be exactly as they always were. Anything I could use must just be something that concerned myself, like the way Giselle moves forward when she encounters Bathilde and sees the court clothes for the first time. In our production, it was just, 'Isn't it lovely?' The way Karsavina showed it was both less kittenish and less arch than that. She did it with absolute amazement, as if being drawn forward, not wanting to go at all. In fact, the movements can be almost the same, but if you have that attitude and try to get that across the vista to the people out there, it has a quite different effect.

So. I had very few rehearsals, comparatively, just with Alexis as Albrecht, and never on the stage at all. We could never get the stage; the opera always had first call, or else the stagehands. And there was no proper rehearsal room in those days at Covent Garden, so we were farmed out to drill halls and basement halls of quite different dimensions. Well, never being able to place it properly or with an orchestra, you get onto the stage — and of course that is your per-formance — and you can feel a little bit at sea. But you know it's going to be like that, and you must make the best of it, so you do.

Alexis and I rehearsed just on our own, with whoever was ballet master at the time, and de Valois didn't see me 'til the matinée that I first went on, when she was in front. At the end of the first act, she was 'round to my dressing room and she waded in. Although I'd done only minute things, she was absolutely furious and thought that this was just my own idea. The temerity of someone my age to do this! She really bawled me out — and I *had* got the second act coming up, and I'd never danced it before. Then she said, in the general tirade, Who did I think I was? What did I think I was doing? and Where had I got these ludicrous ideas anyway? So I just said, "Anything that you find unacceptable I got from Madame Karsavina, whom I went to see because I was interested enough to find out her view of the part."

That stopped her absolutely cold. She didn't say another word; she marched out of my room. And the next thing I knew, Karsavina had been invited for special rehearsals with Margot and whoever she was dancing with at the time, on the stage. She came I don't know how many times, but again none of us were allowed to get anywhere near her. Wasn't it odd? Wouldn't it have been fascinating for the whole company, or even the other people dancing Giselle, to have watched those rehearsals, say, from the front of the house, and seen Karsavina demonstrate? What a weird way of doing it. But then, all sorts of little changes crept in, so I was able to continue. I was glad that it brought Karsavina in again; I think she was terribly pleased. I think it also did improve certain aspects of that production quite a bit, although there was still a set form to it.

I always had a great interest in the history of ballet, and I knew the funny old critic called Cyril Beaumont quite well — we all did. He was a very prissy old boy, and I think his attitude to the ballet was always a rather narrow one, a very English one, but he nevertheless had seen a terrific lot. There's always a great deal to be got from somebody interesting like that, so from time to time I asked him about various things he'd seen. I had his *Complete Book of Ballets,* and all the old Chalon lithographs showing Carlotta Grisi, the original Giselle, and so on.

Beaumont was writing frequently as a critic at that point in 1948 when I did *Giselle* for the first time. Now, into at least two of the many books he'd written and edited, he had incorporated Théophile Gautier's physical description of Grisi. Unlike most Italians, she had what was known as an 'English rose' complexion, curly hair, and blue eyes. But since her day, there had been a succession of black-haired, olive-skinned, aquiline-nosed ladies as Giselle, and this had become the classic idea of how Giselle should look. Well, up I get with my red hair and fair skin, and all the wretch wrote, in spite of Carlotta Grisi, was that, yes, I'd danced quite well, but you really couldn't consider me in this part because the coloring was so wrong. As far as he was concerned, I was just wiped off the map. So I thought, 'Just look up page whatever in your own book. What would you have said to Carlotta?' I thought it so odd of somebody to be that prejudiced. Because he loved Markova's dancing and appearance, he couldn't see past them to anybody else's interpretation. Margot was *just* acceptable because she had roughly the same look, but I was so wildly off the mark, just in appearance, that he wouldn't even consider mine a genuine performance. But I was lucky in that I knew quite a bit about the ballet, and I knew in the back of my mind how I thought it should look. That's the only way anybody can ever do anything; it's impossible to make an overall blanket thing that will suit everybody.

The act I had to work on most was the first act; you can only be really successful in the second act if you've got the first act right. You have to portray this girl in a series of situations leading up to her death, and there is no corresponding choreography of that kind in any other ballet. *Sleeping Beauty* has no acting in it at all, and what acting there is in *Swan Lake* is the old-fashioned, mimed acting that fits in with that very formal arrangement of dances that was the structure of the late nineteenth century. But it would be a really bad performance of *Giselle* if the acting were separate from the dancing, because the way you move or dance in that first act must be absolutely correct for the point you've got to in the story. It must reflect what you're thinking. The second act is so much more like *Sylphides* or any of the Romantic ballets. But the difficulty with *Giselle,* because it's so old, is that many aspects of it are ridiculous, and impossible to make believable to the eyes of today. For instance, although Giselle is supposed to be totally a spirit in the second act, nevertheless she retains enough of her human self to want to protect Albrecht. That's quite a big difference from *Sylphides,* where you have absolutely no character or personality; you're just a pure dancer.

When you first see her with Albrecht, they're engaged, and she thinks he genuinely is this ordinary young peasant lad. She does flirt with him, but in a very youthful way that's almost teasing, almost like hide-and-seek. It is, alas, arranged in such a way that it lends itself all too easily to coyness, but she is not arch and coy, not at all. All that teasing and nonsense at the beginning is terrific high spirits and youthfulness, and a certain slight shyness that she has still, although she knows him well enough to have become engaged to him.

Poor Giselle is in a very difficult situation where Hilarion's concerned, because she appears to have fairly natural good manners. She would obviously not be able to return his feelings, but she would be embarrassed at having to rebuff and repulse him, and she would never make any rough or rude gestures to him. This was slightly glossed over in our production, and it's one of the things I remember talking to Karsavina about. She seemed to feel I was right in feeling that way about it, and that one would never be too rough but just try to make one's feelings clear somehow. But you can't be too subtle. You have very little time, very few bars of music, in which to do this, and everything has to be over life-size if it's going to come over at all in an opera house. So you are a bit caught, but with any luck what you think does help. Hilarion's a very sad character. It's so wrong when he's played like a villain because, in fact, all he does is tell the truth. He's tactless, that's all. He tells it, from everybody else's point of view, at absolutely the wrong moments, but from *his* point of view at the only moments he can.

Because she's going to be the central character, Giselle has her own special costume, she's singled out all the time, and she's always in the center. This is obviously the principal dancer — which is a slight difficulty, but you can't get 'round that — but I think she was just one of the village girls. As it happens, it's her story that's being told rather than any of the others'.

According to the libretto, she's supposed to have a weak heart. All that rather ancient mime the old crone mother does — in our production, like a nonagenarian — is that she mustn't dance too much because of her weak heart. But quite honestly, I don't see how, in ballet terms and in the kind of acting you must do within those terms, you could convey a weak heart without being quite clinical, which would have again been quite wrong. You cannot be too clinical, even in the Mad Scene. It's got to fit into the convention of an old Romantic ballet.

She's constantly saying, 'I want to dance some more,' because she's very young and very high-spirited. But I also felt that the act must have a beginning, a middle, an end, and a progression for her through the various stages. If you didn't give a tremendous feeling of bounding energy and real delight in dancing at the beginning, there was not much contrast as you came through to the end, where, in her rather crazed state, she has to repeat the same steps before she dies. You want to heighten the difference between the two. The music is the same, taken more slowly, admittedly, but you want to show such a feeble echo of what's been before that it is genuinely tragic to see.

I'll tell you what is devilish, and it doesn't show at all. It's one of the most winding acts of anything, because you never stop — jump, jeté, jeté, balloté, balloté. When it comes to the quick, big dance with all the corps de ballet, Giselle is on the end of lines, having to go right 'round the whole stage, while some of them are just doing it in place. You are jumping, jumping, jumping, on and on and on, until really you feel you can't go on for another minute. That's the difficult thing in the first act, not the actual steps. The solo that begins glissade, piqué arabesque was to me the best solo for a woman ever. It was heavenly to dance, and I knew, always, that it was working. You know, I adored doing the Rose Adagio, but I had kittens, right 'til the very last time I ever danced Aurora, over the variation that follows it. If you break it down into the actual steps, there's nothing so very difficult in it, yet I was so nerve-wracked over it that I never once did it perfectly. This solo is technically more difficult, but I had no problems with it at all. I loved it.

The only way to do all the first bit of the first act is to show total absolute trust in Albrecht so that the shock is great enough to cause her to react as she does. Otherwise, she would go off and have an immense crying session and perhaps feel terrible for days, but she'd get over it. It's got to be such a shock: to discover that he is also engaged to the grand princess, that he is not the person she thought he was, and that there's no question of ever being able to marry him or have anything further to do with him. It's absolutely the end for her of that whole chapter, and her entire life is now going to be something quite different — and, as it happens, very short.

But I didn't feel remotely that she could have died in that short space of time just from a shock. Would she not have died immediately from shock? Or not died at all? To me, it just didn't seem sufficiently realistic within the convention of the ballet. And why the business with the sword if she wasn't going to stab herself with it? Karsavina told me, "Oh yes, she stabs herself. It's the sword that kills her." And then Giselle does this sort of wiping with her hands. When Margot did it, it was as if she was looking at her hands, as if her sight was getting less good and she couldn't quite see them. And as the Mad Scene was absolutely set, this was the way it was always done. Now, I don't know . . . She'd have stabbed herself. There would be a lot of blood. She goes 'round, with her hands on her side, and she then finds she's got blood on them. Well, this is a frightening thing for anybody, and you do this, you try to get rid of it. Isn't that what she's doing? I wanted to do it like that, rightly or wrongly, so I asked Karsavina about it, and as far as I remember, she told me that was the right reason for this hand-wiping. It just made more sense.

This may sound very prosaic, but the minute the curtain has fallen, that's finished, and you don't think another thing about it. You've got to get back to your dressing room, get everything off, try and tidy up your make-up — you're sweating like a pig — get the next headdress on so firmly it won't budge. People come in and out: "Can I borrow this?" "Can I borrow that?" You get your shoes off; you never keep a pair on during the interval, and anyway you have to change tights. I always wanted the oldest shoes for Act II, because I hated the tap-tap sound a lot of people would make. Although there was all that hopping on pointe in the first-act solo, I actually liked old shoes for the first act too. In fact, I liked old shoes for everything. Anyway, you just get on with what you've got to do until you get into the wings, and by this time, you hear the Act II music, you're in the clothes, and this gets you back into the ballet again.

But the mood of the first act is totally different from the mood of the second act. You know that people are seeing it as one complete ballet, but it is so different. I adored the second act. All you have to convey is absolute lightness, like gossamer blown away, with just the slightest suggestion of the human element of the character when she realizes Albrecht is there and is going to be drawn into it by the Wilis. You see, the audience does it by then — you don't have to do anything. Very often it's better to leave certain things to an audience. By that time, they know who you are, and they can see it with the eye of the first act, which you can't. For you, it's surprisingly like *Sylphides*, because it's just effortless dancing. Of course it's very difficult, but it must look effortless or it fails completely. It's got to look absolutely the easiest thing in the world.

And if you show too much towards him, you're canceling out your own death in a way. Margot used to run all the way down the line of Wilis and go *whomp*, throw her arms out to protect him, terrifically, as Giselle would have in the first act if some situation had cropped up. It was too much as if she were really living, really strong. For this act, you can't do that. It's got to be much smaller, almost with the head down a little bit, doing it but knowing this is all you can do as your spirit self.

I was always sorry the first dance in that act was there, the whirling in arabesque, because that's a stunt. It didn't really fit with the rest of the act at all. Maybe it was meant to convey the sudden whirl into activity, as she's just come from the grave, but it seemed like a nineteenth-century set piece that one had to do. All the rest of the dancing is soft and elegant, all of a piece, and that one bit seemed to stand out rather like a sore thumb.

One thing I did find difficult, and was always nervous before and very relieved when it was over — successfully, with luck — was where she stands absolutely still in the center of the stage and starts, as if in class, the slow développé. By herself, on the flat foot. And then into the arabesque, promenade all the way around, close, entre-chat six and around to one long arabesque. The end's easy enough, but for the first développé and then through into arabesque, you have to take your foot exact, exact, exact. It's rather like not coughing or sneezing in church. Because you knew you had to do this very slowly and very exactly, it made you want to wobble; inevitably one was going to make a mess. Perhaps this has to do with my being rather over-light. I was also very thin from the side through the middle, so the air gets at you when you turn, deflects you much more. Your arms are up, and if you turn fast enough with them like that, the air is like somebody with great weights pushing on each forearm. Perhaps from being a little too thin through the back, I would waver a bit in some legato things. I wasn't actually going to wobble or give a little hop, but I'd feel as if I were going to. It's a very unnerving feeling, and of course it sometimes causes you to do the very thing you're trying not to do.

But I loved doing the second act. I also realize — and I never quite realized this before — that I infinitely preferred dancing in the softer, longer skirt to dancing in a tutu. The Romantic, Taglioni-type skirt felt much better, and one could dance, in a way, much more easily. There was something very constricting about the other, because it's so plate-like and stiff.

I did *Giselle* with Rassine, with Bobby Helpmann quite a number of times, and I think with Michael Somes, but there were two partners I enjoyed working with much more than any others. One was an Italian-Swiss, long dead now, called David Paltenghi. I don't know how he actually found his way into the ballet, but he was about nineteen years old when he did, and I don't think he'd ever seen it. This must have been just before the war, and with the great lack of male dancers, he rose very smartly up in the company. He was never a good dancer, but he could get by and he was a wonderful partner. John Hart was the other one. He had been trained fully and I suppose was always a better dancer than David ever was. He wasn't really a premier danseur noble — that was not his forte — but he was a marvelous partner. They were both definitely totally male, no two ways about it, and the whole way they presented themselves on the stage was masculine. That was very important to me. And they were rock-solid, so one felt just weightless. They could carry one about and it was all so easy. I'm sure they were working infinitely more than you realized, but it gave an impression that you were almost standing there by yourself, putting hardly any weight on their arm or shoulders. It was a lovely feeling. Others, of course, partnered you too much, maybe because they were accustomed to other partners themselves. That I always found very difficult; it became a sort of grappling business. But there's very little partnering in *Giselle,* so it doesn't make too much difference there.

I did see a broadcast of *Sleeping Beauty* quite recently from Covent Garden, and the male dancing was technically much better than in my time. But with Western European companies, you don't get the tough, strong virility or the particular way of miming that the Russian and Slav companies can do. I find that strength, that style, very believable, and you must make the audience suspend disbelief at the ballet. We haven't got that quality as a nation, so it's no wonder none of our dancers have it.

To me, the music for any ballet, or certainly any ballet up to fairly recent years, is the all-important thing. None of those ballets could exist at all in a vacuum, without music. It is the music which has caused the choreographer, Petipa or somebody much more recent, to want to compose movements and dances. And one is caused to do what one's doing because the music does what it does: becomes fast, slow, loud, soft, whatever. That is the mainspring. This may be old-fashioned, but when you see a very modern ballet today, with squeaks, grunts, and groans or no music at all, to me it's a contradiction of what dancing's about. Something, surely, makes one want to dance. I don't want to make it sound as if I think music has got to be there the whole time, but you want to use it, or the lack of it, with real effect. Like the film *Rififi,* with the marvelous twenty minutes of silence. Brilliant.

I would have thought just straightforwardly that a musical dancer is someone who responds absolutely to the music and phrases well as a response to it. You can't be taught it. It's in you or it isn't. Many dancers would think they were being musical in the way they danced, but they were simply hearing music as accompaniment, and that's not quite the same thing. It can be very effective, but there is another way of doing it where the music is the first thing.

I have heard conductors say how they discuss tempi and so on with the leading dancer, and — well, this is just something that never ever happened to me in all the years I danced. I could count, on one hand I think, the number of times I actually saw the conductor — literally; to say "Good evening" to — before the performance began. There was no discussion at all; that wasn't part of the set-up. You danced, frankly, the conductor's tempi, so it was a little difficult. There was a set way of doing it, and you just did it like that. I don't know about Margot; as she was first cast in everything, perhaps she did discuss it, but I never experienced that myself.

The music is no *more* important with an abstract ballet, because the music is always totally important. *Symphonic Variations* is simply steps, pure dancing. There isn't anything else for the public to hang onto; but that, surely, is what you learn to do as a dancer. You are simply there in *Symphonic*, on a stage, and you have to try to create a series of geometric patterns, to music, that are genuinely beautiful to look at. And create some kind of illusion or mood of . . . I don't know what . . . of coolness or excitement. That's why it's terribly important to have exactly the right scenery and costumes, because the mood and atmosphere of those abstract ballets are all-important. There isn't really anything else to help the dancers create something. Ashton presumably had an overall picture in his head of what he wanted in *Symphonic*, but he didn't let us know what it was.

Ninette de Valois is exactly the reverse. I was first cast in *Promenade,* the Haydn ballet — oh, way back, 1943 — and she had every single detail in her head, meticulously, when she arrived at the first rehearsal, and she could tell everybody exactly what she wanted. I remember thinking at the time that it didn't give one much leeway for individuality, but by dancing in her ballets and seeing them from the front, I discovered they were almost the most satisfying of all. They were one person's vision, right the way through. It's terribly sad that because she was such a good administrator she is rather forgotten as a choreographer. She had an enormous gift and a very particular vision of her own.

One's tempted to say that a character was more fun in every way, and that there was more to be drawn from a part that had a definite character to it. But it's not always so; it depends on the character. Giselle would always be my absolute favorite because there's so much meat there, but I really did not enjoy dancing Swanilda at all. And, funnily enough, I absolutely adored dancing *Ballet Imperial,* although that was nothing but technique and I was always nervous of something supremely technical. Mr. Balanchine came to rehearse it, and he was a great figure, immaculately dressed — this was something we were not accustomed to at the time — in a beautiful suit and a little flower in his buttonhole and lovely polished shoes, and the hair so beautifully brushed. I had never worked with him before so it was very exciting, but it was very much him with Margot and Michael Somes of the first cast. I was second cast, and Violetta Elvin was third.

In the third movement, Michael had to do a step three times, traveling diagonally backward and landing in arabesque from a double turn in the air. He did it one day and it was all right, but Balanchine said, "No, no, you don't understand it. This is how I would like it." Whereupon he went to the corner, and in his suit and outdoor shoes, and with — I thought at the time — a great age, did the step with no warming-up. To me it was miraculous, because he did it very much better and more gracefully than this warmed-up dancer in the prime of his career. That was good enough in itself, but slightly later in the rehearsal there was something he was not happy with about the tempo of one piano passage, and he couldn't get through to our pianist — and she was very good — exactly what he wanted. So he said, "My dear, would you move over?" He then sat down at the piano and played the section perfectly. By that time I was lost in admiration; that really gained respect in a way that nothing else could. This man knew exactly how it should be, and he actually could do it himself.

There was one very interesting thing about *Ballet Imperial*. When he started rehearsing it, it was clear to me — just from watching from the back and picking it up — that the part for the leading female dancer was not straight classicism. Everything was off; there was this extraordinary diagonal angling of the body the whole time, and you had to appear to be falling. It had to look dangerous. It could be done straight up and down, and then it would just look like a modern *Swan Lake* or *Sleeping Beauty*, but that was not what he wanted. He wanted you at an angle, and if you stayed too long at that angle, you would fall down.

I could see him trying to get this, and quite honestly, Margot did not do it. She did it absolutely straight up and down. She must have seen what he wanted, surely, but anyway she decided against it. I felt, 'If and when I come to do it, I must try to get this because this is the whole point of the part.' Then Balanchine stayed in London rather longer than anyone expected him to, and on discovering that I was doing the matinée about ten days after the opening, he evidently said to de Valois that he would like to rehearse me. Now, this was unheard of, but de Valois had no option but to put a call up on the board, which staggered me but I was thrilled. This was the only time, apart from *Cinderella,* that I ever had a stage call, and with the choreographer too. I think he saw right away that I had got this point, and he worked on and on with me. He was there for my first performance too, and I know he was pleased.

I loved doing it, although it was very nerve-wracking because it was so difficult technically. There was one little thing, for instance, which I don't think I necessarily did well, but I was determined to do it. You know how female dancers don't usually have to do any double turns in the air. Well, towards the end of the ballet, one had to come on fairly near the back of the stage, stage left, take preparation, and just with one step do a double turn, land on one leg, and then something else. And then, with your back to the audience, you did it again. Four times. It was very, very fast. They hadn't to be high, but he wanted a double, and it had to look brilliant and astonishing. And again, he hadn't had this before, so I just thought, 'Well, if I break both legs, never mind. I'll have a go.' And of course if you are determined to do something, if you feel it's wanted for a certain effect, you find you can do it.

Because he expected it from you, and because he didn't think it was in any way beyond you, you found you could do things that most other people couldn't even have asked you to do. And that was a great experience. I'm sure I reached a particular standard of technical dancing in *Ballet Imperial* that I never reached in anything else. He expected it, and you couldn't let that man down — you just couldn't. It's very un-British, someone's giving you that feeling that you could do anything. Here, a certain standard is required and you would meet it, but there's not the same daring about it.

There were always just a few people whose opinions one respected very much because they really knew about it. Quite frankly, the critics never. If it doesn't sound too patronizing, the majority of them do not know anything at all about ballet. They will try to be technical and pretend they know. If only they didn't; if only they'd go to it and just receive the total impression, and then say either I like this or I don't and why. But this fearful peppering of reviews with little technicalities — which are almost invariably wrong — makes any dancer or choreographer reading it realize it isn't worth tuppence. It's just done for effect on their part, which is terribly sad. Of course it's very nice to get a good review, but if it's not a good one, you want it to be an informed one that you can actually get something from.

What *is* nice is much later on, perhaps when one's away from the ballet completely. You are in an airport or walking on the street, and somebody will come up to you and say, "Forgive me, I don't want to trouble you, but I just wanted to say that I was at Covent Garden in 1948" — you know, some way gone date — "and you danced" — whatever it was — "and I've never forgotten it. It gave me such pleasure." Now, that is what's valuable. You actually gave somebody pleasure, and that's really all it's about.

I hope this doesn't come out wrong, but the audience has no effect on the way you dance — none. You can dance absolutely as well, sometimes better, with no audience there at all. It's a totally self-contained thing, the ballet. You don't rely on laughs, you don't have to work on an audience, it isn't *to* them. You are creating something within the stage, and the concentration has to be total on what you're doing, all the way through. You can't let up for a minute. You create an illusion and the audience receives it. At the end, you know roughly whether it's been successful or not by the kind of applause you get. When you act for the straight theatre, the audience is all-important. Sometimes you get a very sticky batch of people and you have to work and work on them; your timing, everything, is dependent on how they react. Of course you rehearse without them, but that's not a performance in the way it is with them sitting there. But we could give as good a ballet performance to a totally empty auditorium as to a perfectly full one. It's lovely if there's a full house, with that electricity in the air; it gets the adrenalin going, but it doesn't alter your performance.

If I hadn't gone into the other branch of the theatre, I would never have known this to the extent I do now. During the war, we had such full houses the whole time that we expected it. But when I became aware, acting, of how dependent one was on one's audience and how one valued them, I felt we'd almost been slightly contemptuous of ballet audiences: 'Well, it was nice if they were there, but they could go — it would make no difference.' I don't think we thought that *like* that, but we certainly hadn't appreciated them as we should have done.

I know there are some who sit in front counting the pirouettes, who aren't interested in anything else, and that really is pathetic. They might just as well go to a classroom and watch, because this has got nothing to do with the theatre at all. You might look like a student on the stage no matter what prodigy of technique you produce. Any great dancers I've ever seen did something else. They had so much of their own to bring to a part, and they made it such a complete entity, that one wasn't really noticing whether they were also the technical virtuoso. It didn't matter. The quality of what one sees on the stage has always been more important to me than anything else. When there is a particular quality which is that person's own — nobody else could produce it in the same way — it gives a performance something so different. It gives it style.

There's one role I would absolutely love to have danced, and I feel I would probably have been dead right for it — and that is Fokine's *Firebird*. There, for once, people couldn't have found fault with my coloring. And that part should be strange and odd, and quick and light, with just a little unearthly quality, which was something I rather enjoyed trying to get across, a feeling of not being human in any way. That would have been lovely to try.

But the ballet is an intensely selfish career, and if you're going to do it absolutely one hundred percent, as you must, it's a twenty-four hour a day business and everything else takes second place. Well, if you're going to be married successfully and have children, this is just not possible. Your marriage is going to go to pieces or else your work's going to go to pieces. This I felt was hopeless. So I did about five years of theatre, thinking it was perhaps a more reasonable career to pursue and still have some kind of marriage and life with the children, and I discovered even that was not possible. To me there wasn't really any question about the decision. One was one's own life and other people's life, and that was infinitely more important. So I just quietly removed myself into domesticity.

It's an awfully long time ago, and one doesn't really miss it. I've grown away from the ballet; I find it incredibly narrow. Even when I was dancing I thought that, because technique was all. It was the only thing given time to, it was all you could do. No time or energy for normal life or any of the other arts. And even when you go to see it, you find it's a little constricting. There's only so much that can be conveyed, and it's not enough.

Who was I doing it for? I've often wondered. It's what you know, it's what you've been trained for, you must do it. Ideally it's a compulsive thing — somebody has a compulsion to paint or write music or dance or be on the tightrope in the circus. If you choose it yourself, you're presumably doing it for yourself as much as anybody else. In my case, although I didn't choose it, one wasn't totally unsuccessful at it, and this reconciled me to it as a possible career. Then of course it's exciting to be in your first professional job; and again, if you have some success, that is a satisfaction and a pleasure, and you just want to make it more and more and get better.

Sometimes, when you run into a bad patch and when it seems to be nothing but criticism and the tears running down the cheeks, you do wonder perhaps why you are trying to do this very, very difficult art and apparently failing dismally. But of course on you go, because it is your work, it is what you know, and you must.

October 1979
Edinburgh

Beryl Grey

Beryl Grey (b. London, 1927) auditioned for the Sadler's Wells Ballet School at the insistence of her first teacher, Madeline Sharp, and entered it at the age of nine. Having joined the Sadler's Wells Ballet at fourteen, she was almost immediately awarded leading roles in Les Sylphides, Façade, Les Patineurs, Helpmann's Comus, and de Valois' The Gods Go a-Begging. She danced her first complete Swan Lake on her fifteenth birthday, her first Giselle in London on her seventeenth birthday, Lilac Fairy in Sleeping Beauty in the company's opening performance at Covent Garden in 1946, and her first Aurora and Myrthe that same year. Her range encompassed dramatic roles like the Black Queen in de Valois' Checkmate and demi-caractère parts like the Miller's Wife in Massine's Le Tricorne as well as standard ballerina roles; in her first ten years with the company, she danced forty-three leading roles in thirty-two ballets. In 1957 she resigned from the company, now the Royal Ballet, to freelance around the world; later that year she was the first British ballerina to appear as a guest artist with the Bolshoi and Kirov Ballets. After retiring from dancing in 1977, she served as artistic director of Festival Ballet from 1968 to 1979.

Beryl Grey and Swan Lake have been connected so variously for so long — whether by plan or coincidence — that together they symbolize the way dance and dancers conspire unconsciously to baffle time. Grey entered the nineteenth-century classical repertory in this ballet. She also opened the new production of it at Covent Garden in 1952 and made her farewell performance in it in 1957. Her final performance with the Bolshoi, on January 1, 1958, marked the ballet's 800th performance in that theatre; her coach there, Marina Semyonova, had been a noted Swan Queen herself. The connections go on and on. Grey's debut in Swan Lake was the first performance Philip Chatfield ever saw of the ballet; he would eventually partner her in it at Sadler's Wells. Grey danced Swan Lake as a guest artist with Festival Ballet in 1958, in a new production by Vera Volkova in South Africa in 1963, in Peking in

1964. In 1972 she staged her own production for Festival Ballet, and in 1979 Festival Ballet danced in Peking. I loved the modesty with which she said to me, "It's lovely to feel that one is a link."

*F*ate is extraordinary. I always wanted to go on the stage — not necessarily as a dancer, but to act. That's why I prefer the acting-dancing roles to the plain, pure abstract dance. I had speech training and acting lessons as a child, but I never did any acting. I showed an aptitude for dancing very early on.

I do feel everything's already organized. Because I didn't get the RAD scholarship — I got mumps and missed the exam — I was auditioned at the Sadler's Wells School by Ursula Moreton and accepted, which was much better because it meant I would have daily training instead of once a week special training. But my parents couldn't pay the fees, so because of *that*, I was re-auditioned by Ninette, who gave me this quite unique eight-year contract. It was for four years' training in the School to be paid back by four years' dancing in the company, starting at the godly sum of ten bob a week for one performance a week and working up to four pounds a week when I was eighteen and could do four performances a week. The contract was actually drawn up when I was nine. By that time, I was completely sold on Ginger Rogers and Shirley Temple, so of course my imagination was greatly aroused for dancing. I felt I must go on the stage and dance, or go into films and dance, or do something and dance.

I've always liked music very much too; I had piano lessons and singing lessons. It was always music that made me want to dance, and when I have arranged things, it's always to the music I turn for direction and inspiration. It went right through my dancing. From the practical point of view, approaching a role, I always used to buy the records and steep myself in them, from very early on, when I was fourteen. And the other inspiration that has always been vital to me has been nature. I absolutely adore trees. I've always had to go out on a Sunday and walk amongst trees, and that goes right into my dancing too, definitely. I have to feel one with nature. It's very helpful for things like *Sylphides*, where I created a mental image of sylphs flying through branches and trees swaying in the wind. I like the dramatic works much more because I like to infuse movement with a character, and for the abstract ballets, I've always had to find some mental picture for myself.

And I've always had to have music. I can't bear dancing in silence. My favorite ballet — which is *Swan Lake* — the music is Tchaikovsky's, and Tchaikovsky really is the dancer's dream composer. Very clear rhythms, very inspiring melodies, and great swaying orchestrations which carry you and lift you. Oh yes, they do. There's no doubt about it. I think dancers are much more fortunate than actors, because actors only have themselves to get inspiration from and to create the whole atmosphere and jog the memory, whereas dancers have the music to do all that. I played Beecham's *The Gods Go a-Begging* the other day, which I hadn't heard for ages, since I last did it when I was sixteen — I did it first when I was fourteen; Ninette revived it for me — and when I heard the music, it brought all the steps back immediately. Quite extraordinary. To me, the music and dance are one.

I saw a lot of ballet before the war, the Wells mostly, but I used to go to Covent Garden when Ballet Russe arrived. I remember *Sylphides* very well there — I saw it from the gallery, so it looked really magical — and *Prince Igor*. And I used to queue up for the baby ballerinas' signatures at the stage door; I got them all. That was a great inspiration. And then the war came, and for two years I didn't really see anything. But when the School reopened after the company was put back on the road, I used to go from the country down to London and take a class on Friday and Saturday. That's all I did for those two years until, the very month I was fourteen, Ninette had me appear in London with the company in the corps de ballet. I was telegraphed to join them because the very tall girl in the company had got appendicitis. And then about six months later, the same tall girl, Moyra Fraser, twisted her ankle, and I did some solo parts: Prayer, *Patineurs* White girl, *Façade* Polka, and all that sort of business. And then, when we were in Oxford about three months after that, Margot wasn't well, so on the Monday I did *Sylphides*, and on the Tuesday I did *Sylphides*, the Lady in *Comus*, and the second act of *Swan Lake*.

I was told when I went in on Tuesday morning that I was to do *Lac* in the evening, and I thought that Ninette meant the big swans, because that would be the natural progression. I'd never even done those. I was still in the corps, and being the tallest, I was right in the back row. And I had never done any double work in my life, because one wasn't trained to do double work in those days. I was only fourteen; I wouldn't have done it anyway. I learnt Act II in the morning with Bobby Helpmann, and I shall never forget the evening: on the finger fouettés at the end of the pas de deux, I couldn't remember quite what to do, so I just let go and turned 'round. Couldn't believe Bobby's face. It was terrifically funny.

I had no nerves at all that night. I was never nervous — I could never wait to get on. When I did my first full-length *Lac* in London, also with Helpmann, I was in the wings and I kept thinking, 'This is a dream and I'm going to wake up,' and I was longing to get on before I woke up because I wanted to know what it was like.

I'd really only seen Margot in it, because only Margot did it. Well, you just think of nothing else, of course, except that day when it's going to happen, when it's going to be you. And I was terribly ambitious. I was so disappointed when the company first put on the full-length *Sleeping Beauty* — that must have been in 1939; they called it *Sleeping Princess.* The Vic-Wells was quite small, thirty-five people, so it was a small *Beauty*, but Sergeyev, the man who had come from Leningrad, had the notation and put on a production which was very much acclaimed, actually. Practically all the dancers in the School were in it as something, a page or a court lady or a peasant, but because in those days you weren't allowed on the stage until you were twelve, with a special license, I didn't get on. I was bitterly disappointed. I remember going home and dreaming that Margot would fall ill and I would have the chance of doing the Princess, which is practically exactly what happened to me a few years later when I was fourteen and flung on in *Lac*.

I did Act II then for a week, and Ninette was pleased with it at the end of the week and said I should learn the other two acts. I had three months to do that, and of course she trained me. Oh yes, heavens, I was very much . . . we all were, very much, under Ninette. She did the initial work of telling me what one was supposed to feel when and where, and when to look frightened, etc. I guess I did a very superficial interpretation, but from my point of view, the real challenge was the dancing and all the technical things in the third act, and having the strength to get through it all — it's very tough. As one got older, I was always very concerned about having enough strength. But I think that's partly tied up with the fact that the older you get, the more your standards go up and the more you see that you can put in, and therefore the more you *want* to put in, so the more nervous you get. I was much more nervous at twenty-five than I was at fifteen: one has a responsibility and one's built a reputation. And also, the role means so much more to you because you love it. You grow to love it, and you can't bear to fall below your own standards.

When I was nineteen, I was allowed to go to outside teachers, which wasn't really encouraged, and I went to a teacher I've been to ever since called Audrey de Vos. She was wonderful at producing one in a role, at discussing and working on the dramatic nuances within the choreography. There was never the time for that in the company. One was rehearsed technically, and they would say a few obvious things about the interpretation, but I liked to study it in depth. Audrey would give me an attitude from which to approach a role. She would draw you out and make you think and understand why you were doing things, so the whole role was analyzed. That is particularly important when you have a role like Giselle, with the Mad Scene. For much of that — in fact, even the dancing parts at the beginning — you really have to know where you're going and why. I don't think you should ever do a meaningless movement onstage. Oh, you do initially, of course, for the first ten years. Then it's a question of mastering the technique, because it's so difficult, so all-absorbing and demanding. The first priority is to get through it, do your turns, do your beats, do your *manèges* 'round and finish in the right place and not hit anyone. But after a time, you begin to demand more from yourself than just the technical results. You begin to live with the role and think about it and talk about it and play the music.

You have to remember — and otherwise you get stale — that the dance is not made in itself. You're using it as your means of expression just as a musician uses an instrument. Your body's your instrument. When you realize that, it's just limitless what you can do with a role. I would go on playing the music, and I would often write things down. I've got books and books of ideas that my teacher and I spoke about, and also of the technical corrections she gave me.

I'm supposed to be a very lyrical dancer, so presumably slower movements come more easily to me. But that second-act pas de deux in *Lac* is the most difficult of any of the classical pas de deux, because it has to be restrained and withheld, and yet you have to give out so much emotion. It's technically restrained, but emotionally the opposite. It's much easier to make a flamboyant gesture to express a depth of emotion, as you can in Act III, than to find exactly the right, most telling gesture with the right amount of weight behind it, as you must in Act II. After all, Odette's an enchanted being; she isn't really able to do anything for herself. She feels everything she does is about to be finished by the magician, who can return at any time and destroy her.

When you first see her, she's part swan, part woman, and throughout the second act you've got to remind the public all the time that for most of the twenty-four hours, this creature is a swan. During these hours of night she returns to being a woman, and yet the knowledge is always there that all too soon she's going to be turned back into a swan and that she's not a free agent. I used to feel that Odette was submerged by the magician, that she was such a captured, pathetic creature. Although she has a heart and falls in love, there's an air of doom and tragedy surrounding her. So she must show purity and tremendous dignity, and at the same time have this feeling of pathos.

To me, on a different tack entirely, the Swan Queen epitomizes the ballerina. The ballerina is beautiful to look at, and yet underlying that apparent softness must be tremendous, steely strength. That's what a swan has: it looks so beautiful and graceful, gliding along with its lovely soft feathers, but when you get closer, feet are working hard, it's very strong, and if it gets cross, it can come at you. So I never see the Swan Queen as a little fluttering bird, but as someone with tremendous power and strength — very like the dancer.

Really, she trusts the Prince by the end of the first mime scene. You see her change. She enters diagonally into the center and then progresses gradually. The runs and the jump should be her landing from the air; with the pose, she's flicking the water off and trying to preen her feathers; and by the last arabesque, she's almost human. Then someone is there, and she's naturally, instinctively, frightened. But even as she runs away from him, she tends to want to run less, because of curiosity. So each time she runs from him, she runs less far. And the fact that he is interested in her, and is showing his curiosity by asking why she's there, gradually breaks down the wall of her suspicion. She eventually tells him the story, and he gets quite carried away and swears to marry her. At that point, she feels the magician coming, and when he does materialize, she pleads with him not to harm the Prince. When she takes the arabesque over him, she is defending him, so you know already, quite near the beginning of the act, that she has some feeling for him.

The mime scene is most beautifully designed. Of course many companies now don't keep to the original, and since I've been director here, I've had a great deal of trouble with my ballerinas who also want to discard it in favor of steps. I think we're in a period of homage to the steps. I didn't find it difficult at all. Mime is very much a part of dancing; one is a natural development of the other. When you're doing a ballet like *Swan Lake*, you have to realize that it is a period piece. It was created in the 1880s, when mime was as important to the audience as dancing, and you have to approach that role giving as much importance to both as you can. The moment you start thinking of them as separate, that's the mistake. Mime is such an integral part of this ballet. It's quite possible to make it understandable for today's audience; most of the gestures are pretty obvious. At the School, every Saturday morning from the age of ten, we would have mime for three-quarters of an hour and character dancing for three-quarters of an hour, sometimes longer. I knew all the mazurkas and czardases from

Coppélia and *Swan Lake*, and I think I benefited enormously from them.

Then, in Act II, as Odette gets through this pas de deux which is quite exhausting because of its restraint and the technical demands, you also have to see her beginning to trust the Prince more, coming to him more and allowing him to caress her. You see her love for him developing, and by the end of the pas de deux you must feel that there is something binding them to each other. It's quite difficult to do that in a technical pas de deux because everything is so very pure and clear. You can see immediately if something goes wrong, and whatever does go wrong spoils it for the audience, spoils it for the dancer too, of course. It's a very clean, balanced pas de deux, and it has to be taken at the right speed. This is so important. If it's taken too quickly, there's no time to develop her emotions or to establish a rapport between them. Conversely, many dancers like it very slow because it gives the chance for the love development, but if it's taken too slowly or too heavily, it becomes too long and in a way almost boring. It kills the beauty of the love itself that you see springing up. Because that love is new and young and tender, it mustn't be labored and heavy.

It was very difficult to explain to myself, after that lovely pas de deux, why she came on alone and danced a solo. I used to tell myself that it was her yearning to be free, because the movements are sort of flying away, the sissonnes and also the ronds de jambe at the beginning when she lifts her head. When I put on *Swan Lake* here, I got the Prince to bring the ballerina on for her solo, so that she walked in in his arms and danced the solo *to* him. That way it could be a means of expressing not only her desperate wish to be free of all the shackles of her spell, but her love for him and her yearning to fly away with him. Not necessarily just to fly away as a swan, which is what it's suggesting, but to go with him.

The third act is a much more obvious role to play. I never thought of Odile as something the magician has produced out of thin air. I thought of her, very definitely, as the magician's daughter, a very real spirit or being, but an evil spirit and one who takes great delight in deceiving people and being wicked. You wanted to show the much freer agent, the more direct, flamboyant assurance, which the White Swan doesn't have. Whenever Odette is on the stage, you have the pure love and the hope of good triumphing over evil coming through, and when Odile is on, you see a very sensuous, scheming woman, someone who delights in evil — and there are people like that in the world.

Everyone has different ideas about *Swan Lake*, but I have grown up to believe that the relationship between Odile and the magician is that of father and daughter, and that she is free as much as any daughter is free of a father. He is obviously also dealing in magic and evil, but you never see Odile dominated by him. She comes on with him and exits with him, she plays with and to him, but she's not controlled by him. She has free rein to do what she wants, to entice and capture, to mesmerize and enchant. I used to play to him a great deal; you can have your aside. The Queen and the magician would be sitting on the left, and you could get your different expressions to them both.

One of the things that was very important onstage was how you stood when you were not doing anything other than standing. The character emanates from you whether your back is to the audience or your front. You should be able to speak to the public as well through your body as your face. That's why it's so important that you *are* the character all the time. You're not just Bill Moggs doing *Swan Lake* — you are the Swan Princess. You must be; every minute that you're on the stage, you have to be that magical creature. The audience should know from the moment she comes in and from the way she walks that this is Odile and not Odette. The walk, the run, the stance are all important. Of course, when you're in movement it's easier to express something than when you're doing relatively little or nothing at all.

The magician presents you, and the Prince comes off the throne and takes you presumably for a cosy corner chat. In the version I grew up with, we went off together; in the version I put on for Festival Ballet, no doubt influenced by [Vladimir] Bourmeister — one is so influenced by everything one sees that one tries to take the best — I had her almost disappearing through von Rothbart's cloak and coming up between him and the Prince, who would then go off after her. The idea was that they would be together then, but that he wasn't always quite sure if she would be there the next instant. She is totally in command of the situation. It's really her act. She dominates not only the Prince, but the court too. She has to dazzle everybody, otherwise the court would see the swan in the window. And she knows her powers; she's totally assured. She never for one moment thinks she's not going to succeed. There's never an element of doubt in anything she does. She has to be assurance personified, quite apart from evil personified.

That pas de deux's been so played around with now. Everybody has a different version. When I put on *Swan Lake* here, I insisted that everyone do my version. Slowly but surely . . . Well, we had guest artists in, and someone said, "Do you mind if I do this step?" and being soft-hearted I said, "Yes, do, if it suits you." It's interesting that in Russia they do let their dancers alter the choreography a little bit — not necessarily alter, but . . . 'adapt' perhaps is the word — which is not the tradition I grew up in at all. One was very frightened to change anything. But after all, when it comes to a performance, the audience wants to see the dancer at his best, and it's foolish to go on presenting yourself at a disadvantage. Which isn't to say that you shouldn't work at trying to master the original choreography; one should, ultimately. But there are some things which some people will never do really splendidly, really effortlessly, and therefore I think they should be dropped for that artist. It's the artistry that counts in the end. The technique is one thing, but the artistry is just as important, if not more so. Really and truly, in the last instance, how do we know what it was originally? The notation Sergeyev brought over was probably very near, but he obviously had to adapt and alter to a company of thirty-five. I wouldn't tamper with the choreography myself. I've always had enormous respect for the past, which was something I was given as a child. So if the choreography is set, I believe in my heart that one should do one's utmost to do it, but as a director it behooves you to let some people alter it as long as it's within the style and shows them to advantage. When I get very upset is when they alter it and they still don't do it right. Then they might just as well go on trying to master the original.

The fouettés in Black Swan are traditional, and I was lucky — I could always do fouettés. I used to enjoy doing them. Most people get terrified, but they never worried me at all. I was much more nervous about the second act, probably because there was so much I wanted to do in it.

That pas de deux builds, absolutely. That's why it saddens me to see the way it's tampered with; it's almost unrecognizable now. The one I grew up with was, to me, so wonderfully developed. You came in together. In the Bolshoi version, she does the first step alone, and he walks behind — I think that's a mistake. They should do the step together, because the whole point is that she should be with him from the word go. Whenever she runs away from him, he goes after her immediately. That makes so much sense. And all the technical steps, the grands jetés en tournant, and the double pirouettes with the grand rond de jambe when the leg and her arms twine 'round him, are all meant, I'm sure, in Petipa's mind, to be the spell, the evil she's trying to wind 'round him to tie him to her. Even the fouettés can be approached like that. It all builds up. She does the turns all the way 'round the stage, getting quicker and quicker, and then he comes in and leaps, and then she turns on one spot. I think you should aim

121

to do it on one spot because that's what's so hypnotic about it. After all, she is hypnotizing him and everyone. And you don't have to say, 'Now I'm going to do thirty-two fouettés.' You can think, 'Now I'm going to whirl him and the whole court into such excitement.' He, particularly, should be delirious with happiness and the court should be blinded. The whole structure of that pas de deux, the solos, and the finale is so logical and so beautiful.

Then, when you come to the last act and Odette's one hope of breaking the spell is gone because the Prince was tricked by Odile, she can be so pathetic and yet she still has to have the dignity and beauty of the swan. The dejection that she feels has to be told through the hold of the head and the dropping of the chest and the shoulders, utter dejection. When you see people who are totally miserable, everything is collapsed, isn't it? And onstage, everything has to be larger than life, one way or the other. The ballet is an artificial medium, so of course it's all exaggerated. But in that last act the music is so powerful. It is a great tragedy, the fact that she really thinks she's free at last and then it all crumbles the moment her freedom is achieved. She's totally heartbroken, and she feels the only thing to do is kill herself. In fact, it wasn't his fault, because he was so blinded in Act III that he didn't see the swan at the window — which one does think is very strange, but that's balletic license. It wasn't that he was frozen by her, though I quite like the idea of her being able to immobilize him, blind him from reality. It was just that he was so charmed and overwhelmed by her beauty that he would turn to the Queen Mother and say, 'This is the girl I want to marry.' He is made out to be rather a fool in the end, isn't he? But then, if you consider that the power of evil is so strong, he isn't such an idiot after all. If you believe that everything is predestined, then he is not behaving stupidly. It's just inevitable what happens.

For the fourth act, in Moscow they have this strange idea . . . It isn't strange — it's a very good idea actually. What I mean is that it looks strange because it doesn't, in fact, work. Their idea, which was the original idea, is that she kills herself, and he makes the ultimate sacrifice and kills himself too because he loves her so much, and they are reunited through their love. In the Sergeyev version, this reuniting was in the land of never-never. But the Bolshoi insisted that when they were reunited, they were also returned to this world, and that all the swan maidens take on a natural form again as well. So they all take their feathered headdresses off and throw them on the stage, which looked frightfully untidy to say the least. I always believed that they died first, because it seems to me that's what's needed to prove the ultimate sacrifice. Death so often is needed to prove things.

I enjoyed dancing that version tremendously, the Moscow one. That's not the version they do now, I add hastily, but the one that first came to us after the war and that I danced there in 1957. It was remarkably close to ours, but one or two things in the order of the third-act pas de deux were different. What was so wonderful was that they all acted with one all the time. In the third act, everyone was so excited when you came onstage, and talking. The reaction, the inter- play, is something that I have never experienced in any other company. Incredible. I hope it still exists there. Act IV was totally different. They had much less mime, much more dancing for the ballerina with the Prince, and then a lot more activity for the magician, who actually has to leap about and have his wings broken. Which made quite a lot of sense, because what that version showed was the breaking of his power. And one danced with them both, which was very exciting.

You need a very strong back for those lifts. I had a fantastic partner, but even so, we had to do quite a lot of work to get my back just right. They have backs like iron really, and they seem to hold them tighter and lower down than we do, which gives them tremen- dous control and style and those wonderful arched arabesques. In one way, they were much less disciplined: in class, people came and went whenever they wanted to, which surprised me. Today anything goes, but in '57 it did not, and certainly not under Ninette. You know, you either did class or you were on the sick list. But their whole training is so different. In class, their *enchaînements* were freer, very much more dancey than the ones I was used to at the Wells, and the height of the leg was much greater, absolutely up there. I enjoyed Semyonova's classes tremendously, and [Asaf] Messerer's too. They were both lovely people to work with, very generous and out-giving.

I felt much more confident when I came back, dramatically much freer. I think English people are always slightly inhibited. One is not encouraged to show emotion as a child — or at least you weren't in my day — and that childish inhibition does tend to stay with you even on the stage. I think I got it out of my system in Russia, because nobody is inhibited there. The moment rehearsal starts, everybody acts his heart out.

And another thing that was wonderful was that the conductors always came to all the rehearsals. For most of the time I was at the Royal, Ninette was the boss, and she wouldn't allow any of the dancers really to speak to the conductors. When we got to Covent Garden after the war, we had perhaps grown up a little, and then we were allowed to talk to them and they would come to some of the rehearsals. But when I was in Russia, I had the feeling that that was a matter of course. Yuri Faier came to the classes and the rehearsals so he got to know me, and I always think it's frightfully important that a conductor knows how a dancer breathes. There has to be such a close rapport to get a really good performance.

When the curtain goes up, the performance is in the conductor's hands, and you must always follow him. That's why you must know each other. My gosh, I've done so many performances with crummy conductors, going along at a gallop or crawling along at a funeral rate. It is so unutterably depressing, because you're totally helpless. There's nothing you can do. And if you're going slower or faster than the music's being played, you're going to look wrong. Even though you may be right, it won't appear that way to the average member of the public.

Whether you are a musical dancer or not, there's a certain speed which is right for a ballet and right for the dancer to be seen at his best. I was always told I was a musical dancer. I hope I was. I think it means being with the music totally, being able to feel the music and hear it. So many dancers don't actually hear music. I don't mean that funnily; I really do mean it. It's not fun to watch. A good conductor breathes the music and feels the little breaths that you take. It's something that you really want to develop together.

It's the same with partners. It has to be a give-and-take relationship with any and every partner. Some couldn't be bothered even thinking about the role. Lots of men are mostly concerned with the technique and the partnering, and they think that's probably enough — if they think at all about it. With others, I could talk the roles through, and we would build up a very fine partnership, dramatically as well as technically. It's absolutely essential that you talk with your partner so that you do have a rapport. There's always time to talk — depends how badly you want to do it. In life there's always time for everything if you really want to do it. And again I come back to music: it's awfully important that you breathe the music the same way. But it's so difficult to find someone who is tall enough to show you off in the right way, someone who is strong, who is musical, who is a good dancer, who is a good partner, who's dramatically ringing true. Some partners would believe very much in what they were doing, but somehow it never quite came across. Acting is a gift too, like dancing. To have a sensitivity for music is a gift. And to find everything in one partner — and a tall partner to boot — is asking an awful lot.

I always felt much more comfortable dancing alone, because of being tall and always having partners who tended to be shorter than me. Bobby [Helpmann], my first partner, was really too short; David Paltenghi, who was very strong, was also short, and so was

Alexis Rassine. So it was only when I got to John Field and Bryan Ashbridge and Philip Chatfield that I started getting the right height. And Oleg Briansky, who was quite a bit later in my career.

The Russians were wonderful partners, too. They do know so much more; the science of training there for the pas de deux work seems to be so much better than it is in the West. They could cope with a ballerina off balance, which you never get here, and they knew how to lift. In the West, you have to find your way. [Vakhtang] Chabukiani was just exceptional. He was a beautiful strong partner without looking heavy, so sensitive and musical, and very refined to look at. And he had wonderful hands. I loved his hands. I was so sad I didn't finally dance with him. Mark you, [Yuri] Kondratov was very good too, a wonderful partner, very strong indeed, and a good actor, but Chabukiani just had something that no one else had. Immediately, you could feel that.

The Russian men seem to be trained to act as well as dance, and I don't think many of the dancers in the West are necessarily trained that way. Ballet can become very stolid, very stiff and artificial, but I believe it's possible to keep the traditional confines of the technical ballet and yet make it totally expressive. But if it's not in the mind, it won't go into the body, and if it's not in the body, it won't happen. It won't be there for people to see. You have to convince yourself before you can hope to convince anyone else.

I was very lucky. I was so carefully produced and so sensitively worked on there. One had the feeling of timelessness. It's lovely to feel that one is a link, that it's carrying on through one. And I think that's why one gets so nervous tackling a classical role, because one does feel in a direct line with some of the greatest exponents. There's a certain awe in taking that on, and a tremendous responsibility. And also, you realize the audience knows jolly well if you go wrong. *Giselle* was a very important role for me. That I didn't do until I was sixteen, just over a year after I did *Lac*. It took a long time to get anywhere with it. There are very few ballets in which you actually jump. Most of the roles are more *terre à terre* for the ballerina, but *Giselle* is jumping from the beginning to the end, so you need a different sort of stamina. I used to enjoy it. I often think that I enjoyed *Giselle* far too much. There's not a nerve-wracking, difficult technical bit in it anywhere. It's just sheer dance for which you've got to build up your stamina. And I used to think it was such a wonderful progression: her joy at being alive and in love, her doubts, her fears, the horror of finding out that she's being deceived, and then it breaks and she goes mad. Then she's exhausted, completely — and it's very easy to come on as a spirit in the second act. You see, again you come back, like the swan. She's got to have that control and inner strength all the time, and yet appear totally relaxed and weightless.

The roles all interchange, of course they do. There's something that sparks off something in something else. That's why all dancers long to have new roles. It's not just out of sheer boredom, wanting to do something different. It's because they instinctively realize that the more experience you have, the more the roles you have are strengthened and the more you grow.

It seems to me that in the best of art, in all great art, you have to trim away so that only the essence is left. That's what one aims for after a bit, doing more by doing less. That is very difficult to put into words. Words can be very misleading when you're training a dancer. What will mean the right thing to you may mean something quite different to someone else. I do feel a little shy in passing on all my personal feelings about a role because each dancer must, for her own self-respect, search out her own meaning. One can guide and suggest, but each person comes to it a different way. Their interpretations must be governed by their physical structure, inevitably, and each of us reacts differently to the same different situations. I try to help more on the technical side. One can say, "Well, if you're going to do these double ronds de jambe from two feet, you want to push off here." If they want to discuss the role with you, that's another matter; then you can start lots of ideas going. But I've always been hesitant to do that, because I don't feel one should put one's own thoughts and personality into someone else. It has to be something of their own. There's nothing worse than when someone says, "So and so reminds me of someone . . ." — "another [Maya] Plisetskaya" or "another Fonteyn." Nobody wants to be another so-and-so. Everyone wants to be themselves, and they must be.

Once you get up on the stage, you are alone there, so you might just as well start thinking of it alone. You have to think for yourself. Of course you want to discuss it with your partner or your teacher, or husband or lover or whoever it may be. But in the end, it has to be your final reaction, either to the story, the role, the music, or to all three. What I try to do when I coach is suggest different ways of approaching it. It's so interesting to see how different accents get brought out in the music, in the dance, with different dancers. Some people don't find anything in an area that would have given one enormous inspiration, or they find other areas that one hasn't actually thought about oneself. I love it.

Who I've listened to most in the past years is definitely my teacher, Audrey de Vos, and from the age of ten 'til that time, Ninette.

The audience encourages you enormously, and critics usually depress you. Well, you always want perfect critics, and who gets those? You have to have a teacher in whom you have total faith and respect and trust, and then you know yourself if you've danced well, so in the end you have to be your own yardstick.

When you have developed as an artist, as a dancer, you have to give more than a technical performance. You've got to say something. And there is a tremendous amount of emotional energy that you've got to store up. I'm not one of those people that can sit and chat in a dressing room before a performance, or rush around all day. I always felt I had to withdraw and rest and be quiet. That wasn't just physical or so I wouldn't be tired, but so I would have the strength to get through the performance and do it beautifully and excitingly. You've got to have something within you to give out.

I would very much have liked to dance *Symphonic Variations*, because I think it's one of the classics of this century. That's the one role in the Royal that I would like to have done. We never had *Romeo and Juliet* in my day, but I would love to have done a Juliet. I think all ballerinas wanted to do that. And I would have given anything to have worked more with Balanchine after *Ballet Imperial*. His choreography is so dancey; it's a dancer's dream. And I've never danced Tudor — such an exquisite, sensitive choreographer. I would adore to have done *Lilac Garden*. Still, it's always nice to have something you haven't done. I would think it would be awful to have done everything. And really, *Swan Lake* to me has meant more than anything. One always was wanting more; once you finished one performance, you wanted to do something more with it. I think it's a role you could go on dancing, if your body allowed you to, forever.

Who did *I* dance for? God. Yes, yes, I did. Well, it's a God-given gift, and I think if you're given something, you have to do it as well as you can for as long as you can. And when you think you're not going to do it well enough, then you must stop. I used to love dancing. What is so sad, when you run a company, is that so often you see the person with the least talent longing to dance more than anyone else, and the person with the most talent not really caring very much and not working very hard. That is a tragic situation. You can't make a person work. If they haven't got that inner drive, that inner wish, that inner longing, nothing will give it to them.

July 1979
London

Nadia Nerina

Nadia Nerina (b. Cape Town, South Africa, 1927) first studied ballet with Eileen Keegan and Dorothea McNair in Durban; after her arrival in London in 1945, her teachers were Marie Rambert and Stanislas Idzikowsky. She spent a year with the Sadler's Wells Theatre Ballet, often in solo roles in such works as Les Sylphides, Le Carnaval, *and* Façade, *and in 1947 transferred to the Sadler's Wells Ballet at Covent Garden. There she quickly stepped into featured parts, created her first role for Frederick Ashton, Fairy Spring in* Cinderella *(1948), and was promoted to ballerina in 1951. By 1953, she was dancing the leading roles in all six of the company's full-length works:* Swan Lake, Giselle, Sleeping Beauty, Coppélia, Cinderella, *and* Sylvia. *Her association with Ashton continued as she created roles in his* Homage to the Queen *(1953),* Variations on a Theme by Purcell *(1955), and* Birthday Offering *(1956), and culminated in her creation of Lise in his romantic masterpiece,* La Fille Mal Gardée, *in 1960. That same year, she danced* Swan Lake *and* Giselle *in Russia as a guest artist with the Bolshoi and Kirov companies. She appeared less frequently with the Royal Ballet after becoming a permanent guest artist in 1966, and retired from dancing altogether in 1969.*

Frederick Ashton's La Fille Mal Gardée *is one of my 'desert island' ballets. It's bad enough living in New York without it, but even a hypothetical eternity without it is unthinkable. Ashton once credited his own "longing for the country of the late eighteenth and early nineteenth century" as a factor in his decision to re-create this pre-existing work — Dauberval had choreographed the original* Fille *in 1789. Musing further on the inspiration for his 1960 version, Ashton continued, "There exists in my imagination a life in the country of eternally late spring, a leafy pastorale of perpetual sunshine and the humming of bees — the suspended stillness of a Constable landscape of my beloved Suffolk, luminous and calm." You and I would have to resign ourselves to seeing such an idyll only in imagination. Ashton lifted it intact from his and put it on the ballet stage in the form of his* Fille Mal Gardée. *Since he has also said, "I think the choreographer should always try to work with his dancers, drawing expression from them rather than imposing actions on them," it's safe to assume that Fille would have been a different ballet had different dancers created it. Talking to Nadia Nerina was like approaching the source of my own enchantment.*

I started dancing in Bloemfontein, which is in the middle of South Africa, in the *bundu,* which means "the back of beyond." I was about seven, I suppose, and I twisted my ankle. My mother knew nothing about the dance or ballet, but the doctor said, "Oh, she must go into dancing classes because that will strengthen her ankle." And, of course, I loathed it. It was terribly difficult exercise, and all this business of pliés and turning out never made sense to me. It was uncomfortable, it hurt, and I'd much rather have been playing in the swimming pool with my school friends. But I just had to keep going; once I'd started, they sort of kept me there. The studio was a church hall, all white, white curtains, and the teacher had appliquéd dancers in felt on little squares, and those were around. And of course the studio was lined with pictures of famous dancers. At the back, they had a lovely garden with pomegranate trees, so if we'd been good, we were allowed to share a couple of pomegranates. But that was the only good thing about it.

These rather unpleasant classes went on and on and on — Cecchetti classes. I was trained Cecchetti. Then the war came, and my father was transferred to Durban — by that time I was about thirteen. And there I was very lucky; again I had a marvelous teacher. Training makes a tremendous difference. You can have a lot of talent, but if you have bad training when you're young, that training stays with you, and it's very difficult, when you're thirteen or fourteen, to undo it. Joyce Smerdon was marvelous in Bloemfontein, and in Durban I went to a teacher named Dorothea McNair. Now she was extraordinary because as a young girl she'd come over to England to study with Rambert, and she'd also studied Central European dancing and Greek dancing. I'll always remember her telling me that when she first went to Rambert, Mim [Rambert] said to her, "My dear child, you've got a lot of talent but I better tell you now, you'll never be a ballerina with that jaw. So I think you'd better be a teacher." Can you imagine saying that to somebody young come all the way from South Africa?

It was really kinder because she wouldn't have been able to make the stage, but she was a marvelous teacher, a very strong personality, and she'd also done a lot of mime.

And it was my good fortune that there was another Cecchetti teacher in Durban at the same time, who amalgamated with McNair. Eileen Keegan had left South Africa to tour with the René Blum company, so she was very professional, and she'd also studied Spanish dancing with Elsa Brunelleschi. All the dances Elsa had learnt, years back, my teacher had written down when *she* was a student. So we learnt Spanish and Greek dancing and classical ballet and mime from both of them, and they were so different as personalities and as teachers that we benefited enormously from the two.

Then my parents were transferred again and we lived in Johannesburg, and of course I went to dancing schools there. That's when I discovered — and I was fourteen — that really what I wanted to do more than anything else was dance. I'm sorry to say it about Johannesburg, but the schools weren't up to the standard of those two outstanding teachers. So I ran away. I wouldn't go to school or do anything. I went back to Durban with some friends for the weekend and decided I wouldn't come back. I ended up begging Dorothea McNair to keep me down there. She spoke to my parents on the phone, and in the end they said, "If she's so determined, she'd better stay there." You see, I had made up my mind.

Now, I hadn't finished school, even junior school. I couldn't go to a convent school, which I had been going to before in Durban, because they wouldn't let me out to do morning class. But there was, and still is, a brilliant drama professor called Elizabeth Sneddon at the University. My teachers knew her very well, and she arranged with the educational authorities that five of us would take our drama exams in place of school exams. And once she'd got us, she treated us like students from the University — she didn't talk down to us at all. Our studies consisted of studying a play and learning a bit about what it had to do with or the geography of where it was written, but we didn't have geography lessons as such. We had to spell and write, because occasionally we had to make up monologues which she'd correct, and we had voice training and we learned to act. That was my education, and it was very good for me because it prepared me to leave South Africa when I was seventeen: I'd already been treated like a student from the University.

I'm telling you all this because I think training is so important, and what was so marvelous was to have two teachers with this very varied background, plus the acting. As it turned out, I lost my mother when I was fourteen. I'd taken all the ballet exams I could take in

South Africa, elementary and intermediate, so I continued with the dancing but I switched my interest more and more to the drama, to keep my mind occupied, to take it off my sadness. And then I entered for a bursary in everything I could enter for, and I won the lot.

The trauma about that period was whether I went to England to study drama or whether I went on with ballet. So, at about fourteen, I had a nervous breakdown and was sent into the country to recuperate and think about it. And it's strange, but I realized then that the challenge was not acting. I was never nervous about going on in performances of the Greek plays or Bernard Shaw or Shakespeare, and I'd remember all my words with no problem. But for dancing, I was always nervous, so I worked out in my mind that the challenge was the ballet. I decided I would continue with it and gave back the bursary.

Then I joined a pantomime to learn professionalism, to learn to tour, because I was determined to go to England. And that was interesting because I had to speak and dance and swim, and I met professionals from England. One of them, Ivy Collins, wanted to go home, and my father managed to get us both on a boat that had come over to bring war brides home from the East. I couldn't go alone, you see; I was underage, so I had to be chaperoned. So I arrived in England not knowing a soul, and I'll always remember the endless chimney-pots and the fog, which after South Africa was quite extraordinary, and how old everything looked — all the buildings were dilapidated. I know it was just after the war, but I was used to a young country with modern buildings. And I went to Rambert because Dot McNair had written to her about me.

Ivy took me to the Mercury Theatre, which for me was very moving; *that* I did know about, because Dot McNair had told me about it. And Mim said, "Well, take off your coat and stand on the table. Let me have a look at you." Mim is a very strong personality, and I felt rather like a prize horse being looked at. Then she said, "Good, good, good. Now, where are your practice clothes?" "I haven't any," I said. "They haven't arrived." So she called her daughter, Angela, and said, "Get the child some practice clothes and take her into class immediately." So off I went, and that's how I started at the Mercury. She also, very kindly, said I could stay with her. I had nowhere to go; I'd been staying with Ivy and her friends. So I moved into her house and stayed at the top, and I'd never been in a house that went up five floors. I remember being terrified of the gas because it popped, turning on and off.

Another thing that was extraordinary. I always felt I'd wasted time coming over to England. I was seventeen on the boat, and when

Mim asked me how old I was, I immediately said, "Seventeen." "Oh," she said, "what a pity. Our company's going on tour, and you could have come with us in the company." Well, my heart sank because of course I was *not* seventeen. I had turned eighteen on the boat, literally ten days before, and I said I was younger because I'd felt, 'When I come here, I must say I'm younger than I am.' But I couldn't turn around and say to her, "I'm really not seventeen. I'm just eighteen by a week or so." So I had to go into the school, and the pity was I obviously would have been in the company. It was rather fate that I stayed behind.

From there, I went into the Sadler's Wells, also by chance. I love the story. I saw Mim the other night and she said, "You are such a naughty girl. If you'd stayed with me, you'd still have had a marvelous career."

In South Africa, I'd been used to studying all day. I'd get up at six, have my breakfast, and go down into the garden under the pawpaw trees and practice voice control and breathing for about an hour. Then I'd take the bus to the studio and work for an hour and a half by myself, then have class for an hour and a half. Then we'd go to the City Hall and listen to music. Then I'd go to a drama lesson, kind of a school lesson as well, then come back for a four o'clock dance class, which was Greek or character or Spanish. And get home around six, absolutely exhausted, and study lines for my lesson or do my homework. But here, at the Mercury, I only had a morning class. I happened to shuffle down Shepherd's Bush one day, kicking the leaves, and there was a house with a sign saying 'Idzikowsky giving class.' I knew the name from *The Dancing Times*, so I went in and asked if I could do a class.

The Mercury was professional, so it wasn't Cecchetti as I'd been brought up on it. Professional classes aren't academic in the same way as sticking to a syllabus. Madame Rambert did study Cecchetti, but with professionalism, it changes. You're not doing the set exercises, whereas in a country where there are no professional companies — I had never seen a professional company in my life — they have to stick to the syllabus in the studio. But when I went into Idzikowsky's class, it was thoroughly Cecchetti. I went absolutely wild. I had a marvelous time, and I wasn't being corrected all the time either by Rambert or her daughter.

And then a lady said to me, "Where do you come from?" and I said, "From South Africa." "Well," she said, "I think you should go to the Sadler's Wells." Which I'd never heard of. So I got to Sadler's Wells just because I went to Idzikowsky by accident. It would probably have been very good for me to have stayed with Mim another six months or a year. It might have matured me a little more quickly on the expressive side. She's so brilliant in bringing the personality out of dancers. But as it was, I went straight into Sadler's Wells.

And you must remember, we had two companies. There was the Sadler's Wells Ballet at the Sadler's Wells Theatre, and Madam — de Valois, that is — was forming the junior company, the Sadler's Wells Theatre Ballet. Just before Christmas 1945, I went over to the Sadler's Wells Theatre. And when I arrived, they were all in their white tunics, all young, grand piano, huge room — I thought this was marvelous — and I did a class with Peggy van Praagh. That's where they saw me. Then I went off for Christmas and got the mumps or something. They nearly had a fit, because they thought I'd given it to all the girls. And when I finally came back after about six or eight weeks, there was nobody but a few tatty students. All those beautiful white angels that I thought I was going to be with had gone into the Theatre Ballet, and of course, having just arrived and done one class, I wasn't with them. So it was back in there for me with what was left over. I was heartbroken.

And then I was called to be an extra with the big company. I didn't understand anything about it. I went to Covent Garden, and it wasn't what I'd seen with the juniors; it was a different company altogether, and they were rehearsing *Sleeping Beauty*. I turned up early, did my barre, and a fascinating girl at the other end was looking at me as much as I was looking at her. That was Violetta Elvin, who'd just arrived from Russia. I stood one end very nervous, and she stood the other end very nervous.

I wasn't part of the company, but I was on the stage for that first night in '46, as one of the two Nurses. And because they were short of dancers and I was around doing class, they put me in the Vision scene as well later. I'd only been there for a few weeks when the junior company was ready to go on tour. So I went too, and I stayed with them after that for a year. Madam's idea was to bring the young dancers and choreographers all up together. John Cranko arrived from South Africa, and Kenneth MacMillan was there and Peter Darrell. But then, I was the first young dancer in the system to transfer to the senior company.

I don't know how it happened but the first thing I did there, within a week, was the lead in *Sylphides* with Alexis Rassine, who was then dancing with Margot and Moira. And I was put up in the Number 4 dressing room. Number 5 is our première ballerina's, and the other ballerinas are in 4, 3, 2, and 1. I was only in Number 4 because I was doing the lead in *Sylphides*. And then, not very long after, I think it was Alicia Markova came over to the Sadler's Wells, and of course somebody had to move out of that top floor, and of course it had to be me. Down I went but quick! Into the corps de ballet dressing room and, obviously, into the corps de ballet. You can imagine the reaction of all the girls. Madam was so strict. It took a long time to get to the front of the corps de ballet in those days, let alone to get into the third cast of a solo. And this little upstart not only arrives out of the junior company which everybody's talking about, but in a week she goes straight into the second lead dressing room and into *Sylphides* with the premier danseur!

When I came down, it was the worst time in my life or my career. You see, I'd never done the corps de ballet, in *Swan Lake* or *Sylphides* or anything. I'd only done the little Waltz or the Prelude or the lead in *Sylphides*. There were so few of us in the little company that I'd been dancing Sugar Plum Fairy and the leads or second leads in the ballets that were being created for us. And suddenly, I had to learn *all* the corps de ballet — I didn't know a step. And they didn't rehearse because they all knew it backwards — they'd been together as a team for so long — and nobody was going to show me. So if anybody from the front could see one white swan dithering from one line to the other, that was me. I'd say, "Which way?" and they'd say, "Find out." I used to be in endless tears, but they soon realized I wasn't as dreadful as they thought I might be.

When you're young, you want to do everything. You just dream about it. And then it's a matter of luck to get something, like Madam putting me into *Sylphides*. I had danced it in South Africa and in the second company, so they knew about that. But you don't think clearly; you just hope you'll get something. I didn't sort of say, 'I *will* get them,' even when I was younger. Madam once said to me, "Why is it that all the dancers that come from abroad get on so quickly?" And I said, "You must remember that there are a lot of dancers in Canada and the Dominions and Australia and South Africa, but it's only the ones who give up a lot and leave their parents that actually get to England or into the company. We've got a lot of determination and we've got a lot to lose. You don't want to go home having not achieved anything." So that's why one kept at it.

We were taught very early to work very hard. Eileen Keegan gave us such enormous respect for the stage. She told us we were never to walk across a stage in high heels because so many dancers give their lives to it that it's almost a sacred place. And she always said, "It doesn't matter how talented you are. It's the work that you're going to put into it. You can't just arrive because you've got talent."

And as far as I was concerned, it's not being better than anybody else, it's being better than myself yesterday. That's the whole reason to keep going. I love to watch other dancers, because you can learn from everybody. They don't have to be ballerinas for you to learn from them. And if somebody else can do something, there's no reason why *you* shouldn't, in your own way, if you're better than you were yesterday. And hopefully, one day you'll be better than most. Everything had to be right. It never was — because it never is, it can always be better — but anything that was not right would have to be worked on until it was better. I didn't want to be like anybody. But if they could do it, there was no reason, if I worked hard enough, that I couldn't do two, three, four, five, six pirouettes. I'd just have to keep at it.

It's the role that's important. Whatever role it is, you can make it into something if you respect it. That's a terribly important thing that I think gets lost today. That's where Madam was fantastic. She trained the audience here to respect the roles; therefore, the dancers respected the roles as well. You didn't get a role easily. It was unusual that I got *Sylphides* like that, and once I started again from the corps de ballet up, then it was soloist roles plus the corps de ballet. You were very lucky if you got a matinée solo first, and then you hoped you might be given an evening, and *then* a Saturday evening, which was *the* time to dance.

If you ask me which role I loved best, I can't say. I have a special affection for *Fille* because that was something I created with Fred, but I loved them all. They were always fresh and within their context. I suppose I approached each one from the music, because from the music you have a feel. For instance, try to explain *Giselle*. *Giselle* is very close to *Fille* because the music is the same period. To me, Giselle is a very young, simple girl, not strong — she suffers from her heart — and she loves her mother very much. She's a person of nature, and she's superstitious. For instance, when the Prince swears he loves her, she stops him and takes his hand down. It's too grand for her, to swear like that. She gets the flower to say whether he loves her or loves her not. But when you get to Lise, she's quite a different girl. She's also a farm girl and she loves her mother too, but she's already a little mother herself. She churns the milk — she's like a lot of little girls with their dolls and prams. If I'd picked a flower as Lise, I couldn't have picked it as I did as Giselle, and Lise turned out with the music.

The day Fred said to me, "We'll start," the first bit of music I remember hearing was for the ribbons. Well, immediately you know it's light but it's romantic. It's not *Coppélia*. Swanilda was one of the first roles I did and I loved it, but she's still another girl. She's a tomboy, a naughty, saucy girl with an enormous amount of cheek, and the music tells you she's like that. You cannot compare her to Lise at all. They're both sixteen, and so is Giselle — they're all the same age — but Swanilda's naughty, Giselle is not naughty at all, and Lise is mischievous. That's the music, too. It's the music that always gave it to me.

Here's another thing. There are laughs in *Fille*, but it's not a comedy ballet. One's more conscious of the comedy in *Coppélia*, but it's a different kind of thing. *Fille* should be romantic. It's the sort of ballet that should make you laugh and cry at the same time. Alec Grant's Alain was always on the border, and the same with Mother — Stanley Holden never played it for laughs. If we'd been doing it for weeks and we were all tired and having high jinks, Stanley would go to town. But even then he never outstepped it to the degree that it could be outstepped. The Clog Dance was a humor. It wasn't funny: it was humorous, which is a difference. And if it's pushed over to the comedy side, you lose the delicacy of the ballet and of the music.

Fred said he was doing *La Fille Mal Gardée*, and I knew from Madam that he was doing the ballet for me. But until he started, I didn't know anything about *Fille* or Lise or the story. It was an extraordinary experience. I've created ballets with Kenneth MacMillan, Peter Darrell, Roland Petit, and various other people, and worked with Balanchine too, but Fred is different. One created a role *with* Fred much more than *with* most choreographers. He knows what he wants before he starts; he knows exactly how the ballet begins, the middle part, and the end — I should think it's rather the way a writer plans a book. He knows the music, and he worked with Jack Lanchbery on it for *Fille*, translated it and arranged it. But when he starts, Fred will say, "Well, here are the ribbons, here's the music. Do something. Come down the stairs and play with the ribbons." So you start to fiddle about just doing what you think the music does. And Fred will say, "Hmmm," and then he'll do what he wants but using something of what you did, so that it's actually your personality he's bringing out in the steps. It's only his genius that decides what stays and what doesn't. Another choreographer already has the steps worked out exactly in his mind; that's what he wants and that's what you do. Obviously, you do them — as a person and as a dancer — your own way, but those steps have already been decided upon, formed. Whereas with Fred it's creative as it goes along. For instance, he's done a great deal of creation for Margot, and you might say that Margot's a color — say, pink — so all those ballets are shades of pink. But then he comes to somebody like me, who is 'blue,' and it's completely different. After Margot and Michael [Somes], suddenly he had two completely different colors; Nerina and [David] Blair.

So the first thing I remember was that bit of music, and that gave me the clue to Lise. The music was Lise's personality. All I knew was that it's a bright, early morning, the dawn's breaking, you come down the stairs, and you've got these ribbons. I'm quite sure I hadn't read anything about it, and he wouldn't clutter up one's thought with too much history. You're very nervous when you start to create something new, and I find I don't want to be cluttered up with preconceived ideas. It's like . . . Bobby Helpmann phoned me one day and said, "Nadia, I'd like you to do Electra." I happened to have been in Greece that summer and seen the Greek Theatre. I couldn't understand a word, but it impressed me so much, the way they spoke, the atmosphere. And I had done *Trojan Women* when I was a girl. So when he said that, I said, "Bobby dear, you must have got the wrong idea because I'm blonde and blue-eyed. You wouldn't cast me in that role." He said, "No, don't think about it. We'll just start on Monday, and you'll do it. Don't think about anything." That was much better for me, to start like that.

All I need is the music and an idea. If somebody just says the one right thing that happens to click, then I've got the key, the core of it, the essence of the character. The first thing Fred created for me was Fairy Spring in *Cinderella*. We were in a dreadful rehearsal room in the King's Road, down in the basement where there was leaking gas so it didn't smell very nice, and it was pouring with rain outside. And he said, "There's the music. Now, what do you think of first?" I said, "Buds bursting," and he said, "Right. That's what the dance is." And when I first did *Firebird*, I found it very difficult. *Firebird*'s like *Swan* in a way, and I couldn't get it; it just didn't feel right. And then Dame Ninette came in, and she said, "It's got to be your fingers. There are sparks on your fingers." And that was *Firebird* for me. That meant the whole of the interpretation I did. So it's the music plus an idea that sparks off the whole.

Fred always had ideas. For instance, he had the ribbon and he said, "You know, a cat's cradle." Well, I knew nothing about a cat's cradle. So he showed me; he and David did a cat's cradle with their fingers, and we had a lot of laughing about it because they couldn't get it quite right. Then Fred said to us, "Well, now do that together." So within twenty minutes we'd worked out the cat's cradle with ourselves and the ribbon. And when it came to the 'Fanny Elssler' pas de deux, he wanted big lifts. David could lift me all over the place, and I'd been to Russia by then and done lifts with [Nicolai] Fadeyechev that nobody had done here, which I taught to David. So when Fred said, "I want you floating around. David, lift her somewhere. I want something like smoke," we did various things that looked like smoke.

But, as I say, it's Fred's genius to use something that would happen out of spontaneity between us and the music and the excitement of creation.

When you get a generative atmosphere like that, of real enjoyment and fun, things just seem to happen. In *Fille* they did. You know where the girls promenade me in attitude with the ribbons? The girls were running 'round and Fred just said, "Keep running." The music kept playing and the girls kept running, and I had the ribbons and I stayed there. Fred was getting more and more excited, and then he said, "That's lovely. We'll put that in." But I mustn't mislead; it wasn't an accident. It came from the fact that Fred already had an idea and he had me in the center with the girls supporting me in some way. And then he's poetic enough with his creativity to allow things to grow out of the music with the colors of the artists he's using. We had so much fun doing it. It was marvelous.

And then, when the 'Fanny Elssler' pas de deux was finished and all put together — the ribbons, my solo, David's solo, and then the coda — we didn't know if we'd ever get through it. But jumping is a natural quality that I'm fortunate to have, amongst others. I'm always saying to dancers that you must be in love with the floor if you're going to jump. You mustn't jump off it; you must jump through it, use it with a demi-plié, and really feel it. I think that mental approach is probably why I found jumping a joy and no effort. And you also have to breathe with it. When I learnt acting amongst those pawpaw trees at six o'clock in the morning, I had to take deep breaths and count to ten or twenty very slowly, letting the air out. At that stage, I could talk in a huge hall without raising my voice, and you could hear me in the back. My training with Miss Sneddon was not 'How now, brown cow' elocution. It was diction and breath control. And I was a swimmer, too. 'Til I was about eight, I used to race for the school, swim underwater — we used to compete who could go furthest. So that gave me a lot of breath control just by chance, and as a dancer I was always grateful for that.

Within the ballet, Lise falls more and more in love. She's just fun in the beginning, and then she's that little mother when she's thinking about getting married and all those children, and then she falls in love. She's very fond of Alain. He's the village idiot down the road, he's got a lot of charm, and he's so funny with his silly hat. Everybody in the village loves him, but as a friend, as Alain. It's very pathetic when he comes with the ring; one feels sorry for him, but we all love him. But to marry him? Never! I mean, to marry Alain?! You can't . . . I couldn't marry Alain. You know, he's a bit bonkers. Ah yes, but the other boy is a very good-looking young man, and one has a feeling for him. He's one of the village lads and one of the most handsome. It's Mum who wants the money from Alain's father, Mum who's mercenary, Mum who wants the feathered hats. She's got a lovely daughter, and Alain's father's got bags of gold. So Mum decides she's going to marry her daughter to Alain when she gets to a marrying age.

When Mum goes off and locks her in, Lise has a tantrum. You know, children get in a paddy where they suddenly kick because they can't get their own way. That's why she bangs the chair. But she's not a person to stay cross for very long, and she realizes it's all silly. And then, she starts to daydream, talk to herself and play and imagine growing up and getting married.

Fred spoke to Karsavina about the mime; she taught him, and he taught me. Diaghilev didn't do *Fille*, so probably Karsavina saw it or learnt it when she was, herself, studying at the Maryinsky Theatre. The children growing up is a natural, Marcel Marceau mime. It felt absolutely natural, to explain it like that. I wasn't conscious of miming at all. But with all these roles, the big classical roles, you've really got to believe in that person you're portraying. To me, Lise is a person. If you're Odette, you aren't a ballet character. She is a woman, expressed as a swan, yes, but really a woman. The *Swan Lake* that Leslie Hurry designed, our first production, which I was in at Covent Garden, did have the real classical mime that came from the Maryinsky Theatre version. We learnt it from Sergeyev, who had been in Leningrad. And then, everybody thought we shouldn't have it in any longer because it was old-fashioned, but actually it's rather beautiful.

The mime roles are just as important to the ballet. It makes no sense to have a girl of fourteen as the Queen in *Sleeping Beauty* just because she's tall. She doesn't have the weight to make the whole balance of the performance. When I danced Aurora, also very young, there were always older artists as the Queen. I always remember Pamela May, who had been a ballerina in her own right, being the Queen. When she came on, she *came on*. She *was* the Queen, and therefore the whole performance had weight.

The full-length ballets are much more difficult. You have to grow into each one because you have to create a character to hold the interest right the way through. I danced all the big classics, and that's what's so satisfying about them: to be able to mature through a ballet as a character. For instance, after the mime in *Fille* . . . He's heard her — him, of all people! So she cries and hides her face; she's so embarrassed she doesn't want to look at him. And then, of course, they're together alone for the first time, really alone, and he kisses her for the first time. Now, earlier on when he tried to kiss her, she was off. And when she did kiss him quickly, in between the petits tours, it was just a quick peck. But he kisses her here very seriously, and that's the first time she knows anything about it; she's absolutely in a swoon.

And then, it's panic stations because of Mum. Lise is in a state anyway, having been kissed for the first time. So she says, 'Go to my bedroom,' thinking, 'When Mum's out of the way, I can get him out.' But it doesn't work out like that, as you well know. She doesn't want to go in there at all; of course she doesn't want to go. To change her dress? In front of him? Disgraceful! How can she change into another dress when he's in that room? She's forced in there. Mother *pushes* her up those stairs. Then she does change, and by that time she's gotten over her embarrassment because they're both in love and they're determined to get married whatever happens. Alain opens the door when he's kissing her. For the second time! For the third time! That's why everybody's so horrified.

Isn't that pas de deux music gorgeous? The whole ballet is beautiful there. It's very calm and quiet because she's grown up. She's in love now, really in love, as a grownup. She's been kissed more than once, not only on the haystack but upstairs as well, and she's going to marry him. That's why I said she grows up during the ballet. That music is grown-up. That love pas de deux is very serious; it's not like the first bit when they're playing together with the churn, which is mischievous and great fun.

It was really a happy ballet to make — Freddie would say the same. And it happened so quickly; in six weeks, the whole ballet was done. It really is something where I was onstage all the time, and if I wasn't onstage, I was running 'round to the other side or changing double-quick. Sometimes I wasn't in the mood, and I thought, 'My goodness, I've got *Fille* this afternoon.' But once it started, it just picked you up with it because of the music and the logical way Fred arranged everything and the little jokes in it. The whole cast always enjoyed it so much because, whatever you felt like, after a few minutes with *Fille*, you forgot everything.

David and I were always together in *Fille*, but I always loved dancing with different partners. It throws a completely new slant on the role you're doing. That doesn't mean that it changes *Giselle*, but if the partner is stronger, then Giselle changes slightly towards him and is probably a little more emphatic. Whereas if he's softer, Giselle is even more delicate in the balance, softer still, to complement him.

I would say the partners with whom I danced more naturally would be Alexis Rassine, Fadeyechev, and Erik Bruhn. Alexis is a romantic dancer, very gentle and very musical. And Fadeyechev is also romantic, but taller than Alexis. Physically we were all three very much alike. We moved in the same rhythm, all very soft, very easy in moving, it's not an effort. More like a cat — we've got soft, pliable muscles, not strong muscles. If you dance with a partner who moves in the same rhythm you do because of his physical make-up, you naturally go together with him more easily. Otherwise — and I'm just talking about physical types — it means more rehearsing. Though David and I danced marvelously together and loved dancing together, we had to rehearse more. If I put my head on his shoulder, we had to decide in rehearsal how it would get there. But if I did it with Fadeyechev, I never thought about it — neither of us did. Whatever he did, I'd react and he'd react. The same with Alexis.

Now, Erik was also very exciting. I didn't do *Fille* with him, but we did do *Swan Lake* and *Giselle*. And Erik was such an elegant, pristine prince, the prince out of fairy tales, that one was pure with him. With Alexis one would be softer, with Fadeyechev, melting, because he was such an outgoing artist, and with Erik, one was pure. He was so elegant that one was almost frightened in *Giselle* to give him your hand. You were amazed he took it. Even though you didn't know he was a prince, you couldn't get over his finesse. With Fadeyechev you felt comforted, but with Erik, you couldn't believe that he would come and even talk to you. So to me, that naturally changed certain ways of doing things.

I had already danced with Fadeyechev before I was invited to dance in Russia. He came to London in '58, the first time a Russian came out alone, after their first tour here with [Galina] Ulanova in 1956. For the BBC production of *Giselle*, Margaret Dale, the producer, said to me, "Who would you like to dance with?" Well, just having seen Ulanova and Fadeyechev, I said, "Oh, Fadeyechev!" and she said, "Why not?" So she asked, and they said yes. He came out with no escort at all. We looked after him the whole time he was here, not that I can speak a word of Russian or he a word of English — he had an interpreter. We had a week to rehearse, and he came a day late. Margaret Dale said to me, "Just do whatever he wants you to do in the second act, because we would love you to do the Russian version" — you know, with all the lifts that we didn't have. So we came straight from the airport, and when we'd changed, the music started and we started Act II. The interpreter was running around trying to interpret, but in the end there was no point. She just sat down and we danced. And I did the whole of the second act through with him, having never danced with him before. His second act. I just went the way his hands made me. We could have danced together all our lives, without talking.

Television's very difficult. You don't see the bits and pieces when you're doing it; you see them afterwards, and one's always disappointed. I always think, 'I should have done this' or 'Why didn't I do that?' And if I see them now, it's not me. It's like a life apart. It's like looking at somebody else.

In those days, television was new here. That program was rehearsed with Fadeyechev, but when it went out on the air, it went out live. We did two acts, straight through and no stop. And when we finished the performance, nothing! Silence. The whole studio was silent. It's a very emotional ballet to do in any case, and everybody was dripping and exhausted, and then to have nothing, no response at the end at all. You were left hanging, sort of void, because there was nothing to relax in. It took about ten days to get over that. But I always think of the audience, so after that doing television never made any difference to me because I always knew the cameraman was there. One danced for the cameraman; I always had an audience because he was there.

When I went to the theatre, it was always, 'Oh my goodness, why did I ever go into this profession?' Just to go through that stage door was a cold sweat; I would be all hot and cold. It gives me goose pimples just to think of it. And once I went in, I knew that I couldn't come out until it was all over. And I'd say, 'Oh dear, oh dear,' and then the night went on. But once I heard all the applause and was taking the calls, then I could relax. The applause to me was when one was able to relax. First I'd think, 'Thank goodness, that was all right.' And then, 'I must remember what I did for next time. If only I could quickly do it again, it could be better. Should've been better. It'll be better tomorrow night.' But by tomorrow night, or next week, or whenever the ballet came up again, I was back in my cold sweat.

We had a marvelous ballet master at one time called Mr. [Harijs] Plucis, and it always gave one confidence that dear Mr. Plucis was in front. He took rehearsals a great deal, and he fussed over us rather like a mother hen. If he came back after a performance — or Fred or Madam — and said, "That was better" or "That should be better," it would make a difference. One would obviously think about it a great deal, because you respected everything they had to tell you.

But applause never tells you anything about your performance. It's just a marvelous time to get the excitement out of yourself. You're all tensed up until that final curtain closes. And then it opens, and that well of applause that comes in like a wave is a sigh of relief. Remember, it's five hours in the theatre for *Sleeping Beauty*. You were in at half-past five, the performance starts at half-past seven and runs three hours. I was always exhausted.

Of course applause during the performance adds to the excitement, because you realize that you've been able to create a response.

And that helps inspire you to do something else. But really, you could always feel whether you were going to have a warm or cold house before you even went on the stage. You'd know. You'd listen to the Prologue in *Beauty* and realize those poor fairies were having a tough time out there because that house was freezing. And that made one nervy — not nervous, nervy — because you knew you had to come on and bring that audience up, get it really involved. If you were doing a three-act work, it was up to you. As the star, you carry a three-act work, because they're written for stars. It's different with a shorter work.

I always preferred doing a role that had a personality in it, because it's more human. But I enjoyed doing *Scènes de Ballet*, and that hasn't a character. It's very Parisian — with the hats and the gloves — it's got a nuance, but one just learnt the steps. I think it's the music again that carries one along. And of course when I did *Ballet Imperial* for Balanchine, I did it with the Berman setting, which I loved. In that setting, the ballet was the grandeur of the tsarist days abstracted. It was a Russian ballet. It was Mr. B., a Russian, with all his love for America and influence from America, but with his heritage coming through. Probably he was closer to his heritage then. I know he doesn't like that setting now, but to me the ballet had more weight the way it was done originally. When I did it again, many years later, it was in wishy-washy blues and pinks. Well, there are so many other ballets he's done since that suit that really abstract coloring. The *Ballet Imperial* that we did first was much more Mr. B. of those years, of that period in his life, when I felt he was closer to his heritage or to his youth. But still, there was always the music.

A musical dancer breathes with the music, and that's what I think a lot of people are forgetting today. They're so busy turning out and putting their arms in the right position that they forget to breathe. If you lift an arm, it goes with the music. If you stretch your foot, it's got to feel the floor and you've got to breathe with it, and close it back and breathe out. As you do grand battement, you breathe in as it goes up and you breathe out as it comes down. I used to love barre and working in the classroom, because it was dancing. It wasn't just exercise. Right, you've got to turn out and you've got to keep your knees straight and you've got to point your toes. And your shoulders should be down, but you're not consciously pulling them down and getting stuck. They're down, but you grow out of them. This is the trouble with dancing today. It doesn't dance. Everybody is so busy trying to turn out over ninety degrees and get their legs higher than their ears. Fine, it looks marvelous if the leg whips up above the ears, but it doesn't mean anything. It would be much better if it went six inches lower but went up with movement, with rhythm, with breathing.

You don't think when you're dancing; you just do what comes naturally to you. But dancing really means joy. It's the only way that you can express yourself. I loved dancing. To me, it was a way of expressing so much. And it was endless. Obviously, there are roles I would like to have done and didn't do; they would have come if I'd kept dancing, but you can't have everything in life. I felt very lucky and very grateful to have the gift, to be able to express the gift that I had, and to do it to the best of one's advantage. If it brings pleasure, that's even better, but I can't say I was doing it for an audience or for anybody. If you have a gift like that, you have to express it.

October 1979
London

Tanaquil LeClercq

Tanaquil LeClercq (b. Paris, 1929) grew up in New York and entered the School of American Ballet in 1940. In 1946, at the debut performance of George Balanchine's company called Ballet Society, she created both the Choleric variation in his enduring masterpiece, The Four Temperaments, *and a small role in his short-lived novelty* L'Enfant et les Sortilèges. *She appeared regularly in Ballet Society's infrequent performances during the next two years. When that company moved to New York's City Center in 1948 and became the New York City Ballet, LeClercq became one of the new company's first principals. She danced a unique assortment of ballets by Balanchine, whom she married in 1952, Jerome Robbins, Frederick Ashton, and Antony Tudor. Many of these works have disappeared from the City Ballet repertory, but the company still performs* Afternoon of a Faun, The Concert, Divertimento No. 15, The Four Temperaments, Ivesiana, The Nutcracker, Orpheus, La Valse, *and* Western Symphony — *in all of which she created the lead or a featured role. LeClercq's performing career was abruptly terminated by polio in 1956. She teaches today at the Dance Theatre of Harlem school.*

When I was quite small, Tanaquil LeClercq engraved her pared-down, pristine, nearly casual elegance so deeply on my mind that I can still see it now. And if you look at the New York City Ballet, so can you. Since her dancing gave as enduring a definition to the company's style as it did to my own personal standards, its shape persists today, like a signature scrawled obliquely across time. She was the first dancer I ever saw who captured movement in her body, enlarged it, focused it, and sent it flashing through the dark, without comment but with an extra edge that was hers alone. At full speed she seemed transparent, pure energy encased in glass; slowing to adagio, she became opalescent. When I first spoke to her about this interview, we were sitting at the back of the City Center, awaiting the first performance of Balanchine's The Four Temperaments *by the Dance Theatre of Harlem.*

I was very young to be in the original cast of *Four Ts*; I was right out of the School. I didn't know how early it was 'til I looked up the program. If it was really 1946 — I thought it was '48 or '49 — I would have been sixteen or seventeen.

I started with [Mikhail] Mordkin because my mother wanted me to start when I was seven and nobody else would take me. She took me to Fokine, who said, "Absolutely not. I don't take them 'til they're eight." Then we went to the School of American Ballet, at Madison Avenue and 59th, and they said, "No, we don't take anybody 'til they're nine." So then we went to Mordkin at Carnegie Hall — my mother had seen Pavlova dance and said that was terrific — and he said, "Fine. I'll take her." I don't think children really want to study, but I liked to dance. I had been to the ballet and I thought it was very nice, I liked it. I was also taking piano lessons, which I was a dud at. I mean, you could tell right away: the kid can't play the piano, so it better be dancing.

I studied with Mordkin 'til I was about ten. Sure I liked it; I didn't know anything better or worse. It was very peppy. It was one of those classes that everybody but the kitchen sink is in. At that time he had his own company — I saw Lucia Chase as Giselle, if you can believe it, with the Mordkin Ballet Company. So she was there in class, and I was there, and Nina Stroganova and Patricia Bowman, sort of the beginnings of Ballet Theatre — we were all mixed in together. It wasn't the way it is today at the School: children, and then children a little better. He just taught a lot of classes, I guess, and they were all mixed.

I don't know why I left. I think my mother thought it was enough, that I had gotten just as far as I could. Then I spent about two years with other people, good teachers but not known at all, and then . . . The reason I went to SAB was that we used to go to Cape Cod every summer, and there was one of those music schools with ballet and stuff, and one summer Muriel Stuart turned up there to teach the summer course with Eddie Caton. And she said, "You should go to the School of American Ballet." So I auditioned. They used to have scholarship auditions that were lots of fun; they put a number on you like a horse, and then you came in and everybody looked at you.

I went in 1940, when I was still at the Lycée Français. The teachers at SAB then were Stuart and Vladimiroff, and Oboukhoff came later — I was there before Mr. Oboukhoff was. Then they had guest teachers: Dorothie Littlefield taught, Danilova taught for a month or a week or something, and then Balanchine would come and maybe he'd teach for two weeks in a year. Upset everybody and then leave — you know, that kind of thing. And then Doubrovska came; she was one of my favorite teachers and one I admired a great deal. She taught toe. Stuart gave a toe class too, and the men gave adagio and variations. I was going regularly then. Often. Then every day. Class was in the afternoons after school so I would get excused from school to go, but then the schoolwork suffered and I had to repeat the same damn class for two years. But I didn't care, not at all. School was like the piano, absolutely not for me. I went to a thing called the New York Tutoring School for a few years, a real cop-out, but I never passed anything. I don't have a high school diploma. My mother didn't care, but my father was a professor — he was translating books and had lots of degrees — so he was upset for a while. But then he had the idea that it didn't matter: "I don't care what my daughter does as long as she does it well." So when he saw, and everyone convinced him, poor thing, that I was talented as a dancer, he said, "Fine." He did try tutoring me in mathematics, but I had a lot of trouble with numbers. I couldn't learn my multiplication tables — I still don't know them — and I think that made him stop.

It was right around then that George did *Four Ts* and *L'Enfant et les Sortilèges* on the same program at the Needle Trades High School. He had professional people for all the Temperaments and Themes, except for me. It wasn't that I was so good; it just came at a time when there was nobody else. Call it good timing. If you needed a body, I was the only one. And I didn't stay in the corps because the people he had in there were worse than I was. It just happened. Ballet wasn't that popular; there weren't that many people training, and they weren't groomed the way they are now. Today, every girl in the corps de ballet has fantastic legs and feet, and in my day they did not. Now it's like a master race, but they weren't screened then, and they didn't drop you unless you were eight feet tall — everybody was there. And then, I *was* more talented than the others, and I was a little interesting, I wasn't dull. So he put me in those two things. The corps in *Four Ts*, like the girls that come in and kick, were just tall girls from the School filling in, but otherwise it was people like Mary Ellen Moylan, Lew Christensen, Gisella Caccialanza, and Elise Reiman, who teaches now at the School. They were all professionals, and they were called Ballet Society.

They couldn't have been nicer to me, telling me how to make up and how to put the toeshoe ribbons in and things like that. Everybody was very sweet. But you know that part where I'm in the middle and the other four women are in a square around me? One of the women, who should remain nameless, who was a lead, didn't turn up for a rehearsal. I heard through the grapevine that she had objected;

she didn't want to dance with a student in the middle, or *she* wanted to be there. And then the very next rehearsal, she turned up and everything was fine. George had obviously talked to her. It was the first time and the only time I ever had trouble with anything like that, but you've got to learn sometime how people are disagreeable or envious.

He worked on *Four Ts* just about the same length of time as anything. He's the fastest choreographer I know; and also, once he sets something, he hardly ever, ever changes it. Whereas a Jerry Robbins changes every two minutes — you have so many versions you don't know what to do. But George doesn't, which is so marvelous. The only thing I ever saw him change was a little bit of *Orpheus*, where Maria [Tallchief] enters. I think she just came in and the other people danced, and then he changed it so that she started dancing when she came in.

The music for *Four Ts*? Very nice. Melodic. Easy to dance to. That's not a hard score. Certainly as opposed to Ives or something, it's child's play. Nothing was a problem one way or the other. You just count the rhythm; it's very easy. What's a little harder about my section is that in the beginning it's just piano — a cadenza or something — anyway, it's a lot of rumbles, and you don't want to get caught dancing when the piano has stopped. There's no conductor at that point; it's just you and the piano trying to stick together. And as it's not something with an even beat, if the piano finishes soon, you've got egg on your face if you're still going. I have never danced since then to anything like that, because everything else is right there with me, with a count. In *Ivesiana*, you don't listen for the clarinet, hoping it'll come in. You don't do it through melody. You do it through the beat, the structure of the music. So if the clarinetist doesn't come in, you don't miss what you were meant to do over the clarinet; you're still exactly where you're meant to be. But this was just rumbles to me. The idea was just to finish the turns and be ready, so that on the chord you can go down in the crouch and not still be turning, like an idiot, as he's finishing.

The steps aren't hard. It's free-style. In one rehearsal for it at Dance Theatre of Harlem, I said, "I didn't really get down on both knees there," and the dancer said, "I feel more secure. I don't like stopping in fourth." I'm not going to tell her, "Don't do it." Who am I to tell her not to do it? It doesn't really matter whether she gets down on her knees or stops in fourth. It doesn't matter. And in that production too, they're throwing the girl up and catching her in those three jetés, and at City Ballet they're throwing her forward. Definitely, in my day, they threw — you do soutenu and they throw you — and here he threw *and* caught. I don't know how that happens. Vicky Simon set it — she looked at some old movies — and she said it had changed. She didn't mention that part, but she said other things they're now doing at City Ballet are different. That's what happens. I see lots of things that have changed, and it's hard to say they shouldn't have because you don't know if Balanchine has changed them. I saw Suzanne [Farrell] hit a fifth in *Symphony in C*, and it's supposed to be coude-pied back. Now, should I say to George, "I saw it, and she's not doing it the way I did it"? How do I know he hasn't thought, 'Oh, I hated the way Tanny did that step, always hated it, all those years. And now I've gotten rid of her and gotten somebody else who will change the step the way I've always wanted it'? I *don't* know. So it's hard to come in and say, "But it wasn't like that," when maybe it's been improved. I don't poke my nose into it. It's a very small thing there, anyway.

But there are people who are worried, I can tell you that. When Arthur [Mitchell] went to *Four Ts*, or another ballet that he did, he said, "They've changed such and such. It's not the way I remember it." Or somebody would see [*Concerto*] *Barocco* and say, "They're not doing that step. We used to do such and such a step." But then in my day when we did *Barocco*, other people who had done it, like Marie-Jeanne, would say, "You're not doing the step we used to do." So you see, each generation is telling the other generation the same thing.

I danced with Arthur in one ballet, *Western Symphony*. When Jacques [d'Amboise] had other things to do, George put him in it and did a step for him in the little variation that is totally different from Jacques' step. So there was a Jacques version of that one step, all alone, and then there was another version that Arthur looked better in. If you revived it, I don't know if you'd take Jacques' version or Arthur's. I always danced my own version, and Diana [Adams] knew it too, so she taught it to the next girl who did it. Diana would definitely teach it step for step, because she was really strict and stern. And then it was Big Glo [Gloria] Govrin, or someone, and it went like that from teacher to teacher.

But I don't think the ballets change very much. *Symphony in C* is just the way it was. I love it; I just adore *Symphony in C*. I haven't seen *Faun*, and I didn't see this revival of *Orpheus*, but I saw the one they did in the Stravinsky Festival and I kind of wondered about it. *Orpheus* was always absolutely lovely. I watched rehearsals of that originally — when I wasn't in them — and I watched that silk curtain come down and Maria do her thing millions and millions of times when I was waiting to go on, and I remember it as being something very beautiful and rather magical. Now at the State Theater, somehow that's different. I couldn't put my finger on it, but I was very disappointed. And they did a revival of *Bourrée Fantasque* a long time ago, and I was also very disappointed in that. I don't know if a ballet wears out, or if he repeats it but in a better way so the original looks passé. On the other hand, you see *Prodigal* or *Apollo* and they're not passé at all. I don't see why *Orpheus* or *Bourrée Fantasque* should look passé, but they did. They just didn't look peppy, especially *Orpheus*.

I don't know anything about the titles of the different movements in *Four Temperaments* — you'd have to ask George. We were just given music and our steps and a terrible costume. Everybody had just awful costumes. They were miseries. I really objected to two things in mine. I had a large nylon wig that came down to about my rear end. It had a large pompadour, and it had a white horn in the middle like a unicorn's, which made it very difficult to do all the things he had made. That was number one. Very irritating. You come to dress rehearsal, and if you swing your arm close to your head, suddenly there's a horn. The other thing was that [Kurt] Seligmann had made wings, red wings, down the whole length of the arm, fingers enclosed, and there was no place to get out. If you got in your costume and then got something in your eye or wanted to unzip yourself to get out, well, you couldn't. Once you tied your toeshoe ribbons, that was it. It gave you a feeling of claustrophobia I can't describe. All enclosed. Not even gloves with fingers — no fingers at all. It was hideous. So I remember crying, and then George came and slit a little piece on the inside palm so I had my index finger out, and that was fine. But also, it made it very hard to give your hand. When you're doing arabesque promenade, they grab for something and they don't know what they've got — it's just a big clomp of material.

And then Seligmann did two sort of papier mâché breastplates. They were light all right, but they were large, and when you'd cross your arms, they'd go clunk. It was just most unfortunate. And I certainly was not the only one; other people were having problems too, swathed in this and swathed in that. At dress rehearsal, I got clipped, and somebody else's wig got fixed, and I think Mary Ellen got unwrapped. Imagine taking a dancer and wrapping her neck up, and then putting half ping-pong balls down her arms. You distort everything, there's no arm there, and it looked so beautiful in rehearsal. But we certainly did it like that at Ballet Society, and then even when we went into our black stuff, the leotards, at City Center, they tried the backdrop for one performance. It looked like bandages coming unraveled, sort of a swirl in blacks and whites and gray. It was nice

— nice? It was all right. You didn't die or anything — but at least we got rid of the costumes. It was much easier with an arm free, and I remember I had that feeling that Mr. Balanchine had saved me.

You don't get pushed around so much in that section, even when the four boys promenade you. You give your arm to one, you do arabesque, then you do soutenu on your own, then you give your arm to another one, and if he's good, he stays out of your way. You do your arabesque minding your own business, unless he's a lump and knocks you off. And then there are the two boys under your arms for that lift in the finale, and it's only done twice. So you feel secure — no problems. When you're young, you don't think as much as you do later on, when you've danced more and you realize all the awful things that could happen. You just go in and do it.

I'm not sure about the different finales. I don't think the soloists were involved in that; it was the other people who had different things. I think the couples always did the glissade, jeté across, and we always did that massed group, kick, lean. At one point he had it like a circle, and they used to go up and down in waves. He said it was "my Radio City Music Hall number," sort of Florence Rogge style. I remember it distinctly, but it doesn't seem to me that I was in that circle. I wouldn't swear, but I have a feeling it was all the corps people. But my part always remained exactly the same as he originally staged it. Needle Trades was a very skinny stage that had no depth so you went from side to side a lot, and my part does go from side to side. I never worked out anything with him together. He came in and showed me what he wanted me to do, and that was it. He never changed a step. Mine was absolutely set.

As we continued to do it and we got out of those costumes, I wouldn't say I danced it differently, but I danced it better because I was better technically. I could take more chances, throw myself around. I knew the music like the palm of my hand. It was very comfy, and it was a nice fast thing — I wasn't on the stage for hours. You zipped in and zipped out and made an impression. In other words, I liked dancing it very much. I don't say that I had a different interpretation when I didn't have a costume — it was the same thing. I had the choreography and how it should look. It should look maximum, 100 percent everything: move 100 percent, turn 100 percent, stop dead. Kick legs as much as you can, straight knee, pointed toe. Zip 'round. Fast. Nothing slow, no adaaahgio. It would be the same style to me as *Orpheus*, the Bacchantes, same idea. Kick, wham, fast, hard, big. You have certain steps that you have to do in a certain amount of time, and the certain steps give it a certain flavor. But you can't interpret because you'll be late, you won't be with the music.

I had no sense that any part of what I was doing was any more important than any other part, or that any step was pulling anything together. And if people write about it that way, I think they're wrong. I think they're just writing because they have to write. If you said to George Balanchine, "Those three ronds de jambe pull the ballet together," he would faint. He would absolutely faint. I know from having sat with him and read reviews. He said, "What is this man talking about?" Third movement Bizet [*Symphony in C*], all they're doing is plié and up, plié and up, and someone wrote something about 'The Danes did it a certain way.' George said, "What the hell is he talking about? All they're doing is demi-plié, up, demi-plié, up." People read into something. Everybody takes away a different impression. Fine. But they're all private citizens, and it doesn't make it so. It's very nice in *Serenade* — she falls down. And somebody thinks it's death and somebody thinks it's life and somebody thinks it's so-and-so. Fine. But to write and say, "This pulls it together" — that I think is idiotic. It's certainly not true from the dancer's point of view, unless you're a very pretentious dancer and say, "I'm doing three ronds de jambe and I'm pulling the whole ballet together." It's nothing like that. It's very primitive, banal. You go on and you do the best you know how, and you don't worry about other things, other this, other that, anything. And if Balanchine has a master plan, he doesn't tell you that he has it.

He said somewhere that he doesn't know how he does his ballets. It must be a gift. What I can see is that, since he obviously chooses the music, he's influenced by that kind of music, and the movement will look a certain way. He gets the score, and very often he makes a piano reduction himself that the pianist can play from. Maybe he doesn't do that anymore, but he has done it. And I think that while he's doing that, reducing it, he's probably thinking, 'Now, I'll have Maria and so-and-so,' let's say in *Bourrée*. 'She'll be slow at this time, maybe an adagio. And we'll have Tanny being funny — we'll get a short man, Jerry or whoever.' And then he comes in and does it. I don't think he can explain it himself because he doesn't know.

But he didn't say, nobody said to me, when we were doing *Four Ts*, "This is Choleric." They called me "LeCholeric," and said, "Ha, ha. Isn't that funny?" He said, "Oh, look at that. Your name's LeClercq and you're being Choleric. LeCholeric." That's all. That was it.

Now, I've seen Karin von Aroldingen dance it and Colleen Neary and this black girl at Dance Theatre of Harlem, and I can't say that anybody gave me any idea of how I would have done it differently. Somebody could do something differently and you could say, "She's different in it, but it's a really good performance. It's nice." Somebody else would do it, and you'd think, 'It's different, but it's really not so hot.' I didn't think these other performances were particularly anything. I saw Maria do *La Valse* once, and it was different from me. I wouldn't have changed, but I couldn't change anyway. When you're very tall and skinny and angular, how can you change physically to make yourself look small and soft? There are things you just cannot change, things like being pretty and being ugly, and it is a physical thing finally. So she was different. I wouldn't have changed, but what she did had value. It was different, but it was O.K.

Remember, when we were dancing, somehow we were dancing all the time. The company was very small at City Center, so you had at least two or three ballets a night. It was Maria, myself, Melissa [Hayden], Diana, and Patty Wilde — that was about it — and [Yvonne] Mounsey and Jillana; say, seven or eight people. If you gave a ballet like *Four Temperaments* that takes four or five good girls, and then you give *Symphony in C* at the end, which we would, which again takes four or five good girls, then you were already dancing twice. So there wasn't much time to sit out in the audience. In rehearsal you'd sit out and watch other people, but usually you were in that ballet. And there wasn't that much switching. That came later, as the company got larger, but it took a while. When you had a role done on you, you did it for at least two years before finally you hurt your ankle, and then Melissa would learn it or Pat Wilde. By the time I was almost stopping, by about '54, quite a few people were doing *Firebird*, but before that time Maria had not been replaced. I was in *Four Ts* the whole time — I can't remember anybody else doing it. I was in *Orpheus* the whole time, and *La Valse* too, except when I had appendicitis and then Maria did it.

There's a slight eeriness in *La Valse*, a little more mood than coming crashing in like in *Four Ts*. I used to watch the waltz before me. It was terribly pretty to me, the way the stage and the costumes looked — *Faun* the same way, with the fan blowing and everything. I used to wait for *Faun*. And I don't mean to sound stuck-up or pretentious, but I would say I prepared myself a little bit more for those things. *La Valse* was like a wonderful evening — terrific, beautiful, elegant. Of course I learned it the same way as *Four Ts*: "Here is the step; now, do it this way. No, not enough. It should be like *plastique*, German sort of." Well, I'd never seen "*plastique* German," so I imagined what it must be like. He probably chooses you for your quality anyway, so he wouldn't have to inject a quality into you. He wouldn't take somebody who's one way and force them to be another way, so already you've got 75 percent going. It's a certain type person dressed a certain way doing certain steps. He's not dumb — he's very clever. So for, like, *Bugaku*, you take an Allegra Kent, like a rubber orchid, who can tie herself into knots. She doesn't have to think — she could be mindless. Maybe she is thinking, but already 75 percent is there. The thinking doesn't get you through anything.

The only 'thinking' ballet I did was when Tudor came in and did *Lilac Garden*. He is very intellectual, and you think, think, think. But then finally for me — I was the Other Woman, and maybe I wasn't very good — it was really the nitty-gritty of getting there on time, because he does follow the melody but he's not musical. You have to run, run, run, and when the orchestra hits the high note, you have to be up, mid-air somewhere. But that was all the thinking. You could say, 'You come in and you do this,' like, swish your fan, 'and you look over your shoulder, and you think, "Is he there?"' I had him to dinner once, and he was trying to tell me that I had *thought* all of this while I was doing it, and I just said, "Well, I didn't. Sorry." It just didn't work that way. It doesn't work that way, and I don't see how people can say it does. It sounds better to say it: "Oh yes, I thought of this and I did research and I was thinking," like those actresses who, when they're going to play whores, live with whores for ten months. I don't think you have to. You could perfectly well play a whore, or a saint or a virgin, and not be a virgin and not be a whore. I suppose it's Method acting compared to something else, and I guess I don't believe in Method that much. I've read interviews with English actors — Olivier, Gielgud — and the way they spoke of how they did their roles was exactly the way I would do them as a dancer. They were saying that it's more a technique — you forget your technique, of course; you don't want to be just technical — but not that they went with bums because they were going to have to be an alcoholic.

Somebody may say, 'I dedicate every performance to somebody different,' or that they thought about it or read something. Fine, if they want to. When Jerry Robbins did *Age of Anxiety*, I read *Age of Anxiety*, the Auden poem, and I can't say that it helped me for one damn moment. One was poetry, and one was Bernstein and Robbins and sweat. And *Illuminations* to me was not terribly Rimbaud. You get all dressed up in English, Cecil Beaton costumes, and you have a token black — because Rimbaud went to Africa or something — for Being Beauteous. But Being Beauteous is just one girl and four men struggling, hoping that the tricks will go. *La Valse* was the only thing I did that had any slight story, and *Baiser de la Fée* a little bit . . . in fact, a little bit like *Giselle* maybe. The rest were dancing.

When Patty McBride started to do *La Valse*, she and Nicky [Magallanes] came up here, because she didn't know it and Nicky couldn't remember what he had done. All I did was help recall steps, and whatever George had said to me, I passed on, like that first — I don't know what you'd call it — a contraction. He never was happy with the way I did it. That's when he said, "German *plastique*." I said the same thing to her: "When you come on and you do this contraction thing, it's like somebody laughing." That was all. It was mainly getting the steps right, which way, which hand. Nothing about the character, the girl. Patty will have some other thing that she will hang onto. She will remember how it was when she was in Teaneck or something. I'm not going to tell her anything like that. She did it very well, as a matter of fact. I saw her, and I thought it was terribly nice.

La Valse is an easy ballet to dance. The steps are easy. Easy in *Faun* — that's a cinch — in *Four Ts*, in *Orpheus*. *Barocco* is hard to do well. I'm talking about being able to go up in the dressing room and say, "That was a nice *Barocco*." There's always something that didn't go right. Probably the hardest thing I had to do was *Symphony in C*, because that was not done for me, it was done for Toumanova, who could balance on one leg forever — and I was not a balancer. Plus you wanted to look soft, it must look clean and yet also have some feeling, you must be turned out, hands must be nice. It's very hard. Maybe once I did it nicely, to my satisfaction. My heart would always sink before the balance, but then of course, the balance doesn't mean that much either. Except I've seen people *not* balance, and it does. I don't know. It's all very confusing. Well, you stand on the left leg and do développé with the right leg, and he's got hold of your hand. And you're meant to stay, and he's meant to switch sides. When Toumanova did it — she balances so you have to knock her down off pointe — she apparently did let go and just stand there while he slowly went around and took the other hand. I had been told about how fantastic she was, so at least I tried . . . not to balance so long, but not to clutch his hand when he came around. It used to scare me, but I got it down, and Frank [Moncion] also helped a lot, so that even if I didn't have a very good night, I never came off pointe. Once in Chicago I did a nice *Symphony in C*, and George wasn't there. But he might not have liked it, you can't tell. But I liked it; nice bourrées, moving like the wind, and Frank partnered well, and the whole thing just clicked very nicely.

Partners make a great difference, definitely. They make you look better and they help you. Other partners get in the way; you're on balance and they knock you off. I danced with Jacques when he was just starting — when I was finishing, he was starting — and he was excellent, and Nicky was a very good partner, and Frank; those are the three I mostly remember dancing with. Also, it's nice to have a partner who wants to rehearse with you. I did one or two things with Eglevsky, who was a marvelous dancer but didn't really like to rehearse. He liked to do his own variation, you know, come out and do his jumps, and he would save himself for that, which wasn't so comfy to dance with. I couldn't say, "Hey, can we go down before the curtain? Would you try so-and-so?" He'd say, "Oh, it'll be fine." This young thing wanting to rehearse just bothered him; it was annoying. But Jacques was young and enthusiastic, and he loved girls. That's also nice, people that like women, that don't just like boys. So he would take the time, like for *Nutcracker*: "What do you think? Could we squeeze out one more pirouette here? Yeah, let's try for four." *Nutcracker* was hard, but I always had fun doing it. I remember throwing up in the afternoon the first time I did the leading role. That's the only time I ever threw up — I was really nervous. But once I got it down — and it was short, and half of it was Jacques — I just loved doing it.

I didn't have stagefright when I was young. Maria said the same thing: she said the older she got, the more frightened she got, because the more responsibility was on her shoulders. I felt that way too. When you're a nobody, you dance. And then you get discovered, and they start, for instance, applauding when you come out onstage, before you've done anything. That's always death. I know it's nice, but you think, 'Oh my God, just wait 'til I do it. Don't clap now.' It's unnerving. I'd rather come in somehow in silence and do it and then have them applaud afterward, but they like to greet you. And you always get nervous on opening nights. After you've done it once it's O.K., but I can't think of an opening night when I wasn't nervous. No, for *Bourrée Fantasque* I wasn't, because it was funny. I figured that no matter what I did, it didn't matter. Now, in *Concert* . . . well, at that point Jerry had one variation that was serious. I had a very pretty mazurka — it's gone now — and that one I wanted to do nicely, so I was nervous about that. I remember being nervous about even Dewdrop in *Nutcracker*, and the first night it didn't go well — I mean, I didn't dance so well. You have to be an idiot not to be nervous.

But you can't be too nervous because it robs you of everything, it robs the muscles; you stand and you feel weak. I didn't get horribly nervous. Diana was a nervous dancer. If Maria was nervous, which she said later she was, she certainly never showed it. The first *Firebird* was like she'd been doing it all her life. She was incredible, burned up that stage, and before she did it — George and she were married at that time — she had baked an apple pie. Now, to me that shows that you don't have any nerves. I would never bake an apple pie before I danced. I would be lying on my bed, and then getting up and eating steak, and then taking a little powdered dextrose for quick energy. We all used to take it in those days, though nobody I knew was really involved in fad diets then. The fads were for those people that crack your bones — osteopaths — or for a certain masseuse. I never had a massage so I don't know, but other people said they were great. But no fads about food — just this powdered sugary stuff that everybody took. Maria would always have half a lemon in a Kleenex on both sides of the City Center stage because her mouth got dry. When she'd go off, you'd always hear her slurp. And Melissa had smelling salts because she always said she was going to faint. But none for me. I crossed myself and I knocked wood before I got on the stage, and I figured that would cover everything.

Later on I didn't care as much, but in the beginning, when I was starting, I'd get the newspaper the next morning to read the critics; it was really nice to be mentioned and to see that you were good. Of course, they like you when you're young — they think they've discovered you. Everything's fine when you're young, but then you get a little older, and they start to pick, pick, pick, pick. Or they pigeonhole you: I was "young and coltish." They kept saying "coltish" — sort of a cliché, which is annoying. If I'd kept on dancing, probably at forty I'd still be coltish. But it's really only Balanchine that can influence you; he's the only one I would trust absolutely 100 percent. If you think you've done something very well, and he says, "Dear, it was very nice but you didn't move. It's English-style. It's small. It looks very pretty, but you're meant to travel, cover space," you would remember that. As for other dancers saying anything . . . Well, Maria came up at dress rehearsal of *La Valse* and said, "Do more," and I did more, definitely, with the bunch of flowers and dressing and putting on the gloves. I thought, 'She's right. I'm probably doing it constipated,' so I took her word to heart. Other people didn't say; they were too busy with themselves. Melissa would never say anything — I don't think she cared. Nicky was nice; he would say things a little bit. But Balanchine really is the one, and the critics finally don't matter.

Oh, the gloves are very simple. Again, what they write sounds terrific on paper, but it's a very simple thing. We had the glove and I couldn't put my hand in it, so we wired the top. That way, when he hands it to you, it's open, so you know where it is and you can really go in. That's all it was. As you pull it on, you pinch the wire — just a little, little wire — so that it fits. It looks like you're drawing it on, but in fact you're just getting it straight, and then you go pinch and nobody sees. So finally it's not as terrific as it sounds.

You can teach somebody steps, you can teach them how to hold their head, but what you cannot teach is whatever it is that makes a person step onstage and look interesting. That's absolutely innate; it's Mummy and Daddy banging, and genes, or it's God or whatever, and it is unteachable. You have to have the technique because the technique frees you to get on to dancing. But people get all caught up in the technique, and they think that's it. It's not at all. If you're going to be thinking with every glissade, 'Are my knees straight? Am I turned out? Are my toes pointed?' you're going to look like Coppélia, stiff as a stick. But once you know you have that under your belt, then you can listen to the music, throw your hands in gloves, bend back and know that you won't fall, and know it looks O.K. You can't express yourself if you have nothing to express yourself with, and you're expressing yourself in any role. Yourself — the way you look, the way you think, the way your mother thought, where you went to school probably — whatever is you. You put your own stamp on it.

It's definitely a physical thing also. No two people are built the same way: long legs, short legs, big calf, little calf — so many different variations. And of course you never have your technique down. That's simplifying a lot. You have it down somewhat, but that's the challenge — I hate that word — that's what you aspire to. More technique, better technique, so you can forget it the whole time. And it's a very funny thing, because by the time you've gotten your technique, you're going downhill already. Arabesque isn't as high, knees are bending. At thirty-something, you don't look the way you did when you were twenty-four. Some people last longer, some less long, naturally, but it's one of those awful things that by the time you can say 'I've arrived,' you're starting to diminish. You never really catch up with yourself. You never do, and that's also what's so nice about it. If you did, if it were that easy, you wouldn't bother. It's a goal that you never reach, to do it beautifully, to be as perfect as . . . to dance like your image of you dancing. You have an idea of how you should look and how it should be done — and you never can do it, ever. I suppose if you did it, you'd be a mess, and if you think you've done it, you're wrong. But, oh boy, you can get close, and it's lovely, it's heaven. It's like climbing a mountain; they do it 'cause it's there. Why do you dance? Because it's there and you cannot do it. That's why you keep trying and trying.

Once in a while, especially as a younger dancer, I would occasionally think, 'There's another life. Wouldn't it be nice if . . .' I'd be on a train, and I'd think, 'What would happen if I got off here and got a job in the five-and-ten?' — this was before I was married — 'And I'd meet some man . . .' But I didn't. And certainly when I got married, it absolutely never occurred to me. When I was young and didn't have too many boyfriends because I was busy, I thought

I was definitely missing another life. But you go to a few parties *with* boyfriends, and you see the other life, and you think, 'I don't think I'm missing so much anyway.' Nothing's perfect, and the life I had was a hell of a lot better than the rest. For instance, when I was sixteen and I'd already done *Four Ts* and the Ravel [*L'Enfant*], I certainly knew a lot more, was exposed to more, than another sixteen-year-old who was going to school and the prom. So I didn't know about the latest records or Frank Sinatra . . . yes, I did. I knew about Frank Sinatra, and I did go to movies. Maybe I couldn't dance the latest dance. But you can learn a lot; it's a very good education. You're exposed to one thousand fabulous composers, so you really know music. First thing you know, you go to Europe; you're getting a salary plus you're going to Italy and France, meeting famous people and being in famous theatres, and everybody else is sitting home going to high school. It's a wonderful profession, especially now when you dance a lot. We didn't dance that much; at Ballet Society, you'd get all excited for two or three performances, and then there'd be months and months of not doing anything.

I liked doing two ballets a night. I would be scared doing just one, because one was like a warm-up. With two, if you disgrace yourself in something, you have a second chance. Plus your muscles are warmed up. To know that I would have to come in and do second movement of Bizet and only that, as the last ballet, would make me horribly nervous. One shot. But if you had a first ballet, like a *Barocco*, then a rest, and then you went into *Faun*, which was usually in the middle, you'd be really ready, loose and enjoying yourself. If you came in just to do *Faun*, it would be hard — it's over before you can say boo.

There were always a few dancers that were dying to do a certain role. Maria got all the technical roles, say, and I got the geeky ones, and other dancers would be saying, "Oohh, I want to do *Firebird*. If I could just do *Firebird*." I had no desire to do *Firebird*. I never wanted to do it. It was done for Maria, it was one thousand turns, and I wasn't a turner. I was never dying to do anything. I had enough to do of my own. I got shoved into *Swan Lake*, and I didn't want to do it and I didn't feel I was ready for it. But George had nobody else at that time; Melissa would have been the logical one, but he didn't want to use her. O.K. So he shoved me into it, and I felt totally incompetent. I danced it off and on, not often, not often enough to ever feel comfy in it. I always felt, 'I shouldn't be here.' *Scotch Symphony* I think I could have done, but other people were doing it fine. But I'm also not an ambitious person. I don't work like a dog. When I was dancing, I did not work like a dog, I could have worked harder. But everything came easy to me. By that I mean it came easy, but it was hard work. People don't realize that; they just think, 'Oh, it came easy to her.'

But remember, I never was in the corps. If I had been, I would have thought, 'I just wish I could do *Four Temperaments*,' or whatever somebody else was doing. But I never had that feeling because there I was, doing it. All I thought was, 'I hope to God I'm doing it all right.' It was a feeling of trying to catch up with what people had given me, rather than sitting back, knowing I could do it, and being denied it. I was never denied a role that I thought I could do.

When I was very young, people said — they always say — "Oh, Balanchine is ruining you. It's cold and it's calculated and it's all technique. Oh, it's terrible. You should be doing *Giselle*." So when I was maybe seventeen, eighteen, nineteen, I thought, 'It would be nice to leave Balanchine and do a *Giselle*.' But then it passed and never occurred to me again. They always say, "He doesn't want any personality from his dancers." Of course, he's the last one in the world ... He always wants personality. Also, when I was studying at the School, they said, "You should study with Margaret Craske. She's English. It's Cecchetti. You should be Cecchetti. This is terrible, legs flying, oh, so vulgar." Well, you have to make up your mind. You can't listen to everybody. You can't do everything, this and that and the other. You have to go one way or the other.

They don't come and stay if they're stars. Do you think what's-his-name is going to stay — Baryshnikov? I wouldn't think he'd stay. Erik Bruhn came to stay with us, when we were still at City Center. He'd had Ballet Theatre, he was thinking of his future, he was going to teach at the School, he was going to be ballet master, he would do anything for Balanchine. They always say that: "Great man. Anything — give me anything." And he lasted awhile, and then he went back to Ballet Theatre. I think you have to be brought up on it young and not come from the outside. But I'm absolutely wrong: Peter Martins fit in beautifully. But the other Dane didn't, [Peter] Schaufuss. I would say it's an exception if you come from the outside and stay. Melissa, of course, was from the outside, and she stayed. She was real Ballet Theatre. She wasn't 'prima prima' — it wasn't like having Alicia Alonso coming to stay — but she was right up there. And Diana stayed; she was pure Ballet Theatre, and she converted. She was Craske, she was Tudor, and at that time she was married to Hugh Laing. But when she got into the company, bit by bit Balanchine convinced her to dance a different way, think a different way, and she ended up being 100 percent Balanchine style.

Once I got into the School of American Ballet, I never studied anywhere else again except those few lessons I took from Craske when everybody had convinced me that I was being "ruined." But that was it. When I was married to George and we were on our . . . 'honeymoon' I guess you'd call it, he went over to set some operas and ballets at La Scala, and there was an English lady called Esmée Bulness and I took her lessons. She was nice. And then when we went to London in 1950, he dragged his ballerinas — Maria, myself, and I think Janet [Reed], maybe Melissa — to [Vera] Volkova. But all together, they were just different teachers, nothing that added up to anything important.

Now, working with Jerry *was* something different. Certainly he's less musical than Balanchine; I mean, he cannot read a score. He has to play through records over and over again. Balanchine never plays a record. We never had a record machine in our house. When I was married to him, I never could find out when he invented anything. Never could find out how he did it. Amazing. I mean, he'd be at home, I'd be at home, he would go through the music, maybe play it once or twice, and the next day he'd have a whole thing. He'd feed it to you as fast as you could learn it. Jerry is more intellectual, more like a Tudor. It has to be a certain mood and a certain way. He used to have an annoying way of saying, "Well, you've lost it." And you'd say, "Lost what?" "You had a certain feeling, a quality, and you've lost it." And you'd think, 'Oh, my God.' It's like losing your doorkeys. 'What the hell . . . What quality . . . What was it I lost?' And then maybe a week later, it would come back. I don't mean to belittle him at all; I don't mean to give that impression.

I think he uses things he sees more than George. He would see me do this with my hair, pick it up off my neck and let it drop, and then suddenly it's in *Faun*. Balanchine uses you because you're the way you are, but he tries to push you into doing something hard that you can't do. Jerry takes exactly what you can do, your qualities, and makes something of that. I always felt with *Faun* that he'd seen me in rehearsal, tying the shoe and certainly fiddling with my hair — I'm always doing that. And this kind of 'It's so hot' thing, pulling at the neck of my blouse — it's just something I would do. I think he uses everyday things. He's a type-casting person.

Actually, Jerry didn't change *Faun* as much as *Age of Anxiety*; we had version one, version two, version three of that, and you didn't know what you were doing. But he started *Faun* when I was away — I was on my honeymoon — and when I came back, he didn't know, for instance, if he was going to have it facing front or facing the corner. Now, when you think of it after the fact, that seems to me absolutely major. I remember he'd say, "All right, let's do it facing the corner," and we'd do it diagonally, facing the corner, entrances, the whole damn thing. Then he'd say, "Facing the front." He wasn't too sure whether he wanted Jacques or Frank either. They both learned it; Frank did it for a long time, and then Jacques did it. George would never do that. By rehearsal, he would know exactly if he wanted it facing front or diagonally, and he would know exactly if he wanted the look of Frank or the look of Jacques.

I liked *Faun*. I liked most of my repertory. I did not like the Mozart, *Caracole*, I don't know why. Having four other people dancing with you, you always feel incompetent somehow. Well, one girl has prettier legs, and one girl jumps better, and finally you're left with yourself. I never jumped very well. I was not a beater, like a Pat Wilde, never beat very well, entrechat six I didn't do well at all. My feet weren't that good, and I could have had nicer arms. There were lots of things. I liked the adagio in the Mozart, but I always liked doing adagios anyway. That came very naturally. I didn't mind the other Mozart, *Symphonie Concertante*, which I used to do with Maria. In that one we didn't have variations — maybe that's why I didn't mind it — and it was very long, which is more of a chance. But all the other stuff, I really liked. *Lilac Garden* was lots of fun to do. It was different from George, all that looking around — it was just a change. I liked *Pied Piper*, a jazzy one that Jerry did; that was easy and fun. But I liked all my roles too because they were different, so I got to be different, or as much as one can be looking the same way. To do *Barocco, Pied Piper, La Valse, Metamorphoses, Nutcracker* . . . it's a lot of different things.

It also helps a lot if you like the music. That has a great deal to do with it. I liked the *La Valse* music, and Stravinsky, all those composers. I had absolutely no musical training — I can find middle C and that's it — but practically every score I ever danced to, I liked dancing to. *Ivesiana* was fun; the music was like a puzzle. And the Schoenberg thing, our monster ballet, *Opus 34*, was fun too, because you would lean on that music the way you would lean on *Nutcracker*. I mean, when you come out to do *La Valse*, you hear the melody and champagne and lots of flowers. And the Chausson violin thing that Tudor uses for *Lilac Garden* is like a thousand lilacs or Shalimar perfume. They both help you. But the Schoenberg was more like background music to you than something that would bolster you up. We did it twice; George used the same piece of music, played over twice — I think it was fifteen minutes or so — and we did two completely different ballets. Fascinating. One ballet was just forms doing things, all dressed up in white tights, and the next one was a monster operation, like a German science-fiction film. Herbie [Bliss] and I started out on stretchers, wrapped in bandages, and I had a stocking over my head so my face was all mushed. It was lots of fun. I don't think half the public knew they were hearing the same Schoenberg twice. You'd have to be an awfully good musician to realize it.

I never really felt lost with the music because I had Balanchine. Not because I had the choreography, but because I had Balanchine, who's a musician. With anybody else, you'd definitely feel lost with it. You'd say, "What count?" and they'd be saying, "Sixty-four, -two, -three, seventy-four, -two, -three, eighty-four, -two, -three," and then it wouldn't come out because they didn't know. With him, you're absolutely secure no matter what. You could dance to a drippy faucet with nothing left to chance. It's like your technique: there's nothing left to chance and you know it, which makes you very secure. And you learn all about music. When I see something like *Agon*, I figure I've heard the music better than if I'd just put a record on. When I see the music illustrated so well, it makes sense even to a complete layman like me who doesn't know how it's constructed.

I had a chance to see a lot of other dancing when I was dancing, but I didn't. Dancing tired me, so when everybody else would be rushing to see another company, I'd be at home. And there were evenings when I'd go to the theatre and I'd want to be any place else. I'd think, 'Oh, if a taxicab would just hit me a little bit, just a nudge. Then I could call, and I'd have to be replaced for a week. It would be so sensational. Just a small nudge.' That's why it's such a good discipline, because you're doing something that you sometimes don't want to do at all. By the time you're on the stage, in the costume, and with the music, you're fine, but if you say, 'I have to be inspired,' . . . well, inspiration doesn't come each night. So you go and do it when you don't feel like it, and your technique, your mannerisms, whatever, pull you through. They've paid their money, and you have to give a performance. To say, 'I don't feel like it. I'm not inspired. I don't feel it' — well, tough. Pretend. Pretend and do it. Feel it? Who cares!

Half of dancing is showing off. When I took class, they never let anybody watch, but, boy, if somebody came in — Balanchine or Jerry or Lincoln [Kirstein] or just a cute boy in uniform — wow, of course I danced better. It's a form of flirting; you want to look attractive, devastating, sure. And you definitely need an audience, although they are not your measure of success. It's not that you don't believe in them, but that they're only the measure of outside success. 'This person got an ovation; he must be terrific' is not necessarily true. Somebody else could get less applause and, in my estimation, still be better. Same thing when you do something and know it was wonderful but it's not a popular ballet — say, *Metamorphoses* — so you only get one curtain call at the end. And then somebody does some pas de deux and it's all shouts and applause. Fine. You don't care. In that way the audience doesn't matter. But you have to dance for somebody. You don't do it for yourself; that's like contemplating your own navel. You do it for people. That's why I could never understand those modern dancers, dancing away in lofts for just a few people.

In *Nutcracker* there's a lot of noise going on, because the audience is little kids screaming; they intrude, but it's kind of cute. But I don't like it when audiences clap in between stuff, and you can't hear. If you're the person that's got to enter and they're clapping for the one who just left, it's annoying. You think, 'When is my music going to start? Will I be able to hear it?' That's when you find touring is strange, because then you get different audiences and different responses. Ballets that have been a smash hit aren't, and ones that weren't, are.

You spend an awful lot of time on tour worrying about the conditions and not your performance. There was a beautiful new theatre in Florence, a lovely thing, better than City Center. Covent Garden is also better than City Center. And the raked stages, like the one in Spain, are nice — you really jump. It's hard getting uphill, but coming down you're a goddess. But we also danced in Red Rocks, outside Denver, which is one of those god-awful open air theatres. It had no curtain so you felt funny rehearsing or chewing gum or wearing legwarmers, because there's your audience with their frankfurters and dinner. It's up high — they had oxygen machines — and it's cold, and there's lots of wind, which was very attractive in *La Valse*. I didn't know, luckily, but apparently bats were flying around in the background too; people said it was one of the best *La Valse*s they'd ever seen. But the stage had a cement floor, which was hell on your legs, really not nice at all, and it had no crossover. If you wanted to cross over, you had to go way down and come around. So nobody did it — you would finish whatever you were dancing and dash across the stage with your arm over your face.

Constitution Hall in Washington didn't have a crossover either. And I fell there, flat on my ass, but it was all right because they told me Margot Fonteyn had fallen there two weeks before. They wouldn't let us put rosin down — "they" being the DARs — because it was going to ruin their floor. So we were all jam-packed into this dumb place doing *Symphony in C* finale, and I fell with such force — I guess I'd been turning — that I spun around on my rear end and got up the next time. It was really quite stunning.

And when we went to Monte Carlo, the stage was as big as this table — tiny — and the dressing rooms were tiny. I remember that

Yvonne Mounsey fainted and they wanted to lie her down flat, but the dressing room was so small that she took up the whole space with her body, and these little feet, like the Wicked Witch's, were hanging out in the hallway. You had to step over them to go on for the next ballet: "Who is it? Oh, it's Yvonne. She doesn't feel well."

But we always had a chance to rehearse, so you knew exactly what you were up against. In Monte Carlo, you just didn't move onstage, that's all. When everyone got on for something like *Western Symphony* finale, in all those ruffles, it was unbelievable. People were turning in the hall, in the wings — there just wasn't enough room. But also, you don't have to cover any ground, so it doesn't take so much out of you. You just do it in place. You don't have to run across the stage because there's no place to run. It's much easier.

You see, what Oboukhoff, Vladimiroff, and Stuart taught at the School was fine, but when you got into the company, it wasn't what George wanted. You almost had to learn a different technique. They were teaching old-fashioned style; you put your heels on the ground and you did lots of stuff that you'd never use, long adagios, forever. But in his classes he says, "I hate those teachers who give long combinations. It's ridiculous. All you have to do is eight and eight." When he teaches, it's all don't do this and don't do that. "Don't put your heels down — it makes too much noise. Run faster. You're not turned-out enough." At the School, they don't insist. They say "turn out," but they don't come and see that you have turned out and then wait for you to do the left side to see if you're still turning out. George would just be like a gnat, and annoy you and annoy you.

Before we went to England, in 1950, he obviously thought his lead dancers weren't good enough, so we used to have a two hour class after the School was closed in the evening. It was just maybe two boys and three girls. No piano — he would play it when he felt like it, and otherwise it was just him snapping his fingers. He was young at that time, he had all this energy, and he insisted. "No, dear. Turn out. No, dear. No. Once more. Once more. Once more. No. No. Now let's do this." It wasn't a well-rounded class; he didn't do a little of this, a little of that, a little adagio. It would be — I don't know — how to do rond de jambe. How to do double. How to do on toe. How to do off toe. How to do jumping. Or how to start a gesture. We'd always just done développé, but he said, "No. Begin. Show the beginning from fifth. Show. People want to see what it is, what you are going to do." And hands, because we had very bad hands. All the details. And insisting on it. Not just giving you the details and then walking away and smoking a cigarette, but standing there, with no music, 'til you did it, in perfect silence. "Again. Again. Again. Try again. Again."

It was amazing. Every night for at least two weeks. That's where I really learned to dance. Started to learn. You'd have to be a cretin not to have improved.

He cannot help but do interesting combinations. If he's working on turns, somehow it's an odd turn, it's a cou-de-pied back where you think it should be front. Anyone else would make a ballet out of his classroom steps, ten ballets. I've written some of the classes down; the steps are amazing, unpredictable the way his choreography is onstage. What could be better than to have a choreographer teaching? You've got the man that is going to use you and make up the steps for you, teaching you. You've got the whole thing made.

February 1979
New York

Toni Lander

Toni Lander (b. Copenhagen, Denmark, 1931) studied ballet for two years with Leif Oernberg before entering the Royal Danish Ballet School at the age of eight. She graduated into the company at seventeen and was promoted to principal at nineteen, in 1950; she married Harald Lander the same year. Having left Denmark with him in 1951, she appeared as a guest artist with the Original Ballet Russe during its final season and then as a principal with the London Festival Ballet (1954–59) in such works as Coppélia, Nutcracker, *August Bournonville's* Napoli, *Harald Lander's* Etudes, *and Fokine's* Les Sylphides. *She left that company briefly in 1957 to create the leading role in the dramatic ballet, by John Taras and Don Lurio, of Françoise Sagan's* Le Rendez-vous Manqué. *As a principal with American Ballet Theatre (1961–1971), she enlarged her repertory with leading roles in* La Sylphide, Theme and Variations, *and* Miss Julie, *among others. She was frequently partnered by Royes Fernandez or by Bruce Marks, whom she married in 1966 and with whom she made her debut in the complete* Swan Lake *in 1967. She returned to the Royal Danish Ballet as a principal (1971–76) and is now principal teacher at Ballet West in Salt Lake City, Utah.*

For years you couldn't see a complete Swan Lake *in New York unless the Royal Ballet came to town. Then American Ballet Theatre mounted the first ever staged by an American company, a four-act production by David Blair which opened in New York on May 9, 1967, with Toni Lander in the dual role of Odette-Odile. At the time, the possible incongruity of a Danish ballerina's leading a troupe of Americans in an Englishman's version of a Russian classic didn't strike me at all. What struck me was Toni Lander's giving a performance of the role which decisively wrested it from its familiar, almost predictable, Anglo-Russian confines. I'd already seen Lander in* Etudes, *nonchalantly whipping off double fouettés without putting her heel down in between, and in* La Sylphide, *floating through Royes Fernandez' hands like smoke. I can still see her standing on the kitchen table in* Miss Julie, *calculating Jean's seduction with arrogance. But I'd never thought of her in* Swan Lake, *and I'd never seen anyone dance* Swan Lake *whose individual talents and previous repertory enabled her to do so with such riveting drama and power.*

*I*t was the process itself, doing the everyday work, that got me so enthusiastic about dancing. I started with folkloric dancing, and did ballroom dancing, but it didn't matter what I was dancing because I loved doing it. I never really went into ballet thinking, 'I'm going to wear a pink tutu and a tiara and be the first ballerina.' When I watched Margot Lander, who was a wonderful example both as a person and as an artist, I might have dreamed, 'One day I would like to be like her,' but I never in my whole career thought, 'I want to be prima ballerina.' It's just something that happened.

When I joined my teacher, Leif Oernberg — I was six years old — he wanted me immediately to go to the ballet because he felt I was musical and paid attention. But my mother said, "No. She's not going into the ballet." So I kept having a weekly lesson or two, and when I was eight, he again mentioned it to my mother, but she still said no. My family didn't know much about theatre except what they watched from the auditorium. They were afraid, I think; they couldn't follow me there and guide me. When we came home, my mother said, "You know, Toni, you're in a wonderful academic school, and I don't think you will like going to the ballet school. Here's one kroner" — it was a lot of money in those days — "and you can buy whatever candy you want, and then we won't talk more about it." We didn't have much money and we didn't have much candy, and for me to get one kroner was tremendous. It must have been like giving a little child ten dollars. But I thought it meant go there and dance or not dance at all anymore, so I said, "No. I want to dance. I want to try. Please let me go." And finally she did let me.

When I was eleven, Harald Lander produced *Swan Lake* after having been in Russia in 1932 with Margot Lander. For a number of years he had tried to do other things but Bournonville because the interest for ballet in Denmark was dropping, but people were not ready to see these different styles. So. When he decided to mount *Swan Lake* for Margot Lander, I was chosen to be one of the cygnets. Now, in those days we didn't perform as much as they do now. We only had one theatre, and maybe we performed once a month, maybe four times — it varied. It meant that we did our daily classes, we rehearsed — a lot — for a performance, and we did it once or twice and that was it. So a year and a half went by before we got *Swan Lake* on, and in the meantime I grew as tall as I am now, and of course I couldn't do cygnets. That was a great disappointment, because it was the first one, but I ended up in the corps.

When I came home crying over cygnets, my mother said, "Well, maybe the ballet's not for you. Maybe you should go back to that wonderful school." I was absorbed in something she didn't understand, and she didn't know whether you were supposed to be that unhappy. But the minute she mentioned it, it really wasn't that bad. I said, "No, no. I want to keep dancing."

I was one of the tallest girls in the School and I was always teased about it. They used to call me "the long, thin spaghetti." I wished I wasn't tall; I used to sleep all curled up, and I wouldn't stretch because I'd heard that if you stretch, you grow. I was thirteen and a half or fourteen years old and just under 5′7″, and I couldn't hold things very well together because I grew so fast. But they were paying me a lot of attention because I had a technique that nobody had in those days. Therefore, I was considered a strange one, not only long and thin, but I could also do turns and all sorts of tricks. I could do five pirouettes from fifth to fifth, in both directions; fifth was my specialty. That's what I did in *Etudes* when it was created in '48. In the corps were about six girls, all very strong, and we did all the difficult parts — pirouettes, relevés, piqués, fouettés, chaînés déboulés, and coda. We did everything, because there were only six who could really do it well.

But that was later. In *Swan Lake*, I was taken into the corps at thirteen, and then I mounted up to do the soloists' roles and then eventually the pas de trois, which Harald made into two white lady swans and one black male swan. I was a little nobody, but in that I got to dance with Erik [Bruhn], who already had a big name in Denmark. When I first joined the ballet, Erik was in the oldest group and I was in the youngest group. The other woman, Inger Mosfeldt, did the jumping variation, and I did the pirouette variation.

At that time too, Harald introduced the Russian style into the ballet in Denmark. To do *Swan Lake*, he had to introduce the company to a longer line than the small, rounded lines of Bournonville. Madame Ulla Poulsen, whom I study Bournonville with in Denmark when I have to teach anywhere, still speaks about it: "Do you remember those Russian things? Boy, did we sweat." I did the first Russian classes when I moved up as an aspirant. It was very, very hard and quite a novelty for the company. We learned to do all kind of pirouettes that we hadn't had in the Bournonville school, and lots of pointe work.

Long adagios we had, but partner classes were new. The jumping was not new; Danes have always jumped better than most dancers. The way of jumping in Russia can be spectacular, but when you have to walk up to the corner and then do run, run, run, run, run, halfway across the stage, to do one big split — that, any gymnast can do. It's not as difficult as Bournonville having a whole repertory of small jumps and then suddenly a big jump in the middle of nowhere.

And in the Bournonville school, you do everything forward and backward, you reverse everything. Cecchetti school does the same thing. It's wonderful brainwork. Most people think dancing is just physical, but it has a lot to do with brainwork. If you don't use your head, you can't do it. As children we only did things once; you had only one chance. We did the step once, that day, and then we went on to the next step. Then the next Tuesday we came back and did that step again. So you better learn fast. Even if it's hard, it has a very valid point. It teaches you things without your knowing. You learn to stand right as a child, or to turn out properly, and then you go and dance. Of course we loved it — we had an extraordinary joy for dancing.

Dancing that *Swan Lake* was Margot Lander, Harald's first wife. Although she was a soubrette and did many wonderful character roles — she did a splendid *Coppélia* — she was the first one who was really able to do beautiful pas de deux work, and it was since Russia. I remember as a little girl in *Swan Lake*, watching her and Hans Brenaa in the pas de deux. We had never seen anyone do so many supported pirouettes; they must have done eight or ten with absolute precision. And of course we all fell backward, because when a man did three pirouettes alone, we considered that brilliant. In the Bournonville school, there are no supported pirouettes, or only one or two. To do five, six, was unheard of. So when we saw eight and ten, we all gasped. We couldn't believe it. Is it really possible? So everybody tried; as kids, we stood there and tried to copy the grownups. That was my introduction to *Swan Lake*, and it was really a turning point for the whole Danish company.

So you can see that from my childhood *Swan Lake* has been standing up there as a symbol. I have a photograph of Margot Lander as the Swan Queen, because it was something extraordinary for me. So when I was asked in 1954 to substitute for Nathalie Krassovska in *Swan Lake* at Festival Ballet in London, when they sent me a telegram saying, "Could you come and do it? Do you know *Swan Lake*?" I lied. I said, "Yes, I know *Swan Lake*." I knew that Harald would help because he thought I should have the chance, but I was petrified. I rushed to Madame Egorova in Paris and had a few lessons, and then went off to London, scared stiff, and did *Swan Lake* with Oleg Briansky. I'm sure it must have been awful.

What I was doing was the Markova-Dolin version, the way English people do *Swan Lake*. I was so petrified I don't remember much of what I felt; I think Oleg and I had only one day together before we did it. But I knew it in my mind. I had seen it danced and I learned by watching, not thinking that I was going to do it, but I had rehearsed in it a hundred times. I probably adjusted the pas de deux to Oleg, adapted the rest, and did my own variation and coda, which of course were what I'd seen Margot Lander do and probably very close to what the Russians did, with the drooping wrist. They must have thought it was terrible, but they were very polite and nice, and they were grateful that they had somebody to put on even if it was bad. I felt it was an awful performance, but it couldn't have been that bad because they asked me to stay with the company. When I later read the reviews I had had, which didn't quite accept that *Swan Lake*, I could see very well why. In those days, the English did it very straight and proper. I had watched Margot Lander and wanted to dance the way she danced, which was not accepted in England until the Russians came and did exactly the same things.

The time with Egorova rehearsing was just time to go through it in your mind, and I didn't have a partner there. I was too young and too immature to start making any character. Having been brought up in a strict European disciplined home and in the strict discipline of the ballet, having been brought up to respect the olders and the people who had knowledge, and going straight from my home to marrying a man who could have been my father and who protected me in many ways, I didn't really have much chance to mature on my own. The first time I was away from home, Harald was in Paris, and I had to leave him for two months to be with the Ballet Russe in London. It was Christmas, and for the first time in my life I was alone. I remember crying for a week, going up to the Red Cross nurse in Festival Hall and sitting crying with her until I had no more tears for loneliness and homesickness. Then the company folded and I went back to Paris, but what was I, nineteen? Very young. For being alone, I was very immature. I had to handle situations on my own, to make decisions, and I had not been exposed to that.

While I was in Paris, I studied with Madame Egorova, Madame Kiss — Nora Kiss — and Preobrajenska, and I think it changed me. Madame Nora was very concerned with technique. Madame Preo, who I worked a lot with, was more concerned with executing. She would, for instance, say, "All right. Finish with the hands opening forward, open palms." Then when you did that, she would say, "No. Like this," and she would raise one arm over the head. So then you did that. And she said, "No. Not like that," and she would finish in an arabesque. She wanted you to try to do something spontaneous. She wanted to train you to be aware that it's all right sometimes to do exactly what you've been told, but occasionally, as an artist onstage, you should also be able to change and do whatever *you* felt like doing. Which now, or later on in my career, I agreed with. There's nothing more wonderful than knowing something so well that it's second mind, second nature, and you can afford to play with it. At the time, it was very strange for me. I thought, 'I'm trying to do what she wants, and she says it's not right and she changes it.' I think she tried to develop individuality, personality.

The *Swan Lake* that I did then was probably a copy of a dream — Margot Lander was my dream — and just doing steps. I still had not seen a full-length version; maybe Royal Ballet did it, but I hadn't seen it, and Ballet Russe de Monte Carlo didn't even do second act. And because I was so nervous, I probably went back, without knowing, to dancing the steps Bournonville style, perhaps specifically the arm movements. I only became aware of it after I had done lots of *Napoli* third act and *Flower Festival* [*at Genzano*]. In contrast to the stretched-out arms and very long line, I might have done it rounded and shorter though I always believed in long arms to make the illusion of wings. Being more rounded could have been part of my complex of being so tall. When I became more mature, I could afford to stretch out.

I knew Odette was a suffering princess, and in my performance there was probably a lot of inside feeling without knowing how to put it out, a lot of melodrama. Now you laugh at that because it's not the face that shows things, but I was brought up in a pantomime school. It was a different way of expressing yourself; you danced with your body and you expressed with your face. Now you express with the whole body, the face becomes one with the body. Many times I should have changed that, to make it come from inside, but when you're that young and immature, you know what is supposed to be, you just don't know how to express it.

When I arrived in England, there was Oleg Briansky, who was very tall, very handsome, and a wonderful partner, but he had a bad knee, so he left Festival Ballet. Many of the others were very small, and here I was, a very tall Swan Queen. When you have to feel frightened, and you want to be protected, and you have to put your head down on the level of your own shoulder to reach the Prince's shoulder and then pretend you are little, you cannot make a good *Swan Lake*. One must have been able to see my inner conflict: 'I don't want to be tall. The partner's too small for me. How can I look dainty

and frail and protected by him when I'm a giant and look very healthy?'
All those things must have shown in my performance. Of course
immediately you have a tall partner, you feel great. Flemming [Flindt]
came at nineteen years old, and we did a lot of *Swan Lake*s together.
We were the same style, brought up in the same schooling, and if I
did something unexpected, I knew I could count on him. We didn't
have to practice so much together because it just came so easy. Flemming had short arms, so we couldn't do finger pirouettes very well,
but it was never that bad. Coming to Ballet Theatre, it wasn't until
Caj Selling and Bruce that I really got partners that were tall enough.

The years with Dolin were a great change for me. He was a
wonderful personality when he wanted to be, but he didn't coach that
much. There wasn't much coaching at all; you were left on your own.
And coming from a secure upbringing in the ballet where when you
went onstage you knew you could do it, I was lost. I had never dreamed
that anybody could go on with two rehearsals. I couldn't understand
why there was nobody to coach. Tchernicheva, Grigoriev's wife,
coached a few things which I later thought back on and understood,
but I didn't quite know what she meant at that time. She was there
too little for me to have gotten real benefit from it. I remember,
specifically in *Les Sylphides*, she was saying that we had to be more
forward, reaching out, almost as if you wanted to embrace the audience. Otherwise there was no communication; when you are pulling
back, you remove yourself. Madame Volkova, to get that point
through, told me, "Think about throwing flowers in front of people's
feet."

Then I went away for one year doing the Sagan ballet, and
when I came back [Vladimir] Bourmeister had been there setting the
second act of *Swan Lake*, and I loved it. It was beautiful. There was
no pantomime in it; instead of the pantomime, they dance. It was a
feeling of being let free — there was much more freedom to let your
own personality come out. We are not all the same, so there has to
be allowance for individuality because that's what's interesting for the
audience. We must not kill that. We have to get away from that putting
in a box, that 'It has to be done this way and it cannot be done any
other way.' Perhaps I felt that there was more in me than I could give
in the Dolin version. With the Bourmeister, for myself, I felt more
free.

But, you see, when I did *Rendez-vous Manqué* it was 1957, and
I wanted to give up dancing. I was stuck. I had done *Swan Lake*,
Sylphides, *Nutcracker*, *Etudes*, *Napoli*, and a whole lot of other things,
and . . . I don't know, I felt it was slipping out of my hands. I couldn't
match myself anymore. Of course we all need changes; I hadn't had

a holiday in almost four years, and there's a limit to how long you can tire a body. You have to load up the batteries sometime. My marriage was slipping, which has a great part psychologically to do with your performing, but I also had reached a point where I was a little tired of hearing, 'It was virtuoso. It was crystal clear technique. It was slightly cold.' You start wondering 'What's wrong? Why is it like this? Why is it cold? Why can't I change?' I also needed new roles. Every dancer should have a chance to be exposed to another style, because even if it's a failure we learn so much. You can make a tremendous illusion if you're given the chance. While physically I didn't look like Swanilda, I did it and it was tremendous fun and one of my greatest successes. I battled it; I didn't want to do it, I was not small and coy and cute, and Harald Lander pushed me into doing it. And I loved it; perhaps because it was a struggle to find my own way, I had more satisfaction from it than I ever had with *Swan Lake*.

So when I finally agreed to do the Sagan ballet, it was very hard for me because, always being typecast, I thought I couldn't do an acting role. Doing it and doing it, I realized I had something to give, so when I came back to Festival Ballet they said, 'There's something new about you.' I had lost some of the technique — I wanted to lose it — and perhaps I was a little more confident that I could act. When finally I joined Ballet Theatre, I was immediately cast as Miss Julie. And then when I came to Europe and Dolin saw me, he said, "I never thought you could do anything like that." So I said back to him something that a few years earlier I would never have dared say: "You never gave me a chance."

Dancing has a lot to do with how you feel in yourself. Living in a marriage where we had drifted apart, and not being able to face that, had also made me feel insecure. Then a little bone tore loose in my foot when we premièred *La Sylphide* with Ballet Theatre, and I thought I was never going to dance again. The more I worked, the worse it got. Then Flemming offered me a contract in Denmark as a ballet mistress, and I decided to marry Bruce in the meantime. That was change in my life where I had to make a lot of decisions and stand on my own. All these things were going through my mind, and it wasn't until then that maybe I got more grip on *Swan Lake*. It does take experience to express *Swan Lake*. The best *Swan Lake*s are usually by older or more mature dancers — we see it constantly. So the foot, the divorce, all of it, forced me to think about other things but just steps. And after all that, I don't know really whether my *Swan Lake* was valid or not. But on the scale of feelings, having to figure out *Swan Lake* was a tremendous experience and joy and sorrow: first the experience with my idol, Margot Lander, then having to cope with failure with my favorite dream-role in London, and then being exposed to the difficulties of partnerships in it.

Most ballerinas, if they do *Swan Lake* very young, haven't had any life experience, so very rarely does anybody have the feeling at that age. Usually what happens is that when you cannot technically do the second act, you do the best interpretation, and people feel you're doing a better *Swan Lake*. Which is very hard to accept — that you're doing a lousy technique but a most fantastic interpretation. You have tried to improve your technique for so many years so you *will* be able to dance the second act, and then nobody likes it. And by the time you become thirty-five or thirty-eight, everybody raves about it but you feel you just can't get through it. There's usually an age where the transition happens, between thirty and thirty-five, when you are able to hold both things. You're giving up some of the technique, finally realizing, or your body is realizing, that it's not all technique, and you're beginning to be expressive.

Also, as you reach a certain age and you have been a technician, if you want to go on, if you're not content, you look for new ways to do a role. You can't keep doing it the same, because that's boring and it's automatic. So you fiddle around with it in your mind, and perhaps you unconsciously put your own life experience into it. You're much more conscious of the interpretation. And as you get older still, you realize that the minute you're focused on an interpretation, you do better technically. That's exactly what Bournonville was saying: technique is not there for the sake of technique; it should be there to be forgotten. I think those who never had a great technique were probably forced to think of the interpretation at a younger age. To get through a role they had to cover up, and they ended up doing a fantastic performance.

When I first came to Ballet Theatre, I danced Act II by itself, switching partners constantly — one time with Scott Douglas, another with Royes, another with Igor Youskevitch, a fourth with Ivan Allen — though we pleaded to have the same partner for one specific thing. Dimitri Romanoff was there and Fernand Nault was ballet master, but I wonder how much I was actually coached since I already knew it. It was very much like Dolin's version, which could have been because Markova and Dolin had danced it in Ballet Theatre. Most of the time it was a question of getting together with your partner and figuring out what you were going to do. The real coaching came with David Blair. In many ways, not just in *Swan Lake*, David meant an awful lot to me at that point in my career. He was somebody I think I had been searching for, as a coach and as a teacher, for a long number of years, although I had been going to excellent teachers, like Dickie [Thomas], who also meant a lot in my whole approach.

I'll tell you a little story that is very significant to how I approached things. In Dickie's class one morning, I was very tired. He did one of those crazy little fast steps in the center that are wonderful for the brain, but I was just not up to doing it. I thought, 'I have no energy, and I have to save a little for tonight. Well, I'll just get through it, do what I can, and if it's no good, so it's no good.' After we did it, he said, "I want you all to see how it's really to be done. Toni, would you please show it to the class?" I said, "You mean this step?" "Yes, I mean that step." "But Dickie, I didn't do anything. I was marking. I'm sorry. I was so tired. I can't do it." He said, "You did it exactly the way it should be done." That made me realize I was doing too much. I was trying to be a perfectionist, and unless I was sweating and feeling dead tired, I didn't feel I'd done a good job. That really clicked for me. I thought, 'I'm trying so hard to do everything so well and to be a good girl. Forget about it. Maybe I should just be a little more relaxed.' Having a self-awareness of what is good for you and how your body functions, you can avoid an awful lot of injury and pain. It doesn't have to hurt. I know that many teachers say, 'Even if it kills you, do it, because it's going to kill you for the rest of your life.' That is not true.

There are times when we must be on our own to absorb and develop; we are trying ourselves out just like children. We all need a coach at other times, and David was, for the first time, somebody who coached the way I was brought up in Denmark. Here was somebody who could see what you had within yourself, what looked good on you, but without being possessive about it. He didn't put himself completely on top of you and say, "It must be this way"; it was a give-and-take. He taught *Swan Lake* very specifically, and it was wonderful; for the first time it was explained to me. Before, I had tried to figure it out myself, but you don't know yourself too well. You don't know how you look. You have to have other people's eyes to tell you, and I was ready for whatever David had to say.

We started with the second act on its own, before the full-length was done. And then a year later, let's say we had a week to learn the basics of the full-length, another week to go over the details, and then we started having run-throughs. And as we were doing it, he would polish, because sometimes we knew what he meant but we didn't know how to communicate it. Emotion you cannot teach; it's either there or it's not — and of course we all feel differently. The only thing

David could try to bring out is that sometimes, through a certain way of doing a movement, you can give the illusion of emotion. If you lift the shoulder up to the head or lean down towards the shoulder, it can give the emotion of enjoyment or the feeling that you're dreaming of the Prince's touch on you.

Well, Odette is an entranced princess, and when she lands, I think she has probably accepted the fact that she's entranced. The first jump, the saut de chat, is coming down from the flight, slightly tired, and with the first glissade she is in her own thoughts. She knows that at night she will have her own body back. When we first see her, when she does glissade, piqué arabesque, maybe she is half swan, cleaning herself up from the flight, but also a transition is slightly happening. She is already half woman when the Prince sees her, which is on the third glissade, arabesque. She's rather shocked by him, rather frightened, because she's not used to seeing young men. As a princess, she might have seen *grown* men, but she hadn't yet made the transition from girl to woman. So encountering a stranger, a man, a young man, a good-looking young man, is perhaps a new feeling for her, and she doesn't know how to handle the situation. Half bird, therefore she reacts as a bird, but the feeling is young girl, shy, frightened, and distrustful a little. He tries to approach her and she constantly runs away, and little by little becomes more comfortable with him, finding out that he's not trying to harm her. And finally she feels confident enough to let him know what her story is, in the pantomime.

The first time I did this pantomime was when David brought the Royal Ballet version to ABT; Festival Ballet didn't do it. In Denmark, Erik and I were some of the last to have mime with Valborg Borchsenius, who was a pupil of Bournonville — she died in 1952. As children, fourteen and fifteen years old, we had to stand and say to the boys in pantomime, 'I love you,' and if you happened to be opposite the boy you really were in love with, it was terrible. We were very innocent and we stood there blushing, but we got over all those things that so intimidate many dancers when they have to say them for the first time. I can understand how Margot Fonteyn felt when she was first dancing with Nureyev, because Nureyev, from childhood, stood there and said to the girls, 'I love you,' and looked at them, knowing he had that charming look. When he looked at her, she must have been amazed, almost frightened maybe, because she had not been exposed to that as a child.

You really have to have done an awful lot of pantomime or you have to concentrate an awful lot on it, how you're going to express it, if you want to get it across. Because when you say in pantomime,

'This Evil One Makes Me Cry and Out There My Mother's Tears Make a Lake . . . ,' to me, it's too much. Even dancers don't understand what she's talking about if they are not brought up with it.

I found that I was doing a lot of it up on half-pointe. She's working herself up. When you get excited, you cannot stand down. Your breathing starts becoming faster, and you move to get it out. I tried to make it quite exciting, because I think it has a lot to do with your anger for Rothbart. You cannot stand on a flat foot, saying these things slowly and deliberately. If you're upset about being a swan — you don't want to be this way — you will be to the point of crying almost, all through, until she says, 'Unless somebody loves me or swears he will marry me, I will always be a swan.' There, there has to be a downhill, because she doesn't see the possibility of it. And because the Prince is a stranger, she has to feel tremendous trust for him just to be able to say this. For her to completely submit to him has a lot to do with how the partner speaks too. There has to be enchantment in his eyes, and very strong feeling, and this you cannot teach a partner.

If real emotion is felt and expressed, the audience will feel it. But if you don't know how to phrase a pantomime, it doesn't come across — even to me, who has been brought up in it. It can go like a monotone, and then the audience doesn't have any idea of what it is about. They say, 'What is all that old-fashioned stuff? What are they doing? What does it all mean?' and then you have to have written in the program, 'This gesture means such and such a thing.' Phrasing, yes, making phrases: taking the time to pause, to think, getting the idea and then saying it. A lot of things go on before you do a movement. But unfortunately — here we are again — when you are mature enough to realize these things, perhaps you are too old or you've already finished dancing. And if you do it too often, it can even become self-conscious.

When you do a role like *Swan Lake* or *Coppélia* or *Miss Julie* or *Lilac Garden*, where you have to express emotion, it's much better to get away from ballet and think about other things, meet other people, so it's new. You must get away from talking about it and from rehearsing it. The last years I was dancing, I felt there's too much rehearsing when you know a role well. I don't think it's good. If it's going to go wrong, what does it all matter? When you go onstage, you have to learn to fix it. I didn't like to rehearse *Swan Lake* when I did it twice or three times a week; if I had to do it, I would go in and practice *Theme and Variations*. I knew it inside, and all that counted was spontaneity with the role. It's a little Zen, too. The unconscious, the new approach, is the real approach, with the steps and also, in a way, with feelings.

Odette is falling in love maybe without knowledge of what falling in love is. How could she possibly know when she hasn't encountered it before? When you are shy and uncomfortable in a young man's company, you don't want to get hurt. You have to think of it in terms of the old-fashioned way; you would like to have something else but just going to bed with somebody. You want to have confidence in a person; you want to find out whether there's trust and mutual respect. And through that the feeling of love grows. The pas de deux expresses the love very well and . . . sorrow. There are moments of pure joy, for being close with him, for the feelings that she has never experienced before, and then occasionally she has this fear of what's going to happen, and the sorrow for the future breaks in.

I've always felt very strongly about the phrasing of the pas de deux, trying to put feelings in the movements. It might have looked better when I could forget about partnering. Sometimes you have a partner who doesn't feel the phrasing the way you do; it has a lot to do with emotion and breathing at the same time. For instance, a lot of people like to do the battu at the end very strongly, bang the foot and do many strong pirouettes. But to me it was almost like a shivering — without touching the other foot — almost like having sex, in a way. And I always wanted to avoid noise; I hated the noise. I wanted to make it like quiet love. The Portuguese say, 'When I'm happy, I'm crying,' and that's what I meant by this battu. Sometimes love or emotion can be so refined and true that you are caught in it. You want to just barely touch because it's so sacred. I always specifically thought of that whole last part as the climax of real, true love and very still, almost as if she wanted to keep that moment forever in her mind. I wanted to make it one continuous movement until the fall at the end.

The solo was a different kind of emotion, more an expression of joy but still with the thought of being caught. Perhaps she's thinking about him, daydreaming of the moments they were together. It's a moment of freedom when she steps into the arabesque with the arms back. She is then part bird but mostly woman. She becomes the swan again gradually, halfway through the bourrées going out. It's very impressive the way Cynthia [Gregory] does it: she freezes and suddenly she's a swan and that's it. But I felt more she's wanting to be with him, changing slowly as she goes out, really pulled away from him.

Odile is an entirely different woman. She's von Rothbart's only daughter, an evil person, selfish, wanting everything she points at, and of course she's grown up with an evil father. Perhaps underneath she's been jealous of all these beautiful girls that her father has taken under his spell, and has looked down upon them all. Maybe she's a countess, not even a princess — anyway she's less and therefore trying to be more. She acts above them; they're just trash. She's having tremendous fun snatching this young man away from somebody else. I don't know if she expects to get him for herself. Maybe she's just playing around, like a person who has a ball breaking relationships between other people and not caring about them afterwards. I don't think there's anything good in her and there's everything bad.

Rather than doing it as a straightforward pas de deux, I liked the concept of David Blair's version where Rothbart is involved — he's advising her — because it means the story is carried through. When she does step over, pirouette, grand arrondi, leaning back to him, I thought of it as, 'She's seducing him.' It's a seductive way of doing the steps. And it's progressive; when you have a whole evening, there's a certain way that you build it up. There's got to be some kind of bravura somewhere. But I never really thought of the variation, the fouettés, or the coda as really having anything to do with the story. They're a little outside the story.

When you do Odile's variation and the fouettés, you're not thinking of the interpretation. If you're used to doing a lot of fouettés on the stage, it's nothing to do it. If you're not used to doing it, you think you can't, and then you either have to take your mind away from it or give yourself a way out in case it goes wrong. I had gotten used to doing no more than sixteen fouettés — that was in *Etudes*. So in my thirties, I suddenly had to start doing thirty-two, and I started worrying about how I was going to get through them. Nobody gave me a way out, but when I panicked, I switched and did something else, which all the Russians do. Unfortunately, so many of the audience wait a whole evening to see if she can do thirty-two fouettés, as if the whole evening depended on them. Then you think, 'Well, what's the point of going through the whole ballet if that's the way they judge whether you've done a good performance or not?' It's ridiculous. If somebody has done a beautiful performance, who cares whether they do thirty-two fouettés or not?

Apart from the fouettés, I've done versions of the variation and coda that I like better than what we did, more bravura. David's was the English version and it was a lot of hard work, having to do all the changements at the end when you're dead tired, and I didn't think it came off as bravura. Many people have changed it to the hops on pointe or the sliding back and balance in arabesque or the *à la seconde* pirouettes. I would rather have done that. God bless David, who's not alive anymore, but a lot of us changed things when he was not around. Perhaps I was held back a little more than most in changing things, but eventually I did. I finally felt, 'The changements are absolutely unnecessary. Why should I do all this? I hate doing it.' It's a lot of baloney that is not showing off, and you're tired so you can't do it as well as it should be done.

In different versions, you have happy endings, tragic endings that become happy, or tragic endings that are unhappy. For me, in David Blair's version, there is finding the Prince all over again. She hasn't seen him since the end of the second act, so she thinks she has lost him. She *has* lost him. She knows she's been betrayed — in the vision, she's seen him fooling around with Odile — and realizing that perhaps he isn't the person she thought he was, she's deeply upset. She's not thinking about her survival or coming back to being a princess, because before she met him she's already thought, 'I'll never get beyond this point.' That's what the fourth act starts with, her realization that he has not been faithful and the swans trying to console her.

But seeing him again, she forgives him. It's a pas de deux of forgiving. It's also about learning about life; you live with people, people make mistakes, we can't all be perfect. Act IV is about quiet love, happiness, forgiveness, peace. After the fight with Rothbart, she realizes that she doesn't want to live anymore. It's *Romeo and Juliet*, isn't it? She has known the greatest happiness she could know, she wants to capture that moment forever, and only through death will she feel peaceful. Little does she know that the Prince wants to die too. Nowadays I think they jump together, but when I did it, she jumps alone and they find each other in the next life. That's the way I thought about it, but it might be too idealistic to imagine that one can possibly get it across.

You know, in Denmark, right from when I was very young, people said, 'Oh, she has long lines . . . *Swan Lake* . . . Swan Queen.' And sometimes what you set as a goal to reach doesn't come off with your dreams of what it should be. Occasionally I think it got across, but I don't say that it always did. I've seen performances and thought, 'Gee, that's beautiful. Why didn't I think of that? Of course. That's the way you should do it.' As you get older, you experience more and you see it from a different point of view.

If you have a good partnership, it's never the same twice even with the same partner; a good partnership never becomes routine. With a bad partner, things become routine because you're not allowing yourself to be free enough to use the spur of the moment. Many times, when you have a complete relationship with your partner, you don't have to say anything. He just senses things. This is a true partnership.

The ballets without a real story are more difficult. The Sylphides section in *Etudes* always stood for purity for me, because Harald felt that very strongly. It was church, it was humbleness, respectfulness, Gothic lines, prayer, everything you can include with those feelings. And I think the pas de deux of *Theme and Variations* is about love. But there again, you have to have a partner. If you have a struggle in your partnering, you can't relax, you're too self-conscious, and a pas de deux has to be a unity where you can forget about yourself. Only then can you get the expression through, only when you can forget about what's around you. Some performances I don't remember who was in the wings or if there was an audience. I remember I saw lights like a hot summer night where the heat was creating a shimmer, a vibration, and you heard the insects' sounds and it was a stillness. You wonder afterwards, 'What did I do?' It was a wonderful feeling, almost like what you think Paradise must be, or what people say about when you drown. I think the music is in there with you. I don't know. You're carried away. It's something you cannot explain. Whether it's in dancing or music or everyday life, it's the moment that you'd like to capture, but when you reach out for it, it's not there.

The music is everything. If there wasn't music, I don't think I would be dancing. I always wanted to play the piano; I don't know if I ever will, but if there's another life, I hope I will. If I would choose something else in life, I think I would be a musician or maybe even a conductor. To a dancer, the conductor means everything. He can make you or break you. If you are on the same wave as the conductor, he senses what is right musically. Then a thing can be fast or slow and it doesn't matter — it's still phrased musically. After all my experience, I think the best ballet conductors are musicians who have played string instruments. Maybe the bowing teaches them; the tone of a violin is carried through, then there's a breath, and a new phrase starts. When many pianists play, they just put a beat, a beat of nothing, where that breath should go. Also, if a conductor conducts for a dancer the way he conducts for a singer, everything will come out right because you breathe the same way when you sing as when you dance. No matter what the tempo then, it is never out of musicality. It's a collaboration between conductor, musicians, and me.

With *Swan Lake*, most of the people know the story, and if the story doesn't come across you still have beautiful dancing. When you have a role where the drama comes before the dancing — the opposite of *Swan Lake* — it's a whole different approach. You *have* to get the story across. Now, in *Miss Julie* the choreography is not very varied.

So if you were interested, you had to try to put different feelings in every time you did an entrechat quatre or a little brisé or a pas de chat. Miss Julie does brisé when she is very angry, she does it when she is trying to seduce . . . How do you seduce doing brisés? You had to use your fantasy if you wanted to end up doing anything but steps. It can be a challenge.

The first thing I did with *Miss Julie* was read the book, but it takes time to get into a role and I learned it in two days and then I did it. I had never learned anything so fast. It was frantic, and unfortunately nobody counted the music for me. It would have been so easy, especially in the first scene where she's trying to urge her fiancé to jump over her whip, if somebody had laid it out. Because when you have music in your head, thousands of different themes, it can be very confusing unless it's a waltz or a march. You have all these steps going around and people going around . . . I don't know how I did it. It was only over the years that I figured it out, and I don't know if it succeeded even then.

With Tudor, I did Caroline in *Lilac Garden, Gala Performance*, and then *Undertow*. He always wanted no emotion showing; it was the *movement* that had to be done, and the emotion had to come from within. We do it in everyday life, but it's very hard to carry onstage the simplicity of the everyday movement that you're born with, that you learn as a child, that emotion makes happen. When he would demonstrate, whatever role it was he looked like that person. He did very little; it could be a shoulder, lifting or going forward, that could give an incredible impression. If you were inexperienced or had not worked with him before, you would do too much, too melodramatic. I think he wanted you to think. I learned tremendously from him.

As a matter of fact, Tudor should probably direct many more things. It would be fantastic if he got his hands on *Swan Lake* because he has a way of getting things across — he just touches the right thing. And his direction of his ballets is not so far from *Moor's Pavane*. The way they must be done is very, very similar, because *Moor's Pavane* is also physical expression, bodily expression and not facial expression. I found that the more I was absolutely natural in it, without trying to do 'ballet,' the better it worked. I didn't try to turn out or pull up; I tried to feel the ground, be absolutely relaxed, and let the movement carry my body, which I wish I had learned way before. It's the same with Tudor. You have to be natural. You don't have to be perfect, or a perfect classical dancer, to do it. With *Moor's Pavane,* the less I tried, the better I did. It just happened. And it came at the perfect time for me. I had really decided to stop, and then *Moor's Pavane* came as the crown of the cake.

When I came to Ballet Theatre, Dimitri Romanoff had a lot to tell me. And Royes Fernandez was a tremendous coach; he had the right psychology of how to get things across without putting people down. Many times we think we have not done a good performance — you get so worked up in technique — but we have to learn that we have a certain standard we don't go below. When we have reached the top class, it will always be good; even when it's not so good, it's still good. When things go wrong, you accept it. There are other things that go right, and you should appreciate that.

For my part, I was always very involved in whatever I was doing. And when you're very involved and let's say you get a bad review, one person's opinion can absolutely crush you. The critics can make you and they can also kill you, and I don't think they always do the artist a favor. Cyril Beaumont, in England, did the right thing. He said to me, "I never go on the first night, because you can be lucky the first night and never make it again, or you can be so nervous you can't get anything across. I go maybe the fifth night. Or when a dancer is doing a new role in an old ballet, I go the fourth or fifth time. To be absolutely fair." He didn't have much space, only a small column, so whatever he said he came right to the point. And he didn't try to crush you. He tried to guide you because he figured out that if somebody was chosen to do a part, it must be because that person was able to do it. Many times the critics write that it was absolutely wrongly cast. How do they know? The choreographer is the one who has picked that person. I wouldn't like to be a critic, but I think that at the same time they're guidance to the audience, they might be guidance also to the dancer.

You dance for a lot of different reasons at certain times of your life. When you're very young, you try to dance for the people you love, the people you respect, or the people you want to please. Sometimes you just dance for joy, you dance for happiness, you dance for sorrow. It can be a fantastic way, if you're very unhappy, to get rid of frustrations. It's a wonderful vehicle for people who are not in balance with themselves or with others, a marvelous outlet. I think dancing attracts a lot of people with more or less psychological difficulties, but that can also make it very interesting.

I danced because I like dancing. I love to be involved in movement — that was a joy. As you progress in a ballet and feel the response of an audience, that can egg you on. You feel they're with you, and it sometimes makes you do unbelievable things that you never thought would happen, which is very exciting. One carries the other; it's give-and-take constantly. But I think to go in and dance for yourself . . .

starting off thinking of yourself . . . I don't know. Maybe through all this I do it for myself, I don't know. But the greatest joy is giving something. What the pleasure or happiness of others does to you, that you can call selfish.

August 1979
Long Island, New York

Donald MacLeary

*Donald MacLeary (b. Glasgow, Scotland, 1937) began his ballet training with
Sheila Ross in Inverness only shortly before he entered the Sadler's Wells Ballet
School in 1951. In 1954, he joined the Sadler's Wells Theatre Ballet, where
he was promoted to soloist a year later, created leading roles in Kenneth
MacMillan's first commissioned work,* Danses Concertantes *(1955) and his*
The Burrow *(1958), and made debuts in both* Swan Lake *and* Giselle.
Early in 1959, following a performance of Swan Lake *with Svetlana Be-
riosova that christened their enduring partnership, he was almost immediately
promoted to principal and transferred to the Royal Ballet at Covent Garden.
Within his first ten months there, he learned and performed* Sleeping Beauty,
Cinderella, Sylvia, *and* Coppélia *and originated major roles in MacMillan's*
Le Baiser de la Fée *(1960) and Cranko's* Antigone *(1960), partnering
Beriosova in all of them. Best known for his repertory of noblemen, which
included Romeo and Solor in* La Bayadère *(Act IV), he also danced ballets
as diverse as* Song of the Earth, Apollo, *and* La Fille Mal Gardée *with
distinction. Having announced his retirement from dancing in 1975, he remained with the Royal Ballet as ballet master until 1979. He has appeared
since then with the Scottish Ballet and several other companies.*

---

*Today's craze for physical virtuosity threatens dancers like Donald MacLeary
with extinction and renders superfluous the rarest qualities of their performances, qualities like dignity, modesty and refinement. Many men at the
Royal Ballet have danced with greater charisma and more spectacular technique
than MacLeary, but no one in my experience has seemed as intrinsically aristocratic or consistently gracious. With a partner, he was attentive to the point
of self-effacement, flattering her as a finely wrought setting flatters the jewel
it displays. Because he was always where he was meant to be, physically and
dramatically, you trusted him. Trusting him, you were all the more quickly and
willingly persuaded by the illusion he so convincingly created. The Royal Ballet
is lessened without him, as ballet itself is diminished without dancers like him.*

I obviously was an instinctive dancer from the word go. I wanted to learn to do highland dancing, though I never competed because my parents didn't think that rushing around to competitions was on. But when I heard music around the house, I danced. Made it all up, really, improvised everything. I started off in ballet with somebody called Sheila Ross, in Inverness. But in fact she encouraged me to go away because she knew she couldn't teach me enough, and she encouraged my parents to write to the Sadler's Wells School, as it was then. I had several teachers at the School, but Harijs Plucis was the main one, and he was a big influence.

He was a good teacher, but he was also a fantastic gentleman; he had wonderful manners and he expected wonderful manners. Even though he was training one as everybody does in a classical class, his manner was very much like a cavalier all the time, and he always talked about you as being the cavalier. He related everything to what you were going to be, and to the theatre. Actually, I feel that a lot of teachers don't do this to the young kids. From the minute you go into the classroom, the teacher must associate what you're doing with a stage. The classroom is the stage, and the front, the mirror, is the audience. It very seldom happens with the young teachers — they forget it. Many teachers nowadays haven't had a career so they tend to think a class is all technique, but Plucis was very aware of presence and manner. In between exercises, he never let us slouch, and he never let us put our hands on our hips, never. He used to go mad: "How you be a dancer if you slump like that?" Well, it makes one aware of what the end product should be, a rather gallant gentleman.

We did study partnering, but not with him. We had pas de deux classes in which I was a disaster. Well, I found them very difficult. Everybody thinks that I was a natural-born partner, but I wasn't. If it looked that way, it was because I worked very hard at it. When I first went to pas de deux class, I was horrified that I couldn't do two pirouettes with a girl, and I couldn't get her on my shoulder. I thought, 'Well, God, one's got to do something about this,' and I just knew that if I worked hard enough, hopefully I'd get it right.

The minute I saw *Swan Lake* for the first time, I began studying it. It was probably Margot and Michael [Somes], but I also saw Moira Shearer, Violetta Elvin, Nadia Nerina; and the men were Michael, John Field, Philip Chatfield, Alexis Rassine. I saw lots of people. I was a huntsman as a student, and I was also in the Polonaise, and I think that's when I started studying the role of Siegfried. I watched how everybody did it, because at the back of my mind I knew I was going to do it; I never had any doubts about not having the opportunity. So in the classics, in the *Giselle*s and the *Swan Lake*s, I watched absolutely everybody I could, any visiting company, watched them all, how they presented themselves, how they did certain parts of the choreography. So I had a good idea of it before I was actually in the rehearsal room. I knew I was headed that way. It sounds terribly conceited, but I think you have more confidence when you're young and ambitious — gradually you get it knocked out of you. It wasn't any sort of arrogance; it was just that that was my aim. I didn't go around telling everybody that I thought I was going to do the Prince, but I watched. You have to have a goal and you have to work for it. I think it's sad that dancers don't. I mean, I'm amazed, when they come to do one of these really famous roles, that they don't have the first idea about it. They wait until they've got it and the cast is set, and then you have to teach them the walk-on — they don't know the ballet. I'm always surprised about that.

Before I did the full *Swan Lake*, I did Act II in the touring company, the Sadler's Wells Theatre Ballet, with a girl called Anne Heaton. And I was coached by John Field, who had done the Prince with Beryl Grey at Covent Garden and with several other people. Now, Plucis was the company coach at Covent Garden, so all the ballerinas and all the principal male dancers were coached by him in the pas de deux work in the classics. So it was a good extension for me to have *my* first coach, John Field, be someone who had been trained by my teacher. Plucis coached him, so what he taught me was in Plucis' style; it wasn't foreign to me. It wasn't something that I thought, 'Oh my God, I can't take this.' It was the right progression.

The touring company didn't have the full production then, so I had to forget about the rest of the ballet for a bit because it wasn't in the repertoire. You have to be convincing in what you're doing at the time. If the story's condensed, you have to tell it like that; that becomes the whole thing. And then I started to work on the full-length ballet when it came into the repertoire, immediately it came in, although in that production I first did the center boy in the pas de six in the first act, and I also did the Mazurka in the third act. But again, as I was on, I was able to watch all the performances and make my own impressions while, at the same time, start working with Lynn Seymour on the full-length. And I stole like mad. I stole what I thought was good from everybody: a walk here, a gesture there, or how they got into a position in a pas de deux. We had already worked together, Lynn and I. Kenneth MacMillan created a ballet for us called *The Burrow*, so we were more or less the new young partnership in the company at that time. But she had never done *Swan Lake* before either, so John Field took us both through it. Again, it wasn't a case of teaching one the steps; it was producing us, really. I had always known the steps — you don't forget what you've learned. But when I was doing the second act, I was thinking only in terms of that act, and usually one was doing two other totally different ballets the same night anyway.

In a way it was good that, although we'd neither of us done it, I had had much more experience than Lynn. I'd been in the company that much longer, I'd done *Giselle*, I'd done a lot of one-act ballets, so I felt like I was the person who could be helpful. And it's also good to work with somebody who's never done something before, because they will work harder than somebody who has already done it. For somebody who's done it before, it's a bit like going backward. So we were able to work a lot of hours on it, and when we didn't work with John Field, we worked on the technique ourselves. We tried to get really comfortable technically in all the pas de deux, so that one wasn't aware too much of technique and you could start thinking about characterization. The thing that I think about all the classics is that, from the moment you come on the stage, you have to start telling the story. Those pas de deux are simple classical dancing, really, things that you have been training in class to do for many years, and that isn't what makes the performance in the end. It's the extension of that dancing that makes the performance, and the characterization. In fact, what grows in your performance isn't the dancing — it's the characterization and what you do with it. I never changed my variation or anything else from what I first did, never. They were set. Young people can do these difficult things, but what they can't do are the other things and that's what you grow in.

And the other thing I was thinking is that I was very fortunate to do it so young. A lot of people come to it later on, or if they get the opportunity it's because they've become quite well known dancers. But they've only ever done the pas de deux as concert pieces, and the thought of doing the whole thing frightens them. I always had a different approach, that it was a whole piece and that ninety-nine percent of the audience wanted to be told the story. One percent will know the technicalities, but nobody's so superhuman that every performance can go well technically. What you *can* do is get so in tune with the role that you make the audience sympathetic to you.

The great thing was that when I first did the whole ballet, we were on a tour of Australia and I danced it twice a week for eight months. That was the best thing that could have happened. I did it on Tuesday nights with Lynn and on Wednesday afternoons with a girl called Susan Alexander — for eight months. So I had a lot of groundwork. And therefore, the role was less frightening when Ninette de Valois asked Lynn and me to go and do it with the big company. We were very young and it was our first time doing a full-length ballet at Covent Garden with the parent company, but one wasn't terrified — one was elated. Because you'd got those months of solid groundwork behind you, it was much less scary. At the time, I didn't think of that occasion in terms of anything dramatic happening in my life. What I didn't realize was that Svetlana was at the performance and she asked if I could do one with her. So she came out with the touring company to somewhere like Streatham, in London, and I did one with her, and then she asked if I could be moved from the touring section to the big, parent company.

My Prince did certainly change. Everybody talks — or everybody did then — about how wooden the princes were, and I kept thinking, 'Well, one has to remember that although he's a prince and although it's a ballet, he can be a real person.' So you forget about doing the 'I'm a prince and everybody must bow when I come on' look. The Prince is a human being, so you must break through that balletic stiffness. You have to break that down, and it takes quite a lot of courage. It also takes quite a lot of experience to stop rushing around everywhere. You can tell the audience masses of things by standing still and listening with your eyes. You can feel something behind you, and they can see you doing it. You do it to *them* because you're telling *them* the story; you're not doing it for the people in the wings, and you're not doing it for yourself. You always have to tell the audience, and you can't do it if you're busy walking all over the stage. A lot of people find it very difficult to have the courage to stand in the middle of the stage and not move, to create an atmosphere by using your eyes, listening with your eyes.

Lynn and I had a lot of preparation — certainly we had enough. But, as I say, it takes performances to make a role, and that's what was really a help. I probably was quite different after six months, but not different enough because I was twenty. I wasn't like I was at thirty or forty, but I couldn't be. That's the other thing: you can't be. I couldn't play the Prince the way Michael Somes did, because I would have looked wrong — Michael was twenty years older than me. I couldn't play Siegfried like a heavy. In fact, I was the right age. And as I kept doing it, I think it got simpler. I got to having more courage, to knowing that I could do nothing and get an emotion across, whereas I probably would have been a little bit more 'silent movie' when I was younger. Even then I believed in what I was doing, but I was probably a bit more anxious, trying to please.

It's nonsense to say the Prince has nothing to do. To me, he just wasn't complicated. He was a real person who hadn't, until he met Odette, fallen in love. But because he has been brought up to know that one day he is going to be married, he accepts it when the Queen says, 'You're going to marry.' He's not going to be difficult about it. He starts to say, 'Well, do I have to at this moment?' and when she says, 'Yes, you do,' he agrees. He knows he's going to have to go through with it. It's the same today: Prince Charles will marry who they choose. And this is a nineteenth-century ballet — people knew about these things. But I never saw him as a rebel, not in the first act. O.K., he has a little bit of a drink, but who wouldn't? He's popular, it's his birthday, everybody likes him — that's why they're all there. I don't think anybody should overemphasize too many nuances of his character, because it is a romantic ballet, and the more simple but real you are in the first act, the more the audience will be moved by you building up the romanticism later. If you're very busy in the first act and you have all these nuances, the audience is going to get terribly confused.

That solo that Rudolf introduced later on was rather nice because it added more dancing. But it's the sort of dance that you must do with emotion — you can't just go posé, arabesque, chassé through — which is what I loved, to have something that you can get your teeth into. It wasn't a virtuoso variation; you could have pauses, use your face and your eyes, but at the same time you are doing an *adage* solo. It didn't become a problem. It added to the melancholy of the Prince; it made him a little more down than he would have been without it. He was probably indulging a bit, thinking, 'What a mess. Why can't I fall in love? Why doesn't Miss Right come along?' But there's just a little more time to say that than in the other production, and at least you have something dancey to say it with. Some people used to do it with the tutor on the stage. But I always used to say, 'I want to be alone' and send the tutor off, because I don't think the Prince would show his emotions to his court. He was expected to behave like a prince, so any indulgence comes when there's nobody there. You don't do it in front of your people; they expect you to be perfect. When you come on, you might be thinking, 'My God, it's my twenty-first birthday. Who needs this?' but you don't show it. You put the façade to your court; they never see you looking glum.

During that whole first act, he hasn't got a *big* problem, but there's a slight problem: it would be nice to marry somebody he liked. But he simply hasn't met anybody, and when the tutor says, 'Don't be low. The ball isn't until next week,' or 'Who knows? One of these princesses might be wonderful. Why don't you go out hunting?' he says, 'What a good idea.' And then, it's only when he sees this creature that the problem in fact begins.

The problem is that suddenly he sees somebody that he loves, and she's a bird one minute and a human being the other. That's the biggest problem of all! That's a hell of a problem! There she is, but there's this terrible curse on her. She does tell him that there's a solution: 'The only way the spell will be broken is if somebody loves me, marries me, and swears that he will do it.' That is the solution. But to make the ballet into four acts, you don't say it then — you only say it when she forces you to. Odette says it in Act II, but *you* don't say to her, 'I love you and I'm going to marry you and I swear' until the third act, and of course then you're saying it to the wrong person. And the reason you don't say it before then is that she tells you this in the mime scene, before you've danced with her, before you're absolutely under her spell. You're fascinated by her, but when you meet somebody you usually don't say, "I think you're terrific. Will you marry me? I love you, I swear it." You wait; you go out for dinner a couple of times. But by the end of the second act, when he *is* under her spell, she's transformed into a bird again. And when, in the third act, Rothbart says, 'Will you marry this girl and will you swear?' and Siegfried *does,* the spell of course isn't broken. She's destined to stay the swan. He's said it to the wrong girl.

What she's saying to him is an incredible story. He's amazed. She's saying, 'There's a lake of my mother's tears,' and he says, 'It's incredible. Tell me more.' He absolutely can't believe it. You go along into the wood and you see somebody who's a swan and then suddenly, before your eyes, is a woman. It's an incredible thing. You are mesmerized by her. When I rehearse anybody, I say, "Never take your eyes off her." You are waiting for the next thing. It should get really urgent: 'My God, I've never heard . . . What the hell happens next?' And he's just about to say, 'I'm going to protect you' when von Rothbart comes on, so he can't. Plus the fact that he hasn't had time to think, 'She's the one I'm going to marry' before Rothbart enters. But then they do the pas de deux, and by the end of the pas de deux, he's hooked.

We did the ballet for a while without the mime and then it came back in, thank God. I think Fred [Ashton] preferred it. In a way, it's not as satisfying without it. I love the simplicity of the mime, and it's a very good opportunity, again, to tell the audience what's really happening. If you feel uncomfortable with it, you're not doing it right. You have to believe in the character. Whatever you do on the stage, whatever ballet, if you don't believe in the character, the people in the theatre aren't going to believe you. So whether you think the mime's all codswallop or not, you have to take hold of it to make it work, and do it with sincerity, real belief. If you go around thinking, 'What a load of crap it is,' it'll look like a load of crap.

The pas de deux is all part of the story too. When I rehearse anybody, I say, "For the Swan Queen, that pas de deux is the first time anyone's listened to her." They don't start that off like a love duet; they shouldn't. She's gone through such a horrible experience that she's really afraid. She should be, like, 'Am I all right, staying with you?' That's why there are so many movements of 'I'm going away. I'm not sure of you,' like all the running forward. But he keeps saying, 'Don't go. Come back,' until, by the cello solo, she starts giving in. All the way through she's wanting to, she's getting more and more confident, but it's only the very last fall at the end that is her submission to him. It isn't an indulgent love pas de deux; it's him wanting her to stay and her looking at von Rothbart's rock and thinking, 'He might appear any minute. We must be careful.' They're telling a story throughout that pas de deux. It isn't just that music and those steps; you tell the story the whole way through it. And I say to any girl I've ever done it with, "You have to do that, because it doesn't work for the Prince if you don't." In the later version, he's not onstage for her solo — that is something we all have to live with. It's not a perfect ballet, but you try and make it as convincing as you can. You have to try and make even the imperfect bits as believable as possible.

He doesn't come on in Act III thinking, 'Oh, this is wonderful,' but he's not snubbing people. He's behaving as they expect him to behave because he's so trained that way. Definitely there's a down there because he's thinking of her, but you mustn't look bored, you mustn't. Maybe some princes think they've got to feel down, but again I feel that his training would make him acknowledge everybody. It's not until the fiancées come along that he has his first problem, and of course he dances with them. But when his mother actually gets down to the nitty-gritty and says, 'Which one is it going to be?' he finally says, 'I can't go through with it.' That's why she gets so furious: 'How dare my son behave like this, especially in front of our court.' It's something that would never ever happen, but he's desperately in love by this time. And just when he doesn't know what he's going to do and how to explain it all to his mother — she's in high dudgeon — he's saved by the bell. Von Rothbart comes on with Odile.

Now the thing about *that* pas de deux is that it is wrong for Odile to be in full control. It's von Rothbart who's in control. She's been told what to do, but just when the *adage* starts and Siegfried goes to kiss her hand, she thinks, 'My God, now what do I do?' So she goes over to von Rothbart and says, 'This is getting a bit tricky. What do I do?' and he says, 'Just go ahead.' So then she gets more confident. But she shouldn't be 'Aha! You're mine!' all the way through it; she should play, 'I must go and check.' It's sort of teasing — well, he thinks it's sort of teasing, but she's dead worried. It's important that Odile has this not too confident feeling, because you get confused about the fact that she's constantly leaving you and it gives you time to wonder if this girl is really who you think she is.

You're not completely sure to begin with. The first thing you say to von Rothbart is 'Who is she?' and he says, 'She's mine.' You can't quite believe it's Odette because how could she suddenly be appearing there? You've just seen her, but she was a swan. And she didn't tell you about the father — von Rothbart has changed from a bird into a man. So you're really confused, and during the pas de deux you're still trying to figure it out. That's important to do for the audience. It's not just happy-happy dancing. During the vision, you're really wondering, 'What *is* going on? This is very strange.' And then when she imitates the swan, you begin thinking, 'Well, thank God. She *is* Odette. It must be her,' and the variation and coda are just an expression of joy. She finishes the pas de deux on a triumphal note because she knows she's got you, and your variation is a celebration of your happiness that you've got her. I don't start thinking that she's dazzling me with her dancing. I'm just so happy that it's her. I'm dazzled by the fact that I find my love again.

Everything seems to be going all right until von Rothbart says, 'Wait a minute. Do you love her?' And you say, 'Yes, I do.' 'Do you want to marry her?' 'Yes, I do.' 'Will you swear?' And you swear. And at that moment, Odette reappears, and von Rothbart says, 'You fool, this is all a giant hoax. Look at her.' And you realize the horror of what you've done, that you swore to love somebody else and that *she* will be doomed forever unless she meets somebody else by the lakeside. It was so nearly going to happen and you've ruined it, for yourself and for her. And you go tearing off.

The whole of the fourth act is sheer tragedy, no joy at all, because the inevitable is hopelessness. I have done productions where, when you kill von Rothbart, she changes back into a princess — certain countries like happy endings. But it's not really about that because the story is a tragedy. Well, maybe it isn't a tragedy, because they're reunited in their death — you can look at it that way. But the fourth act is very melancholic — it's pure desperation — because he *could* stay alive, and she feels the torment of the terrible situation she's in. I suppose to begin with she's saying, 'But you mustn't come with me,' but he's a true hero, a true romantic.

Basically, my characterization has only grown. My idea of him is that he's a real, true romantic who would throw himself into a lake because of love. So I tackled him as a romantic without too many problems. He's waiting for love, and when he finds it, it becomes a tragedy. And because he's a romantic, he's prepared to kill himself. Growing into the role is simply cutting out the unnecessary, making stronger the things that are important to tell the audience. You suddenly find ways of disregarding unnecessary things. Simplicity is always the best. And, as I say, the more one can be in contact with the audience to tell them what's happening, the better.

For example, I always delayed my entrance in Act IV. I waited for the harp strings, and I came in on a little glissando on the harp, and then I waited again. And then I only moved when the harp strings went. You don't look-and-go; you look, and then you go. Even the searching of the swans — you can rush up and down lines of swans, but it doesn't really mean anything. Once you've gone up one line, the audience knows that she's not going to be down at the bottom of the other. So you almost disregard the second line; you get dejected before you even bother to look at it. It's like looking for my passport today: I know it's not going to be there, because I know I've lost it. The more you look, the more convinced you are that she's gone. It doesn't go one line, two lines, 'Oh my God, where is she?' because you know she's not going to be there. You might start to go through the movements, but it's only to lead yourself into a natural position before she comes. Then you hear her coming, you hear her with your eyes. And then she's there, and you've sort of engineered a way that you arrive there in the proper mood. You have to make it feasible.

There are things that you can never plan, really, and my partnership with Svetlana was one. We were fortunate that we were similar physically, similar types of dancers, and she's an extremely intelligent woman, very easy to discuss things with. So apart from the styles being in harmony, we were in harmony mentally, which is a great help. It's difficult to find that with someone. There are partnerships now, of course, and there always will be, but there seemed to be more of them when I started off. A good way of developing a partnership is just to find one, to find that you're right for each other.

Svetlana made dancing very easy; physically, it was a good feeling. We seemed to know when we were going to breathe and when we were going to hold things. She was very good at stillness because she had an exquisite line. I mean, she could afford to get in positions and hold, hold — and people would take photographs — and never look ugly. There are some people who will say, "I'm not going to stop there because I haven't got the right back," or "I must move." Then you have to adapt. But we built something up as we got to know each other — I knew her body so well. And I liked dancing with a tall girl, because the waistline is better for my height. It's a fallacy to say it's easier to work with a smaller girl because she's lighter. If she goes into a plié arabesque, on a short leg, you have to go underneath. You're working below yourself. If she's taller, she's just there for you. So that was also fortunate with Svetlana.

Certainly you change yourself with different partners; certainly that happens. But that's quite refreshing. It was lovely doing *Swan Lake* with Margot and with Natasha [Makarova], and with [Antoinette] Sibley and Deanne Bergsma. There wasn't anybody that I really hated doing it with. With some, I didn't quite like their reactions; some of them didn't have the subtleties that I rather like in it. It would be wicked for me to say names, but I don't want to anyway, and they may have felt the same way about me, I don't know. I do know I always made them feel comfortable, because most of them were sweet enough to tell me. But dancing only with one partner is like having steak and chips every night. It's good to have a different diet to stimulate you. We did one tour when I danced *Swan Lake* one night with Margot and the next with Svetlana, for six weeks or whatever. That really keeps you thinking, which is not a bad thing because you must never be cosy. You must never feel, when you're in performance, 'I've done this a hundred times before.' Each time it should be like you're doing it for the first time; it never becomes a bore that way.

You learn the hard way. When I was very young, about eighteen, I did the White pas de deux in *Les Patineurs* — it was almost one of the first things I did. Obviously, the first performance one was really concentrating, and it went well. And the next night I thought, 'I must put a little bit more into this,' and we missed something. Because I wasn't concentrating on my partner — I was selling it. Well, you absolutely don't forget that; it goes right home. I always used to approach everything like, 'This could go wrong.' You don't just stand there thinking, 'Isn't she divine? It's all going to work,' because there is going to be the time when she will suddenly step in a crack and come at you all wrong. You can't stop things going wrong, but you can make them go less wrong if you're prepared, and you can cover up. It's like driving a car. You must be ready for the idiot who's suddenly going to come down the road. I don't think anybody worth his salt should go on there thinking, 'It's all going to be terrific.' People say, "Oh, but you must be so into the part that you lose yourself." Never. Absolutely never. You have to make the audience believe that you're in the part, but if you lose your concentration it's indulgent performing, a real indulgence. You think, 'Oh, isn't this wonderful! I'm really . . . Ooops! Where is she?' You must concentrate all the time, all the time.

I used to get nervous before *Swan Lake*, but not because I thought at any point, 'Oh God, I hate that bit.' The Black Swan is always nerve-wracking, but it's much less nerve-wracking when you do the whole ballet, because by the time it arrives you've either got the audience or you haven't. Some people are very happy to go out and do the Black Swan by itself. I'm not that sort of dancer. I don't get a kick out of getting up and just doing tricks. Dancing is a real art form, not just a technical thing. Ballet is not just steps. Anybody who becomes a really great artist is the person who's been a success in the big ballets. The people who have gone down in history are the people who have done the big roles really well, and doing them well is what I call artistry.

With anything, even an abstract ballet, you don't even think about the style at first. You learn the choreography, learn the basics, get that right so it's all there. Then you find where you can do something with it. You exaggerate the style, in fact; you stretch it. Instead of just putting your arm out, you let it flow out. The choreographers will tell you if they don't like it. If you do the choreography, you can't go wrong; the performance is going to be halfway or three-quarters of the way there. Then you just find places where you think something might make it look better, like having your head back rather than down.

It's all the music. The music is the whole force. The most difficult thing for me is to dance with a girl who's unmusical. If you're both musical, you'll suddenly find yourselves instinctively using the music, even if you haven't discussed it before or thought about it. *Song of the Earth* is all there in the music. Again, he's a romantic man, and there are lots of very good still things that make him look very strong. The whole accent is staccato and you make it as staccato as possible, without fidgeting around. You might learn it and go sliding along, all lyrical and soft, but then when you get more with the music, you make it more sharp and rough. The music makes you feel it like that — or it makes me anyway. It's absolutely from the music.

It's funny you should mention *Ballet Imperial*, because after the original production, we did a new production of it. Balanchine didn't want it in the old costumes and sets; he said, "I want them in body tights." Well, they were shitty brown and everybody moaned, everybody carried on. And one boy asked me, "How is it that you still manage to make that look elegant?" And I said, "I'll tell you how. I get the make-up on, I put the costume on, and I go dance on the stage. I don't see what I'm wearing. I don't go, 'Oh, this shitty brown thing!' When I come on, I *feel* that I've got the old costume on." If you believe in what you're doing, it doesn't matter *what* you're wearing; you can still make the audience believe you're elegant. I have no patience with people who say, "I'm not going to wear that costume.

I don't like that." That is an excuse. Nothing will cover up what your dancing is or your interpretation. I've worn some horrible costumes, but if you let that influence you, you won't do the performance.

I also don't agree with people saying, "I don't like her classes. I hope she's not going to stay very long." You can still work; you can still do your tendus and your pliés, whoever's giving them. You just have to readjust mentally a bit, but there's no reason why you can't get as much out of it as you would with some teacher you adore.

I never thought about Siegfried in terms of being satisfied with my interpretation. Each performance is a new challenge. Sometimes at the end of a performance I would say, "Oh, that was nice. I enjoyed that," simply because it went well. But you don't enjoy it at the time. You can't afford to — you can't indulge. You see, when you do a big ballet like that, every performance one wants to do better. I never got complacent. There was always a bit of fear, and it's not the sort of thing that you can get lost in. There are too many pitfalls. You can't go on and just toss it off; you have to treat it with respect. *Romeo's* much easier and so is *Giselle*. In *Giselle*, the dancing is more submerged in the acting, whereas in *Swan Lake* it's like separate numbers. That's the dangerous part, and that's why you've got to make it all join up. In *Giselle* and *Romeo*, it joins up on its own much more.

It's been fun having the *Giselle*s and the *Swan Lake*s and the *Romeo*s and the *Song of the Earth*s. It's the great thing about being with the Royal Ballet — it's not *just* a classical company. I know people think of it in those terms, but there have always been other things as well, and that's what keeps one alive and not getting stale, the switching. I never found I had a problem with that. And I always think it's strange when dancers go on about 'I haven't done a classical ballet for so long. I've been doing *Voluntaries*.' My dear, they do class every day. That's your classical dancing. So there should be no question of having to adjust. It's a sort of excuse, again, preparing you for how they might not be good in something or for forgiving them for their performance. In my capacity as a ballet master, I've said to a girl, "You may have to do the pas de trois at the end of the week," and she's said, "Oh my God, I haven't done it for three months. I don't think I'll have the stamina." Well, I hadn't danced for two years, and at three days' notice I did three *Swan Lake*s with Natasha at Covent Garden. But I'd done class every day. I had retired, but she wouldn't dance with anybody else, and they said, "Will you do it?" and I said, "Fine."

May 1979
Baltimore

Bruce Marks

Bruce Marks (b. New York, 1937) began his career as a modern dancer. He made his professional debut at fifteen in Pearl Lang's Ironic Rite *(later* Rites*) and majored in modern dance at both the High School of Performing Arts and Juilliard. He studied ballet at the Metropolitan Opera Ballet School and the School of American Ballet. After spending only two years in the corps of the Metropolitan Opera Ballet, he was promoted to principal in 1958. As a principal with American Ballet Theatre (1961–1971), he assumed such disparate roles and identities as Jean in* Miss Julie, *the Peruvian in* Gaîté Parisienne, *the Moor in José Limón's* The Moor's Pavane, *the cavaliers in* Theme and Variations *and* Etudes, *and Siegfried in* Swan Lake. *He danced Siegfried for the first time in 1965, while appearing as a guest artist with the London Festival Ballet. Together with Toni Lander, his frequent partner and his wife since 1966, he resigned from American Ballet Theatre in 1971 to join the Royal Danish Ballet, where he was the first American to dance as a principal (1971–76). Since 1978, he has been artistic director and principal choreographer of Ballet West in Salt Lake City, Utah.*

It's become a cliché: "I've felt as if I'd known him all my life." But that's exactly how I felt watching Bruce Marks dance, as if I'd gone to school with him for years and home to meet his family and out to the movies on Saturday nights. Even at his most regal, to me he was a mensch *first and a prince afterward. But everyone could see that he peopled his dancing with flesh and blood men, and infused it with the kind of genuine emotion that many people spend their real lives trying to deny. Most dancers refine their art until it looks natural; Marks seemed to refine his nature until it became art.*

I don't know that I ever thought about switching from modern to ballet. I didn't sit down and say, 'Am I going to be a principal ballet dancer?' It never occurred to me to think about it — I was much more existential than you would think. I loved going to the ballet. I went to the New York City Ballet, and I'd been to the old Met and seen the first performance of *Giselle* that Erik Bruhn ever did, with Alicia Markova. But at Brandeis University, where there was only modern dance, I was still speaking as if I were a confirmed modern dancer and commuting to New York to dance with Pearl Lang. Then, when I decided to go to Juilliard, I began training with Mattlyn Gavers and Margaret Craske. Of course one was a modern dance major in Graham technique, but the discipline and wonderful training of [Alfredo] Corvino, Craske, and Gavers got me interested in ballet. And when Tudor arrived in 1955, he took one look at me and said, "You're going to be a ballet dancer." Well, I told him definitely I wasn't, but it was the start of our friendship. And you never work with Tudor, if he is interested in you, without a very deep involvement. He taught me what to eat and drink, changed my tastes, my life. Tudor changed everybody's lives.

He added something to Juilliard called production class. I'm not sure *what* it was. It was group therapy or . . . an encounter group really, before anyone ever heard of an encounter group. We did things like awareness exercises, sitting in a kind of lotus position and opening umbrellas inside our bodies — no one was doing this sort of thing. He'd say, "All right, now the umbrella," and he'd place the imaginary umbrella so the point was up near your neck, and then make you open the umbrella and change the shape of your body as you felt it open. And he made me battle; he made us all come out as if we were coming onstage in battle. Production class was so embarrassing, and so were the things that Tudor was saying.

But you have to remember that male technique at that point was very different from female technique, and he was also teaching that difference. For instance, for a man to lift his leg higher than hip level in extension just wasn't done. A man's leg was to be kept at a forty-five degree angle. And men were not to stretch. There was always a mystique about losing your jump if you stretched too much. Tudor didn't like the modern dance bow because it looked like you were stretching — you know, when you drop your whole upper body with your hands touching the floor. He said, "Why that bow? How does that relate to the audience?" A year later, I went back to dance with Pearl — because even after I got into the Metropolitan Opera, I danced with Pearl — and I stepped onstage after *Appassionada* and stood as I'd done at the Met, one hand up, looking around the theatre and bowing just from the neck and the upper body. Pearl nearly died. I heard her screaming, "Where does he think he is? At the Met?! Disgusting! What was that bow? What does that mean, with his arm up like that?"

There were ballet evenings at the Met Opera during the five years I was there — well, there was *one* — and I did other ballet things outside the Opera. The first time I stepped on the stage in a classical role was in Zachary Solov's *Soirée*, and I'll never forget it. For the first entrance, you had to turn around and stand point tendu back in fourth position. I turned around and turned out *so* much — and I had to wait quite a while — that I thought, 'I'm going to tip over.'

And then we went and did a benefit concert with Eugene Ormandy and the Philadelphia Orchestra, and Tudor taught me Black Swan. Yes, Tudor. He knows all those ballets. He's been working for two years on *Sleeping Beauty* at ABT. It hasn't helped — the Garland dance is still dreadful, and they keep saying, 'Is it the left arm or the right arm?' — but he's been working. He taught me just the steps, because the only drama, when it's done as a pas de deux, is where she takes her hand away from you and you reach for it and kiss nothing. So I had the steps and the enthusiasms and the jump to do it, and I was spoiled out of my mind by having that orchestra play. The orchestra was onstage, on platforms behind a scrim. I didn't know how much space you were supposed to have for Black Swan, so it didn't bother me at all. We set the tempos with Ormandy, and when the coda music started . . . I tell you, if Rudolf had that orchestra now, he could jump again. It was electrifying, and I had so much fun.

And of course Lucia [Chase] came to see it. I guess she wasn't wildly impressed, but she did offer me a corps de ballet contract — and I said I wouldn't accept it. I was pretty feisty in those days; I had never been in a ballet company. Nowadays, with the technical level they have there, if I were offered a contract at all I'd accept it, but then I said no. I would be a soloist or nothing. So she had me come in and dance for Fernand Nault, who was ballet master then, but I did not do Black Swan. Ted Kivitt and Eleanor [D'Antuono] and I auditioned at the same time, and we learned *Theme* [*and Variations*] and maybe some of *Billy* [*the Kid*], I'm not sure. After the audition they had a little talk, and Lucia said yes, they would hire me as a soloist. And within a week she had made me a principal; I had never appeared with the company before I was made a principal.

Well, Toni chose me for *Etudes* — which I've never let her forget. We had never met, but she had seen me in class and Lucia had told her that this guy from the Metropolitan Opera was coming and maybe he could do *Etudes*. So Toni walked up to me at the barre and said, "Are you Bruce Marks?" I said "Yes." And she said, "Oh. Then I don't need to see you dance." I knew she was staging some sort of ballet, and I thought, 'Then I'm not going to be in it.' And she turned to me not only to be in it, but to learn both parts and do them, and there was never any question that I would partner her.

There was almost no choice. Scott [Douglas] wasn't there at the time, and Erik [Bruhn] wasn't there, and Igor [Youskevitch] had retired, so it left Royes [Fernandez]. It left Royes and Royes to do both parts. What Lucia did not know was that all the New York dance critics — *Dance Observer* was going then, and Walter [Terry] and John Martin — had seen me for ten years as a modern dancer, and here I was in the American première of *Etudes*. I was scared. Had I known more, I would have been more scared, but I was pretty scared opening night, and I had reason to be. I had been condemned at the Metropolitan Opera for doing this one ballet evening. I did *Les Diamants*, partnering Lupe Serrano, and a piece of John Butler's called *In the Beginning*, an Adam and Eve thing with Bambi Linn, and for the classical thing I got dreadful reviews. And Herbie [Ross] did a piece to the Poulenc organ concerto which was about Christ in long red underwear and an angel — that was Scott — and Nora [Kaye] goes to bed with the angel . . . The Catholic Church was ready to ban it. The whole evening got dreadful reviews, but I took them very personally, and those were almost my only ballet reviews when I opened in *Etudes*.

I had also done a waltz in *Gypsy Baron* with Violette [Verdy], and danced in *La Gioconda* with Edith Jerell; those got better reviews. But still, Walter had decided I was not a ballet dancer. He had a friend at the Met at that time, Tommy Andrew, whom he was kind of pushing. And he wanted Tommy to dance these roles, so my reviews were worse. When we finally did the full-length *Swan Lake* at Ballet Theatre in '67, Walter said to me the next day, "I have to take it all back. You've done it. You have become a prince. I'm going to write a full-page article about it next Sunday." And of course that Thursday the *Tribune* went out of business!

You see, until then, my performance in *Theme* and *Etudes* was questionable. From the start I had been told — and it was said in print about things like Alias in *Billy the Kid* — that I brought modern background to the modern repertory and could do it like nobody else. But it was only with *Swan Lake* that the eight years of work *and* the background that I had before were brought together.

Don't forget, my first *Swan Lake* was not done at Ballet Theatre. It was done at London's Festival Ballet, which *I* almost forget, the summer of '65, during the time I was with Ballet Theatre. John Gilpin had been a guest at our first State Theater season. We had danced in *Etudes* together, and I guess he had seen some of my other work, and he said, "Why don't you come to Festival Ballet? It would be exciting." And I said, "Oh, I'd love to do that." I had never guested as a ballet dancer, so it was really prestigious. And what they happened to be doing was a full-length *Swan Lake*, which Gilpin taught me. The reason I was so excited about going was that they had a second act by Bourmeister, and I had heard from Toni all about what he had done. He had taken out all the pantomime; it was all done in dance terms and, in a sense, almost modern in approach. So I thought, 'This is going to be wonderful, a Bourmeister *Swan Lake*.' But when I got there, it turned out that Bourmeister could not come, and a man named Vaslav Orlikowsky came instead.

That summer was terrible for me. I hated it. I didn't want to be on the stage, and yet I was going to force myself to get through it. But I felt like an also-ran; I really felt very inferior about the whole thing. There was Gilpin dancing with [Galina] Samsova, a Russian-trained woman. There was Lucette Aldous, who did it with John too, and Irina Borowska and Karl Musil from Vienna Staatsoper. These were people who were ballet-trained from when they were children and were accepted ballet stars. And then there was me, American-trained and not very princely, and the British-trained Carmen Mathe. We did a matinée here and two performances there, and I felt like I was eighteenth cast, like I shouldn't be doing it at all. The reviews were kind, but there was very little interest in what we were doing.

That was my first *Swan Lake*. It was to be history later when I came back with Ballet Theatre and opened Covent Garden season and took home all the reviews. The headline in the *Times* was "Noble Prince: An American *Swan Lake*." It was astounding to me . . . I still don't believe it. I really had that feeling of, 'The underdog has done it.' Done it! Turned the tables on them; proved it could be done. It was the first time a modern dancer had ever done this. Glen [Tetley] made the transition from modern into ballet — one of the few of us who did — but he never made the transition from modern to classical. He did one or two *Theme*'s, but he never stayed on to do the big classical repertoire.

One thing helped me enormously at Festival Ballet: everyone wore wigs. I wore a wig for the first time in that *Swan Lake*, and after that I *always* wore a wig for *Swan Lake*. My curly hair was not fashionable at that time, and when it's straight, I look very different, so the wig helped a lot. And when the company folded and they couldn't finish paying me, I said, "I would like to take my wig," and I took off. It's funny how a physical thing like that could help me get into *Swan Lake* in New York, and I think it's part of the reason I was accepted: I did not look like myself — I looked like Siegfried. It somehow gave me a more romantic look, and it allowed me to feel like someone else.

Those are the things you get to hold onto, like the magical Noguchi bones that Martha Graham puts in her hair which transform her into another person. Perhaps it's part of a theatre ritual, like the Kabuki dancers putting on their make-up and becoming someone else. In a sense, when I went to the Royal Danish Ballet, Henning Kronstam was my ideal because you could never recognize him. You never knew who he was. Is that Henning Kronstam? That handsome man, that old man, that woman, that toreador with the big teeth? They're all Henning Kronstam. Is he not the ideal dance-theatre performer? That's always what I hoped would happen for me. It never did as much, because I never had the same support in terms of a theatre make-up department or the time he had to look different in all those roles. Here, everyone looks the same in every role.

I've always believed that the only good dancing — all dancing really — is character dancing. Even an abstract ballet is character dancing. The way I've gotten through all the abstract, highly technical ballets is through the infusion of a character. It gives me something to hang onto. I've always felt terribly insecure about classical ballet, and there are many people who have hated my work in it. 'You dance like a frog,' they've said. Very nice. But I can understand that, given my background and given the fact that I do not have the perfect instrument — or did not have. So I had to give something else, and the something else was a very concentrated and very dramatic approach. I don't mean dramatic in terms of making everything into a drama, but in terms of going out and doing something other than the technique. That's why I felt marvelous about *Miss Julie*. I used to make jokes in Ballet Theatre: any time anyone had to be raped or killed, that was a role for me. *Pillar of Fire, Sargasso, Miss Julie* . . . any time they needed someone who could be angry or nasty onstage, that was my role. And also, after four years in Ballet Theatre, I got reviews saying I was as good as Eglevsky and Youskevitch in *Helen of Troy*, and that I had great comic sense. These were really fine reviews for something with more classical dancing. And because of the comedy in it, *Helen* was something I could latch onto and feel free with.

Obviously, all this is about the Prince and the forbidding thing about the Prince for me. David [Blair] made it happen. That's funny, because a lot of people didn't like David, didn't like his approach. He was aggressive, he had his feet on the ground, and he didn't play a ballet-ballet prince. His approach was personal, dramatic and non-posing. I had always admired him on the stage because I felt him so direct and strong, and I felt his communication with the audience. When I saw *La Fille Mal Gardée* for the first time, I thought he was a knockout, a real charmer. I had great faith in him. He was the right person for me.

In 1966, a year before we got to do the whole thing, we did just the second act. Working on that with David was helpful, but I never liked doing Act II alone, and I never danced it — or Black Swan or any pas de deux — as well as when I did them in the full-length. It has to do with relaxation and allowing my plié to work, getting a very soft finish. Having done first and second act and the little princess dance, then getting into Black Swan I'd be right on top of my legs. With only one act, I was never able to get warmed-up enough to get the kind of plié I got in class. But I got it when I danced a lot, and I understand why Nureyev danced so many ballets. It's easier; those legs just relate to the floorwork, they go up easily, and they will do anything, always soft, always beautiful.

And that's why Black Swan worked so well in the full ballet. That's when I started flying. That's why I could do grandes pirouettes in the coda, just stay there and float around, which happened opening night at Covent Garden. It was the thrill of all time. In those days, people weren't doing four or five grandes pirouettes ... and I did two, then one half-tempo staying on that point around, stopped dead, and then pulled in. It got that gasp that happens to you once in a while — it was that kind of evening.

So that's one reason Siegfried started to work for me when we did the full-length. And here's another thing. We rehearsed in the Japanese Gardens on 96th Street above a movie theatre, inside the theatre but on the roof. Now, when I rehearse in front of a mirror, I think I don't hold on to that image and what it feels like. So when the mirror's taken away, I don't dance as well because I can't see the line — perhaps it isn't in my body. Having rehearsed *Swan Lake* but never seen it, in a dark place where there were no mirrors, the transition to the stage was effortless and not frightening in any way. So luck was with me.

The other lucky thing, of course, was David, who never played the Prince by putting his nose in the air. Some princes dilate their nostrils and look as if they smell something bad, but obviously I didn't feel like that kind of prince because of my background and the roles I'd been given. I wasn't going to be the aloof kind of prince, but the kind of prince who was essentially dramatic and involved. My problem with birds or with my mother was not an aloof problem; it was a problem of passion and rebellion and involvement. I couldn't do the cool, languid, pale prince, and if David had reacted to Siegfried as some effete, distant young man, the role wouldn't have worked for me. But David and I agreed on him — we were naturals together from the beginning.

I've seen men pull up and stick their noses in the air to do Siegfried — it's never interesting to me. I want to see *people* on the stage; I want to feel things. When I go to the theatre, unless there's some point where I have a tingle or something happens in my stomach, I've wasted my evening. I need to gasp once during an evening. Usually it isn't about a jump; it's usually about a concept, the way of doing something. Not how high or how many, but the way it's done. I love those things, and that's what I wanted to do. I wanted to have people say, 'We felt something,' instead of saying, 'It's decorative' or 'He turns a lot' or 'It's nice to see a traditional ballet again' or 'I like *Swan Lake*. It's a pretty fairy tale.' I didn't want it to be a fairy tale. I wanted it to be a drama in the sense that anyone could relate to it.

I hadn't seen any performances that really impressed me. Of course I had watched the Festival version from the front at the New Victoria, but I was already involved. I had seen the second act with New York City Ballet and Ballet Theatre, and the full-length when Fadeyechev and Plisetskaya did it for the first time here. But I was never impressed because I didn't like that kind of acting. If my Siegfried ever related to anybody, it had to be because I related him to a twentieth-century person. I didn't princify him: I humanized him, so that someone could feel something about him. In that sense, I would hope that if it were seen in twenty years, it would look terribly dated. Isn't that a funny thing to say? It *should* look dated. That's why I'm not sure I like films of ballets, because a performance should relate to people of its time. If I moved anyone, it would be because they could relate what I was doing to themselves, to a mid-twentieth-century idea of what a prince was like.

Have you ever seen any of the John Barrymore films? Or Valentino? Everyone was melting all over the place. They would faint. That obviously related, was realistic, in terms of that period, and now it seems wildly dated. There are some performances that transcend time, but I wonder if they really worked when they were done. I guess they did — we're talking now about a Garbo. In most of her performances, like *Anna Christie*, the moments work, but no way could the whole thing work. The only thing that works over time is comedy. *Ninotchka* still works, exactly. And the Bette Davis role that works all the way through is *All About Eve* and not *Jezebel* which is so stylized and dated.

David worked hours with me on how to walk, just in the second act, getting in, looking for the swans. And he gave me the relief of not having to walk toe-heel, point tendu. I could come out and stand with my legs apart; I could walk on my heels and look. And we spent a lot of time on thought, the process of thought, partial reaction, and reaction, so the body was broken up and looked more natural than doing 'You. Me. Love,' the great model look of the too-pulled-up dancer. He got me down into the ground, and through conviction we made a Prince who walked on his heels and stood firm, a Prince who was a person. I was still pulled up, my chest was still lifted, I still had a sense of myself, but it wasn't a tiptoe-ing Prince. For the run in, in the fourth act, I'd start twenty feet offstage, get up steam, and *run*. You see, I think you can do anything on the stage — you can walk toe-heel, you can be lightweight — and if you believe it, it works. Rudolf walks around a lot toe-heel, and stands in fifth position, and it's accepted from him as the way he looks. I couldn't do that. It wouldn't look right on me.

My feeling about the role was that I was the central character and that Odette-Odile were part of my life and my fantasy. Isn't that funny? I felt like number nineteen in line in Festival Ballet, and here I felt it was my ballet. Which is probably why I got that review in London saying Noble Prince in American *Swan Lake* — because that's what I believed. The ballet was about me, or David had convinced me that that's what it was about. And it is! It's not about Odette-Odile.

I made the Prince as much like myself as possible. I used the conflict that I've always had with my parents, the rebellion that I had as a teenager which I feel is natural when you're cutting the umbilical cord. I remember crying because they made fun of the art I was looking at then, Picasso. One *has* to say that one's parents are stupid, that they don't know, they're not up to date. I'm going to get it from my children: 'What are you talking about? That's such old crap, so conservative.' I thought my performance would have to relate to that. As a Prince I would have to use a kind of reverence for Lucia as my mother but also become irreverent, make fun a little with Benno, look and be a little sly. When Lucia used to say to me in mime, 'You drink. Why?' I couldn't say, 'No,' couldn't lie outright. So I would say, 'I drink . . . ?' and then shrug my shoulders. Do I drink? Do I not drink? Are you sure I drink? or Why are we discussing this? My friend Priscilla Stevens said I always looked so Jewish there, because I would spread my hands as if to say, '*Nu?*' After that it was a smallish shrug, but I still couldn't do it without looking Jewish.

I will tell you a marvelous anecdote about my first performance of *Swan Lake* with Ballet Theatre. Nadia Nerina and Royes danced the opening night, in Chicago, and Toni and I the second night. Obviously, the ballet was to be terribly important to the company

— that's why David brought in Nadia — and it had to go really well. Considering it was my first full-length *Swan Lake*, I wasn't that nervous. It was one of the few times I had gotten a stage rehearsal for anything in Ballet Theatre — it's still like that. I talked to Marianna [Tcherkassky] about *Giselle* last night, and she said, "Oh no, we didn't have a rehearsal." "When was the last time you did it with John Meehan?" "Months and months ago" — so for Ballet Theatre I was in pretty good shape. By Royal Danish Ballet standards, I was unrehearsed, because you always had two stage rehearsals and one orchestra dress rehearsal for every new thing. If you're new in a role, the stage is right there, the stagehands are there, and you just go down and do it. Anyway. Lucia did the first one with Nadia, and David had worked very hard with her on it. Then, the second night, Lucia and I got to 'You drink. Why?' and then she says, 'Wait.' And she's supposed to say, with the mime gestures, 'From over there, are coming here, 1, 2, 3, 4, 5, 6 beautiful princesses, and you must marry.' We got to that point, she said, 'Wait,' and her face went blank. She looked at me. She did none of the pantomime. So I said, 'Just a minute. Do you mean that, from over there, are coming here, 1, 2, 3, 4, 5, 6 beautiful princesses, and I must marry??' And she stood there and nodded her head, yes, that's what I mean.

Then the Prince is being commanded, and he says, 'I marry? No. I will not do it.' He's obviously a very sensible young man — we'll talk about his *mishegas* with birds later. Since you can't show what's in your mind, which is 'What's it going to be like to be married? I'm not in love with anyone, and I don't particularly want to get married just to get married,' he simply says, 'I do not love.' If you were among the serfs, arranged marriages might have been common, but he's someone with an education, a literate person who had read the Greeks and Romans. So he's emphatic, because this situation has nothing to do with personal liberty. He's also used to power and to saying what he wants. So there has to be anger. I'm in touch with my anger. I can't always let it out, but I can use it on the stage because I know I have a lot. I get very angry, and it usually takes an outburst . . . I can't be angry in small quantities. With my own company, either I'm having a love affair with them or I'm slamming the door, saying, "I can't work with you. That's it. If you want to do that, I'm leaving!" and then coming back to apologize. I'm very offhand to the Queen when she leaves, but I'm involved with what's been told to me. An edict has been given, and he's incensed by it. He's reached his majority, and his life, his individuality, his manliness, are being controlled by a woman — don't forget, there's no father. And marriage is not one of his considerations at the time — it's too soon — but for his mother, it has to happen the day he hits his birthday, otherwise they're going to lose control around there.

The Waltz is done as a peasant dance in David's version, and the Polonaise is done by the nobles. In the middle of the Waltz, they say to him, 'Won't you dance?' And he stands up and does temps lié en arabesque, waltz, chassé, double saut de basque, chassé back, assemblé, goes up to the corner, does a cabriole step coming down, cabriole center, pirouette, stop. Then they dance around him, and he does a *manège* of temps lié arabesque, pas de bourrée, coupé jeté. But there's no solo. That music where Rudolf sometimes does a languorous Hamlet-type solo wasn't there then. And not considering myself to have great line, I never wanted to move that slowly. I was a much better dancer later on than when we did *Swan Lake*, but it touched on all the things I could do well. I could turn well, I could jump well, I could move quickly, and I could portray a drama.

And so, given that last quality, the mime was really no problem. You have to remember that at the same time that I started dancing in the High School of Performing Arts, I started studying acting. I was asked to leave the dance department and join the drama department — I guess at the end of my first year — and I said no. David believed so much in the mime and in the idea of thought, idea, bigger idea, and action. And Toni helped me with it too, because mime at the Royal Theatre in Copenhagen is taught exactly that way. You never do something unless you tell or show the audience that you had a thought about it. And the way to have a thought about it is to let something happen so they know you're thinking, and that something is a movement. You could easily stand still and say, 'You, me, love,' instead of looking back at her when she speaks and then moving. For most people, pantomime is totally unnatural, and you get this robot look. David and Toni both spent a great deal of time with me making it all real, working on individual details until it became natural. I hadn't seen it. I didn't grow up with it the way Toni did.

The only point in the first act that I became committed to something was at the end, after Benno comes running down. You sense in the change of light a magic time of evening when things begin to happen for you. I don't know what seeing the swans means or why it should become exciting. There are just magic moments in natural phenomena that happen like that. It has to do with the feeling, that I only understand more now, that happens to me when I'm in New Mexico. I'm driving along and I sense in the landscape and the air a kind of magic, a Castaneda kind of power, that you get in the Southwest but that you can't get anywhere else in America. You feel wonderful about being there even though death lurks in all those places — Snowbird, where the avalanches can come down, or rock climbing, or in the mountains where you can freeze from exposure — but it's not like the desert. And in New Mexico, as you look across hundreds of miles and see just empty desert and then a mesa and a red sky with blue on top of it — and you can really see Georgia O'Keeffe paintings — you sense that there's something very strange at the pueblos in Santo Domingo and Taos. You sense that something's going to happen. I've got goose-bumps talking about it. And in a way that's what happened at the end of Act I, even though I didn't know then what it was.

Many people find the crossbow to be the symbol of power. It sounds very Freudian: he's been given his power by his mother. Dr. Freud says arms, weapons, are that kind of symbol. I never got excited about the crossbow. I thank her for the gift, but I don't feel that's the exciting part. The exciting part is when the fantasy takes hold. I've always tried to make that run off, at the end of Act I, as exciting as possible. It's the high point of the act for me, the moment of release and freedom. You want to feel that the run off is going to hold the audience through the intermission.

I don't think he runs off to look for the Swan Queen. He has a premonition, and I don't think it's a feeling he's had before. Why else would he not keep everyone with him in the hunt? He doesn't. When Benno says, 'Over there are swans for you to shoot,' the Prince says, almost on reflex action, 'No. I here will shoot alone. Go.' Friendly, always friendly, never commanding. I see him as a very benevolent prince and not, certainly, as despotic or haughty or snobbish or arrogant. But there is some instinctive sense in him that's saying, 'This has never happened before. Everyone must leave. I must be alone.' He doesn't say, 'I think I'm going to see some strange transformations or some mystical thing.' I don't think he knows anything about that. And you don't see Prince Charles doing impulsive things. Everything's rather thought out; one is a representative. It's simply that for the first time Siegfried's felt some kind of predestination in his life, this kind of mystical, magical awakening.

The magical place and the mystical things were things I could relate to without a doubt, and I had no problem with the idea of a mythical creature. I don't know why; it certainly isn't part of my background. But most of my life is based on the premise that the truly real things happen in your head. The most important things to me have always been the things I fantasize, and even when I make them real — materially real, like ballets — I tend to find them less real than when they were in my head, and less absorbing. *Sanctus* took me four years to make, and now that it's made, it isn't part of me anymore.

216

It is itself. The process was the exciting part of it. But the process has always been the exciting part, in seeing if I could do what I set out to do. What I tried to do as a performer was make my real fantasies visible to other people. Since Odette and Odile exist in my imagination, they are very, very real things. They're ideals.

Maybe Act II is simply saying that a human being that you're fascinated by and with is a creature, has magical properties. Or maybe it's about love being a magical or mystical experience since it's not measurable in any way. Why could that not come through a fairy tale? When you love someone, you're transformed by the giving of your love. I had grown up on that in the movies, like *The Enchanted Cottage*, where this couple who live in a cottage were terribly scarred but to each other they were beautiful.

It doesn't matter if Odette's a bird or a woman. That's something for the audience to be thinking about; it's not something for me to be thinking about. I feel desire, and I tried to show real lust in the second act, which is not the usual approach. The cello solo in the pas de deux, and the sway, to me had to be the most sexual moments in the act. It was important for me to close my eyes and hold her. And the way you touched wasn't rapid — it had to be an embrace. It couldn't be simply the wrapping of these ballerina arms around you and a polite sway-sway-développé.

I believe what she tells me because I'm in the fifteenth century or whenever it took place. It's like a woman explaining the story of her life, saying to you, 'I used to be married to a terrible man who did these things to me.' Well, certainly you don't sit there and think, 'I wonder if I really believe her.' This is a time of enchantment; the story — in the twentieth century — is the story of her divorce. Here's this desirable, beautiful, strange, exotic creature — nowadays, maybe a film star — who's saying, 'Here's what my life is like. My life is a nightmare because I'm locked into a situation with a man who uses me.' I never questioned it.

His feeling grows. He comes on searching for what he knew he was searching for, that love, and by the end of the act he's totally committed to her. When that one creature comes in, you step back and gasp. 'This is it.' And you go up to her, you unfold her, and you look. It's a first look, a first feeling that you offer. You take hands, and finally, when you get to the cello solo, you have your first opportunity, without her pushing your hands away, of holding her. During sway-sway-développé, there's a little push, maybe a little residual, but almost none.

I'm onstage for her solo. David and I talked about that a great deal, and the way we motivated it was that she was dancing for him:

'Here I am for you.' It ends with him catching her in arabesque before she runs off. Later, people began saying, 'I don't want to be touched. It's my solo. Let me do the arabesque and run off, and you follow me.' We talked about a lot of things like that with David. One of the things we agreed was that we would not bow to the audience then, after the pas de deux, but only to each other so as not to break the feeling.

I take my lead from her with Rothbart. In a sense, Odette controls the second act just as Siegfried controls the first act. Here it's like a woman with another love, another man in her life. What she's saying is, 'I know best how to handle him.' She's already told me the formula: 'If one loves me, and will vow faithfulness and swear that love, I a swan no more will be.' And he says immediately, 'I you love. I swear.' The swearing is definitely a serious business. Oaths were much more serious then, because one believed that if one broke an oath, bad things really *were* going to happen. It wasn't just in name only, you know, 'People will think I'm a bad person if I break my word.' There would be retribution. But now, with von Rothbart, she's saying, 'This is the way to go about this. Here's the formula to get me out of it.'

One responds to the music too. I'm not terribly musical except in the sense that I can respond to the style, what the music means, and to the phrasing. What you hear when Rothbart appears on the rock and she breaks away from you heralds a big change. She's now coming under his power again and acting by his command. The music sets the way; it says, when Rothbart is controlling her, that the controls are on.

I never thought about seeing her as a bird; no bird images were needed or wanted. So when I finally have to break from her and she is transformed, it was simply, 'I now have to go home to my husband, go to that apartment and pretend that I'm involved in that life. So you will see me now, as we get set to part, changing my face.' I felt someone drawing back from me, assuming a role — I felt the guilt. The audience sees her as a bird, but I can only see what I feel, and I only approached her as a woman in that situation.

At the end of the act, he feels that obviously this is *not* the end and that something is going to happen. He felt that from the moment he saw the swans in the first act, and certainly he feels it all the way through to the end of the ballet, that he's now involved with powers bigger than human powers . . . as we still feel, even though we give very little credence to non-human powers these days. Predetermination has a lot to do with this fifteenth-century story, and since I feel it so much in my own life, my Siegfried had to feel it. Remember, I'd been doing second act for a long time, but I never approached the role in its totality until I did the full-length ballet. I certainly didn't go and read the legends and the fairy-tale stories and get involved in that, as many people do when they're doing a new role. I approached each situation as it arose and, in the creation of the character, did it more or less instinctively. I knew what I could be, and David helped me get away from what I should not be.

I did not, as other people have, end the act in dejection, which is an important point in terms of how the whole role worked out. I ran to the wing to follow her, followed her from the upstage to the downstage wing with my eyes after she was off, and began scanning the audience. I started from the lower box stage left and went to the top balcony stage right, ending with my face and body up as if to say, 'I still see her.' When we get to Act III, I will sit on the throne and look to exactly the same place so the audience will have that continuity.

In the third act, I spent quite a bit of time sitting on the throne and staring into space at images of the second act. I played movies in my head. Princes sometimes come on, cover their legs with their capes, and sit back sort of hand-to-brow, trying to look like Hamlet. Siegfried's not Hamlet; he's not given to that kind of musing. So I sat up, kept my energy going, and projected my thoughts into the second act, which was where I wanted to be. You see people sitting at a party and they're a hundred miles away. That's what I wanted to do instead of sitting there bored.

Tanaquil LeClercq was one of the few dancers that I ever went to see and wondered what was going on in her head. It had to do with the kind of concentration she had onstage. And I thought later, 'Somehow that relates to Siegfried. If, while this whole act is going on, I can get an audience to wonder what I'm looking at in space, if I can focus concentration so strongly on the picture screen in my mind, then they'll understand more who I am.' Then I have to be called back and play, 'What? Oh, them. Oh yes' — try to concentrate on what's actually going on and then lose myself again. If you're in love and you're that passionate — obviously it's sexual — you're ready to explode. Well, then you're not sitting there saying, 'Gee, am I bored!' He is not bored or disillusioned; he's wrapped up, and that's why I wanted him to have to be hauled back all the time to the action until the Black Swan appears.

Lucia was always wonderful and a terrible distraction. She was Lucia, and that was in a sense what performed. After a while I got used to her whispering, "The Mazurka, from Russia" — and I'd have to say, "Poland" — and "The Spaniards, from Granada." And she'd say things like, "Why so sad?" or "Here are the princesses. That one's very rich. And that one can cook, I'm sure" — as if a princess had to cook. So when she leaned over to tell me that the Neapolitans from Italy were coming — or whatever — I would try to reawaken each time, until finally the princesses came and I had to seem involved and bow. That was when I was most diffident and most automatic, in the bow. I really wanted to be left alone because now I did have a passion, I did have something I was really committed to, which I didn't in the first act.

And then the fanfare happens. He turns, and there's von Rothbart and then, there she is. And he bows and runs after her. Of course he thinks it's Odette, because he's mesmerized, bewitched, tantalized. It's like one of those Hollywood movies where you meet the same girl twenty years later, or meet a different girl and think it's the same girl, one of those switched identity things. I always wished there had been more music, or that Petipa had had time to do something right before the pas de deux itself, so Siegfried could say, 'I see who it is. I know.' Because the Black Swan music happens, there she is, and he goes, 'My goodness, I'm going to dance.' He's never said, 'This is Odette. This is the person I'm in love with, Mother.' He only says it to the Queen after the pas de deux: 'Here she is. I her love and will marry and I swear,' and then the whole place starts crumbling.

The pas de deux is the explosion. All the energy's been there waiting to happen, and the confusion and the willingness to be confused. I don't know if that point's quite clear onstage, but when you're that wrapped up and that passionate, strange things can happen. She can pull her hand away, she can be a little mean, and you can dismiss it, because you've been waiting so long to see her. You're so involved that you're willing to say, 'Oh, nothing really happened.' In the adagio itself, I tried very hard to play the confusion: 'She's fascinating, but what's going on? Maybe it's just her way.'

I never changed what David gave me to dance. Never. Now that version has been changed and changed. I disagree with allowing that to happen, because there can be an integrity to a production, and if you're going to tamper wildly, then you should do a new production. I don't mind changing something from left to right, as long as you don't change the intention of the work. Also, I needed the security of not changing it. It all worked for me; the variation was something I felt totally at home in. In David's *Sleeping Beauty*, the steps in the variation did not suit me at all. I did them, and I had a disaster in it. Everyone said I looked out of shape. I wasn't out of shape; I just wasn't the malleable kind of dancer that could do any step and make it look beautiful. I needed to be taught to do certain steps in a certain way or with a certain rhythm that worked for me. I could do good grands jetés, I could hang in the air, good pirouettes, so Black Swan worked for me. And because it did, it gave me the kind of relaxation and authority that I didn't have when I came to that *Sleeping Beauty*, and I didn't need to worry about it through the whole ballet.

The coda is a dance of joy. You look up in those jetés because 'I've found my ideal.' All Siegfried's joy springs out. Don't forget, he's never done an open, uncontrolled movement like that. You see, I approached *Swan Lake* sexually as well. I wanted to touch her, to make it as basic as possible. I did not want to partner formally: I wanted to get close, hold in, grab, form my body to her body. That's what I think helped make it real. You don't want to give a pose; you want to do it like a real person, and the audience could feel that. They can feel the shoulders forward, the body trying to make the shape of the other body, which you do when you want to make love. They understand that. I understood it — what I'm trying to analyze now and put into words is something I did instinctively. In all three acts, when we touched each other, I would try and get as close as possible, which seems natural.

During the vision in the window, he's confused again. It's another of those teasing things. She says, 'Don't look.' What's she going to do, take off some clothes? I don't know. She turns him away, and there's a freeze. Rothbart enchants the whole court. It's not that I choose not to see, but that I'm enchanted. Then everyone wakes up, defrosts, and she does bourrée — like Odette — assemblé. But after Black Swan, when I say, 'I her love and will marry, I swear,' Rothbart grabs her and they point: 'There, look!' You come around, you see that you've been tricked, and you run off to look for Odette, whom you've betrayed. It's a point of betrayal. It's like thinking I've been married to Toni and one day waking up to find that she's still waiting for me somewhere or that I've been married to an impostor. It's kind of a wild idea.

From the time I run out of the palace to the time I run on in Act IV on the drum roll, I've been running. And searching and trying to find the place that we stopped at in the wood, and there I find it. Opening up each group had to be a very immediate moment, and when you find her, you have to be so contrite and really try to explain in the pas de deux. There's something bittersweet about the pas de deux we did. She's distraught, destroyed, upset, unhappy, and yet at the same time I feel she's asking to be loved again. I wasn't wild about the choreography before the pas de deux, but no one ever is; David did as good a job as I've seen. And I actually loved the ending. I loved fighting Rothbart; I enjoyed grabbing her and being violently passionate. That was wonderful. We said the same things too often, but

I could still say them with compassion: 'I here will die,' and then 'I there will die as well' after she jumps. I loved throwing myself off the rock. It was very much bigger than life, but I liked to do that. I liked the fourth act. I liked the whole ballet. I can relate to all of it.

I'd like to lie and say I thought the Prince grew and developed, but it only did inasmuch as I was able to show more of it. I don't think I ever consciously said, 'Hey, I'm on the wrong track.' Small things would help me revitalize it. After you've watched [Raissa] Struchkova do *Nutcracker* pas de deux four times, you realize that her eyeballs look diagonally up to the corner every time she does a relevé on a sixteenth note, and you say, 'Gee, that's studied.' You feel this very often with the Russians, that they've done something a thousand times. And that's always a danger, especially with something you're successful in. I had about three roles that I could really keep alive: *Julie*, *Moor's Pavane*, and *Swan Lake*. Maybe those three were the most important to me as far as my career was concerned. *Etudes* was technical dancing. I had to make ways to make it work for me so it could work for an audience. But I brought such love to those three roles, and they meant so much to me.

I danced with all of them, Eleanor and Lupe and Toni, and Cynthia [Gregory] a lot. I felt very similar in terms of portrayal with Cynthia and Toni, though in the beginning I was not comfortable with anyone but Toni. Before our marriage, dancing it with Toni was wonderful, but later on we had terrible trouble with it. We became very competitive, or at least I did, and we had to stop rehearsing together. Rehearsing tended to be bickering and then, later, marital things and nastiness sometimes, so it became easier to dance with other people. I'd like to give you the romantic answer, that dancing with Toni inspired me, but I can only say that we did beautifully in it together when we were not rehearsing.

Certainly this was one of the few ballets that everybody left me alone about — my successful ballets people left me alone about. The other ones . . . I'm thankful they helped me, or tried to help me, with their points of view, but they were all supportive about Siegfried. Even the critics who had hated me for years in ballet-ballets were now highly supportive, including the London critics who did mention that I had done it before at the New Victoria with Festival. I remember the phrase "he has fleshed out the role." Interesting and very British, that "fleshed out." And also, in terms of what I had tried to do, "fleshing it out" seemed to be the right expression.

I couldn't use what I learned from the other classics in my Siegfried, because I was never allowed to dance *Giselle* or *La Sylphide* in Ballet Theatre. After the great success of my Siegfried in London,

I went to Lucia immediately and said I would like a crack at these other two roles. Technically, *Giselle* is really easy, and partnering I did well. We had talked about it and not talked about it, and it certainly didn't help my confidence to know that I was tucked away from certain classics. I had learned an awful lot since 1964; we were now in '70, six years later. So of course part of the reason for my leaving to go to the Royal Danish Ballet was to do *La Sylphide* and the Bournonville repertoire. As it happened, I used *Swan Lake* in *La Sylphide*. Clive Barnes happened to see my first James, and he said, 'We now understand why Bruce Marks is leaving America.' Much as people want to quibble about my being a classical dancer or a non-classical dancer, and was my background right to do this or not right, it's interesting that I got to do them and had a point of view.

Going back into the modern repertory with *Moor's Pavane* at the end of my career was then a pleasure, because I had proved what I had to prove . . . if I had to prove anything. It wasn't originally a competition between me and the critics. It was simply that I wanted to be a ballet dancer and they weren't about to allow that to happen until they could say, 'If we didn't know his background, we wouldn't know. He's doing this well.'

If I were to dance Siegfried now, or to coach it, sure there are things I'd do differently, but mostly in terms of dance and not so much in terms of interpretation. There has been an enormous change in dance, in dance style, even in the twelve years since that production was first done, and you can say whether you like that stylistic change or not. My wife doesn't tend to like it. I don't judge it that way. It is. It's the way people are working. Men's legs now go up very easily in a stretch. There was no one who could do a split on the wall, like Mischa does, when I started studying ballet — no men. None of them wanted to. The first year I danced, I remember Pierre Lacotte came from the Paris Opéra and stretched constantly. I had never *seen* a man so stretched; it was considered taboo. We made fun of French male dancers for that. They were considered effete because they were looking for a kind of line that was forbidden to us as men. And, as a man, you turned in a coupé position. To turn with your foot at knee level was like donning women's clothes. I sound like ancient history, but that's what Tudor and Craske and Corvino were teaching. A lot of that is getting lost. People are dancing more and more technically. They're so interested in making their line. A whole different emphasis is being given. That's all right. But for that reason, you would have to do a different Prince. You'd have to.

I would teach some of my performance, but the role would always be in transition. Look at the film of *The Red Shoes* and at the legs and feet of everybody dancing. My goodness, those people couldn't get a job today! Then look at a [Fernando] Bujones and a Baryshnikov. They're lighter-looking. And it's happening all over the world. I don't think anyone gets together and says, 'We are now going to get them to look like this.' But they begin tending to look alike, just the way Youskevitch and Eglevsky and [David] Lichine all had a wonderful bearing and the low arabesques. And when a dancer goes to the ballet now and looks at a Bujones, he tends to shape his body more like that because that is the current mode of dancing. It's handed on by watching other people. You tend to look like what you see.

But coaching, now, it still seems very important to me to talk about the Prince as a non-prince and about finding the person within the stereotyped figure. I still want some princely qualities, but I don't want them to transcend the humanity of it all.

But no one does *Swan Lake* like I did it, and no one is going to, and that's wonderful. It was made from whole cloth and it was made to be truly dramatic. I took chances on doing things in a way that was un-princelike, on the feeling that if it was done with conviction, people could understand it and they could relate. I wasn't playing him as a 'prince.' 'Prince' was not involved in my playing the Prince.

April 1979
New York

224

Lynn Seymour

*Lynn Seymour (b. Wainwright, Alberta, Canada, 1939) studied ballet in
Vancouver before winning the scholarship that brought her in 1954 to the
Sadler's Wells Ballet School in London. In 1957, after a year in the Covent
Garden Opera Ballet, she joined the Royal Ballet Touring Company, where
she created the dramatic leading roles in Kenneth MacMillan's* The Burrow
(1958) and The Invitation *(1960) and in Frederick Ashton's* The Two
Pigeons *(1961). As a principal of the parent company at Covent Garden,
she continued to originate roles: for MacMillan in* Romeo and Juliet *(1965)
opposite her frequent partner Christopher Gable, in* Anastasia — Act III
*created in Berlin (1967) and the balance at the Royal Ballet (1971) — and
in* Mayerling *(1978), and for Ashton in* A Month in the Country *(1976)
and* Five Brahms Waltzes in the Style of Isadora Duncan *(1976). She
also danced such dissimilar works as* Giselle, Raymonda *(Act III),* Apollo,
Dances at a Gathering, *and Cranko's* The Taming of the Shrew. *But
for extended leaves to dance with the Berlin Opera Ballet (1966–1969) and
to direct the Munich Opera Ballet (1978–1980), she remained with the Royal
Ballet until her resignation in 1981. She began to choreograph in 1975 and
made her latest work,* Intimate Letters *(1978), for the Sadler's Wells Royal
Ballet.*

---

*Lynn Seymour is widely acknowledged as the foremost dramatic ballerina of
her generation. That's what the history books will say about her — and it's
true — but it's hardly the all-out celebration her dancing warrants. Over the
years, she has short-circuited my reason so often with the immediacy of her
emotion that she has permanently altered the expectations I bring to ballet. As
Juliet, she sits on the end of the bed in Act III staring ahead into her shattered
future. Immobile, she makes me understand why all the words, film, and
photographs on earth can neither duplicate nor replace live performances.*

*T*here was no chance in Canada to be fully decided on a career. That came not long after, with the scholarship, and then I was determined. I had wanted it badly, and once I knew the chance was there to escape Canada, I really was all for it. I came in 1954, and I was two years in the School . . . If only I'd been able to come earlier and study longer. I was very behind everybody of my age. I'd done my two or three classes a week, after school, but I'd missed everything. It wasn't only feet and ankles; it was placing and equilibrium, and I knew nothing about *épaulement.* And I've got the sort of muscles that don't build up quickly. That's been the problem right up 'til now. If I'd had that training behind me, several years of it, life would have been much easier later. It's always been missing.

So I had a lot of lost time to make up for in a very short time, and Winifred Edwards, who was sort of the top teacher and had the graduate class, which I was in, taught me an awful lot. Even later, when I joined the company, she took me for private lessons when we were in London to help top up what I didn't have. She taught me to own up to one's physical disadvantages right away, to see them quite clearly, and to work quite honestly through, over, and on top of them. Recognize the problem right away, see that it's a weakness, and tackle it, not try to disguise it or cheat by working on the things that are easier.

I went into the Opera Ballet first — it was absolutely the dregs in there — but that wasn't the first time I was onstage. I'd had a few experiences in Canada with competitions and Sun-Ray Revues at the local cinema and things like that, and I also used to tap dance when I was a kid. From what I've heard, I was an absolutely natural ham. I used to be very bossy, and I always knew what I was doing; if anybody made a mistake, I would correct them. I don't remember anything about it, but that's what my mother told me. I must have been an absolute monster, with glasses and curls and a very round fat face, tapping away.

Anyway, the reason they put me in the Opera Ballet was because I did need time. It would give me experience to be onstage, but I could still do a good curriculum of classes. So really, I was getting the best of both worlds. Our ballet master was Peter Wright and he was marvelous. We were all young kids then, almost like extras if we were doing something like *Rigoletto,* and he made us frightfully interested in the period. We'd study the costumes, make our hair and make-up right, and then he'd see and criticize after. He was doing it very consciously. And then he gave lots of classes and organized little performances elsewhere. In fact, the first time Christopher and I danced together was in Gluck's *Orpheus and Eurydice.* We did an excerpt, without the opera, at the Arts Theatre in Cambridge. We were in the same class at the School, but we hadn't worked together. I was terribly studious in those days, and life wasn't meant to be like that. Christopher said he hadn't liked me much then, but I think he'd exorcised that dislike by the time we danced together.

Then I joined the touring company, which was wonderful. It was so busy, and one could improve as one went along. The first year I had just the classical repertoire to learn, which was hard enough — I was so weak I could hardly stay on pointe. The only thing that was on my side for those big roles was youth; you're sort of fearless then. I think I'd feel now that I didn't want to do them with that weak a technique, but in those days I just said, 'Well, all right. Let's have a go.' I've never believed in myself that much that I thought I could do those things, until I was presented with them, and then I had to. I was much more conscious of getting things together technically, because they didn't come naturally to me. I probably have to work harder than most people just to keep from muffing turns and all that sort of thing, and that makes you much more aware of what you're doing. Much, much, much. But if you have to do it onstage, you have to find a way to do it — you just have to. If you're lousy at doing certain things and you screw up several performances . . . well, you don't want to ruin the thing. You don't want to damage ballet by doing it badly. But, you don't make a conscious personal choice to develop along different lines just because your technique is weak. You don't suddenly decide "to act." No. Actually, I think this acting business is a whole lot of balls. I don't feel that I do act. I couldn't act as a straight actress; no talent that way at all. It's just dancing that does it; it's the dance itself. It's not "acting" in inverted commas — it's the way you dance it.

Kenneth used me for *The Burrow* that first year I was in the touring company, and I think he did know that I couldn't stand on pointe because he had seen me do the peasants in *Giselle,* sort of unable to stay up in a soutenu. You see, I got into all the corps de ballet things straightaway because I learned very quickly. It's just the way I was trained, from before the School probably. It's part of the old, hard, American school: if you know it, you're on. So he was seeing me in all those things and in rehearsals.

I was this lonely kid from Canada, I was frightfully homesick, and while I made a few friends, in all the hardships of going to school and coping with life, it was hard to. When I got in the company, Kenneth was very, very helpful to me. And then later, after *The Burrow,* I wanted to get to know him better so I more or less forcefully joined his club, which was Nico Georgiadis, Jeffrey Solomons, Kenneth

Rowell, people like that. They were all sort of like daddies to me. They took me to the theatre and to exhibitions and things, which meant my lonely weekends were filled, which was very nice. And I went to see a lot of things that were very influential. For instance, I saw Ionesco's *The Chairs* at the Royal Court. Joan Plowright was doing it, and all I can remember about it — and it's rather an odd thing — was that she was wearing these terrible bedroom slippers and I couldn't take my eyes off her feet. When I was doing *The Invitation*, I remembered that for the Young Girl: the way the feet went, the awkwardness when you're nervous. All those little things sink in. You file them, in a way, and then suddenly snap your fingers and think, 'Oh yes. That's something.' Very odd.

Donald MacLeary was in the company then, and Kenneth used him a lot too. He was my first partner and also a friend; he was really nice to me when I got in. He was a principal, and I went up to him one day and said, "Look, I've done hardly any pas de deux. Can you help me with my pirouettes and things?" and he said, "Sure." He was working terribly hard, but he did — he was absolutely fabulous. In fact, he did his first *Swan Lake* with me, in Australia. David Blair was my first partner for that, but then he had to go back to London so Donald made his debut with me. In my very first performance of *Swan Lake,* I did eight fouettés in Black Swan, and then David came in and jumped and jumped and jumped. Then the second performance, I did sixteen, and he came in for the last sixteen bars and jumped and jumped. And then the third performance was Donald. We had a stage rehearsal before, and I did maybe twelve fouettés, and he came in and jumped and jumped and jumped and then he fainted. So on the performance, I did thirty-two for the first time. I had to. He's such a sweet man. I was never able to do them in the rehearsal room. I used to just get on the stage and do them — I don't know why. It was something up here, in my head.

You have to take a pretty pure line with the classics. You can't fiddle around with them, because it gets affected and dishonest. The atmosphere has to be there, the allure, the glamour, the ease, and making the difficulties look graceful. You have to think, 'I'm going to do the best I can as honestly as I can,' and that's got to be it. Otherwise you've sort of ruined yourself before you start out. I just slogged. I could always move, I had speed, but I always had trouble staying in one place, especially on flat foot, actually. I had terrible difficulty just standing on one leg doing *adage*. On pointe it's rather easier, especially if you're moving. Then it's really all right.

At that time, I was still going through that young period. Nothing really bothered me. I was just getting on with it. I don't think I really learned a lot from any one dancer until Rudi came. I couldn't learn from the women, really, because I was so different from them all. Physically we had nothing in common. Naturally, Ulanova was amazing when the Bolshoi came, totally unaffected and completely believable. In life, I suppose one would say she's almost plain, but she became incredibly beautiful on the stage, magically beautiful, with of course this exquisite dancing. And the spectacle of it all was mind-boggling for everyone that saw it. Margot made a big impact on me too, and so did Svetlana. All of them did, but I don't think I used them for my model.

When he made *Two Pigeons* on me, Fred set a lot of things that weren't comfortable but that one had to contend with. It was very good; it sort of pushed one on. It's not an easy ballet, although it looks it. The first act's awfully hard, killing actually. Fred's very demanding and his things are always very puffy. What with extra bending and flinging and backbending and moving your head, there's no chance to relax, none at all. You can't really compare his style to Kenneth's, but they're both into doing these intricate, footsy solos for me all the time, all sort of knitting downstairs and not able to drop a stitch. But they actually work very similarly. When he was young and a dancer, Kenneth was sort of one of Fred's guinea pigs. Fred used him a lot; he used to make suggestions, and then Kenneth would say, 'Well, what about this?' and Fred would say, 'Yes, that's fine, but do it that way.' That's part of the birthright. And Kenneth works very much the same. He and the dancer just start out together from scratch.

What's nice, you see, about creating things is not, in fact, performing them. It's the working together in the rehearsal room that's really the greatest joy. When they finally get on the stage, they're suddenly something else. But those times of working on a thing are one's happiest. You're without the horror of doing it in public, and you're creating — just simply that — together. Somehow it's a terribly satisfactory process.

Then John Cranko invited me to come to Stuttgart and do his *Romeo and Juliet*. Well, he knew me from the touring company. The first year I was in there, he and Kenneth and Peter Wright and Andrée Howard each put on a ballet during the tour because in the Christmas season we were going to be at Covent Garden for the first time. So while doing eight shows a day on that tour, we also had three newly choreographed pieces and *Veneziana* to learn. We were in them all. I was in the corps de ballet in everything but *The Burrow*. Andrée Howard revived *Veneziana*, and I did a tarantella pas de quatre in sort of a melted LP wig, very black. Cranko did a piece called *The Angels,* with Desmond Heeley designs, and Peter did *Blue Rose.* They all went on at the same time.

So I went to Stuttgart and learned *Romeo* there. John had created a tremendous family atmosphere, and he was in the fabulous position of having a wonderful *intendant,* [Walter] Schäfer, who was behind him 100 percent in furthering the company. So in a sense, John had *carte blanche* there. He was freed of a lot of worries, and the company adored him. They were locked in this provincial town, they were trying to build up something from nothing, and they'd created their own world within the theatre. They were a motley group — American, French, German, English, oh, from everywhere — with one thing in mind, which was to make it all work. So of course it was exciting; we had tremendous fun. Marcia [Haydée] taught me the role, and I danced with her partner, Ray Barra. I just did one performance, but I loved it. Kenneth loved the production too, and I think he longed to do one after that in England. It got his juices going. Cranko took one rehearsal in a part that I was confused with, just at the point before Juliet decides to take the poison, back in her room. I forget what he said actually, but that was the one moment we discussed. I remember it was a very different conception from Kenneth's, so I don't think there was anything there that I used later.

Then I saw Zeffirelli's production here, with Judi Dench and John Stride. That impressed me a lot, because Zeffirelli took the non-romantic side of it. The ballet's very romantic, and he made it more tough and hard, which was a good combination. So when Kenneth started on it, I think those two things — Cranko and Zeffirelli — made me decide, 'There are so many hundreds of romantic heroines. Let's try to make her more real and not so heroic.' That seemed to me a better way. The music's all romantic and heroic anyway, so you doing it as well would be, you know, almost wanking on the stage. I thought I'd try and avoid all that if I could. And of course I'd seen the fabulous Bolshoi production too. They're all impressions that get saved away somewhere, and God knows when one draws on them. It's sort of underneath your conscious — intuitive.

Kenneth did the Balcony pas de deux first, for television in Toronto. We didn't really know then that that was the beginning of the whole thing — it wasn't in the bag — but later it did stay in the ballet. Fairly soon after, when he started on the entire thing, I knew he was going to use me to work it out, but I also knew that Margot and Rudi were going to do the first night.

We started with all the pas de deux, out of context. We just started doing steps, and I read the play. He wanted a lot of it to be very realistic, very true to life. Like, he wanted me not to keep my legs together in the crypt. He wanted it to be awful, almost revolting, not pretty. That was one thing. And the Bedroom pas de deux in the third act should be different from the Balcony pas de deux, not ecstatic.

I should think Juliet's life must have been quite a lot of fun — not as much fun as a boy's, but pretty carefree. At the ball, dressed up as a young lady for the first time, she feels rather pleased, with the dress and the whole thing, but also a bit nervous. The family greetings are very formal, but that first dance she does with Paris she's sort of sussing him out. She probably knows they're trying to make a match for her, but being the type of person she is, she doesn't want to think about it. But she has a good old look; that's the first time she's met him. I used to take it that one *was* interested in him, because in the play she talks about 'the face looks all right. Not a bad type.' She has a little monologue about it to herself. So I used to do it like that. But then this conductor [Yuri] Ahronovitch came from the Bolshoi a few years back, and he said that Prokofiev had in his score that she took an instant dislike to Paris. So I tried it that way, and it felt better. As soon as I saw Paris, right away I went, '(Gulp), not for me. Time for a cold stare and drawing back.' I thought in the context of a performance that might be better, because then when you see Romeo, you can . . . you know, fall apart. That was many years after the first performances, but little things always get changed.

When she sees Romeo, she's stopped dead. Unlike the play, where they see each other but it's not the sort of magic this is. Christopher and I used to phone each other up in the middle of the night with sudden ideas about it. About everything. But I try not to work out that moment at all until each performance happens. It's one of those places that I don't plan. I play it by ear, and everybody you do it with does it a bit differently anyway. All that's set is that you've seen this thing for the first time, and you don't know who he is. Time stops for a minute . . . and then resumes, but something's gone clunk. I think she's wondering about it all, but she doesn't change until they meet again later, during the Madrigal.

Again, Ahronovitch had something to say there. I used to do it as if I were coming back in looking for Romeo. But Prokofiev actually had in his score that she wasn't looking for him at all; she was looking for a hankie or something she'd forgotten, and then he's there. I guess you can play it either way. Now I play it as if I wasn't looking for him but for something else, and there he is. Then she gets more and more excited as the music goes on, until finally, when it starts into the big melody, she's completely lost. You're really committed to him by the end of the Madrigal, before you know who he is. One of the things Christopher and I found together was the kiss of the hands, where the hands meet, which is in the play. But they don't actually kiss until the end of the Balcony pas de deux. Of course there's physical attraction, but not only that; they talk a lot.

Finding out who Romeo is was something I worked out for myself. When Tybalt comes in, when the Madrigal's finished, the Nurse comes to me and I ask her, 'Why are they all so angry?' She says, 'Well, it's him,' and I go, 'Ohhhhh, I see.' Juliet's very aware of the feud, and I would think she takes it pretty seriously. It is *the* problem. But it probably isn't a serious factor until Tybalt's dead. That's when the tragedy starts. The marriage might have been all right had Tybalt not been killed. It would have been the way of making peace, and everybody would have approved. But the trouble really starts with those stupid deaths, Mercutio and Tybalt. It might have been O.K. otherwise.

Romeo's solo at the ball is a lot of fun, full of derring-do and flirtation. And Juliet's terribly pleased, squirming with delight, both because of him and because of his audacity to do that solo, to flirt like that. She has her own little solo after that, and they get together again at the end of it — she likes that too. I don't think it's really a deception of her family. It's the sort of thing a young person would do if they're interested in someone.

When you leave the ball . . . well, you never know what will happen, do you? You just hope you might meet around another corner one day. That's how it always is, isn't it? The Balcony scene isn't arranged by them. She thinks she's alone for her whole soliloquy, but he overhears it. He's left his mates and gone back to see if he can just catch another glimpse of her. And she's overcome with mortification when she finds out that he's heard every word of her outpourings, but her desire overcomes her mortification. That's expressed before the big, waltzy thing starts, in their meeting. He gets her to come down the stairs, and she presses his hand to her heart: 'hear it beating.' She dares to do that and then decides to flee. 'Don't go, don't go,' he says, and after that it's just all out. The whole thing's giddy — just general *extase* really. And she only goes because she has to go, before they're discovered, before anything happens.

At the start of Act II, she's getting all her notes ready and writing a hundred letters. Her letter to him just says, 'Meet me. Meet me at Friar Laurence's place. We can get married there.' That's all. She's pretty sure that he'll be there, but a little worried that he may not. I think she probably wants a good legal fuck.

Anyway, she marries him, and then Tybalt's killed. Of course she knows about it. He's carried back into the house, and her mother's tearing her hair and heart and breast and weeping and wailing. And Romeo has to go — that's where the trouble starts. I'm sure the banishment intensified her feeling for him. It's very sad, you see, their parting. It's very weighty, that. She knows he has to go, and she's not sure if she'll ever see him again.

Then she has to face her family. That's hard. She hasn't become a different person — I don't think people change that much — but she's no longer carefree. And she wants something she can't have, which has probably happened before but not as serious as this. And she's on her own, as it were, for the first time. I think she hoped for *some* understanding. The mother must have had the same thing happen, a pre-planned marriage at thirteen or whatever it was. Had Juliet married Paris, her life would have been very much like her mother's, and even now the mother can't have been that old. And Nurse isn't helping; she betrays Juliet by insisting that she go to Paris. Nobody's helping. The important thing is that she's completely alone. Completely. All she can do is look for help, and Friar Laurence is the only hope.

Kenneth was afraid to have me just sitting there on the bed. He wasn't sure it would work. But I said, "Let's try the sit and see if it works," and he seemed to think it did. What am I thinking there? Nothing. Nothing as Juliet and nothing as me. If you're in a predicament like that, it's very hard to think. She's in a terrible tension at the time. Something's got to happen. It's just like squeezing yourself together until suddenly you snap your fingers, you find the only thing to do.

She's a bit frightened of the potion. First she refuses it, but there's no other way out. It's the only way. It's a risk, but the only way to do it. Then she goes back to her room and dances with Paris and accepts him. I think that's the first time she really practices deception — then — when she says yes to him. She knows jolly well she won't marry him. Her accepting him makes it even more important that she has no way out. But then, she's just a stronger version of what she was before. I daresay she might have become that person anyway, but not the same. She's heading for a tragedy, yes, but I do think she must have been pretty headstrong in any case. I'm sure she feels the decisions are necessary; without them, everything would be intolerable. And if she brings the tragedy on herself, she does it unwittingly.

The Tomb scene does have to be ugly, in the sense of not dying traditionally in fifth position. I thought it was much more important and more honest to be ugly and dead there than pretty, and I don't think she's ever meant to be a stunner. The stabbing is, again, something I've changed. The music goes on, so you can't just die immediately. I used to contemplate stabbing and then make it hasty, and a huge surprise when she'd done it. But I've changed it; it seemed to work better just to plunge the knife in, right away, without thinking, and then there is that shock: 'Oh my God! This hurts much more than I thought it would.' Yes, she's pretty impetuous throughout, but she's sympathetic too — anyone in love is. And that's what it's all about: love, a very strong love.

My Juliet's changed quite a lot, as with everything one does over the years. It makes me cringe at the moment to think that one has to sort of hop around pretending to be young, but you have to think that way — there it is. I know everyone always talks about not being able to dance Juliet fully until one's 'mature.' I suppose there's some truth in it, but I'm not really convinced. Given the technique, I don't see any reason why a fourteen-year-old couldn't dance it, none at all. I think you just get simpler and simpler. The danger with all those romantic tragedies is becoming too over-sentimental. You've got to beware. So as you come back to a role, you cut down and cut down, just because the other little bits seem extraneous or false and not important.

It's always good to come back to something having left it for a bit and done something else. When you create a lot of things, what tends to happen is that you find you're making everything the same. So when you go back to an old role, you think, 'Oh, I was just doing that bit. Can't do that again. Somehow it's got to be different.' There is also a process that goes on about defining a character, but I prefer not to think about it. I know it's churning around in there, but if you actually express it, then it's already gone. It's better to leave it all lying and waiting.

You know, everything Juliet does is separate from everybody else, really. Except in the ballroom, she's not involved much in group scenes; it's all private scenes. So your performance also changes if you change your partner. It's better that it does. I like dancing with a partner by far the best. You add up to more than two people when you're dancing together. When you're by yourself, you're just one. But when you're two, you can elevate somehow. Still, I try not to plan things too much because it gets a bit sticky and false — sort of laid on top — and not honest.

I've been so lucky with my partners, all of them. With Donald and Christopher, Desmond [Kelly], Rudi, Anthony [Dowell], David [Wall] — you can't have better. Christopher and I based ourselves on the music a lot, and we were able to take death-defying risks, each knowing almost intuitively what the other was going to do. I felt fearless with him, but I think it's more temperament than anything. It makes a great deal of difference if you like your partner because it's hard work, and if it's a fight, then it's really rather hopeless. You've got to be working together. But I'm rather easygoing that way because I tend on the whole to like everybody.

Partnering's a technique from the girl which you learn largely from experience. The boy has to have the technique too, but you can do endless things to help. One helps in the Tomb scene in *Romeo*, for instance, but it's still hard for the boy. For some boys, partnering's a natural thing. Donald could always do it, and he's got great big hands — those things become important. Especially doing the new ballets, I've learned how to cling like a leech, so that even if the boy let go I'd still be up there, holding onto something.

In rehearsal you play it by ear, and then something different usually comes out with another partner. When David and I did *Taming of the Shrew* together, he'd been working with Merle [Park], who's much lighter than I, and I'd been working with Wayne [Eagling], who, although he's very strong, isn't as strong as David. There's a simple thing, a little throw into the air from a lying position, which David and I had never actually rehearsed. I'd found a way of helping Wayne with it, but Merle hadn't had to help David because he could just do it alone. So when we came to that bit in the performance, I pushed and David pushed and I went waaaaay up, right behind him, and landed crash, flat on my back. And he lost me; he couldn't find me. He was looking all over, and I was looking the wrong way myself because I should have landed in front. Well, the whole audience stood up and gasped. It was awful. I was pretty shaky when I got up. He said, "Are you all right?" and I said, "I think so, but I'll get even with you later." I couldn't move my whole body the next day. It was horrible.

But there can be nice surprises, too. That happens quite often. For instance, when I was doing Rudi's *Romeo and Juliet*, I learned it awfully quickly and didn't really rehearse it with them. He wanted her to be a rather different type of person from Kenneth's Juliet — much more tomboyish, playing jokes — and I didn't realize it in the first few performances. When the penny dropped, I suddenly started putting those qualities in, and Rudi was quite astounded. He's taught me a lot, about dancing and about solving technical problems. He's another incredibly honest worker, so he just backed up or reinforced all that I thought anyway, plus encouraged and guided, all the time that we've worked together.

I did three *Beauty*s with him a couple of years ago, the first I ever did at the Opera House actually. I went back to it — it was seven years since I'd done it — and I was very pleased with how they went. But they didn't go down. Everyone said, 'It doesn't really suit her.' I thought I'd come a long way since the last one, so for myself it was a personal best. Maybe not in terms of the world, but I was quite chuffed with how I'd dealt with it. I'd gotten stronger and I had my head in a better place, with Rudi's help.

I danced them with him, which helped very much. He was very keen for it to work. So much so that on my first performance he was watching Act I from the wings, and in between the Rose Adagio and that horrendous solo he was so nervous and caught up that he walked on the stage and into the next wing to get a better view. Just like that! I didn't know, but the two girls who were standing there did a real double take: 'Did you see what I just saw?!' They came and told me later. And he was very pleased. We had three in a row, so by the third one I had started to get somewhere with it. I would have liked to keep doing it, but there was no chance — another six months was going to go by. Well, Trefilova came back at about age forty-six to do it for Diaghilev, and she'd been doing barre on her bedstead or somewhere to stay in practice. So keeping in mind that she came back and jumped into that, I suppose there's still hope.

I think *Giselle* and *La Sylphide* suit me more than the other classics, because they're all jumping rather than staying poised on pointe and I'm better at moving. But we haven't had *Giselle* in the rep here for a long time. I did do a couple of *Swan Lake*s, but they didn't go down very well either although I was quite pleased with them.

I don't think one should approach those ballets as one would *Romeo and Juliet*, because they're a different kind of dancing. The classics aren't expressive dancing. You might say a role like Juliet is inspirational and free, but the classics are very formal, more like the classroom but with a little extra on top. The mime scenes are very formal too. It's what you put into them that makes them come alive. They're a technique in themselves, and you have to do it correctly within the context of the ballet. It's a stylized thing the whole way through.

Music is the key to everything, what you do and how you do it. I think a musical dancer is simply someone who takes his dynamics from the music; if the intent of the score is one thing, they change accordingly. I hope I do that. It's very important. And the conductor is very important as well — vital. I prefer to follow him, especially if you've got a sensitive conductor. If you've been rehearsing to one tempo and it's very much different on the stage, your muscle memory is put out of sorts a bit. Sometimes it's impossible to contend with, and sometimes it's quite okay and you just get on with it. But the music is the only rope you've got.

I am quite musical, but I think it was my tap dancing that helped me with that. It's mostly intuitive. I can't read a score though I've tried to learn. I did take music classes when I came here because I was determined to get it together, but I've got this awful thing about my voice, and my teacher made me sing instead of doing it on the piano. These little squeaks used to come out — I was so uptight — and then the tears would start, and I thought, 'I can't go on. This is too much. I just can't persevere.' The next thing that probably helped was that I was one of the first people to learn dance notation, Benesh system, at the School, and in order to notate you have to know your rhythm and your score. They've still got simple notation that I did for them, the Red Pawns in *Checkmate*, I think, and all the Hours from the third act of *Coppélia*.

I learned *Las Hermanas* from notation in Berlin, and it worked fine. When I did get into trouble sometimes, it was because I was trying to do it too pedantically. The notation tells you exactly how it should be done instead of just saying 'a whiz of spins' or something like that, and I was breaking it all down too far. But I tend to do that in any case, be too analytical because of my own difficulties.

What happens when you haven't got a character? Again, the music is the thing, and the intent of the choreographer. Somewhere in the abstract ballets there's always something to hold onto. *Laborintus* was all alienation and searching, that sort of stuff, and each little piece in *Dances* has a theme to it that Jerry [Robbins] wanted, at least all the bits I did.

The only ballets I could never really get my teeth into were those Massine ballets. I don't know why. It was all terribly like puppets. I did *Good-Humored Ladies*, which he taught us, and recently I learned *Boutique Fantasque*. It was odd. They always evaded me somehow, so I didn't do them very well.

Also, it's no fun to do comedy. It's so tenuous, you see. You have to be on your mettle terribly; you can't relax. You've got to be all ready for the situation; otherwise, it'll drop like a lead brick. It's the situation that's funny, not the person, so if you try to be funny it just backfires. You have to be completely earnest about what you're doing, the reaction's got to be real. Like when the lady comes in with the same hat in *Concert* and you go off all dejected, you've got to be so *dégonflé* about the whole thing. But *really* so. You can't just schlep off.

The way things happened, there were a lot of new things done all at once when I came back from Berlin, and one just did them. It's just luck. I suppose they're all different sides of one. I don't think you ever completely separate yourself from a character. That would be real acting, but I don't think that happens. Fred must have chosen me for *Month* for a reason. Of course, he had the idea originally many years before, and I think he had Svetlana in mind for it then, maybe for her Russianness. But by the time it came to fruition, she wasn't dancing anymore, so it fell to me. Fred did it awfully quickly. But then, there was the trouble of executing it, because it's all very difficult, swift and precise. There was a lot of struggle going on for me, but finally it got better. Unlike Juliet's problem, this one is completely social. It was an older woman too; she's about my age in real life, probably a bit younger actually, but in those days if you were over thirty, you were over the hill. That was part of the tragedy, that her juices were still flowing but there was no way out of the spider's web.

All the situations are things that could have happened to one. With Anastasia, the problem is much more contemporary: loss of identity. Just imagine you walked into the place you go to work every day, and all the people you've worked with for ten years suddenly didn't know you, or they said you weren't who you were. That's Anastasia's problem.

That's one reason I so loved Tudor's *Romeo and Juliet*: it just made such sense. I loved that she saw Tybalt's death, because I think she loved Tybalt and I'm sure they had a bit of fun at home. And she knew Tybalt much better than she knew Romeo, so his death must have been the beginning of the horrors. And I loved the scene where she's getting dressed to be married — it's that hopeless, ghastly, inevitable feeling. She can't do anything about it, and she has to. Tudor's just got her like a dummy at that moment, which shows her total helplessness beautifully. She's not a romantic heroine; it's all more stylized.

He just taught me the steps and talked a bit about it. And he changed a few little things too, because Fernando [Bujones] had never done it before either. It was quite good, actually, that we were both new to it, because we could find our own way. It just emerged. I think it helps to know the story well and realize the moments, and then find new ones — there were lots of new little ones. It's a hard ballet to do because he wants something very simple and unaffected, but I thought that was lovely. Oh, he went into all the background, but I just understood, so that wasn't a hassle.

But later, with *Pillar*, he abandoned me at one point. I was in class and I missed a rehearsal; I didn't even know it was scheduled. And he was furious with me because I still didn't know the ballet. He was busy on details and I still didn't have the whole thing together in my mind, and time was getting short. Anyway, this horrible afternoon came and he said to me, "I don't think you can do it. You're not going to get the interrelationship. I don't see anything happening." He dropped that like a ton weight at my feet. So we went through the whole rehearsal and I was fuming. I went back to my friends all, 'Mutter, mutter, mutter. Interrelationship, interrelationship. *I'll* show him interrelationship,' but for the rest of the rehearsals, he wasn't there. He did come to the performance, and he came back after, very pleased, and said, "You are a naughty girl. I've heard this about you, but I didn't believe it possible until I saw it." I was equally stand-offish and said, "Well, you should have trusted me a little more." I didn't get a chance to do it again, but he said he liked it and we finished good friends.

What you're wearing can make a big difference, and the costumes helped in the Tudor, particularly in *Romeo*. But in that case, we hadn't rehearsed in all that stuff and the steps are jolly hard without anything on, so it did affect one a bit. It's hard on you and the partner too. But I'm not egoistic enough to peruse myself and decide if a costume's right or wrong for a character. As long as it's comfortable and it's what everybody thinks is right, I'll just wear it and get on with it. You can't see yourself; you don't know what you look like. Something might feel fabulous but it might not look any good. You have to depend on another eye to guide you if you're on the wrong track. Margot's got a wonderful eye for the way things look. She's got eyes you can trust, absolutely.

I always listen to whatever Margot and Rudi have to say. She was very good with helping me with *Beauty*, and she just helps with courage. The teachers are all very helpful as well, really: Brian Shaw, Gerd Larsen, Michael [Somes]. They're always coming up with something good. But the best measure is probably oneself . . . and a trusted eye that knows what you've been working on at that particular time. The critics don't make any difference. I don't read them. I'd just rather not, in case it's hard. And on the whole, awful as it is, I don't think one takes an awful lot of notice of the audience's response. The only time you notice it is when there isn't enough applause — like in the classics — to recover for the next thing. Then, as you pant, you think, 'Oh God, I wish there was a bit more.' But from an egoistic point of view, I don't think you notice it. You're too tired. I don't go in there actively thinking that I'm dancing for the public, which is sort of horrible. It wouldn't be the same without the public, but somehow it's a much more private affair.

I never had thought I could choreograph anything myself. It was Glen Tetley who encouraged me to start. It's a difficult process, but I'm still innocent enough at it and childlike enough and beginning enough, like I was when I first started dancing, to adore it. I don't really have any fear; I'm just doing it. If I ever get minimally proficient, I'll probably start to be frightened, but at the moment I'm still like a child making mudpies. It's just delight.

Choreographing, you do learn about yourself as a dancer, just from working with other people. You find out how receptive people are. The last ballet I did, *Intimate Letters*, I had the great good fortune to work with Galina Samsova and Desmond Kelly. You couldn't get two more fabulous people to work with; they just did things naturally without even having to discuss them. They added the right dimension intuitively to something that was just the nucleus of an idea, and one wouldn't have to say any more. There it was. Then, when you're in the same opposite position, as a dancer yourself again with a choreographer, you learn to have less and less inhibition, just to go into it. It becomes clearer and clearer that you must do that.

I guess I taught Juliet to everybody that did it at the beginning — Margot, Annette [Page], Antoinette [Sibley], and Merle — because I was the only one that knew it. I couldn't coach them, because they'd all have their own ideas about what to do. I've never been asked to coach it. It might be interesting, but . . . I guess one could make a few suggestions, but what one's going to make of it is a very personal thing, and I don't think it would be fair to fit one's ideas on somebody else. One would prefer to figure it out alone rather than be dicated to. The reason it's such a nice role is because it has so many possibilities. It lends itself to all sorts of interpretations and still succeeds. Everyone's going to look different in it. It's timing, it's phrasing, it's what you decide to make with the steps. But, as they say, they're the words.

October 1979
London

Antoinette Sibley

Antoinette Sibley (b. Bromley, England, 1939) entered the Royal Ballet School in 1949 after spending five years studying ballet, tap, and musical comedy dancing at the Arts Educational School. She graduated into the corps of the Royal Ballet in 1956, advanced to soloist by 1959 — when she danced her first Swan Lake *at Covent Garden on twelve hours' notice — and was promoted to principal in 1960. Her repertory embraced great story ballets:* Swan Lake, Giselle, Sleeping Beauty, Romeo and Juliet, Cinderella, Nutcracker; *great abstract ballets:* La Bayadère *(Act IV)*, Symphonic Variations, Ballet Imperial, Dances at a Gathering; *and everything in between from Fokine's exotic* Firebird *to Tudor's haunting* Lilac Garden. *Perhaps the most notable of her twelve created roles were Titania in Sir Frederick Ashton's* The Dream *(1964), and the title part in Kenneth MacMillan's* Manon *(1974). The former ballet marked the beginning of her extraordinary partnership with Anthony Dowell, which continued until her retirement in 1979. Sibley's first marriage, to Michael Somes, ended in divorce; she married again in 1974 and has two small children.*

I loved Antoinette Sibley's dancing — as the Quakers say, "It spoke to my condition" — so it didn't really matter to me what she talked about. But since she turned formal elegance and refined breeding into personal trademarks, it seemed only fitting to ask her about one of the touchstones of the classical repertory. Sibley was trained for the classics, aimed at the classics, blessed with the body to dance them exquisitely and the temperament to increase their effect exponentially. Raised to her highest power in Swan Lake, *she was classicism embodied, so serenely at her ease that she made artifice appear artless, and thus natural, and eventually inevitable. Few dancers ever probe both the subtle emotional nuances and the heroic physical structure of the monumental classics. At the Royal Ballet, Margot Fonteyn did, and Svetlana Beriosova, and then Sibley. With a certain impatience, I wonder who will be next, and when. Such dancing is addictive.*

I obviously was ready for a career in the theatre — that was my milieu — but I don't think that I meant at all to go into the ballet. I'm quite sensible, basically, and I realized it was very hard work, too much concentration, and it was exhausting me all the time. It simply wasn't fun, whereas acting was. I was much more fascinated by the acting; it wasn't physically exhausting, and it was making up characters and thinking things out rather than making your body do very difficult steps. Tap dancing was also great fun. I loved all that, and I did everything: tap dancing, character dancing — "national," we called it then — Greek dancing, musical comedy, acrobatics. So ballet was merely one tiny little subject, much the hardest of all of them, and not at all the thing that I chose. But my teachers informed my parents that I was good at it, and I came to Sadler's Wells. I had been away at boarding school since the age of three because of the war, and this meant I could get back to London and be nearer my parents. So for me, it was merely a way of getting nearer them rather than anything to do with taking it up seriously.

I remember as we arrived at the School for the audition, I couldn't go in the door. My mother said, "But here's the door," and I went, "No, I can't possibly go in," and walked right the way past. So she walked me back, and I went right past the gate again. I really didn't want to go in — I was so nervous and ill at ease with the whole thing — but eventually I did. And then my interest became mathematical in a way. I was very good at maths; I loved solving things I couldn't do, and trying to make my body do the steps was really a mathematical sort of exercise. It was only when I got to be about fourteen that I realized it *was* acting. I could actually act through these steps that I'd now made my body do. An arabesque wasn't necessarily an arabesque. It could be a hundred different languages; it could be 'I love you' or 'I'm sad' or 'I'm exhilarated.' *Then* I loved it. I'd always adored music, and I realized I could do my acting through the whole body, not just the voice, so it seemed to me I was getting the best of all worlds.

Winifred Edwards was really the backbone of my youth, in that she was a ballerina to the fingertips. She was a pupil of Pavlova, very petite, very graceful, and she had the stick and the gray hair done in the bun style — it was exactly how old ballet teachers had always been. I admired her and respected her tremendously, but I didn't fit into that picture. I never did understand the picture of somebody like Margot who always looked absolutely immaculate and so beautifully turned out, never a hair out of place. All this was something I loved in other people but couldn't see myself being. I didn't feel like that.

So I was slightly at odds because I didn't have something to follow that I understood.

Then, when I was, again, about fourteen, we had Pamela May, one of the ballerinas in the Royal Ballet, as a teacher. And here was a woman — the long red fingernails, the cigarette in its holder, the very high-heeled shoes. Not a ballerina, not a pretty thing that happens on the stage, but a real, blood and flesh woman. And suddenly I had something to latch onto. This was more like me. I thought, 'My goodness, if she could be a ballerina, like this, then I can understand it more.' So she, in a way, began the forming of my personality as a dancer.

I mustn't get it wrong. I don't mean that seeing Margot didn't appeal to me, because I was absolutely bowled over by her, but I couldn't in any way connect it with myself or my ideals or how I felt. I thought she was magnificent, but it wasn't anything to do with me. There was no way I could be like that, so it didn't help me advance. I adored it on her, but it was something that I could never even approach; it wouldn't fit me and I didn't want it. I watched Markova, of an earlier generation, with tremendous admiration and respect, but she didn't help me either. Here again was a lithograph person, an immaculate person, rather as if she hadn't ever washed up. That is most people's ideal, but I wasn't that kind of a person. From an artist's point of view, Beriosova, although very other-worldly, was one of my great idols when I was young. She was much nearer me in age, she wasn't so ... the top, like a statue on a pedestal, wasn't quite so groomed. I could latch on a bit with Svetlana.

But it was really in 1956 when I saw Ulanova — I had only just come in the company — that I could suddenly see that I did have something to say. She was an absolute eye-opener. Up 'til then, I knew I was good, and I knew people expected a lot. I didn't think I was so good at all, other than that I obviously could do the steps and I looked quite presentable. But I couldn't see where I was going to fit in, because I certainly hadn't got the dark hair and the looks and that kind of personality. Then we were performing at Croydon, and the whole company came back after the performance to see the Bolshoi's final dress rehearsal of *Romeo and Juliet*. They didn't start it 'til midnight because they'd had the usual trouble with sets and musicians and God knows what. We came in, exhausted, and we all packed into the back of the stalls circle at Covent Garden while Struchkova was dancing with [Alexander] Lapauri. Then it all stopped, and this little gray-haired person all covered in woolies came up onstage from the stalls and started pointing to things. We thought, 'Oh, she's obviously the ballet mistress.' That wonderful Yuri Faier, the conductor — you know, the blind man — said something in Russian, obviously about starting again, and this little old woman with the gray hair went up to the balcony onstage and took off the woolies and was sixteen years old. Just like that in front of us. No make-up, no costume. It was a miracle in front of our very eyes, and that was Ulanova. She started with the Balcony pas de deux, and when she did the run offstage, before the Poison scene, everybody cheered her. We were hysterical; we'd never seen anything like it. We were all, by then, so excited that we just yelled and screamed.

I could then see the whole thing. Here was a prima ballerina, not a glamorous woman — which Pamela had been in my eyes — not some ideal, or something in a picture book or looked at through the other end of a telescope, but a real person who didn't seem artificial to me in any way. She was not acting for acting's sake or being over-dramatic, but just natural. Her Giselle wasn't like a lithograph. It was a real person, who had suffered. And she was fair; I'd never seen a fair ballerina. All the others had always been very dark. Here I could see somebody in a mold that I could, maybe, put myself into eventually. I could see her in context with myself.

It was a wonderful generation of dance. One thinks of the French Impressionists, all that glut of talent at the same time, with its rivalry and inspiration and comradeship and a pushing towards a goal. I had that to a tremendous extent at the School. I had Marcia Haydée coming in from abroad in my class, Lynn Seymour from Canada — the talent was just amazing. I was very lucky to have all this around me when I came to a responsive age.

I think the best part of my training was the footwork. It sounds a funny thing, but the English dancers were very strong on pointe work. The Russians at that time had a wonderful jump and wonderful backs, but their footwork was very weak and they were on half-pointe an awful lot. People always remarked on my feet. Not that I had a huge instep like Pavlova or Lynn, but tremendously strong feet, and feet that would speak. I could talk a bit through them. You see, we did pointe work with no pointe shoes, just in slippers. And when I was doing pointe work, my parents lived at Brighton, and I would run along the pebblestone beach always with no shoes on, so my feet were strong. After Tudor had seen *The Dream* for the first time, he said, "Your feet are just like Spessivtseva's. They talk." He went on and on about my feet, and I was so amazed and a bit perturbed at first. I thought, 'Gosh, this is *The Dream*. There's so much you can say about it, and he talks about my feet.' But of course when I see the choreography, as I do now, it's very much the jumping on pointe and

the quick footwork. Fred has always made me do a lot of that —
Dorabella in *Enigma Variations* is all talking with the feet as well —
and Tudor picked it up right off.

Now, *Swan Lake* was the first ballet in which I ever went onstage
in my life. The day after Margot got the DBE, a lovely occasion to
do your first performance, I was the second swan on. And then, of
course, I did the corps many times, but I never thought, 'I would like
to do that ballet.' It is a bit odd, but I didn't. I never thought that
about ballet at all. I never saw myself in any role until I physically
started to do it myself. But I suppose I must have thought I would
do those things; otherwise why was I doing all this work? I did know
that I didn't like being in the corps de ballet. I love being the pivot
of the story or being with the person making the story, and I don't
like to be in the background. I would never have stayed if I was only
going to be in the corps, because it was hard work without the rewards
and that didn't interest me. I must have envisioned doing my own
ballets, I don't know, my own roles. I certainly didn't see myself doing
what I saw other people doing, because I thought they were marvelous
in those roles.

A big example is *Daphnis and Chloë*. It was Margot's absolute
gem of a role, and I didn't know what to do when I found myself
down to do it. How could I do it? She was perfect to me, so I didn't
see another way, a different route. When I said this to Fred, he said,
"How silly. Have you ever read the original?" I said, "No." And he
said, "Well, you go and read the original *Daphnis and Chloë*, and you'll
find that she was fair, she was a very sensual being, and quite, quite
the opposite to the way Margot does it." So I went and read the book,
and then, of course, immediately . . .

You see, always through the written word. The same with *Romeo
and Juliet* — I had the written word in front of me, so of course I
could see my way to do it. I wasn't seeing somebody else; I was seeing,
in my own imagination, my person. For me, reading was an imperative
— I'm an avid reader — and if it wasn't the reading, it'd be the music.
Those were my two ways. Never ever from seeing did I want to do
anything, because seeing somebody else, I was always captivated by
their performance. Once I had done a role, then there was no turning
me back. Then I couldn't see that they were right; then, I could only
see my way, and my way seemed right to me. This is why I used to
find it so difficult taking over roles from people. It was very easy when
they were done on me. That was fine, and I was fortunate having so
many. But I couldn't actually see myself in things until I started rehearsing them.

Before the *Swan Lake*, I had done *Ballet Imperial*. It was a magnificent thing, and a very great favorite of mine. It was, I think, the only Balanchine in our company at that time; very much *épaulement* and difficult angles, but we were used to that. But it's an extraordinarily difficult ballet, mainly because the ballerina is asked to do tremendously difficult cadenzas on her very first entrance. She comes in cold to it, half of it's the speed of light, and then you move so slowly and then quickly. It's very hard to adjust to the different tempi and to do them all right on that first entrance. In fact, you have to make your mark, like the Rose Adagio. That's it — you seal it then, and the whole performance takes off from that or not. It was my first really big role and a big success for me, and the more ballets I did, the more I liked that one still. It was such a hard ballet, it could have defeated one very much at that age, but once I could do that, I could cope with anything. *Swan Lake* became much easier — everything did.

Well, *Imperial* was such a success that de Valois said to me that she'd like me to learn *Swan Lake* and I had two weeks to learn it. And I thought, 'Well, how can you possibly learn *Swan Lake* in two weeks? It's nonsense.' But then I thought, 'You can't let this drop. Maybe it won't come along again for many years.' And she did sweeten the blow slightly by saying, "As you've only got two weeks, I have asked Michael Somes if he will partner you to get you through it." So I thought, 'I suppose I'd better try and do it in that time,' so I set off to do it.

Unfortunately, we were on in the provinces then, every night in different ballets. I had to come in to London before the class at 10:15 to do my rehearsals of *Swan Lake*, because that's the only time we could fit it in. The whole thing was absolutely ridiculous. It was such a worry. I hated just to do 'a performance'; it wasn't a *Swan Lake* to go on and do the steps. There were certain things I knew I wanted to do and others I knew I didn't want to do. But it's such a huge undertaking at that age anyway, like climbing Mt. Everest. You hardly have time to think, let alone do your own interpretation. It was a matter of getting through it. If you'd had time to think, maybe then you'd have got into such a snit about whether you could do it or not. That's rather different from suddenly being pushed on. It's crazy to be pushed on. I wouldn't choose to do it like that if I were given the choice, but that's how it's always turned out. It seems to be my role in life for everything to come as a shock, but there you are. I was going on in two weeks for my first performance, at Golders Green, on the tour.

Well, I did my performance, and then I did another one at Streatham the next week, but with another partner. And then *Swan Lake* was completely off my list, because now we were back at Covent

Garden and there was no way I was going to do it at Covent Garden, age whatever I was, nineteen or twenty. Then a month or two later, in London, Michael Somes rang me one morning when I wasn't very well — I had flu. I was married to him subsequently, but I wasn't married to him then and I didn't know him very well other than having danced with him on this one occasion and he'd rehearsed me. And he said, "Oh, you're on tonight." I thought it was a rather odd thing to say, because of course I was on that night — I was doing the pas de trois in *Swan Lake.* So I said yes, I knew I was on, and that was the end of the conversation. I thought, 'Well, I might not be on anyway because I feel so gruesome,' and then I went back to sleep. When he rang back to say that Margot had very kindly said I could use a bit of her rehearsal time to rehearse, I didn't know what he was talking about. And then, it suddenly . . . I realized . . . He said, "Nadia's off, and you're doing Odette-Odile." I really was absolutely shattered. However, I went along and rehearsed it, and that was it; I went on and did it that night. It really was a tremendous ordeal.

Swan Lake I found very hard to get to grips with because I had a confusion: the kind of *Swan Lake* I adored was not the kind that suited me. What I loved was the very opulent, exaggerated *Swan Lake* — Plisetskaya, back arched, legs up, crazy sort of things — Svetlana's *Swan Lake,* one of marvelous positions and very unclassical in a way. Well now, I wasn't that kind of a dancer. Whereas with *Giselle* the kind I loved was the kind I could do, I was at the opposite with *Swan Lake.* Obviously, the *Swan Lake* that suited me much more was the simpler one, because I was a simple mover. I was a *big* mover for my size, I had an expansive movement, but it wasn't an exaggerated or flamboyant movement. It was tremendously pure in a way — big but pure — and very relaxed, formal. I didn't have the sway-back legs or the arms that bent backwards — I was classical-lined.

I just didn't know how to come to grips with this, so I asked Karsavina to help me with it. I was working on a book with her, early in my *Swan Lake* career. I told her my problem, and she said, "But that isn't *Swan Lake.* You can't do *Swan Lake* like that, exaggerated. *Swan Lake* is the purest of all the ballets." I was absolutely stunned by this. I said, "No, no. *Sleeping Beauty* is the purest of the ballets, but not *Swan Lake.*" And she said, "No, on the contrary. It is *Swan Lake* that is the purest." I then did it that way because, anyway, this is the way I had to dance. To watch it, I do love to see those crooked arms and the bent arabesques, but it isn't my way. And at least I had her saying she had always been taught that *Swan Lake* must be simple and pure.

She also helped me a lot with the mime scenes in Act II; she showed me how the mime should be done. She must have been one of the great dramatic ballerinas ever. As she did it, she became every character. When she talked about von Rothbart, she was von Rothbart, and when she talked about the mother's tears, you could almost see the mother. The way she did every gesture, every movement, was an eye-opener. It wasn't like saying, "You know, the English language." If you read Shakespeare, you gasp, you die. It's a flowering of it, and this was the same with her. I knew the gestures, but to see her do it was like listening to Beethoven after just learning the scales. She had bad arthritis, but the moment she started to move, you understood everything. She had the most beautiful eyes I've ever seen. Those eyes told a million stories. She looked up, and you died with her.

I did most of the rehearsals for that '63 production. That was Bobby Helpmann's and Fred's production, with the Prologue, where you see her as a princess before she is actually changed into Odette. You see Rothbart come and capture her and take her away, and then the ballet goes on. I think doing the Prologue slightly takes away from her wonderful, theatrical entrance in Act II, that jeté on that particular music. The audience have seen everybody else dance, as in the Prologue in the *Beauty* they've seen wonderful things, and now they're waiting for the ballerina. That's how I like my ballets; I'm old-fashioned about that. I like the build-up for the ballerina, and then that marvelous entrance, flying in. It was made to be like that, rather like a crown that is the final, beautiful thing of authority on a queen. I like all the trimmings.

You are a swan when you first appear, and this is why the Prince is trying to shoot you at first and capture you — he doesn't understand. It's only when he gets close to you that he realizes there's something strange about this swan: she's slightly human. Gradually you're a swan-woman, which is so confusing for him, and his confusion is why she starts to tell him the story, that her mother's tears made the lake. I think it must have been the mother that upset von Rothbart; she was somebody he wanted as a mistress, but obviously she didn't want to. So he's gotten his revenge by taking her daughter, and the mother's cried ever since — that's the lake.

It's a formal ballet, and I like the mime. I think it makes sense. Why shouldn't we know why she's a swan? It's lovely that she tells the story, and it can be so beautifully done. I don't think yet another pas de deux is valid there. In a little while, we're going to have one of the most beautiful pas de deux ever created. Why spoil it with one where you're flapping around the stage trying to escape for so long? You've already tried to escape in the beginning, before the mime. I never liked doing that version; I only liked the mime. It's not something people wouldn't understand. You get the idea. If you're watching a film in another language, you'll get the idea of it. And good heavens, it doesn't go on for very long, so you can't be that stupid not to pick up what it's about.

We had mime lessons in the School with Ursula Moreton, who was a great mime artist herself, so one was totally at home doing mime. For young people it's far harder than it is to dance, because it's mainly standing still and, with these few gestures, telling a story. But it's rather like the musicals, which you do so well in America. When we did them in England, you'd have dancing numbers, and then they'd stop and suddenly talk, and then they'd stop again and start singing — it was nonsense. But with American musicals, the singing goes into the dancing, the whole thing's one. It's the same with the mime. You don't just stand still; the gestures are all part of the dancing, but a different form than actually doing ronds de jambe.

Certainly Odette falls in love with him, in that marvelous pas de deux. You are, by then, almost a woman, but you have the mannerisms still of the swan. It's a metamorphosis, but you're never completely — or just — a woman. Now he knows the story, he knows why she's been changed into a swan, and she realizes he would do anything for her. Von Rothbart has appeared and Siegfried must also be scared of him, but he's fighting for her. So she knows his feelings, and during that pas de deux she's getting to know him and trust him and love him. There seems to be hope. She can't quite figure out how, I don't suppose, but there is hope. And when you fall in love, you don't really think of much else — it's such a wonderful feeling.

I have done it with Benno, and he never did seem to interfere, funnily enough. A person always in the court, like a princess, would be used to never being alone, and you have to be natural when your equerry or whoever is around. Not like us mortals — if somebody else came in when we were with our loved one, we would be rather perturbed. But that's very much how it was in the court circles in those days. Benno only did the first part of the pas de deux, and it worked rather well; he would just take your arm occasionally and then give you over to the Prince. He was really rather a help, because I obviously would be rather shy dancing — or talking, as it would be — to the Prince about such deep things for, gosh, absolutely the first time. I never found him an intrusion; it seemed quite natural to a princess to have somebody else around.

A lot of your characterization comes from how you look and how you dance, which is why we get back to my problem at first. I'm a classical dancer, so I have to do it through my mold. I knew I couldn't do that Plisetskaya style, so it did take me a long time to feel the bigness of a movement. I could feel it very much in something like *Sleeping Beauty* because that's purely classical, and 'the bigger, the better' is the right way of doing it. Odette's very big in warmth, and I couldn't equate that necessarily with a classical line. The line of an 'atti-arabesque' as they call it, an attitude-arabesque, and those arms coiled back, all those exaggerated things gave me much more the feeling of a swan than the line of Aurora. One was a swan, the other was a woman, and I wanted a swan-woman.

In the end, I related it more to the music, with sweeping movements done just in bigness and fullness. I have a very long neck, so I was able to use that, and I would always use my arms to quite good effect as a swan. Whereas the legs I never could; they wouldn't look right in those arched positions; they aren't made to be like that. So I had to do a half-change: in the top part I could do some of those, but in the bottom part I couldn't, so it had to be my very own way. Which was lovely because in the end, with every ballet, I got it to be my way. But this did take a long time.

You can't change the way you look. I am very small; therefore, I look very frail. I'm delicate. The kind of life I've led is sad in illness and things like that — one's gone through those tribulations. So one knows about sadness and breaks-up of marriages — all the things everybody knows about — but when one's lived through them, you put this into your dancing. You have to do everything as you are as a person. I couldn't change the way I look or think, no, or hear the music. So much is from how you hear the music. You couldn't do it in a gay fashion; there's nothing gay about *Swan Lake* in the second act.

I loved the black act. I thought it was wonderful. You're putting on the black costume and the black headdress and becoming a total woman, a woman of experience, a voluptuous seductress — that for me was very easy. I could always identify that side. It was how to interpret the side that my body didn't feel that was difficult, as I've explained. But Odile, never. I've always loved women. I'd always wanted, if I had lived hundreds of years ago, to have been a courtesan, in touch with all the power of the time. I wouldn't have minded doing that for a living — I would have adored it. You know, it's not like a prostitute now; it was a marvelous position to be in. You were literally in the seat of power, and you knew all the sides to every question. I've always loved that sort of woman. That's why when *Manon* came to be my ballet, it was a glove. It was my realization of all that.

Odile's wonderfully evil. The more she can do to hurt him, the better. And she's loving it, loves the power she has over anybody. She's enjoying it as much as von Rothbart. She's so beautiful, you see, and a man cannot resist a very beautiful woman however much he loves somebody else. I mean, she's overpowering. She wants him to get confused as well — it's part of her whole game — in case there's a minute of aberration when he thinks, 'My goodness, what am I doing?' — as he does. It's in those minutes she's got to capture him back, and it's imperative then that she foil him with bits of Odette. She must confuse him all the time, because otherwise he would just know. He can't be a fool. And if you have an intelligent-looking Prince, you've got to have an intelligent interpretation yourself.

First, she's just come on and he's absolutely overcome by her. They go off. The next time you see them, they're dancing together — it's as if they're talking together — and she's seducing him. I would say he's gone off to get her a drink or take her cloak off if she had a cloak — you know, just take her around — and now he wants to talk to her. He's desperate to talk to her, find out more about her, and she's gradually letting him know as much about her as she wants him to. Von Rothbart's instructing her, saying she's doing too much or too little, or 'For goodness' sake, get him now. We haven't got much time. Odette's on the way.' She's really having a wonderful time using her power, and when Odette appears, the more she's got to save the situation. Von Rothbart can't. It's up to her. It's all there in the choreography. It's just a matter of doing it.

I always had to grit my teeth to do the fouettés. I never found fouettés easy. I always remember Margot saying to me, "You just go on, and you know when you go on you're going to do thirty-two fouettés. You can't allow yourself to think. You just go on to count thirty-two. That's all. You go on to get through them." In fact, in other ballets, like *Patineurs*, I could do quite extraordinary fouettés, with double turns and all sorts of things put in. So halfway through my career I thought, 'Maybe, if I started putting those in Act III . . . Maybe it's the monotony I'm finding so hard.' So after sixteen, I used to start doing doubles every now and then, and that I enjoyed because it was fun. I would get bored the other way, and I might start thinking I was falling apart, so it was better for me to do something harder.

Then, for the last five or six years that I did *Swan Lake*, I never did the fouettés at all. My knee was starting to play up — it would give way on me. So from then on, I did a big circle of very difficult pirouettes 'round the stage, and I found that was much more exhausting because you were having to move at such a speed rather than stay on one spot. When I would just do the black act, I would do the fouettés, but never in a whole performance because my knee wouldn't have allowed me to.

We had no leeway at all. We all did exactly the same in our own way. Nobody does an attitude or a pirouette the same, but the steps were identical. We had no choice. Whether that's a good thing or a bad thing is a different question. I do think one should have slight leeway. For the opening step in the solo, the first attitude pirouette, I always did a double instead of a single. The step's the same; I merely did a double because I found it harder to do the single and come out of it. But other than that, I didn't change any steps.

The fourth act was my favorite. I always loved that best. You change which is your favorite act and which you're doing better all the time, from one act to another, depending on what you're going through in your own life and how you're developing as a person. I found Act IV so moving. The hope gone, everything . . . the usual in life, everything just hit on the head, total disaster. Right at the bottom, literally, of the lake. Everything is falling apart around you. You see his plight, you know your plight, and yet there is that total binding love. Odette sees the whole thing in the vision. She then goes back to all the swans and tells them, because — apart from just her — she was going to save her whole kingdom with this love of the Prince. She's their queen. She's in charge of all these swans. They are her people. She was not only out for herself. They're all lost as well, and she has to tell them this. He has deceived her. He's deceived them all. It's absolutely shattering.

I did two marvelous versions of that last act. One was Freddie Ashton's with that marvelous pas de deux of hopelessness and desperation and very deep love. The other one was Johnny Cranko's; I did his version, with the most wonderfully moving pas de deux, in Munich. The Prince gets killed in the end, drowned, trying to be after her. You're alone and he's drowned. It's total disaster. I don't like the normal version that's done. To me, it's nonsense — the whole thing's awful. I hate all that Drigo; Fred's and Johnny Cranko's versions use different music, and it's far more expressive when it's all done with different music. All these other fourth acts use appalling music. They're not dramatic in any way, with the swans all piddling around. These two fourth acts are most beautifully explicit and dramatic — for all the swans as well — and have beautiful music.

Act IV is just Act II with the tragedy. She's a sad creature anyway, with all she's gone through: living as a swan, knowing that your mother's gone through hell, that all these people are also swans, and that you'll probably be like that for the rest of your life. You're already doomed. There's no way that you're a young, innocent, happy creature. You find hope and love, which makes you blossom, but then you lose all that too. No, you're obviously a sad creature. Whereas Juliet, for instance, wasn't. She was perfectly happy, because she had nothing to be sad about. Life and the circumstances she lived just gradually snowballed on her, but she wasn't doomed as we see Odette is from the start.

I'd done Swan Queens long before I did Fred's new pas de quatre in Act I, for the celebration of the Prince's birthday. Merle and I created that. But in *Sleeping Beauty*, I did practically all the fairies and most of the numbers in the third act before I ever did Aurora. That's a wonderful background. You feel very at home in the ballet then. I was so used to being in the wings for the Prologue that for me later to do Aurora was just part and parcel of the same thing. It wasn't a terrible ordeal. One was so used to being there, being part of it, hearing that music.

The music, what the music spoke to me about, was always a great key to any interpretation. I would only be happy if they were my own interpretations, I wanted my way, and if I couldn't see a written word about it — as with *Daphnis and Chloë* and *Romeo and Juliet* — then it was literally the music that would be my guide. I knew everybody heard the music differently, and this would be the way I would hear it. I'd listen to it until I knew it off by heart. I was trained with piano, but I really couldn't cope with the scales, so unfortunately I gave it up.

And it matters tremendously that you like the music. That's what sparks me off; that's the start of the whole thing. If I don't like the music . . . For instance, I was doing a ballet with Rudolf that was being choreographed by Rudi van Dantzig for our company, a very modern ballet called *The Ropes of Time*. I absolutely adore Rudi van Dantzig and I love his work, and I was so looking forward to doing this ballet. But it was modern music and, really, it drove me mad. It was like people throwing glass at glass, a shattering sort of music. It was terribly effective when the ballet actually came together, but working with the music all day really hurt my mind. However much I wanted to do it, I couldn't in the end. I didn't ever do the ballet. I couldn't accomplish it. That's one of the reasons I never did the modern ballets: I couldn't pick up the music. I like listening to it while other people are doing it, but I don't find that music inspiring. And the music is all-important, so it's hard to move my body when I don't find it helping me along.

Some people do not dance to the music — they are the music. Their bodies become the music. The music sails through them, through their very souls. That, to my mind, is a musical dancer. Lynn

257

is the music, I am the music, and Monica Mason is the music. Merle
is fantastically musical as well, but to a quite different degree. She has
time to play with the music, which is quite a different thing. It's
amazing. I merely was the music, the personification of the music.
And Anthony was exactly the same as me in the way he heard music,
which is why we could work so well together. We just did the same
thing at the same time without having to think about it, rehearse it,
try it. It just moved the same way.

You do, of course, have a chance to talk the music through
with the conductor. But if we're talking about, like, a big first night,
some conductors go faster when they're nervous; some go slower.
Some dancers go faster when they're nervous; some go slower. This
is the human factor. You can't get it right always, you just can't. There
are so many human factors contributory to a performance — how
often can it possibly jell? There's you, there's your partner, the music,
the conductor, the costumes, the lights, the stage can be slippery. So
many things can literally be disastrous that it's very rare you get *a*
performance that you can really feel thrilled and happy about. That's
one of the joys of it; that's why you keep going on. You're still searching
for it.

Swan Lake I did with so many different partners it was an
absolute joke. I think I'd done it with ten partners before I ever got
to do it with Anthony. It was an impossible situation because you
couldn't develop much in it, either of you. It's wonderful to do performances with different people as long as you're going to have a go
at it, work out something together and make it work, but just to do
odd performances here and there is no help to anybody. And in our
company, the roles were absolutely divided up equally: I did the *Beauty*
and *Lac*, Merle did *Giselle* and *Beauty*, and Lynn did *Giselle* and *Lac*.
Nobody was allowed more than two; it was all actually rationed out.
Nobody did the ballets that often, so we really never had a chance for
anything to get set. And I'm a very spontaneous dancer; I can't do
things exactly the same every time, and therefore the ballet wouldn't
be the same anyway. And then, you do react completely differently
to different partners. I loved dancing with Rudolf, and with Mischa
as well, and one would react completely differently than you would
with Anthony. They're different people; there's a different way of
asking them the questions. If you're strong and they're strong as
personalities, you bring out different things in each other.

Now, Anthony. Well, it's like ... Why do you like certain
people? Why? You just get on very well. When you first meet them,
you click, and with other people you don't. You can't say what it is
exactly. You can be mundane about it and go, 'Yes, our proportions

are exactly the same. Therefore, when I was on pointe, I came up to exactly the right place, so when we had turns with the hands over our heads, he didn't have to stoop or go on half-point. And my waist was at the right level for his arms when I was on pointe.' That's all true, and of course it's all very important. And it's also important if you hear the music the same way. The whole thing can look so easy in that you're breathing together almost. But I think we were very similar . . . our strangenesses, in a funny way, were the same. Although we had opposite characteristics in many ways, and we could help each other by being opposites, we also both had — for instance, in *The Dream* — a strangeness about us.

Certainly ballets help one another. You can't be adding to *Swan Lake, Sleeping Beauty,* and *Giselle,* the ballets you keep bringing out time after time again, unless you have a chance to do a tremendous variety of roles. That's why I was so lucky having so many ballets done for me, which brings out things you never thought you had in yourself. There's a side of you somebody else can see, and then you realize they're absolutely right — you know deep down that, of course, that's how you are. But also, having a very large rep, which I did, you're going from *Jazz Calendar* to Dorabella to *Lilac Garden* to *Dances at a Gathering* to *Scènes de Ballet,* and that's the fascination of it all. And it's all helpful when you come to do those classical ballets, because all that life experience and know-how give you a background to bring down to them.

I've worked with Fred many times, and I did *Triad, Manon,* and the *Pavane* with Kenneth, apart from being around all the time when he was working on *Baiser* [*de la Fée*] and *Romeo.* Kenneth has it very much all worked out in his head when he arrives. He will do it in front of you, and he wants those steps. But I don't mean it's absolutely set there and then; obviously, if you can't quite do them in the way he wants, then he is quite willing to change it. Whereas Fred's quite a different kettle of fish. He'll just arrive in the rehearsal, he knows the music absolutely backwards, and, as with *The Dream,* he'll suddenly go, 'Well, I want a fountain.' You tend to look back a bit blankly and search your mind to what a fountain would be like, and then you do something mad and he goes, 'Yes, wonderful, that's what I want.' So you then have to try and make that into steps. His is a poetic vision of something, and that's why it's very much the person he's done it on. He does the ballet on how you look, on what shape your body is — the whole thing has to be that person. He brings it out of you as you are in that room; you are being molded right then and there.

With *The Dream,* at the first rehearsals Anthony and I thought we were one of the two pair of lovers, because Merle and Austin

Bennett were at the same call and we didn't realize they were going to be second cast to us. We thought we were a pair of lovers, and since we started with the argument, we were even more sure that's what we were about. Nobody ever told us we were Titania and Oberon — certainly Fred didn't. It's quite extraordinary when you think about it. We just assumed, I suppose, as the ballet was done that that's who we must be. I was then a bit disappointed, because I thought, 'Oh, Titania. Whatever is that? Just a fairy. Yet another fairy tale with nothing to get hold of. No flesh and blood.' But the more I worked, the more I realized she wasn't at all just a fairy. She's a wonderful creature of womanhood, very strange, very weird, very supernatural, and at the same time, tremendously proud. She's as great as he is in her own right, and she's not going to let him win anything off her until she finds that he *is* winning, and then she has to completely wilt for him and mesmerize him again. But she gives herself, in that last pas de deux, her way. And it was lovely that you saw that other side of her too, being so foolish when she falls in love with the ass. She's a lovely character. I loved doing her in the end.

Obviously the subjects that interest Kenneth more are meatier subjects; you know that by all the ballets he's done. He's interested in that side of the theatre. Fred loves to make a story as well, but I don't think he necessarily likes to see the unattractive side of life. The ballets can be just as dramatic — *Marguerite and Armand, Ondine* in its way, *A Month in the Country* — but they're mainly dwelling on the beauties of life. Fred loves the beauties, I think, the beautiful side of things.

I loved, more than anything else, being a bit of clay for one of those people. Particularly Fred, in that I had done virtually all his ballets, not only the ones he choreographed for me. I adore working for Kenneth too, but I had worked for Fred in so many different spheres all through my career. I've known him since I was nineteen, since *Ondine*, when I was one of the funny little sprites in the background. I found I suited his kind of choreography a lot, and he liked the sort of things I liked very much. I loved being the clay, but you're not only the clay really — it's what you make out of that clay. They give you the confidence and you give as much back, because you know they trust your instincts, your quirks, and your funny ways of maybe doing something a bit differently. Those were probably my happiest times, creating ballets, and I felt totally jealous of my own creations. They're like your children, very personal to you. And funnily enough, not just created ballets. I felt very like that with *Dances at a Gathering*, which I absolutely adored. It was another side of my personality, total naturalness, which goes back, you see, to when I saw Ulanova in December '56.

When one goes down to the history books — or whatever one does do — I suppose those 'abstract' ballets will be very much a part of my career, of what I've achieved. They did mean such a lot to me — *Scènes de Ballet, Ballet Imperial, Dances at a Gathering, Symphonic Variations* — and they're none of them abstract. To me they're not. They might not have a story, but each has a mood, a feeling. How can *Ballet Imperial* be abstract? The music is so grand and exultant. Oh, it's wonderful. I could only see it as if, in the second act [movement], she was in her private apartment with her prince and just a few maids of honor, and then it's back to the grandeur of the full court. *Dances* is . . . The very fact of the meeting of people can't be abstract. It doesn't mean that you fall in love or you're passionate, but life isn't only that — life has many other sides. *Scènes de Ballet* was sparkling, the most sophisticated of all the roles: a real French woman, with her pearls, total sophistication and then the sultry solo. *Symphonic* is heaven — it's what heaven must be like. It's fulfillment, peace, happiness, beauty. It's not abstract. It's not steps, is it? It's intoxication of everything that's beautiful on another, not human, plane.

I'm known as a classicist, I'd been brought up as a classicist, and I *was* a classicist. I had the classical ballets and the 'abstract' ballets, but I hadn't the chance to try everything — the company was too big — so *Lilac Garden* was one of my first experiences with a narrative ballet. I absolutely adored doing it, and I adored Tudor. I'd heard such frightening stories about him, but I just happened to get on with him terribly well. I thought, 'I can't be scared of him, because if I'm scared, I'm not going to be myself, and he's not then going to like me or get on with me or anything else. So I might as well just relax.' And there weren't any scenes, nothing. Now, he is completely the opposite of Kenneth or Fred. Every second is talked through, every single finger is important, every detail: 'Why is that little finger like this?' or 'Why are you looking up there?' And you think, 'Gosh, I don't know. I just felt I should. It was instinct.' Then you think, 'No, I must put it into words, because that's what he wants,' and you have to give him a reason for everything, which is very good. It makes you positively think. I thought it was going to be very hard. Being a totally spontaneous person in my ordinary life as well as in my dancing, I didn't know how I was going to cope if somebody was going to worry that I would do something slightly different, which I knew I would. But I think his main point was that as long as you concentrated absolutely, you would be with the idea of it. Even if you then did something differently, it would be in the same mood or with the same feeling.

We'd also heard so many things about Jerry [Robbins], but to work with Jerry was an absolute delight, with *Dances* and then with *Afternoon of a Faun*. Funnily enough, I heard I was going to do the *Faun* the night after my first *Giselle* in London. Jerry said, "I'm only telling you so that you don't cut your hair." He wanted the hair down to the waist, and as the summer holidays were coming, I would have cut it off, so it was just as well he told me. And then I spent my holidays with Nora [Kaye], and I must say I did ask her about Tanny [LeClercq], how she did it and what the original was like, thinking that's probably what he'd like. But again I realized that the whole point anyway was that Tanny and Moncion weren't anything like what Anthony and I would be. We'd have to do it the way that we were, the way we reacted. I thought, 'I'd better not have it preconceived.' I probably mentioned it to Jerry at some point, and he said, "No, no. We'll do it as you are."

It's always better not to have seen anyone when you do a new role, oh, absolutely. When we were working on *Romeo and Juliet*, there were, I think, four of us all working together on it. It was choreographed on Lynn, but Margot did the first performance, Lynn did the next, and I did the next. And I didn't know quite what to do, because I wanted to go to the first night and yet mine was coming up so soon after, in the same first week. I didn't want to be put off my track — because by now I'd got my track, in that I'd rehearsed it all myself — and yet I was fascinated to see the ballet as a whole, in performance. I think I went to see Margot's the first night, because it meant I wouldn't see it the night before I was going to do it, but that was quite a decision to me. I didn't want to be influenced in any way by anybody else. When you see a performance, you're seeing a whole; it's rather different from seeing people in rehearsal.

When the adrenalin gets going and you're out there on the stage, it's a magical world that nobody can penetrate but the people on that stage. But, gosh, by profession we're entertainers, so we're dancing for the public. We're only the circus in another form, or like the actors in Shakespeare's time. It's not any more highfalutin than that, really. We are entertainers, so in the last, we're there for the public. I don't mean that if the public clapped because you did entrechat dix you're going to do it every night. I don't mean you would necessarily do what the public wants you to do, to please them. But they're what you're there for.

I think you're like a sponge; you soak up an awful lot and then you spew out what you don't want to keep. It comes at different times from different people. One has so many influences: Fred, Tudor, Kenneth, my teacher Miss Edwards, and another teacher, Miss [Ailne] Phillips, and Pamela May. Everybody gives you something that you latch onto if it helps. De Valois was a tremendous influence, and Michael Somes, of course. And then the people you work with — Anthony, Rudolf, Mischa — all give something to you that helps make whatever you turn out to be. Possibly in the last analysis, it would be from the ballets, or maybe from Fred, that I got more confidence, if confidence is the word we're talking about. I knew he liked the way I did his ballets, and that would drive me on to new goals and to trying different things every time.

I always wanted to do — a silly thing — Czardas in *Swan Lake*. I loved the red velvet costumes and the wonderful *épaulement* arms, the grandeur of it almost and then the quickness at the end. And the other thing would have been *A Month in the Country*. Oh, and *Song of the Earth*, because I was supposed to be going to do that when I had my baby. I was the original Youth in London, but I'd also learnt the second and last movements when I was pregnant and I was actually down for a performance. I would have loved to do that. And I would have loved to dance in Russia again. I had been asked when one of the defections happened, and then it was sort of passed by and we were never asked again. You see, our whole company went in '61, but I hadn't been a principal long then; the Bluebird was the most I was doing. So I would love to have gone back as a flower in bloom. I don't think there was anything else, but I didn't know it was going to end so quickly so I didn't really think what else I would like to do. I did so much.

I have taught people my roles. I just took my little one along the other day to watch *The Dream*, and I was asked to help a bit. I haven't done much of it because I hadn't the time, but I'd love to now. One knows so much about it; you were there when it was born, and you know all the funny things that Fred actually wanted that just get changed — not because people mean to, but then they're lost. If one movement's changed, it loses a meaning in a way. An artist will then do a role not really knowing the reason for that movement, because a peculiarity has gotten lost.

Certain ballets I thought I'd have difficulty seeing so soon after the event — I hadn't thought I'd want to see *Dances* or *The Dream* — but in fact, it proved not to be like that, which was rather a relief. Some bits of music kill me; I know those bits so well. I was that music, and I find it very hard to listen to it and have nothing to do with it. Other bits, though I was terribly fond of the ballet, I can listen to. It's strange, really.

I couldn't have possibly coped with as many injuries or as much ill health if my personality weren't to get over things immediately. You know how funny life is. There isn't another possible route, somehow; this is the only thing you know about, the only thing you can do. And you love it. You obviously hate it as well, but that's true with everything in life, isn't it? This knee was in such a bad way all the last six years, but they didn't know, 'til they took that cartilage out, how bad. *I* knew it was very bad, but all the doctors said there was nothing wrong. So you have to go ahead, if that's what they say. With anything in life, you have to put it behind you and go on. If you dwell on it, you sink below the mire. You just can't. Life is to forge ahead.

And I was so lucky — you see, there's always the other side to it. I had a very lucky body for dancing, other than the constant injuries. My muscles were very strong for such a small person, so I never had that problem most people have. If they're off for a couple of days, their muscles have gone, but my muscles were better from rest. That's what God gave me on the other side. The difficulty was more mental every time, coming back after an injury, more the mental thing of being pushed down and trying to come up again.

It was such hard work, and I have such a heavenly life that I can't honestly say I'm sitting around moping — because I'm not. I'm so terribly thankful. Obviously, you can't get the feeling of those magic minutes on the stage into any other part of your life, because you can't suddenly start walking around being a different character. People would think you'd be going — well, you *would* be going — nuts. But it's been one's existence since one was very young, so for us to go into all these different characters is really as natural as for other people to clean their teeth. And it's a very good cleansing for the blood to do that, because you don't take things out on other people; you tend to take them out on these roles, nasty roles or whatever kind. I do miss that — I miss being able to hide, to jump into characters.

But I really couldn't bear that I never had a whole weekend in the country. I love the country. I love to read. I didn't have time to do all these things, and I didn't have that enormous energy of somebody like Rudolf who can do both. He is an exception. Just as much as I needed so many different kinds of roles, I need those different ways of life. I have to be able to go to the movies and to the opera. I have to be able to learn to drive. I cannot just do the one thing, and I would yearn for these things. I'm sure that's also why I would get ill, because when I was ill I wasn't dancing and I was able to do everything else. And there's the other thing: how would I now go rushing to New York, to Los Angeles, to Rome, to whatever, with my child, with my husband? To me, it wouldn't have worked properly. So I think he knows what he's doing sometimes, the master in Fred's heaven.

October 1979
London

Christopher Gable

Christopher Gable (b. London, 1940) entered the Royal Ballet School in 1951 and the Sadler's Wells Opera Ballet in 1956 upon graduating from the School; he joined the Royal Ballet Touring Company the following year. Advancing from corps de ballet to principal in that company, he danced the classical repertory — Bluebird *and* Florimund *in* Sleeping Beauty, Siegfried *in* Swan Lake, Colas *in* La Fille Mal Gardée — *and also created leading roles in Kenneth MacMillan's* The Invitation *(1960) and Frederick Ashton's* The Two Pigeons *(1961), partnering Lynn Seymour in both. He transferred to the parent company at Covent Garden in 1963 and added* Coppélia *and* La Bayadère *(Act IV) to his repertory before creating the leading role, again opposite Seymour, in MacMillan's three-act* Romeo and Juliet *(1965). Early in 1967, Gable resigned from the Royal Ballet and retired from dancing to pursue an acting career.*

Christopher Gable was unlike any other English dancer of his generation and, indeed, any other English dancer I've ever seen. He had a face like a beacon and a presence so compellingly ardent that you scarcely noticed his considerable technique. He could light and warm a stage with his disposition, with gaiety or grief or exuberance or disarming tenderness. You didn't simply 'watch' Gable's dancing — that's far too passive a description for the experience: you surrendered to what his conviction made irresistible. You didn't sit back coolly and admire his Romeo: you either became Romeo or you fell hopelessly in love with him.

My whole career has been accidental, if there is such a thing. At the beginning, my real ambition was to be a singing, tapping, Fred Astaire–type figure. I was about six when all those escapist American movies were coming over, and those, in austerity Britain, seemed terrific. It wasn't 'til I went to a dancing school and learned to do all that, tapping and singing, that the teacher said it was ballet I should be doing. I fought against that quite a lot — the tapping particularly attracted me more — but then I passed my eleven plus exam and they sent a list of the grammar schools you could choose from, and one of them was the Royal Ballet School. And we noticed there was a bus that went from where we lived on one side of London right to the Royal Ballet School on the other side, without any changes. Since my parents felt they could technically allow an eleven-year-old to cross London that way, they agreed that I should go for an audition. And once you've become part of a school like that, you're on the conveyor belt; you start working and working and you get the same goals as everybody else, which are to get into the company and to become a star.

Of course I had great parental opposition, partly because of the appalling insecurity of dancing and partly because my parents, like most people then, associated the ballet with effeminacy. In fact, when we went for my audition, my mother practically fainted with horror. You know the headbands that Bjorn Borg wears for tennis? Well, in those days fellows just didn't put bands around their hair, and I remember her saying to my dad, "The boys all had ribbons on!" So they were very worried. Also, at that age you're very concerned with what your peer group thinks, and I was regarded as a laughingstock by all my mates because I was going to ballet lessons when they were going off to play football. It mattered terribly to me, and I was miserable about it. And even when I was a star dancer, I still used to get uneasy when somebody at a party would say, "What do you do?" To have to say, "I'm a ballet dancer" slightly bothered me. But anyway, I stuck to it.

It's a complex, difficult language, the language of dancing, so just trying to coerce your body into doing what it's got to do takes up every waking moment for the first several years. Now, a violinist or a pianist can shop around and buy the best instrument he can afford. But ballet is one of those difficult things where your instrument is your own body, and you either have the body or you don't. When I started to dance, really beautifully built men, ideally built for dancing, were very thin on the ground — there weren't many of them — so my body didn't matter too much. It was serviceable in that it was tough, it was built to last, and it would take quite a lot of punishment, but a glorious, aesthetic piece of equipment it was not. So, since you carry in your mind an image of what you'd like to be, I realized very early that what I would like to be was not what I was going to be at all.

That image is a collection of things you see on other people. Inevitably there are basic rules: you want long, slender, flexible limbs, highly arched feet, a good neck, a good head. A man needs a very broad chest because — I'm off on a track already — particularly onstage, the sexual relationship between people is vital. I find it all the time as an actor. In theatre and opera, the male sound opposed to the female sound automatically gives you your sexual balance. In the ballet, where you have two bodies just moving, it becomes more important that one of those bodies gives off a powerful male quality and the other a female quality. That balance has to be there — that's why I think a male dancer should look very male. But that's jumping ahead.

One is the product of the influences that come on you. Probably the first major influence on me was the Bolshoi Ballet. On their first ever trip to London, a few of us, students, were selected to carry bowls of food on our heads to the Capulet banquet. The security was incredible; you couldn't get in the stage door unless you had a card with your photograph on it, and you only got a card if you were in the ballet. We'd go down to the basement of Covent Garden, get into our servants' robes, wait there to go up and carry our bowls of food across, and go back down. That was all we were supposed to do. But I realized that in a dressing gown and a make-up, one dancer looks very much like another, and you could just stay in the wings. So I saw everything, and I was very aware of the contrivance of the productions. You see, when we went onstage as students to be huntsmen and stand 'round the edge, we were told, "React." Blanket term — react. Nobody told you how. So you looked at what the others were doing and tried to do vaguely that, which seemed to be stand still while the solos are on and then get very animated between whiles, while the curtain calls are happening. But there was a jester's dance in the ballroom scene of their *Romeo*, and the ladies and gentlemen sitting 'round the edges had been choreographed. They were all holding handkerchiefs and, as he danced, they all made a swaying-in and swaying-out movement, with a ripple of laughter in it. If you picked it out individually, it was entirely stylized, but if you looked at the whole stage, what you saw was a weaving mass of people that suggested convivial, relaxed merriment.

I watched every *Romeo* from start to finish — I watched Ulanova. Ulanova was the greatest female dancer I've ever seen because she accounted for every second of stage time. She was a wonderful dancer;

she had speed, enormous elevation, great technical assurance — but all of it was only a means to an end. All her technique, all her athletic gifts, were put to the service of the role, and what one saw was an in-depth psychological study of a girl at a real crisis point in her life and how she dealt with it. I suddenly saw, 'That's what it's about,' and that was when I stopped thinking about how many spins I could do and whether I could jump higher than anybody else. I suppose a man should be fixed onto another fellow, but there was too much of a gap between the unformed, very young fifteen-year-old I was then and their far more mature men. They appeared to be in their mid-thirties to forties — which seemed very old — and they had a heavy, grand style that was completely inappropriate to me, so, in a way, one filtered it out. Also, they were dancing so well technically that it was way beyond anything I could ever imagine doing. What I honed in on was the essential thing, the reason you were on there in the first place.

As far as I can tell, that is ignored almost completely at the moment. I find the ballet very disappointing now because, like any athletic form, its technical standard goes on going up and up. Look at Olga Korbut, the toast of the world for a year. The next year, [Nadia] Comaneci can do all she could do and more, and this year Comaneci will be gone and a new, tiny fragment with incredible physical facility will take her place. Well, this happens to a similar extent in the ballet. The thirty-two fouettés in the Black Swan pas de deux were put into *Swan Lake* originally because only one dancer in the world could do them. Now every dancer must be able to do them to the right and the left before they can even take their advanced RAD exams. So the emphasis for the teachers and the students has gone onto technical excellence. And because it's a hard fight and 99.9 percent of your time — job — to achieve that excellence, I think you have to abandon the rest. Which is, in a nutshell, why I'm not dancing any more — I mean, it's why I made the break.

It happened for me when Rudolf arrived. Rudolf raised the technical standard of the game way, way up, which was all to the good and essential and had to happen. And at the time, I was sharing the *Bayadère*s and the *Swan Lake*s with him, often dancing on alternate nights, so it became essential that I raise my game too. I was able to, but the only way I could do it, at that stage in my career, was to devote 100 percent of my time to it. And I did that for a while, until I realized that the essential thing that interested and concerned me was being fatally neglected because of it. Also, there was a swing at that time very much away from the narrative ballet, which was where I was most comfortable and felt I had the most to say, and into a more abstract, Balanchine-type rep that drew the attention entirely onto the physical excellence. So I thought I'd lost that battle before I started it, and I wasn't prepared to fight because I didn't want the prize at the end of it, which was to be the most beautiful dancer that had ever happened with nothing to say. Of course, people who do that would argue that there is something to say, but I couldn't find it and it wasn't what interested me.

I approached the abstract repertoire with enormous difficulty and a fair amount of misery. What I used was music. Another lesson from Ulanova, not that I observed when I watched her — because I wasn't a sophisticated enough observer then — but that I read when I was older, was that the music is everything, even in a narrative ballet. She said that the music tells you where the climaxes are, what is important and what isn't, what to give value to, what to devalue, speed, tempo, everything. The whole shape of every part is built entirely on the music, she said, and I found it to be true. So if there wasn't a story line, I hung entirely onto the music.

Before the School, I studied the piano for eight years; I was quite good at it. But I never felt at home without the narrative. I felt I had enough to do onstage withdrawing my concentration from my physical shortcomings. A dancer has to have this split personality: in the classroom, you have to be able to look with a very cold, reasoning, harsh eye at all your shortcomings and failures, and in performance you have to eliminate all of them from your mind because they're irrelevant. In my experience, you carry the audience primarily on the force of your concentration. It is a fact that you can make them see what you want them to see provided you concentrate on it hard enough. It's like Katharine Hepburn in *The Rainmaker*, when she says, "I'm pretty, I'm pretty, I'm pretty," and her face becomes pretty as she says it. It's force of will. A dancer operates on that all the time.

Probably the greatest success I ever had as a dancer was that I was regarded by the London press as very much on an even level with Rudolf. There was a review that said, 'If Rudolf Nureyev is the Joan Sutherland of the ballet world, then Christopher Gable is the Maria Callas,' and opinion was very evenly divided on whom you'd sooner go and see. Now, I consider that an amazing triumph of concentration and of having an image of what you want, because I had virtually no technique. I had more speed. I could spin more, and I learnt to do a few clever things. I got better later — and I also got very good at faking — but the fact remains that I wasn't within a million miles of Rudolf as a dancer, ever, ever, ever. When I teach — I often teach. I like teaching. I like working with my actor's brain with dancers now — I say all the time, "You must have an image of what you see, and you must concentrate on it so hard that you make the audience see it. The proof is me, because I was total disaster in class." I couldn't get a job now in a company anywhere in the world, and I pretty nearly didn't get a job in a company then.

In those days, if you came out of your training at the School and you were really white-hot, you went straight to the first company, as Sibley did. If you were considered very good but there was a question mark, you were put into the touring section. If you were considered rather poor but deserved E for Effort, you got put into the Covent Garden Opera Ballet. And if you were a total disaster but had been right through the School so they couldn't very well finish your training and then say, 'Sorry, good-bye,' you were put into the Sadler's Wells Opera Ballet. I went into the Sadler's Wells Opera Ballet, and I considered myself extremely lucky to be in a company at all.

Dancers by definition are a very young race — it's over by the time you're thirty. You've got to pack it all in so you're going very fast, and you're always in a hothouse atmosphere of young, physical creatures. What I loved about being with the opera was that one was working with proper adults, who approached the situations on the stage in a far more naturalistic style than dancers did. Opera singers are ordinary people: they're married, they've got kids, and they're in their mid-thirties — that's about when voices come into the right place — and I was fascinated by them as people. And I became interested in trying to find ways of using a more naturalistic approach to the classical style of ballet, and not getting into those bizarre positions that are attractive to look at but which no person in the world ever got into.

You see, dancers have an interesting advantage over ordinary people. If somebody comes to see a play and they don't understand what it's about, they will say either, "This is a bad play" or "These are bad actors" or both, because if they don't understand it, it's bad and there's no question. But people say, "I don't understand the ballet, but I love it." They assume that if they don't know what's going on, it's because they're not cultured enough or experienced enough in the form. So dancers can get away with murder — and do — because nobody challenges them. An awful lot of them make the terms of the classical ballet an excuse for departing from reality. I go into rehearsals and say to them, "What are you doing? It's no good waving your arms about if I don't understand. You must make it clear to me. I'm just Mr. Ordinary sitting there in the stalls, and I want to know what's happening." Unless you apply basic, logical standards of human behavior and interaction to the situations on the stage, you're moving off into a never-never land that never existed. And who cares?

But anyway. At the end of the first Opera Ballet season, I was asked if I would go to the Covent Garden Opera Ballet. I was feeling pretty sick because my friends and contemporaries had either disappeared into the commercial world or got into one of the companies. And I knew I'd got another season and then, because nobody was interested in me or thought I had any talent, they were going to say good-bye. So I did a bit of subterfuge. I called up Simon Mottram, who was in the touring company, and I said, "When does company class start?" — that company was coming back to work a fortnight before the Opera Ballet. Then I wrote to John Field and said, "I have sprained an ankle" — all lies — "and I'm going into the Opera Ballet, but I would like to be in practice when they come back. So may I come to company class until then and just work?" And he said, "Yes." I danced up a storm and tried to be very impressive for the fortnight, and then they went off on tour, where one of the corps de ballet boys slipped a disk. And John Field said, "Who was that fair boy who was in class? He looked all right. He could come in." So they phoned up in the afternoon, and I went on that night and stayed with the company for thirteen weeks. I learned the whole rep and got into everything, eight shows a week, but at the end of the thirteen weeks, the boy rejoined the company and I was fired. John said, "We're not dissatisfied with you, but I'm only allowed so many people." I was dreading the prospect of going back into the Opera Ballet. And then one of the girls in the touring company got pregnant so she had to leave, and her husband got a job in London to be with her, and I knew all the rep, so I was asked back into the company. A fluke again. But it didn't occur to me that I would be anything other than corps de ballet all my life, and I was quite happy with that.

I formed two very close, formative relationships in that company, one with Maggie Hill, who had twenty years of [Ballet] Rambert behind her and was a tremendous source of inspiration and encouragement, and the other with Simon Mottram, who had also been with Rambert. Possibly because of their background — Rambert had a tradition of producing very interesting, exciting people — I became very influenced by both of them, and they reinforced the fact that you must take each step and paraphrase it into what it would be saying if it wasn't a step. Of course, Ken comes into that too, because one of the first things that happened to me in that company was Ken choreographing *The Burrow*, which was based on *The Diary of Anne Frank*. It was Lynn's first opportunity, and I was in the corps. There was a bit at the end where we were running from wall to wall to wall in a kind of panic, and I can remember Ken saying, "We have to find a step that says 'panic.' " He gave a step because it was a ballet — two sauts de basque and a jeté or something — but one suddenly thought, 'This is not about beautiful little sauts de basque with pointed feet. It is about trying to get out of here.' So I started to think in terms of 'Don't ever do a saut de basque because it's a saut de basque,' and I realized you could apply terms like that to every step.

The Burrow continued me in the direction I'd started to go, and I also worked very, very hard. I also was discovered to have a natural stage presence — I was just look-at-able on the stage. And then, when we were on tour in Australia, it was discovered that I was big and strong and a very good partner. One of the girls they were preparing for *Swan Lake* didn't have a partner, so I used to go along and hold her up so she could rehearse the pas de deux; I was just a body to do the lifts and stand behind her. Partnering *can* be taught, but I was a natural partner. Of course, John gave me lots of information, and he had a very simple, direct style that I picked up, but it's also to do with a sensitivity to your partner and with the kind of natural self-effacement I had. Because I didn't rate myself as a dancer very much, I wasn't as concerned with presenting myself in a pas de deux as I was with presenting the pas de deux.

So all these things overlaid one another, but *The Invitation* was an accident too. I wasn't down to do that with Lynn. Pirmin Trecu was going to dance the young boy, but after they'd already done the first ten or fifteen minutes of the ballet, he smashed a kneecap in Bluebird one night, and Lynn suggested to Ken that it might be worth giving me a try. That ballet happened on the road — we toured it — and it was a great success, so it was included in the season the touring company did at Covent Garden. And for that season, Fred Ashton decided he would do a new ballet for the company, and that was *Two Pigeons*, which he created for Lynn and Donald Britton. But Donald was stricken with some terrible bug and collapsed two days before the opening performance, so I did that too. It was all an extraordinary fluke that for me that first season was two ballets, the opposite sides of the same coin.

I was never ambitious for particular roles. At that time, I was just working out a language for myself, entirely insular and self-absorbed. I was just doing the best I knew how and trying to justify every second on stage emotionally. It was self-defense, really. I'm very shy, and I feel cripplingly embarrassed and exposed if I've got time onstage that I haven't accounted for. If I know why I'm there, I'm absorbed in that, and the damaging kind of self-consciousness goes away.

In my experience, the dancers who choose to become dramatic or interpretive dancers, to justify what they're doing on the stage in the way we've been talking about, are usually the ones with considerable technical shortcomings. Dancers who can dance flawlessly are very often seduced into going onstage and dancing flawlessly. The audience loves it, and so it's enough. But look at someone like Julia Farron, who had a desperately suspect technique, or Margot, who was a very pure dancer but never had the kind of bravura technique that would wow an audience. Lynn is probably the best case in point. When I started working with Lynn, she had her work cut out to stand on pointe at all without a boy holding her up. She was given things to do — like the *Swan Lake*s and the *Beauty*s —in the hope that it would develop a technique, and of course, in a make-or-break way, it did. But I'm thinking of her first *Beauty*; I can remember it quite clearly, and it seems important to tell about it because it sort of sums up Lynn's approach to work, which was the same as mine.

The Rose Adagio, where you have to choose one of four young men to marry, has come to be a very assured young girl coming on and doing a lot of clever balances. You grasp their hands with great confidence and balance for a long time after each one, which usually involves spotting somewhere on the floor. The audience loves long balances because there's a circus element in that, and they'll cheer and scream, and you've got a successful Rose Adagio on your hands . . . some say. But Lynn couldn't touch most of that choreography; she couldn't let go of a boy's hand because she'd fall over. So what she did was hold on and look that guy right in the eye, as if to say, 'You're really rather lovely. I quite fancy —' And then she noticed the next chap, and snatched her hand away and gave it to him: 'Oh, you're even better,' and then, even more thrilled, to the next, 'Gosh, you're terrific.' So we've lost the balances, but what we've got is a lady choosing between four fellows, which is what the choreography is about.

Now, my theory is that if Lynn could have balanced, there wouldn't have been any need for her to reassess that situation. That certainly was my approach to work as well, and it was forced on me for the same reasons. It's very uncomfortable to be forced through technical inadequacy to reassess every minute you're onstage. If you don't have to do it, you won't. But if you have to, you go back to the basics, just as an actor does, and think, 'What's happening in this choreography? What am I on here for? How do I feel about these people?' and you play *that*. And suddenly, audiences are going, 'Aha. We never saw this ballet like this before,' because you've actually gotten to what it's about.

The creation process of *Romeo* was a marriage between three people who got on with each other very well and understood each other. We were great and close personal friends, and I'm still very close to Lynn. We have the same artistic ideals and goals, the same way of working, and, probably most important, the same basic response to music — we hear music in the same way. As fully and truthfully as we could, we took on the personalities of those two people and thought that situation through fresh. Of course, we read Shakespeare's play, but we thought primarily about what it would be like if it were happening now, to me. When you work with Kenneth, you decide first on the emotional climate of the scene and the quality of a relationship, and then you try to find a dance vocabulary that will express it and clarify it for an audience.

He often can't bear to start. When we started on *Romeo*, we started on the Balcony pas de deux. We were called at about ten-thirty, and I think we talked 'til eleven, and then Ken said, "Let's have coffee." We had coffee 'til half-past eleven. Then we went back in and vaguely mooched around and set a couple of ideas, and then decided to break for lunch. He couldn't bear starting, because once you start, you're committing it. But when we started on the Bedroom pas de deux, for instance, we talked about everything. Her parents are saying she must marry. She is already married and can't tell them. They're waiting for an answer that she can't give them. She and Romeo have had their first sexual experience together — certainly the first ever for her — which has clearly been terrific. He has managed to kill Tybalt inadvertently in the afternoon. He is under banishment. He has to leave before morning light, and it's quite likely that he'll never come back. We explored all of that together — how it would feel, what it would be like, how we would deal with it — and then we started to look for the steps that would say it. Which is why the pas de deux has nothing spectacular in it. He tried to do it like one long suppressed groan of agony. It was a thrilling, marvelous time.

I've seen the ballet since, and an awful lot of it has gotten lost. This is the sad thing about ballet: things get lost if the people who were there and who know why it happened the way it did have gone, and if the people who are in charge either don't know or aren't interested. If what they're interested in is technical excellence, straight lines and pointed toes, then the very heartbeat of what you did is gone. I've never taught or coached Romeo; nobody's ever asked me to do anything with Romeo.

First of all, Lynn and Ken and I agreed that Italian boys are traditionally the horniest of all and will screw anything in sight. And when the play opens, Romeo is languishing and desperately in love with Rosaline. So what we tried to create in the beginning was a young randy guy with his two young randy mates, rampaging around the town. He's a good screw, he really likes it, and he's horny and sexy, and you need that so you can make the transition when you come upon someone who is different. Juliet is different, and he knows straightaway she's different.

I think they take the feud as seriously as three guys like that can. In terms of the period, it's major; there's a bust-up in the streets every week or so, and you end up with a lot of carnage. But life was cheaper then anyway, and if there isn't a reason to fight, young guys like that will find one. It's really just street-fighting. If you get an opportunity and the rival gang turns up, it's *West Side Story*. You were using swords, and I should imagine a lot of people got mashed around a bit, but it's a good old punch-up. It's fun and it's virile and it's proving you're smoldering — it's very Latin to smolder. I tried to keep it in that context. And they go along to the party in the same context, for a lark. They put on their masks for a lark. It's a dangerous prank. He's also following Rosaline; one of the reasons he goes is that he knows she's there. And it's when he's there that he sees this creature, Juliet.

There was some device, a general dance, when he sees her for the first time, and then . . . I forgot how it happens technically, but he is confronted with her. Lynn and I decided that it was such a huge thing that one couldn't choreograph it. So what we did was stand stock still for a long time. Dead still, just looking, not moving, nothing at all. For a long time. And it was broken by somebody else — Tybalt or somebody came and took her away — but it had set the seeds for another meeting. She comes back into the ballroom and Romeo's there. I think Lynn decided to make it a very definite return because she figured that Juliet is very strong and takes her destiny very firmly in her hands — *she* goes to Friar Laurence, *she* decides to take the poison. So she wouldn't just wait for events to take their course; she'd come back to look for him.

I can't really remember the solo too well. It's a piece of provocation; people are getting suspicious by then anyway, and he's sailing pretty close to the wind. But I don't remember it because I tended to skate across the solos as fast as I could. I'm really thinking about the way we organized the Balcony scene. What we talked about was the fact that when she comes down, she does something very brave which gives the whole pas de deux its impetus: she takes his hand and puts it on her heart, because she wants him to feel how fast it's going. And we very, *very* consciously devised a series of steps there that were all slightly off balance and turning and reeling. You know that minute when you know that you are hugely, deeply attracted to somebody and when you realize that they're feeling the same way? You can't believe it's happening. Oh boy, it's like stars bursting in your head! We were looking for that sort of reeling, spinning thing that never begins and never stops. Which is why I was so distraught when Rudi cut all that and put in a big, virtuoso *manège* because he felt Romeo needed big dancing steps there.

You can make the entrance for that scene work, even with your back to the audience, providing you can hold in your mind what's happening. Yes, you're standing still, but you aren't stopping. You can't stop. It's so difficult to talk about it without sounding pretentious. It's like a held breath, like a suspended time sequence. If music can be described as being made up of sound and silence, dance is made up of movement and stillness. So if you use stillness correctly, it will convey as much. And, you see, I committed to her from the very first encounter. That seemed most valid to me theatrically, and I wanted it very clear, not a slow creep from the tough, horny guy of the beginning into a new dimension, but a complete jump. So when he comes on for the Balcony scene, he's already a different man. There's also something very strange, right at the end of the pas de trois before the boys go into the ball, when Romeo drops out and loses the other two for several bars. It was taken off a direct quote in the play about the shadows of coming events. He has an odd premonition that something is about to happen which is going to change his whole destiny. He doesn't know what — something. He shakes it off and they go in, but that moment is about his commitment too.

So the way I did the start of Act II was that he now knows that he's loved and he is in love, and *that* changes your perspective on everything. I tried to make all the early part of Act II like champagne, like the way champagne makes you feel. That's why it's *so* fast; it's like an explosion of excitement, enthusiasm, possibility. Everything is golden and sparkling and terrific, and into it comes a wedding procession, which is what he hopes is going to happen to him — I tried to link that in too.

Now, Mercutio and Benvolio play with the Nurse when she comes on, but I don't think Romeo does. What he has to do is appear to play — play along — because he doesn't want to show his hand to them. He wants that letter real bad, but he doesn't want to admit how committed he's become to *the* one person because that is going to be shrieked to scorn by them. They'd kill him if he started saying, 'I've found *the* one.' They've heard it all before; Rosaline was that, every week there's a new one. So he has to play two things: play their game, but actually make damn sure he gets the letter.

He goes out like a bat out of hell the minute he's got it, to the Friar. You're not out of breath at that point, but I remember making myself very out of breath because it seemed important to be arriving

breathless and sweaty and urgent. He knows she's going to be there
— that's why he's raced, without pausing, without stopping, without
thinking, to get there. And then the marriage is hugely solemn. Young
people *are* very solemn, and of course they'd be very religious. I think
the combination of meeting the once-in-a-lifetime person, who is going
to be everything for you and change the world for you, and finding
that they feel the same, and then having that consecrated by the
Church, is very deep and solemn. The marriage has to be the most
important thing in that act.

I had to look a long time to find a way of doing that return
to the marketplace. Romeo comes along on the top gallery, and I
wanted the audience to know that a huge, emotional event had taken
place and that the religious significance of that bonding had been very
important to him. I did it the way it seemed natural to me, with my
head down, and I remember Lynn saying, "When your head is down
like that, what your body says is 'dejection.' " But you're not well
placed up there, and if your head is up, you become aware of what's
happening in the marketplace very quickly. I wanted something that
could only happen after a momentous religious experience — which
I thought the marriage was — but I couldn't think of choreographic
terms for it, and I don't think Ken could find them for me. It was
left to me, and I'm not sure I ever quite solved it. It *is* only a few
moments, but one has to account for every second onstage. You can't
have gaps. Ultimately, I kept my head dead straight and tried to do
it in the deliberate pace, the speed, of the walking, but I don't know
how successful it was because Lynnie was never out front to see that
bit.

He's then got this extraordinary situation to deal with, the taunt-
ing and provocation of Tybalt, which he's always been the first to leap
into with both feet and enjoy with Mercutio and Benvolio. It's a very
macho thing to do, but that's just what he is and what he's known as.
But suddenly, it's Juliet's cousin and he's married to her, so it's unthinkable. This is why one has to make the religious aspect of the
marriage so significant; it's got to have made such an impression on
him that now, in front of his mates, he's got to turn the other cheek
and become a peacemaker. Which can only be construed by Tybalt
as weakness, cowardice, and all the terrible things that Italian boys
can't get into, and God knows what his mates construe it as. So he's
trapped. There's nothing he can do but avoid this impossible situation
or somehow stop it developing. And the only way he can do that is
by appearing completely changed. Having tried very hard and been
sneered at by Tybalt and put down, he finally elects just to do a cut-
off from it altogether.

But, of course, the situation gets out of hand, and when Mercutio is killed, everything snaps. Mercutio was very dear. Those bonds between those lads were very close, very tight, and it's important that you establish the bond you have with Mercutio right from the beginning, and the fondness for him, which is in some ways closer — or other or a different kind — than you can ever have with a lady. What fellows have together is kind of special; because sexuality isn't there, in a way it's more open and honest. Mercutio has been an ally, a supporter, and a wiser, older friend for a long time. And he's dead. And he's dead by a piece of treachery — he's stabbed in the back. So it seemed to me that what you have to do is keep hitting the thing that did it until the breath stops. That's why the whole fight is based on only two sword movements. It isn't rapiers, and it isn't craft or style or art. It is hit it and hit it and hit it, on and on and on until it stops. No finesse, no gamesmanship, nothing. Hit it 'til it stops.

I would think he's killed somebody before. Life was very harsh then, and it was held more cheaply than it is now. And it would have been a Catholic country, so there are all those escape routes for Catholics. You can confess and get rid of it all — I'm pretty sure he's done all that. But after he's done *this,* it's like the end of an orgasm. When you have exploded on the deepest level and it's over, there's that terrible place you go into afterwards. There's her cousin, dead. You did it. You just married her, and now you've killed her cousin. I used to just check out. I don't remember getting off at all. Anthony used to do that for me, as Benvolio; he used to deal with it, because that's what friends are for. I didn't do another thing. That was the end of the world.

Fundamentally, the eye of the story is Juliet's, and we have to know the processes she moves through. It is enough to know that Romeo leaves, gets the poison, and then hears that she is dead. He comes back to see a dead body. As far as he's concerned, it's over, she's poisoned herself, and she's dead because she was being forced into a marriage with Paris which she can't agree to because she's already married. So from Romeo's point of view, Paris is largely responsible. Her parents, of course, but Paris is the best focus for why she's dead at all. So it's easy to kill him, particularly as he's the other man and he's right there in the tomb. You know how you don't want anybody there? Romeo's come to kill himself, to die with her, and it's a time to be together and alone. We don't want Paris around. It's our time together.

And then, when Paris is dead and Romeo is alone to grieve, as he must, there's that attempt to make her dance, to make her love, to make the arms work again. You know how totally incomprehensible death is, particularly when you're young? You can't actually believe that that person or that dog has gone forever and is never coming back. You can't get it into your head. So the idea we built on for the pas de deux was that if he holds her in his arms and tries to make her dance with him again, she'll *have* to dance again. She'll *have* to move again. Because she can't be dead. It can't be over. It can't. He tries very hard, and it's only when she can't dance that it really impinges on his brain that she *is* dead.

And then Ken had a wonderful idea: "When you've tried and tried and tried and it won't work," he said, "then I want it to be just like a big piece of dead meat on the stage." A gorilla at London Zoo had a baby — did you read about this? — and didn't know how to look after it, and it died. But they couldn't take it away from her. She dangled it around and played with it sometimes, and it didn't do anything, and she kept walking around with it. It bashed onto chairs and things, but she just kept pacing and wouldn't let it go. Well, that was the image I had in my mind. I used to drag Lynn around the stage, and she'd just let her legs fall apart, all open and exposed and vulnerable and ugly. I think she's the only one who does that; all the other ballerinas make pretty shapes on the floor. And I also used to rock, the way you rock when you go into that bad, grief place.

Then he takes the poison, and there's the awakening for her. And again, we explored what it would be like, at fourteen years old, to wake up in this tomb. It's full of dead people, cold, stone, dark, and you're locked in. We tried to find all that. And finally she takes the knife and kills herself. Lynn always used to stab herself in her womb, because it's never going to make any babies . . . for anybody. Gosh, she was smashing. And also, that way Juliet wouldn't die straightaway. She tries to crawl back across the tomb to get to him, and can't. She dies before she gets there. That's very important; Ken didn't want any suggestion that they would be united in death. So they die apart, not touching. Two beautiful, young lives have been totally wasted. Nothing's been achieved, nothing's better, and they're not united. They're just dead. Just two dead things.

It's a wonderful story. And in the ballet, when you've taken away the words, you can't devalue those emotions and those relationships, because they're your life-blood. You're living on them and the music. I suppose what you actually decide to do with a role, or how you decide to approach it, is more of an intellectual process, but the actual playing of it, your emotion, is supported by the music all the time. If one decides there's a rhapsodic quality to a pas de deux, it's because that's what the music is telling you. If you listen to the music, it will tell you, oh, everything.

There are three kinds of dancers. One kind sometimes dances on the beat, but not if they can do a step more excellently in their own time, in which category I would put Rudolf and Makarova. Makarova I can't watch. She has probably the most flawless dance instrument I've ever seen in my life, and as far as I can see, any relationship with the music is accidental. A lot of people like that, but it's not what I want. Then there are quite a lot of very rhythmic dancers, who dance on the beat. And then there's the kind of dancer which I pray and hope I was — and which Lynn certainly is — who responds to the music on a quite fundamental level, so that the whole way one's body reacts to a Stravinsky score is different from how it would react to a Prokofiev score or to Ravel or to Tchaikovsky. The music is entirely in the bloodstream somehow. That's a really musical dancer, and for me, they're the only kind. And, like all the best things, that quality is something you cannot learn.

Romeo *is* difficult to do well technically, but I don't like that everything-stops-while-you-do-your-dance thing. The idea was always that the variations should come out of the dramatic line and disappear back into it without a bump, like the songs in a good musical coming out of the story and going back into it. The choreography was designed to be an expression of emotion, not an expression of dancing. It ought to look improvised — that's what I mean. In the same way that, as an actor, one tries to make the words sound as if you're coining them fresh, that second, because they're what you need to say, one tries to make a solo in a ballet look as though you're doing it because it's the only thing you *can* do then because of the way you feel. It shouldn't be about beautiful feet — although they've got to be there as well. I was usually guilty of going the wrong way, the other way, but you have to try to strike a balance. That's why it's so difficult. You have to keep the classical schooling good enough that nobody will remark on its absence, but you can't take very careful preparations and then do lots of lovely pirouettes. You don't do pirouettes in a solo like Romeo's: you spin.

If you're doing a play, its nature lives in the relationship you create with the other people onstage. When all is said and done, there's no such thing as speeches in plays; there are just things that you say, and who you say them to makes a great difference on how you say them. You talk in a way that's appropriate to the person you've got to talk to. Otherwise, you just say your bits, and when you've finished, she'll say her bits. If *you* were somebody else, the way I'm talking now would be different because I'd respond to you differently. I'd say the same things, but the whole feel would be different. Well, it's the same with the ballet. I always loved doing pas de deux with Lynn, because

I liked getting to a reality within the frame of the ballet. We once did a gala performance of the last-act pas de deux from *Two Pigeons* for a charity show. We did it as we'd always done it, and afterwards, the dancers who'd been standing in the wings all said, "Oh, you have such tremendous eye contact." Like it was something magical. I said, "What the hell are you supposed to do in a pas de deux? Not look at her?!"

Everything you do, your knowledge of life and also what you've done onstage, gets stored away in your little knapsack of experience. If you've learned there is a technical way of achieving the effect you're trying for, you'll use it, because you obviously aren't going to rip yourself to pieces night after night. I used to watch all the stuff Lynn did on her own, the poison-taking scene and all of that, finding ways to work, because Lynn is very technical. Any professional is technical. You can have a great emotional binge in rehearsals, but come show time, you've got to have something that you can reproduce in coolness so that it has its maximum effect. You have to use a technique. And ultimately, what is important is not that you have a great emotional experience on the stage but that the audience has a great emotional experience. There's a rather rude name for the other thing.

You must be doing it for the people. That isn't to say you allow them to dictate artistic terms to you, or indeed, any terms at all. You are doing it for yourself and the person you're working with in that you are trying to find the deepest, richest truth you can. Oh, all these things sound so crappy. I'm sorry, but they are the facts. That truth is entirely for yourself and personal, because it has to do with your artistic integrity. But having found it, it's no use to anybody unless you can share it with the people who come to watch.

Ah, but the audience and the critics are quite, quite different. The critics are nothing whatever to do with the audience, and I never listened to them. I listened very carefully to a handful of people whose judgment I valued and whose artistic integrity I respected; primarily Lynn, I suppose, but there were two or three others. But certainly not the critics — last of all, them. Because if I spend three, four months preparing a ballet, as we did with *Romeo*, and then I spend two years refining it, changing it, adjusting, working, and thinking, I don't consider that somebody who walks into a theatre has the right — with the price of that ticket — to tell me how to do anything. They haven't put in anything like the thought, time, care, love, concern that I've put in. They have no voice for me at all.

I listened to my family too, and to all kinds of totally arbitrary people I would meet at parties. I was always very interested in what they thought, because ordinary people aren't diffused by what they think is expertise or by what they think they ought to say. Neither are they concerned with projecting their own sensitivity and awareness onto what they're seeing, or displaying their own gifts. For instance . . . Well, early on I did the fight with Tybalt the way I thought it ought to be, which was 'Kill Tybalt and don't think about it.' I hadn't got to analyzing it then. And I met a lady at a party who said, "One of the most exciting moments of the show for me was the fight with Tybalt, because it was like you were trying to kill death itself." And I said, "Thank you very much," and we went on to something else. But I thought, 'O.K. That bit's right. No question.' Oh, Lynn and I spent lots of time changing tiny moments. I didn't get to a Romeo that I was remotely satisfied with for two years. But that's the lovely thing about the ballet, of course — you keep coming back to things. The *Swan Lake* I was doing when I left was nothing to do with the ghastly rubbish I was doing at the beginning.

I didn't lust after parts and want to do them; I don't have that kind of ambition. The only part I've seen since I've retired that I would like to be physically fit enough to have a crack at would be *Mayerling*. But I've spoken to David Wall, and he reckons it's shortened his life by about five years, so I think it's out of the question. But that seems to me the closest to the kind of ballet that interests me, because it's a beautifully constructed story, told in terms of movement and dance, about something very strong. I would love to have had a crack at it.

You can't avoid making a personal statement when you dance, because your dancing is you. No matter how purely you are listening to the music and trying to reflect the choreographer's idea, you nevertheless reflect it through what experience you have, what understanding you have, what sensitivity you have, and primarily, in the ballet, what body you've got wrapped up in. It's got to be a personal statement in that sense. I think really the trick is to efface the ego. People usually want to impose themselves on the music. They don't want the music to tell them what to do; they want to tell it what they're going to do. But when you listen to the greatest musicians talk, they're not interested in doing the definitive Brahms this or Tchaikovsky that. They're interested in trying to find what Brahms was saying, and presenting that. But by definition, most people in the theatre also want to present themselves, to be stars or whatever. So the ego gets in the way. They put themselves between . . . In the middle, between the real you and the work, you put yourself, and that spoils it all.

July 1979
London

Deanne Bergsma

Deanne Bergsma (b. Pretoria, South Africa, 1941) began to study ballet when she was four with Marjorie Sturman in Johannesburg. She joined the Royal Ballet in 1959 after two years at the Royal Ballet School in London and advanced to principal by 1967. Her roles ranged from Odette-Odile, Myrtha, and the Lilac Fairy to the Hostess in Nijinska's Les Biches *and the Tsarevna in Fokine's* Firebird. *Having created leading parts in Ashton's* Enigma Variations *(1968) and Glen Tetley's* Field Figures *(1970) and* Laborintus *(1972), she made her debut as the Siren in Balanchine's* The Prodigal Son *at the first Royal Ballet performance of that work, in 1973. She retired from dancing in 1978.*

Every time I see either the Lilac Fairy or Josephine in Ashton's A Wedding Bouquet, *I see Deanne Bergsma. Luminous as massed candles in one, tart and sparkling as champagne in the other, she slips unbidden between my eyes and whoever is actually dancing, and only disappears if I deliberately banish her. Photographs capture her face and shape but falsify her dancing, which never stopped, never came to a complete halt, even when she was standing still. Thus, memory records her more accurately than print. To my lasting regret, I have no memories of Bergsma as the Siren and I never saw her dance a step of Balanchine.*

I came to the School at twelve and only stayed three months. There was no White Lodge or anything at that time; there was simply a little boarding-house, and my mother just couldn't leave me in a place like that at twelve, so we went all the way home. But they said for me to come back in a few years' time, and they told Sturman how to train me, what to do — it all seemed to be planned. I think mentally I was happier to come later on and be with my family for a longer period. And then I did come back when I was fifteen, but I got diphtheria and I decided absolutely the ballet was not for me. So I went home again for quite a few months to recover, and gradually decided it was for me. So I came back, and I was a student for a few more months and then joined the company. Ballet had been my world, really, since I was four, but I loathed the exams and the competition. I wasn't ever a theatrical person. I always had the other side of life. I always wanted that somehow. If I could get away from the theatre, I always did.

My teacher, Marjorie Sturman, was quite a woman. I did RAD training with her — nothing else was involved — simply classical training, class, and rehearsals — she had a company. We did *Swan Lake* there when Margot and Michael came out, and the whole of *Sleeping Beauty*. I was a fairy in *Beauty* and one of the swans in *Swan Lake* — just corps. I was big, but I wasn't a big swan. Oh yes, when I was twelve I was already pretty tall. And I think Madam [de Valois] and all of them weren't too sure about me because of my height. I used to stand at the barre and pull myself down, try and get down. Svetlana had a lovely trick; she had such a supple back that she could go down a bit, but I could never do that.

I knew I could jump, I always did have stamina, and I could see the sort of roles I'd want eventually to do. But all I saw ever were guest artists who came to join Sturman's company. Just Margot, Michael — we saw Markova — and films, Russian films, Bolshoi. I learned how to do grands jetés and things just by watching the films. And that was really it. And way out in South Africa, one never thought of joining the Royal Ballet or anything like that. It was just a dream. One was simply looking at ballet books and dreaming about those.

It all happened because of an RAD examiner, Claude Newman, who came out, saw me, and just wrote to the Royal Ballet School and asked them to ask me to come over. Otherwise, I'm sure I would never have done so. I mean, I was planning to become a nurse or something.

I was so thrilled really to have such a quantity of choreographers of quality. Nijinska was quite something. She really was a great big tub, just huge. She couldn't really move. She couldn't speak to us. She had no English at all, she could only speak French, so she sort of interpreted to Fred [Ashton]. But just her top half helped us enormously. She would just do a few movements, and you could see the whole ballet in that. She was very precise and she knew exactly what she wanted. To try and get it from her was quite extraordinary, but she jolly well got it from us. I would have worked and worked for her. She was fast, and I was so engrossed, I didn't realize the time was going or that I was tired or anything. Really one of my favorite roles is *Biches* — oh, it's fantastic.

I was not really as happy with Jerry Robbins. Well, I just don't like working with choreographers who are out to make you nervous, and you felt with him that he could, at any minute, chuck you out or say something awful to you. Actually, he behaved quite well with the Royal Ballet, but one knew that he could suddenly attack. It was enjoyable, of course, working with such a famous person, but I don't work well with people who make me nervous. Nerves were a constant problem for me anyway. All my friends said they didn't ever see me nervous, but I was. I always hid it. I think a lot of people thrive on it.

He got the feeling of being nervous into *Requiem Canticles*; you had to be so on your mettle for that ballet, to bring this feeling across. It was quite enjoyable to dance, but there was something peculiar about it. It didn't quite make it.

I also did *Faun*, oh yes. That was the beginning of the end, really. I rehearsed it with Robbins in New York and he was very, very nice then. And I did a few performances, but I always felt I was too tall for David Wall. If I could have had a taller partner it would have made a world of difference, although he's a smashing chap. And then Robbins said via Peter Wright that I wasn't quite suited. I absolutely adored the ballet, the music more than anything, so that hurt a bit. Working in the beginning with him I got that feeling that he could just chuck you out, and he did eventually.

Ashton, of course, was wonderful, and I thoroughly enjoyed doing *Wedding Bouquet*. It only sort of jelled when the performance started; rehearsals were all very loose. I didn't quite know what sort of character Josephine was going to be until she came out on the stage. I always used to make my mother laugh, and if you make somebody laugh when you're young, you must know how, even without knowing it. And I watched a lot of hostesses and a few tipsy ladies at parties, and that helped.

Enigma was the one role I created for Fred, and it seemed to just somehow be written. He worked so fast; he seemed to know. He always liked my bourrées, and he said if only he could get on my back when I was the Queen of the Wilis and see what it was like to travel like that. Can you imagine?! It's the most lovely picture, with him on my back. He always used the best things in a dancer — whatever they were, you know, he hit them — and I always liked bourréeing anyway. It was easy for me.

In the classics, everybody knows exactly what you're supposed to be doing, so you daren't put a foot wrong, and yet you've got to put your own interpretation onto that. Otherwise there'd be no point in doing it. That's what you've got to strive to do.

Oh, I think I was happiest with Queen of the Wilis. The dancers always used to say I'd come out here, to the cemetery, and get my tips. I loved doing that role — I could always get involved. Lilac Fairy I always loathed . . . loathed, loathed. It was such a cold-blooded thing and such a difficult solo. I used to get so scared, I suppose because I did it first when I was so young. When I was eighteen, I did a few here, and then we went to New York and they made me first cast. I had to do it on the first night in New York! I did feel responsibility then and so nervous. You know, if you slip once, it's such a short solo, with those fouettés, that you might as well say good-bye. That's it. You don't have another chance. At least when I last did it, Kenneth [MacMillan] put another solo for the Lilac Fairy in the last act. Now they might've taken it out again. But with just the one, you either walk around in the second act pleased with yourself or miserable — you've got two acts of walking around miserable.

Working with Glen and the New Group came at a perfect time for me because I'd really come to a standstill. I was dying for something new. I was dead sick of Lilac Fairy and just the usual classical things. He chose me for *Field Figures* because of the look in my eyes. That's what he said. I was just at the back of the class, and I thought, 'Well, this is not for me, modern dancing,' but I desperately wanted to do something like that. I just thought I wouldn't be chosen because I didn't believe I could do it. I'd sort of gotten into a rut, and I felt all stiff and ghastly and hideous. I gave up before I even went into class. You know, I took one look at Glen and thought, 'He's bound to choose somebody else.' So it was a great surprise.

It was just complete opposites, three months of opposites, but Glen was the most fantastic teacher. We'd go hours and hours just doing exercises and classes with him, and then gradually he'd take a few steps and start the ballet. It seemed to emerge. *Rite [of Spring]* was the only modern thing I'd done, but that was a different thing really. That was simply a classical dancer doing other steps, but with Glen's, you were actually working on a different technique. You used lots of different muscles, a lot of the stomach muscles. And you're going into the floor with modern work and lifting off the floor with classical work. It helped my back enormously, and it helped to go from Glen back to classical work. One had so many new things to think about.

Glen said he enjoyed working with people who were so highly trained classically because they could just tell the other muscles what to do. For us it was three months of sheer, utter agony, but it was a lovely, lovely rehearsal period. We all just died when the first performance came and he was going to leave us; he wasn't ours any more. Oh, he came back, but it was never going to be the same. He'd given birth. *Laborintus* was different somehow. He wasn't as happy — I don't know why — and we didn't have as long a period rehearsing with him. I don't think it came out as successfully.

Now, Balanchine was quite a different style. It was difficult to get hold of but most enjoyable too, because one knew he liked tall dancers and he felt it suited them. I did *Apollo* and *Serenade* before *Prodigal Son*, but I wasn't first cast for *Apollo*.

And then . . . Well, I write a diary, so I was looking it up. [John] Taras came first, to teach *Prodigal*, and Pat Neary came just before Christmas. They taught it very quickly to us, and then Christmas happened. And virtually the first rehearsal after Christmas and all the holidays, Balanchine arrived and we had to rehearse it with him. I remember I had a bad ankle, as usual. He was splendid. He got the atmosphere for us, and he actually danced — he partnered me. I thought he was going to fall down with the first lift, but not a bit of it. He did a few things, not everything, not all those writhing things, but he's a good partner, pretty strong.

We didn't work on it long at all; I think a month, and we were on. It was just long enough, just. I remember saying, in my diary, we really needed another week. And again, it all just happened on the first night.

I'd only ever seen one performance, and that was Suzanne Farrell. All I remember is that she hadn't pinned her hat on, and it was wobbly. I was terrified that it was going to go. Eventually, I guess, she just had to hold it. Well, I never liked looking at other people's performances anyway, if I was going to do something. I like to have a fresh mind. But I didn't know I was going to do it then. Never crossed my mind, actually. When there was word that *Prodigal Son* was coming, I hoped desperately that I would do it, because I really liked the idea. It seemed like me. And one always wanted new roles, and I was starved of them.

The story was very much in my mind because of Benjamin Britten's *Prodigal Son*, which I was involved with because my husband was involved with the opera side of the Opera House. So I knew the story and I knew who'd done it before, and I looked at photographs of the make-up and everything. I knew just about that much. The music was the biggest thing really, so strong and full. On your entrance, it's so exciting standing in the wings, because of that music, that you're made before you go on.

Balanchine didn't talk about it at all. He didn't mention one thing about how to do it. I think you make the choices. Well, what I wanted to be was seductive but intangible, hot and cold. I wanted to be opposites, not just one thing. It makes a problem for me, yes, and a problem for him too, the Prodigal Son, but that's the way I felt I should be. Sexy I'm not. Cruel . . . yes, I think so. Available and absolutely not — icy cold. I don't know whether I got that across, but that's how I felt.

The first solo you're showing yourself to him, but the rest of the cast are very much involved watching it. And I think there could be a moment that you actually fall for him, when you're sitting at the back, at the table, watching, just looking at him, not dancing. And then you don't — you're far too cruel. I doubt the audience could see it, but it's in your mind, it colors what you do. Technically the solo was quite comfortable. It never bothered me before a performance. *Prodigal* was always a performance to look forward to, with no real nasties waiting 'round the corner for you. And I'd rehearsed the solo, not with the hat, but with the cloak, always, a rehearsal cloak. It had to be very much like the costume because just to unhook that blessed thing . . . now, that really was a nasty moment, always. But the cloak helped to get you into the mood; it was a piece of you, like an extension of you. I think in the beginning the Siren is a dream for the Prodigal Son, like a vision. It's as though he's watching as part of the audience. And then when he comes up to her and actually sees the make-up really close, she's not all he thought she was.

The pas de deux was with Rudi, who is small, but that was fine. I had no problem really with that, apart from sliding down those precious shins. Well, he was worried, so I got to the ground pretty fast. Otherwise he was splendid. The difference in size helped, because you were in command, very much in command, and using him. And he was strong enough to handle me. Actually, I enjoyed all those strange positions very much — after *Field Figures*, I could cope with anything — and I think they're absolutely needed. You must get tangled up because you are snaky.

I suppose one learns things about partnering, but it just comes with your technique, by doing it and getting stronger and stronger. I was lucky enough to have Donald MacLeary for most of my partnering, who is the best. My goodness, he was marvelous. But I was

always aware of my height. I thoroughly enjoyed dancing with a partner for certain things, but it depended on the role and the partner.
And I think I was really happiest dancing by myself.

You're still on top of things in *Prodigal* after the pas de deux.
No matter what they're doing, you're still calling the shots. But part-
nering-wise, it's up to them and you can't do a thing. It *is* rather
frightening, especially when it doesn't work. There was one night it
didn't work: Rudi had put some putty on his nose — I don't know
why. He just wanted a different profile that night — and I landed
right on it, right on his nose. Going over the table. I came right down
and bent his nose. He was hysterical. He couldn't do a thing. And,
you know, the next position is just sitting looking at each other, and
we were both trying so hard not to giggle. But I was never hurt in
that toss, and there were no accidents except for Rudolf's precious
nose.

I would say she's still in command there. But then, when she
gets the Prodigal's necklace, she lets herself down. She just comes
down to rock bottom. She can't stay aloof. She goes right down and
then up again, possibly, for the boat.

I danced it later with Desmond [Kelly], but it always felt the
same. Whether one was on tour, on a small stage or a large stage, *The
Prodigal Son* was *The Prodigal Son* and that music took over. And the
Siren was there. I don't think it altered one bit.

Oh, dancing a role without a character was much harder for
me. I hated it. Dancing Glen's ballets didn't feel that way at all, though
what I was dancing certainly wasn't me. I don't know what I was, but
it wasn't completely abstract, not at all. He gave us certain images, and
you were free to work on them as you wanted to. For instance, he
wanted us to move like insects, without any . . . not 'emotion' . . . any
sentiment. It's very difficult to explain. But when you were simply
doing ballet steps in a tutu or whatever, there was precious little you
could do for yourself but work jolly hard at it. When you are simply
Deanne Bergsma, it isn't really very nice. That's what I miss now,
actually, having given it up — being other people. It was fun, changing
yourself sometimes three times a night; it was lovely.

Critics always made me nervous. I could never wipe out what
a critic had said. And it was always bad . . . well, usually . . . and it
always hurt; it always hurts for every artist. But you always have to
listen to your classroom teacher. I had a private teacher, Winifred
Edwards, and I listened very closely to what she said. And of course
every word Fred ever told me was golden. Fred and Glen are my
favorites, really.

I think I danced for myself first of all. And if the audience wanted to watch, then they could very well come. It was fun to have an audience, but many times you felt awful and the audience loved it, or vice versa. I think you have to please yourself first, apart from the choreographer. Yes, sticking with yourself is the best bet — it's the only bet, really.

I never really thought of what roles I'd like to dance. I mean, one was with the Royal Ballet, and whatever was going to come, you hoped to do. But I never visualized myself with another company, so I never actually thought about other roles. I think I would have loved to have done *Giselle*, although I know I wasn't suitable.

I've put all that behind me now. It's rather hard to call it all up again and talk about *Prodigal Son*, not because it's painful to remember dancing — it just seems such a long time ago. I've always been a great one for shutting one door and opening another. I was never a complete dancer. There's always been too much of life going on elsewhere.

July 1979
London

Monica Mason

Monica Mason (b. Johannesburg, South Africa, 1941) began her ballet train-
ing in South Africa with Ruth Inglestone and Frank Staff and continued it
in London, from the age of fourteen, with Nesta Brooking and at the Royal
Ballet School. Having joined the Royal Ballet in 1958, she was still a member
of the corps de ballet when she created the demanding, pivotal role of the
Chosen Maiden in Kenneth MacMillan's The Rite of Spring *(1962). A*
principal since 1968, 'she dances a repertory so eclectic that it defies catego-
rization; it includes Odette-Odile, Carabosse, Lady Elgar in Ashton's Enigma
Variations, *Webster in his* A Wedding Bouquet, *the Hostess in Nijinska's*
Les Biches, *and leading roles in* La Bayadère *(Act IV),* Les Sylphides,
MacMillan's Song of the Earth *and* Manon, *Balanchine's* Apollo *and*
Serenade, *and Robbins'* Dances at a Gathering. *She made her debut as*
the Firebird in 1979.

Monica Mason is never the same twice, even in the same ballet. Every time
you look at her, you find someone you've never seen before. In a company of
classical conformity, Mason is an original, a dancer of exceptional daring and
uncommon diversity. Like Alec Guinness, she transforms herself from role to
role without reservation, adopting theatrical guises with such apparent ease
that her personal anonymity has become part of her artistic identity. How many
women can capture the classical serenity of Nikiya, the sardonic humor of
Webster, the operatic flamboyance of Carabosse, and the eloquent austerity that
permeates Song of the Earth? *I selfishly chose to talk to her about* Firebird
because I'd never had the chance to see her dance it.

I'm very glad that I came to *Firebird* late. There's so much to it, and when I came to do it, I knew it mattered terribly to me that I should try to contribute as much as possible to what I consider a great ballet. I think I would have been very disappointed to have danced it at a younger age and not appreciated the qualities that are there. And perhaps approached it in a little more facile way. That would have disappointed me.

I was going to do a performance when they revived it in 1972, but I had broken a bone in my foot so I was off, and I didn't do it until they did it again about eighteen months ago. I didn't even learn it in '72. I wasn't at work, you see; I didn't go near the place.

When I first joined the company, I used to be in *Firebird* in the corps de ballet, when Margot and Nadia Nerina danced it. I was one of the Indian maidens, not the white princesses, the Indian maidens that run on and shake in the finale. It was fabulous. Grigoriev and Tchernicheva were there; they mounted *Petrouchka*, *Firebird*, and *Sylphides* at the time. They were wonderful people. My first encounter with them was when I was still in the School, walking on in *Petrouchka*. We were brought in from the School, as graduates, to work with the company, and I used to do one of the rather grand ladies who walked around in the fairground scene. And then later on when I joined the company, I worked with them again in *Petrouchka*, because I became one of the gypsies. That was fun. But in everything they did, they took great, great care and worked in enormous detail. I think I learned a lot from them.

Tchernicheva was especially marvelous with the girls. Later on, when I became one of the princesses, she was amazing. By this time she was a very old lady, very stiff and arthritic, and rather sad in some ways. I think she'd had a great reputation as a great beauty in her day, and now she felt like a very faded flower and was always apologizing for the fact. It was quite sad. And of course to us she was still so beautiful. She had the most expressive face and wonderful gestures, beautiful hands and arms, and wonderful mime. I remember her talking to the princesses in *Firebird*, making each one of them individual. The way she described it, and her face and hands, made everything part of the whole — the moonlight and their white dresses in the moonlight and their own purity, virginity. And also the gentle music and the simple joy in playing with those apples, catching them and throwing and catching. When they see Ivan, they must feel that they've never seen a man before. They're absolutely horrified when his hand reaches out to them with the apple in it, horrified and tantalized. Maybe in the very back of their minds they had imagined a man, but nothing more than that. That's a difficult thing to explain nowadays; we live in such an enlightened, free, morally liberated society — which is wonderful — but the life in the early part of the century was much more protected. And Tchernicheva came from that life, lived it, believed it, and could make us believe it too. In fact, when we were just remounting the production, I asked to take a rehearsal of the princesses to try to pass those things on to them, those feelings that she had made so clear. I can remember her face exactly, and the way she talked.

Present-day dancers find it increasingly difficult to capture the qualities in the older ballets because they were danced at a time when life, the whole of life, was very different. You have to believe in some of the most extraordinary things. All those weird creatures that come out of Kostchei's palace have to be danced so well and with such conviction. And every single one of those princesses has to understand the real conception of the purity and virginity, in the sense that today's young people really don't understand. To explain today to an eighteen- or nineteen-year-old girl that she'd never seen a man before in her life . . . it calls for a great deal of imagination. Whereas I think in the Twenties life was so much simpler and far, far less sophisticated. Even when I joined the company in the Fifties . . . you know, the Fifties were still pretty uptight about an awful lot of things. I was — maybe not at the back of my mind, not quite so virginal — but certainly I was very virginal when I first was a princess. And Tchernicheva explained it so beautifully and made the princesses so magical that I found it relatively easy. I won't say I danced it like she wanted it to be danced, but I found the conception of the princesses very easy to accept.

I remember those early performances with Margot and Nadia very clearly — I saw Annette Page do it as well — and I remember I always wanted to dance the role. Always. I don't think I ever missed watching the first part of *Firebird,* ever, and it used to fascinate me that everybody used to say it was the most exhausting thing they'd ever done. I remember Nadia Nerina, who was such a strong dancer, coming into the wings one night and saying, "Now, if any ballet will kill me, it'll be this one." So it sort of had an extra fascination. I always adored the music and just longed to be the Firebird. I adored the role.

I think I probably watched it with the feeling of retaining what I was seeing, but you can't really pick up those points when you're watching from the wings. You have to be in front really to judge the value of something. You can notice from the wings whether technical things are working all right, but to get the measure of something, I always have to see it from the front. I never pass judgment from the wings. And I never, ever saw *Firebird* from the front because I was always in it.

There were masses of ballets like that, that one didn't see for years and years. One of the boys in our company, David Drew, saw our production of *Swan Lake* last night for the first time in fifteen years. He's never not been in *Swan Lake* in fifteen years! It's amazing, isn't it? I had never seen *Sleeping Beauty* before I was in it. I'd hardly seen the company dance at all when I first joined, and then I was in it and in these things and I'd never seen them. So as much as I might have wanted to know things about *Firebird*, I wasn't able to, really.

When I came to learn it a year or so ago, Michael Somes taught us. And then I said to Norman [Morrice], "I know the role now. I know how to dance the steps and I know what all the steps are. But I just have got to have a link with the past. You've got to get Margot or somebody to come and show us how it felt. You've got to show us what the ballet's about." This is not to knock Michael in any sense at all, but this I felt was the one role where you had to talk to somebody who'd danced it.

Margot had actually been coached by Karsavina, and I *knew* that Margot held the key for the Firebird because she had got it directly from Karsavina herself. And Margot of course, as always, was so busy and couldn't be reached and wasn't available and then couldn't do it and then she'd be in the building and couldn't stay and all this. But I just couldn't accept the fact that she was not available for half an hour at some point in her life. And eventually one day I appealed to Norman: I said, "You know, I have a feeling that if I can't get some time with Margot, I don't really want to do it, because I can't do it without that." I was passionate about it. And so he had another talk to her. And one day, I suppose literally she gave us about forty-five minutes or an hour. It was wonderful. From the moment she started, I knew that I'd been right — I had really, really needed her.

She just used some of the words that Karsavina had used for her; what had been conveyed to her had really stayed. And they have stayed, they will stay, with me. On the very first entrance in *Firebird*, she said, "This is your territory, your domain, and you don't fly over it, you soar. You soar over your territory. Even a sparrow notices if another sparrow comes to perch on his tree, his branch. So imagine what it must be like for the Firebird to have a man invade her territory and actually *capture* her." And immediately one had a whole different picture. And then she talked about the viciousness of the bird. Apparently, according to the Russian folklore, Firebirds actually ate men. She absolutely was a man-eater. So the Prince doesn't really know what he has caught, but the Firebird knows.

And she said that Karsavina had said that from the moment the Prince catches her, she hates him. She hates him for daring even to touch her. Nobody dares to touch her. And another thing Margot said was that when you plead with him to let you go, you still retain this hatred for him, that there's no softening in your feelings. You hate him, and you even hate the fact that you have to ask him to release you. You have to plead, but you plead without losing any of your dignity or your feeling of self-preservation.

So all of that stirred one's imagination, which was really what I knew I needed for the role. Those were the things I latched onto and tried to understand. They all make it very fantastical, which the music is.

I don't think of myself totally as a bird. Maybe the original Firebird is totally just bird, but certainly the way Fokine saw it, the woman also had a part to play in it. I don't think I could play it solely as a fantastic creature, though I don't relate to it emotionally as a woman; I only think of it in terms of a woman inasmuch as it's a woman that's dancing it and the creature's in a woman's shape. The costume doesn't try to turn you into a bird or actually try to make you look extraordinary. It makes you feel very beautifully dressed. But I'm still very much myself, whereas I'm sure Derek Rencher as Kostchei almost doesn't feel like a man. That's what I'm really trying to say: his costume actually takes him away from reality, whereas I think my costume doesn't. In the original design, the Firebird had long plaits and tissue trousers and she wore great strings of pearls. Well, I can't imagine the conception was totally away from a woman in that. There is some element of female form.

If there is anything ever to look at, I try to look it up. I have lots of books myself and I try to talk to people. G. B. Wilson, the historian, is always readily available because he's attached to the Royal Ballet School, so I always get hold of him. And if he's got anything else he can show me, he always brings books in. He's very kind like that.

It's always interesting to fill in the background, but I think the very nature that we are determines how we're going to move. Your body is related in a sense to your nature. That's why positive people walk positively, lazy people walk lazily, and you can't really ever get away from that.

Yet every single role is really very separate and distinctive. And we always say that *Swan Lake* is tiring and *Sleeping Beauty* is tiring and *Firebird* is tiring, but none of them helps another. If you're dancing all of them, presumably you're fit, but the stamina for one is nothing like the stamina for the next. Every one has to be paced a little differently. *Firebird* is extremely exhausting, but it's not by any means for me the most exhausting. *Rite of Spring* is worse. There's no way that I would like to pretend that *Firebird*'s easy; it's very, very demanding. But just before we came away I had two consecutive performances, and by the second night, I could pace it much more. I suppose maybe I've done a dozen performances now — not a great many — and I do find that I can begin to get through it without being totally ill.

Apart from the pas de deux, you're on your own. The first entrance and the whole of the first dance is on your own, and then the final dance is on your own. But I think I'm far more used to dancing on my own than I am in a pas de deux situation. I'm usually more of a loner. Also, the main base of my repertoire has never been in the classics. Although I've performed *Beauty* and *Giselle*, I've done each of them only three or four times. So it's only when I come to do *Swan Lake* that I'm really in the classical ballet tradition.

They're not dissimilar, *Lac* and *Firebird*. I mean, they're completely unalike, yes, but in thinking about them there are similarities. Again, one has the question of creating an illusion of sorts relating to wings, and Odette is a very powerful, rather fantastic creature. It's all very far from reality, although the emotions are real. Now you really *do* have the bird-woman link, with the woman most definitely uppermost. When Ninette [de Valois] talks about Odette, she always says that one doesn't really try to look like a bird because she's *not* the swan; she's only too glad to get away from being a swan. I can remember Ninette saying years ago that there was one thing she didn't understand: why Makarova stresses the bird movements and qualities quite as much as she does in the white act. Choreographically, one is constantly aware that the shape Odette is making relates to what — twelve hours a day — she is. But Ninette felt that one must get away from it there and impress on the audience that it's a woman the Prince is falling in love with, not a bird. So that's where the comparison between *Firebird* and *Swan Lake* doesn't hold at all.

Certainly when one thinks about Odette, I invariably try to think very much about leaving the bird behind, especially when one makes that very first entrance. The moment of transition has only just taken place, so she still must be feeling very much like a bird. And then you should see her change again into the bird, just at the end of that act, in the bourrées. The change is much harder to do in the entrance because it's also the first time you're coming onstage. But the very first arabesque and the folding of the wings — people talk about the last drops of water on your arms and getting rid of them, and there are still a few feathers, and the lingering of the waters of the lake on your wings — it's wonderful, really. I just wonder how much the audience can possibly understand about that when they're watching. You have to convey so much in such a very short time. Of course, the mime explains a lot.

The only thing you have to mime in *Firebird* is the pleading away to be freed. I don't think she explains anything to the Prince, really; it's usually just in the program. When she gives him the feather, she doesn't explain to him: 'This feather is going to give you a great power. When you need me, just wave it.' She just hands him the feather. It's done very simply. As she takes the feather out, she waves it in front of him and that is repeated in the music later on, so it's all signified, I think, by that tiny little theme.

Oh, gosh, don't talk about that feather. Everything happens to that feather. It's been sewn in, it's Velcro-ed in, it's wedged in. Poor Alfreda Thorogood — on her first performance, her feather fell out in the middle of the stage. She had to pick it up and stuff it down her bodice and then retrieve it later on. Of course your whole skirt is feathered and net, and at the moment that you want it, you have to feel around and hope and pray that you can find the stalk of the feather and whip it out. It's really quite tricky. It's the moment you always pray happens; it's so quick and kind of vital to the story.

It *is* an old-fashioned ballet, but then I think Mozart is old-fashioned, and nobody ever talks about that. And the same for *Swan Lake*; it's very old-fashioned. Think of how Ivanov calls on the principals to tell their stories, in this sort of mad arm-waving which nobody could possibly understand, and how Kenneth [MacMillan] gets all his principals in *Mayerling* to tell their stories without a single mime gesture. It immediately puts *Swan Lake* a hundred years ago and *Mayerling* in the present day.

I can't imagine not actually relating in some way to a role; just how depends on how strong the story line is and how strong the role is. If the actual content is strong enough, then you can leave an awful lot of yourself behind, but I don't think you ever totally leave yourself in a box. I shocked somebody the other day by saying, "I wish somebody could do a ballet to *Salome*." And they said, "Why? It's a horrific story." And I said, "Because I can totally relate to that woman." Well, they turned and ran a mile.

But if the character is very faintly drawn, or if she doesn't exist — like the one I do in *Manon* which Kenneth invented in a sense; she doesn't exist in the book — then I think it's entirely yourself. It's created for you and out of you, and obviously, the more you enjoy digging in a role, the more you're made to find. Every dancer relies enormously on himself. I once said to Kenneth, "It worries me sometimes that you've always cast me as a whore. I've done so many in my time. What does it mean?" Yes, there's the Chosen Maiden. She starts out quite pure and deteriorates on the way.

I used to think that the thing that stood me in such good stead for *Rite of Spring* was the fact that I had been brought up amongst Africans, who I saw dance from morning 'til night. They're such a musical, wonderful people; one can watch them endlessly, because even in their conversations they seem to dance. When I visited South Africa again with my husband in 1975, one of the first things he said was, "Look at those people on the corner. They're just standing talking, but look at the way they're moving."

And I'd always been fascinated as a child by the way they danced. We used to take visitors from England to the mines and watch. On a Sunday, various tribes of people who were working in the gold mines used to do some of their traditional dancing, which is still, to this day, some of the most amazing, exciting dancing you could ever see anywhere. Of course the rhythm they have is something totally inborn. They make their own music. They could get through whole numbers, with maybe fifty of them in a line or two lines, with no music except drums. For some of the numbers, they didn't even have drums; they just sang and just danced, totally in synchronization. It was like watching one person magnified. That made such an impression on me.

And I always loved the natural rhythms and some of the more natural forms of dancing. I studied Greek dancing as a child and also Spanish quite a lot, and I was fascinated by the unclassical, in the sense of the pointe shoe bit. So when Kenneth started to do *Rite of Spring,* it was just heaven. I mean, to have something absolutely made for you and then to find that you could really use that music and move to it in a way that was totally natural to oneself. And strangely enough, I find this very much about *Firebird* too, although it's classical. It is so beautifully musical, so rhythmical, and the music gets you through it. Everybody hears music and everybody tries to listen in varying degrees, but some people are helped more by the music than others. You actually can use the music to assist you. Technically, the way that first Firebird dance is built on the music is so helpful. You're never, ever fighting the music, never, ever going against any of the rhythm. It's absolutely in the music. In *Rite of Spring* as well, you're going with whatever the rhythm is at that time. There's something so fabulous about dancing to the music in both those ballets.

I played the piano as a child, and my mother played the piano. And my father's family were very musical people; he had three sisters who all played the piano when I was around, one aunt especially. My father loved dancing; he was a social dancer with tremendous rhythm. Even when I was very, very tiny, he used to dance with me, ballroom dancing things, and always the music around the house. I was forever dancing in the sitting room. I'd dance at the drop of a hat. I remember once, at junior school in South Africa, there must have been a competition coming up, and one of my girlfriends who knew I was mad about it said to the PT instructor, "Monica's going to do a competition this week. Why don't we all sit down and watch her do her dance, because she'll dance for us." And so they did. I must have been an extremely extrovert child; I don't seem to have ever been bothered about getting up and doing my bit for my friends.

Apart from my extrovert nature, I was actually very nervous about competitive work, and I never enjoyed it. I was never a very good competitor at anything, actually. I liked winning, but it always seemed to me that the ballet was about something else. I don't mean to sound pompous, that I thought this at age nine, but my mother tells me that I was always my own best judge, that I was tremendously competitive with myself but that I was never very good about the fact that I was competing against other people. It always seemed to bother me. And when I got to be about nine or ten, I got so distraught about it that I used to get ill and couldn't make it; I'd cry wolf at the last moment. And so she said to me, "Well, let's just give it all up," and I said, "If this is really what it's all about, I don't think I want to do it anymore." So she said, "Well, don't." So I didn't.

For about a year I stopped dancing, and then I decided I missed it too much, I'd like to go back. And I apparently stipulated to my mother that I would only go to a teacher who didn't shout at me — I didn't mind how much she corrected me as long as she didn't shout. So my mother combed Johannesburg to find somebody who didn't actually raise her voice — what mothers will do for their children — and she found this wonderful woman, Ruth Inglestone, who had a relatively small number of students. I adored her from the moment I met her, and I stayed with her until I left South Africa. I did go to other people as well, but she was really my main teacher. She is a Cecchetti-trained teacher, still teaching now. She must have been very young then, in her twenties, and she had a great imagination and created beautiful solos and competitive things. And she was always very particular about her music. I always understood from her that the music was the mainspring of her inspiration, that it was all in the music really, and that it must always be the music that helped us. And then to go to Frank and find all the things that he understood . . .

Well, I continued in competitions and I was a little bit better, but I still wasn't all that happy. I guess I must have wondered if this was really all it was about. And then Frank came to Johannesburg and set up this little company. And it was my teacher who said to my mother, "Why don't you send her along, just sort of Saturday mornings, for another lesson? And if he thinks he can use her in the group, we'll . . . you know, play it by ear." So she took me along, and I used to do classes on Saturday morning with him.

I was thirteen when I went to him, not all that tiny, and we performed around South Africa on tour. And I had a very thrilling experience when I was with him. You see, he had danced the Nijinsky *Faun* — *L'Après-Midi* — with [Ballet] Rambert, and flown out to South Africa and mounted it for this little company of fifteen people — and I was one of the nymphs, at age thirteen. I have to say I didn't understand the deeper sensualities of the man or quite what he was up to. But this was the wonder of Frank and going to work with him, and really what made me feel that it wasn't just about dancing in your sitting room and dancing onstage in a competition. He made you understand what it was like to be in a theatre. He was a tremendous professional and a tremendously theatrical personality. And he really trained us; he made us understand about interpreting things and what his ballets meant and what we were trying to achieve. He explained that this was a ballet done in the Diaghilev era and that Nijinsky had danced it. He told us all about the history of the ballet; we didn't just get up and do the steps.

So he was a terrific influence, and being informed was wonderful. He choreographed some new ballets, and I also did *Peter and the Wolf* and *Faun*. He also did a marvelous ballet to Schoenberg's *Transfigured Night, Verklärte Nacht*; it was about two couples and, I suppose, rather Tudorish in conception. Frank had known Tudor through Ballet Rambert. And, again, this ballet made a great impression on me. I didn't dance in it because I was obviously too young, but I wished I could grow up, to be in that ballet. So the dramatic things have always appealed to me.

Yes, like *Rite of Spring*. I don't know really how that happened. I think that one of the greatest parts of being a choreographer is being able to spot new talent. Ninette believes that the company with a good resident choreographer is the company that goes on and develops. Picking somebody out of the corps de ballet, totally unknown, is really what it is all about. They suddenly see something. It can be a very simple thing, like seeing people dancing at a party; this happens quite frequently. You see a little girl come out of the Royal Ballet School, and she's got a perfect little body and perfect training and she's quite delicious and very classical, and then you see her let loose at a party. Suddenly there's some disco going, and suddenly you've got the most raving hep hippie. A choreographer only needs to see that to think, 'My God, that kid's got something,' and to notice a particular kind of musicality or a particular way of moving. I think at the time we were doing *Rite of Spring,* we were heavily into rock and roll and the Twist. Maybe Kenneth had seen something at a party. I really don't know what it was.

But I can remember it so clearly. He called me across the studio — there was a rehearsal going on, and I was working right at the back — and suddenly he was beckoning me. I said, "Me?" and he said, "Yes, you." And I came down the studio, and he said, "Monica, I'm going to be doing a new ballet soon. I don't know if you've ever heard the music for the *Rite of Spring.*" I said, "No. I haven't." And he said, "Well, you must go out and buy the record immediately and start listening to the music, because it's very difficult and it's unlike anything I've ever done before and I want you to do the leading role." Amazing. In a brand-new ballet.

And I said, "Will I have to grow my hair?" — you know, a ridiculous question. I was really in shock. And he said, "No, I don't think you'll have to grow your hair." The next question was, "Is it on pointe?" He had said, "The movement is going to be very different and modern. I don't know how to describe it, but you might understand if I say it's a little primitive." I guess that's what made me ask if it was going to be on pointe, because it sounded suddenly so strange.

So I went out, bought the record, took it home, and played it. And played it and played it, and almost wore the record out playing it. By the first night, I didn't have to count very much.

I think we did the final solo in about three weeks. So that Kenneth could start with me at eleven, I used to only have to do the barre in class, which was a treat. And every morning we used to work for about an hour and a half in a tiny studio at the Royal Ballet School with Donald Twiner, who had just joined the company as a pianist. Kenneth liked him immediately, and Donald was very clever at breaking up phrases, working very slowly on the music, and counting it in a way that was helpful to us.

And I remember not really being able to grasp the fact that something was made especially for me and also that Kenneth relied so on oneself. He didn't say, "Do this, do that." Because before, when I had worked with Frank, the ballets had been danced before in England, which I didn't realize being so young. Especially with his own ballets, like *Peter and the Wolf,* I imagined that he was choreographing them for us, and there was no question of changing a step.

So I'd not had anybody professional like that change anything for me. I think it was the one-to-one relationship that was so wonderful. Kenneth would say things like, 'Now. You're in that position. How do you feel you want to get out of that place? Can you do something by turning upstage? Or can you move an arm like that?' And it was really like I was making it up. What I've loved so much about working with Kenneth is that just when you think, 'Oh, I know exactly what he wants now,' and you do it, he says, "Oh, that's ghastly." Just when you think you've got him taped.

Doing a Fred ballet is very different from doing a Kenneth ballet. Although the roots are in the Royal Ballet, the actual qualities, the styles involved, are very different. For me, to dance an Ashton ballet and then to do a MacMillan ballet is just as different as to do Nijinska and then Balanchine. We just did *Liebeslieder Walzer*; I adored doing it and I adored working with Mr. Balanchine — he was only there for a week. I'd never worked with him before, and every New York City Ballet dancer I've ever talked to — Pat Neary and Karin von Aroldingen, who came and mounted it for us — has always so, well, worshiped him really that we were very nervous before he arrived about how he'd find us and if he'd be pleased. And I know he wasn't well, but he had so much energy and gave us so much time and, again, was prepared to make little changes to suit the individual and to explain exactly what he wanted. The subtle use of the music I found inspiring, and how he explained tiny changes in rhythm.

I think that's been for me the most rewarding aspect of being with this company for, gosh, it's twenty-one years. One's had the opportunity to work with so many people in such a variety of things. There are two sorts of ballets; the whole dramatic works and the pure dance ones, like the Balanchine repertory. The difference is what makes dancing those Balanchine ballets so fascinating. I'm afraid that without that total form of expression — drama, dancing, music, costumes, everything — something very important about ballet will be lost forever. Of course at the level of genius on which Balanchine is working, the pure dancing is enough. But in the Diaghilev repertory, everything is so important, the sets even. And in Nijinska's ballets too.

Les Noces remains one of the greatest, most beautiful ballets I've ever seen. It's a mystery to me how we ever got the ballet together. Nijinska had no English, and she was this old, very short, rather fat lady, deaf, wearing a hearing aid and muttering in Polish or Russian. She couldn't even count one-two-three in English, and the music for *Les Noces* is so tricky. She would sort of half-demonstrate, but she even had difficulty getting us to understand kneeling or bending over with your arms in fifth position facing the front. So it was very slow, and it was exhausting, absolutely exhausting. She asked for total concentration and maximum physical effort a hundred percent of the time she was in the room. There was no question that you ever marked anything, ever. She was, I think, the most demanding person I've ever worked for. And an eagle eye; she didn't miss a thing. If anybody was slacking, she saw it. Her husband used to sit at the front of the rehearsal scribbling in the back of a tiny little diary, and we were always sure he was making notes of people who were giggling, which one was bound to want to do at points. Oh, it was wonderful.

I don't think it helped at all to have done *Rite of Spring* and been in *Firebird*; I don't think anything could have helped with Madame Nijinska. The only thing that helped was the fact that Michael Somes was her assistant and she adored him. Michael could somehow get her to be a little more patient and a little more understanding if somebody wasn't doing something immediately, because she was obviously frustrated by the fact that she couldn't really explain. She used French a bit and that helped, but even Michael often couldn't understand what she was doing. What he could get her to do was to keep calm. And of course the moment she wasn't in the room, we'd rehearse madly and try to get it together so that when she came back in we'd have it right.

The most fascinating thing was to see her demonstrate, especially for the young Bride, who was then Svetlana [Beriosova], and also for the leading fourth-scene dancer, who was Georgina [Parkinson] and I understudied. For instance, there's this wonderful moment of resting your head on your hands. The Bride does it a lot, but also Georgina's role does it at the very end of the ballet. And the important fact was that your fingers are bent in like an open fist, but it's not a dead position like a fist, it's not a finished position. It's always got a certain amount of life still. Nijinska was always moving her fingers to suggest that they were still alive, still would feel, that they wouldn't just go into a nothing position. It was still very much felt, but it had to be just so, with the thumb pressing on the second knuckle.

When she demonstrated the cupped hands, and the head in the hands position, she suddenly looked like a young bride of twenty. Amazing. And the same thing, much more marked, was when she would demonstrate the Hostess in *Les Biches*. The expressions she could find in her face! I can nearly believe that Nijinsky was able totally to convey whatever character he was portraying, because *she* could do it, as a really old lady, and make one totally convinced.

There's a wonderful spot in *Les Biches* where the Hostess has finished this exhausting dance and sort of collapses onto the sofa, but collapses in a very sophisticated way, with her cigarette holder, and her cigarette still alight. And two very attractive young athletes come onto the stage from the beach; and she sees them and wants to know more about them and beckons them to her. She has to recline on the sofa and beckon, but without sitting up and without moving her shoulders from the back of the sofa. Well, the most natural thing is to want to say, 'Could you come here?' and lean forward. But Nijinska wouldn't do it; she'd do it reclining. And the expressions on the boys' faces! If ever we were tired and just didn't know how we were going to do any more, we'd ask her to do that bit for us, and she never, ever refused. She obviously loved doing it, and it was never the same twice; not musically or in any sense was it ever a repeat performance. It was new every time. She was extraordinary.

I guess the one person I wanted so much to work for and never have done is Tudor. Right from my early Frank Staff days; he talked about Tudor and obviously respected him very, very much. We did *Lilac Garden* not long ago, but I was not involved at all. But when I saw ABT do it with Martine van Hamel and Cynthia Gregory, I wished I could have had a shot at the van Hamel role. Tudor was working on it with us, and judging by the people he had cast, I could see why he hadn't chosen me, but I'm very sorry about that. I'm not saying that I should have been chosen, but I would love to have had a chance to work with him on that. And then, the things I've heard about *Pillar of Fire,* and also Lizzie Borden [*Fall River Legend*]. I'd love to see those, and people have said that they wish I could have a shot at those. Other than that, I think now I would love to have something else made for me . . . I don't know what, but something. The things you feel most comfortable in are really the things that have been made for you.

Oh, I know what helps me very much with any role — words. Some people are very good at finding words, and if somebody can find the right word to describe a quality of a part, a movement or an emotion, that for me is the greatest help, both technically and in interpreting a role. I usually read all my notices and everyone else's too, because I'm curious, I'm interested in what people say, in how people write, in how good or bad I think criticism is. And also because if people write well, they can come up with something — it might be nothing to do with oneself, it can be about somebody else or another ballet altogether that you've never danced — but it can be a word. And that word can suddenly mean something.

When I was doing the Hostess in *Les Biches*, very early on Ninette talked about the sarcasm of the Hostess, and she didn't think I had enough of it. Something like that helps enormously. I remember another example, when we were doing *Checkmate*. As the Black Queen, I had an entrance of very difficult développés, on pointe. And one day Madam said, "You're like a cat walking into a room." It was quite slow and rather deliberate, like a cat picking the spots with his feet. That helped me.

The only time I ever saw Karsavina was at a lecture she gave us about the fairy variations in *Beauty* — each one. I knew I'd never remember the half of what she said, but I do remember this. When she talked about the third variation, Fairy of the Woodland Glade, which I was dancing, she said the opening movement, the port de bras, was like a gentle breeze blowing across a wheat field. Well, there you are.

Sir Frederick is also very clever at finding words to describe things, and a person I met recently, a teacher from New York, Bill Griffith, has an extraordinary ability in this way. His whole business is finding the words. Maybe words don't work as well for someone else; perhaps the music is more important or watching someone demonstrate, set an example, so they can be the mirror image of that. But for me those words, any words, help more than anything.

The audience always helps if they're enjoying it. If they're warm and responsive immediately, it's such a good start to a performance. But then you also have to feel that what you're trying to do is working, because if you feel a performance is not going well, it doesn't really matter to you what the audience does. Even if they're applauding, if you feel that you're dancing below your best, it's very frustrating.

That's why television is so difficult. I've done quite a lot of television, and psychologically it's a terribly depressing situation. We're like children, you know, or sometimes I feel I'm a performing seal. One just expects the applause, and when it's not there, you just faint away. But I think it's important *not* to expect it. If you're in a new city or before a newish audience, and somebody does a beautiful solo, literally takes one curtain call and leaves the stage and the applause stops, often a young dancer will turn to you and say, "Oh, they should have had two calls at least." The "should" is interesting. I don't think there is such a thing.

We notice this very much in London, where we do quite a lot of children's schools matinées. The children are wonderful. They're tremendously enthusiastic and they applaud like crazy for about three seconds and then stop, because now they want to see what's next. That's always a very good lesson, because they're not indulging you in any way. And you have to learn that you can't be indulged. You shouldn't expect to be.

July 1979
Wolf Trap Farm, Virginia

Desmond Kelly

Desmond Kelly (b. Penhalonga, Southern Rhodesia, 1942) began his ballet studies at the age of nine with Elaine Archibald in Rhodesia. He came to London in 1957 on a Royal Academy of Dancing scholarship and studied for a year with Ruth French before entering the London Festival Ballet (1959–1965) where he danced soloist and principal roles in such ballets as Swan Lake, Les Sylphides, Napoli, Etudes, and Le Spectre de la Rose. Between 1965 and 1970 he was constantly on the move, from the New Zealand Ballet to the Zurich Opera Ballet, back to the New Zealand company — this time as both principal dancer and ballet master, and briefly as company director — and then to the National Ballet in Washington, D.C. When he joined the Royal Ballet as a principal in 1970, he was already a preferred partner of Margot Fonteyn and a danseur noble of distinction. He quickly added contemporary works by Ashton, MacMillan, Cranko, and Balanchine to his classical repertory, and created roles in Tetley's Field Figures (1970) and Laborintus (1972). He made his debut in The Prodigal Son in 1973, when the work first entered the repertory. Since 1978, he has been ballet master of the Sadler's Wells Royal Ballet where he dances as well.

What would you do with a strong body, a persistent, probing curiosity, and an adventurous temperament? Desmond Kelly chose to become a dancer and a most unusual one, as devoted to becoming as to dancing. First he made himself a prince; then he remade himself more often and variously than any British dancer of his generation: as Romeo and Dr. Coppelius, as a depraved dandy in The Rake's Progress, as an anonymous abstraction of classicism in Monotones. First he found his way to England; then he abandoned it for five years to explore undiscovered countries and untapped talents. Although I've never seen him in the Balanchine repertory at the Royal Ballet, I knew that he danced it all — Agon, Apollo, The Four Temperaments, Piano Concerto No. 2, The Prodigal Son, Serenade — and I'd read that it fascinated and delighted him. John Ruskin said, "Hundreds of people can talk for one who can think." I asked Desmond Kelly to talk because his history assured me he was a thinker among dancers.

*I*n Rhodesia, I had a very RAD training. It's sort of traditional there. Rhodesia's still old-fashioned enough to think that 'the Royal Ballet is the ultimate.' Still today. If you're going to go anywhere when you leave Rhodesia, you have to go to the Royal Ballet, and if you don't make the Royal Ballet, you're not quite good enough. Isn't that horrible? Anyway, it was entirely RAD until I joined my first company.

When I started dancing, I loved it for a little while, until I found it was taking me away from other things that boys do, like sports and games. Then I thought, 'Maybe I don't like it so much.' But my mother and Elaine cornered me to continue. Here if you go to a school, it's a pastime, little girls being pretty on Tuesday afternoon. But in Rhodesia, from the beginning, it's dedication. After the first year or two, I used to go every day. We had music lessons every week, and mime lessons every week that went on for two hours. I loved those; I was in my element then. We did tap dancing and Scottish dancing, and what else? Pas de deux started very young. We had everything. It was really a big professional school.

And it grows on you. Ballet grows on you, and it becomes indispensable. You can't do without it. I did stop for a year and become a clerk in a fish firm after I entered for the RAD South African scholarship. They took ages to answer, and I thought, 'Well, I couldn't have got it.' We were very poor; I didn't have enough money to come to England. So I took a job for a year, and then the letter came and said I'd got the scholarship so I started dancing again.

But I didn't go to the Royal Ballet School. People think the scholarship's only for that, but it's to further your dance education. As long as you spent it in this country, you could go anywhere. I wish I had gone to the Royal Ballet School because I know I would have learned a lot more. Not that Ruth was a bad teacher — she was a very good teacher — but at the School I would have had other boys to bounce against, which is so important. For most of the year I was with Ruth I was alone, and you can't dance with girls all the time. You have to have other boys to dance with. But it was very professional training and we were terrified of Ruth, so she really did teach me a lot. She also had contact with Festival Ballet, which got me my first job; she heard they needed a boy and she sent me along. In those days, the Royal Ballet did not take you into the company unless you were a pupil at the School. But in the back of my mind I always wanted to be here, and the proof's in the pudding — I ended up here. It goes right back to my training: 'The Royal Ballet is the thing to do.'

So I joined Festival Ballet, and most of my roles then were sort of classical princes. I was very young and I was thrown on at the deep

314

end, in *Spectre*. Fancy doing *Spectre* the very first time you appear on your own on a stage, when all you've done before was corps de ballet, standing in a line of sixteen boys. My God! I remember one of the critics actually saying, 'This poor boy's been thrown in to swim before he can walk.' But at that age you think you know better than any of them. As you get older, you realize how many pitfalls there are, and things start to get more difficult. But there's that wonderful thing of youth: 'I can do anything, absolutely anything.' I never thought about it. I just did it. That's your job.

But you know how you have things imprinted on your brain that you will never, ever forget? My first *Lac* was absolutely horrendous. It was a huge open air theatre, Verona, and it had rained all day long. And I kept thinking, 'Just continue raining a little bit more and the performance will be canceled,' but of course it stopped a half-hour before the performance. And the stage was completely wet, puddles everywhere. Orlikowsky's choreography starts with the Prince in the middle of the stage with a great big cloak, and it was a long way to walk. It took in my mind five hours to get there. And then I stood there, feeling everything, waiting for the lights and the music, and that waiting — which I'm sure must have been ten seconds — felt like days and days. And then the lights went up, and there were twenty-five thousand people out there. Oh, it was terrible.

And I was terrified of Anton Dolin. I used to do exactly what he told me. In the end I rebelled, but if you are frightened of somebody, somebody with as much experience and as good as Dolin was — or is — it makes it so much easier for that person to have influence over you. You believe what he says and do everything he asks you to do, and when you're very young he is able to mold you. That's the sort of thing Dolin had for me. I knew how marvelous a stage personality he was. He could do *nothing* — I don't mean he *could* do nothing — but he could stand on the stage and do nothing and make the audience think he was wonderful. It was amazing. I remember one thing he used to do called *Hymn to the Sun*. In the middle of it, he took something like thirty-two bars of music and he stood in an attitude, demi-pliéd right down and then came back up again. And the audience used to go crazy. Can you imagine anybody doing that now and getting away with it? I still have a base of Dolin to work from. His approach to *Giselle* affected me a lot, and he had a fantastic tradition.

And then, to see those Russians! By the time Festival Ballet did a joint season with them, I had built a small reputation as a good partner and was wallowing in it. And then the Russians came and did their pas de deux, and I remember one of them telling me I was lifting completely wrong. I was using my arms to lift, and you should never do that — you should use your legs and back. Thank God they taught me that. That's why I can still lift now without any pain or worry.

And they prepared for their jumps differently. We take equal time for the preparation and the jump — so it goes 1-2-3-jump-5-6 — whereas the Russians would go And-a-jump-2-3-4-5-6. You hardly see the preparation; all you see is the suspension, and the jump is like a spring exploding into the air. I'm always saying in class, "Please don't do Royal Ballet preparation for grand jeté en tournant," because they do Step-fifth-step, throw-jump-land instead of And-a-jump. It's a basic fault of British teaching.

The split with Festival Ballet came because I was branching out on my own and I wanted certain things to happen in the way that I wanted them to happen. I never felt that I didn't have the roles I wanted; I felt the company was at an artistic low. I could not bear it any longer. As far as I was concerned, it was commercial crap, and I just had to get out of it and do something else.

I went to New Zealand the first time then and didn't really find what I wanted there. They needed a principal dancer and a ballet master as well, and they said, 'Would you like to do it as a sideline?' It was a marvelous experience, I absolutely adored doing it, but I was too young. I hadn't done enough. You can't just be a ballet master. You have to have something behind you first, and I didn't have anything yet, even though I was twenty-five, twenty-six. That's too young. I think I'm even too young now. I haven't done and learned and seen enough.

And then I went to Zurich and certainly didn't find what I wanted there. Ballet was a very secondary, minor thing. I hadn't thought, 'It's Zurich Opera, it's not Zurich Ballet.' We had perhaps two performances a month each. It was absolute death. And then I went back to New Zealand and got completely involved, so that I started to find what I was looking for. And then I went to Washington — I really loved that.

I was scheduled to do *Prodigal Son* there, but I didn't do it. It was the one thing I wanted to do and never got to do. Eddie [Villella] used to come down and do it with us. I should have hated him for that, but I didn't. I just adored watching him. My first thought about *Prodigal Son* was, 'I want to do that role like that, with that much energy,' because from the moment Eddie came on, there was this incredible *energy*. I learned it then, so when we did it here I had that to pull out, but I left before I did it. I did do *Bourrée Fantasque* — but that's sort of un-Balanchine Balanchine — and Freddie Franklin taught me *Sonnambula*. He used to do the Poet, marvelously, when I was there; he was fifty-something.

The musicality is the great thing about all Balanchine ballets. It's fabulous. And I took to the choreography immediately, like a duck to water. I thought, 'This is it. This is what I want to do,' and I did it naturally, without thinking about it. I don't know whether it was good or bad, but I knew when I was doing it that I was right. You often do somebody's choreography and you think, 'God, that just feels awful. It's wrong. It's not in my body.' But every movement I do in any Balanchine ballet feels right, as if that was what my body was meant to do at that particular time.

And then, when I joined the Royal Ballet New Group, Tetley had been asked to do a ballet. He didn't know the company, so he got a lot of dancers in Covent Garden studio, gave us steps to do, and chose his cast from that room of people. And again, I did them and I knew what I was doing was right. I thought, 'What have I been missing all these years?' and I knew, excitingly, knew, 'I'm going to get it.'

It took three months to do *Field Figures*. We had to learn all that modern stuff from the beginning: sitting on the floor, pushing in before you come out, things you never thought of. Danny [Bergsma] and I were lucky; we did it naturally. I don't mean to say it was easy — it was bloody hard. How many times have you watched a Tetley ballet and seen an exhausted dancer on the stage? Every time, right? It's because Glen likes to see the human body go to its limits and beyond. He likes to see the kind of movement that happens to a body when it's completely exhausted. Isn't it a horrible thought? The dread thing about Glen's ballets, the only thing you get nervous about, is getting through them. You get that sheer pain in the chest and the muscles, and the state of exhaustion where you don't care what happens on the stage. Actually you do care, and you carry on and finish, but it's a hideous feeling. Glen likes that. He likes to see the body doing that.

Choreography just flows out of him. He looks at a body and what position the body's in, and he sees another position the body should get to with fluid movements. You go to that next position, and then this one, and then that one, and it all comes, it all happens. I was open-mouthed. I couldn't believe it. Rambert came one day and watched a rehearsal. She said, "It's like a new landscape, new trees. It's like grass that you've never seen before." And it was true.

Glen's got a saying that all movement's beautiful, and it is, if you do it properly. He opened my eyes to a lot, and to something so different from Balanchine. Balanchine's choreography is completely a part of the music, and Glen can choreograph an entire ballet and put the music to it afterward. I know to him it has a contact, but I never found the contact, though I knew that when I was doing a certain step, I had to be at a certain stage of the music. So then, you dance to time, you don't dance to music; you dance to twenty seconds, you don't dance to ten bars. Certainly that was the case with *Field Figures.* When we did our last movements, at the end of the ballet, we were hoping that the music would finish, and it did. But it was taped, it was absolute — that's how we were able to come out at the right time. If that music had been played by an orchestra, at different tempi every evening, I wonder what would have happened to us.

You either have the rhythm of music in your body and it flows through you, or you don't. A lot of dancers have it naturally, and those are the dancers I like watching, the musical dancers. Then there's another kind of dancer — I mean, Margot and Merle — who can take the music and pull it or compress it and play with it, so they and the music are doing something together. It's rather marvelous.

Long before that Balanchine evening with *Prodigal Son* at the Royal Ballet, I did *Apollo* in the New Group. And I became much more confident about dancing Balanchine because of one thing: when he came, he didn't insist that you did a certain thing at a certain time. He left a lot of it to you. And as long as he saw your body was going in the right direction, he'd push you in that direction. Later, I did *Four Temperaments,* Melancholic. Terrified out of my mind. He's sitting there and I thought, 'Christ, I've got to get up and do it for him.' So I got up and did it and he said, "That's right, but more." That's all he said, and I knew exactly what he meant.

But going back to *Apollo.* I learned it from notation and, again, it came naturally. When the dry choreologist gave these steps to me, I did them and I felt, 'That's what Balanchine wanted.' I'm pigheaded, aren't I? I felt it so strongly. So when the two directors, Kenneth [MacMillan] and Peter [Wright], came and watched rehearsal, I knew I was doing it correctly. There were two other boys rehearsing at the same time, doing it in a very Royal Ballet way, but because I didn't have any Royal Ballet background, I didn't have that barrier. I was free. And I remember Kenneth and Peter both saying to the other two boys, "Do what Desmond's doing."

Don't you know how Royal Ballet people do Balanchine choreography? I can give you one word: stilted. It's true. When I saw *Serenade* the first time the company did it, I was shocked. And they were all so happy about what they were doing; they thought it was right. That was the way they'd been taught. But I had seen *Serenade* in America, and it was nothing like what I was seeing on the stage here. Over the years it has gotten much better, I suppose because they've done so many more Balanchine ballets. I'm not trying to put myself above them, saying "I knew." I am a very British dancer. I was only lucky that I'd been exposed to it before and not been bounded by Royal Ballet tradition. I didn't feel my hand had to go there on one and here on two and there on three. I felt I could do it with my body and use the music and make it come out right.

Johnny Taras came to teach *Prodigal Son*, and Pat Neary did *Four Ts* and *Agon*. Before the casting came out, I was called into the office by the directors and told that they'd gone through the people in the company and found there was nothing for me in the Balanchine evening and I was not to be too upset about it because there were going to be lots of other things for me to do. I was upset about it, very upset. And then, I don't know what happened, but I found myself called to an audition for Melancholic. And Pat said, "I want him to do it." I loved her forever for that. So I did *Four Ts* first cast. Came to *Agon,* and John said, "I want him to do the pas de deux in the second or third cast." That was two out of three. Came to *Prodigal.* There were David Wall and Rudolf, and I was in the back because I'd been asked to come by then. And John said, "I want him to do it as well." So I ended up having all three Balanchine ballets when, at the beginning, I had the prospect of not having any.

And then Balanchine came for three days at the end and rehearsed us, and taught me so much without saying anything. I mean, he's not the kind of person who sits down and gives you a half-hour's talk about what you should be doing with this interpretation. He can say one word, or get up and grab a girl around the waist — he adores holding girls up, doesn't he? — and say so much by that movement. I remember him getting hold of Danny, and the way he did it spoke a thousand words for me about the interpretation of *Prodigal Son*. I couldn't take my eyes off him. He has this completely man-woman thing, and it's not very usual in ballet. I'm not saying that because there are homosexuals — that's apart. It's this love Balanchine has for a woman's body and the things you can do with a woman's body in a pas de deux that's so great.

I certainly didn't feel ready for *Prodigal Son*, absolutely not. I've learned it as I've gone along. There's so much in it other than choreography. If you analyze it, there's not that much choreography in it. There are those two solos at the beginning for the boy, and a lot of walking around on pointe for the Siren, and that very slow pas de deux. But it's the what else. And you don't learn that until you've done it. And we can not do it for a year or eighteen months and come back to it, and there's not one detail of the choreography with the music that I will have forgotten. My body will do it naturally. If you count the first couple of solos in time to the music, they're a bit odd — they come out wrong. But if you learn it with the music, when you come back to it, it just happens. You don't have to relearn anything. It's always there.

I only read background material when I feel very frightened about something, if something's got a great tradition behind it, like Romeo. I read the play for that, but I don't know whether it helped me. I don't know whether it's better to have a basic thing to work from or to read a lot and feel bound by what you've read. With *Prodigal*, I had Eddie — this power, this incredible energy — in my head, which was so exciting that it made me want to do it . . . not necessarily like that, but just to make the same kind of impact in my own way that he made.

If I make the first entrance out of the tent in the right way, I know I've set my pattern for the ballet and I'll be all right. That's the only thing I always remember Eddie doing, *bursting* out of the tents. What an entrance! You think, 'God, *what's* he going to do?' And I try to establish 'breaking out,' getting away from the family and the environment. The feeling that there's something else out there that you're never going to see unless you get out will establish the power for the first two short solos: 'I've got to leave. I've got to get out. I can't be under the influence of Anton Dolin anymore.' At the end of the first solo, you turn very slowly and walk back to the Father, and I try and feel that I don't really want to go back. So 'I'm leaning down here in front of you and I really *can't* bear it anymore' is what starts the second solo. If you have the energy and speed, which you build up, those solos aren't so hard. Nice actually, exhilarating, because by the time you've got that last thing off, you're gone.

When you come on with the Munchkins, I have to think of innocence. I'm not an innocent person, actually; I've been through life. But in that scene I try and have an overriding innocence, so that the things I'm seeing, I'm seeing for the very first time. I'm reading a Mary Renault book at the moment about ancient Greece and a man that sings songs. He takes a young protegé out of his hometown into Athens, and when he gets to Athens, this boy has never seen a horse before, and the wonder of seeing a horse for the first time is marvelous. It's that kind of feeling. This is so new. '*This* is what I've been missing home in that dump in the desert. All this has been going on. It's wonderful.'

You're dubious about those skinheads — 'What are they up to?' — but at the same time fascinated by them. It's marvelous choreography when you think of it, the way the Prodigal Son comes onto the group of skinheads and thinks, 'I must make friends. No, I'm not going to make those,' and backs away. Then you give them the gifts, and it slowly builds up until you're carried away. You're doing all the things that they're doing and loving every minute — 'Aren't I great? This is it!' — until you're on the table, and then it completely changes. The music changes, the lights change, the mood changes, and the Siren comes on.

And that's difficult because you can't immediately go, 'Ahh, I'm interested in her,' because you have to build it. You have to think of the end of that scene first, so it has to start very gradually. In your mind you tell yourself that she is really very interesting, and then, by the middle of her solo, you can't help yourself. It's like 'I've got this feeling that I want to touch her, but what's the feeling about?' You're innocent; you've never had sexual intercourse or any feelings like that at all for a woman, so that has to come through.

And then she does that fabulous step with the cloak. That's a climax point for me, because immediately after that he plucks up enough courage to take the cloak off because he wants to see what's underneath. Then you have to build from there again. You step away because she hasn't looked at you. It's been all to the boys. But then she does the kicking, takes the cloak off, and does that movement down the leg, and that's the first eye contact — well, that's the way we do it. I don't know whether it's right, but it makes sense. That's when she's got her eye on you. And that's frightening, because you can watch a person being generally seductive and it feels quite good, but as soon as a person focuses right on you, it's frightening. So you back away: 'Perhaps I don't really want those feelings.' So the very first time you touch her body is a huge climax. She's done that pirouette from pointe to pointe, and you have to make the motivation for that *huge* step of touching her for the first time. That's a difficult part.

The sitting on the bench, when the two boys do their little dance, is quite important too. That innocence has to come back there, because you've got time to think about it. Do you know the character I think of there? Dustin Hoffman in *The Graduate*. It's exactly that feeling. The way we do it, she actually takes his hand halfway through and puts it on her breast. And that's a terrifying moment, absolutely terrifying, but it gives you the impetus to start the pas de deux. After that position behind the table, you actually touch her. It goes with the music — bosom and hand and crotch and hand. You've got to build yourself to the point of touching her crotch, which you know — because your daddy's told you — you must never do until you're married — and here I am doing it. And then you get carried away by the pas de deux. At the end of it, the boy's lying back and she lies back on you. Then she has a rond de jambe with the leg, and there's a movement of the boy's leg coming up. I always think of that marvelous crossing over as the actual penetration, the leg being the penis. So it's really got quite erotic by then. If you think of that being done properly in 1929, they must have been shocked out of their minds when they saw that pas de deux. And isn't that a sign of great choreography, that the interpretations change but the ballet still remains? Theatre now has become so much more blatant, but the ballet's still absolutely valid.

Then, you've just had your first contact with a woman and your first ejaculation and you're absolutely on cloud nine, right? You should be. So that next furious, throwing-around bit is 'It's not happening! Ah! I'm just having a fantastic time. All the drinking.' You think it's supposed to happen and you're not really conscious of it happening anyway. They're kissing on the table, and then there's a moment, after she's carried across him on the table, where they meet in the middle, break, and run to either side. He's trying to get away because a little spark, a thought, has come in: 'Maybe . . . I shouldn't be doing . . . It's completely wrong. I want to go.' But the boys stop him, lift him up into that spread-eagle position, and carry him across and underneath her — which is more sex as far as I'm concerned — which leads into the Siren throwing him against the table. One thing Eddie always used to do was hit his head on the table and fall.

And as you're coming up, you see the boys with their hands waving in front of their faces, and you start to realize it's not really as great as you thought it was. And when they dance with you in the middle, they're threatening you, threatening you, getting closer — 'No, no, don't!' — break out, get thrown from one to the other, onto the floor. The boys stamp, and then you know now it's going to be hell. You're going to be beaten up — you might even be killed. He runs up the table as an escape, stops, slides down, and the boys slam him against the upright table. His thought starts when he breaks away and tries to get out and the boys stop him in that spread-eagle position, and it builds up to when she throws him against the table. Then you really know that that's it. It's turned nasty. It's turned serious.

You mustn't do anything against the table in a physical way. Complete exhaustion takes over then. You've been beaten up — not so obviously, blatantly — but you have been, whether the choreography says it or not. So when you're thrown against the table, you're battered and bruised and almost dead. They do the waterfall thing with the fingers running over you, and you leave that to the boys. Every role you can't be in the fore all the time, because other characters have to take over, right? So the skinheads have taken over, and all the stealing of the clothes you leave to them.

The first knee-crawling, coming forward, and the very first movements, I always think of as a plea for help. Because there's nobody. They've all gone. There's nobody left on your side. That's when you start to think, 'My father was right and I was wrong,' and 'Where's my father now?' and 'Why aren't you here to help me when I really need you? Please, where are you?' Never self-pity, no, but the Catholics say, "*Mea culpa, mea culpa, mea maxima culpa.*" That's the important thought there, that it's your fault. You don't feel sorry for yourself, but you know your father was right and you were wrong, and you're asking for his forgiveness. It *is* easy to turn that into pathos or self-pity, since some of the movements are breast-beating. But you know this marvelous one, with one arm reaching through the other? I always think of that as prayer.

And I love the crawl across the stage to the drinking of the water. I always think of that as being real travel. It's taken days; I've already gone a long way. Hundreds and hundreds of miles are condensed into a few minutes. By the time you come back onstage, it's a year, two years. It's a completely different character then. That's when you've been molded. There are still certain bad, wrong things about the character on the first crawl that haven't been purified. But by the time he comes back on the second time, with the stick and the black cloak, they've been washed out of him; he's pure by then. That much more time has passed by. He's been through much more than you've seen happen, through hell and high water since the Munchkins. They're not his total experience of life. Other things have happened to the poor sod after that. So it's sunk in, over the year or two years, that it was completely wrong.

I don't think he had the thought, 'I must go home.' He's terrified of going home. He doesn't really want to. In the back of his mind he does, because he knows that's the only place for him by then, but he's not thinking, 'Oh, I've done wrong. I must go back home now.' He's resisting going home. At the end of the second crawl, when he first sees the gate, there's a moment when the music changes, where it suddenly becomes much lighter. But when he realizes it's his gate, he doesn't necessarily think, 'I want to go there.' He just goes. On his knees. And when the Sisters come out, your reaction to them is one of pure, complete joy, because you don't have this dominant thing with them. They're the people you love without realizing that you love them, and seeing them again brings this great emotion, yes, and real joy, so you forget about your own troubles.

You're completely wrapped up in that crawling around before the Father comes on, and when he does come on, you're terrified again. You know you've made a big mistake; you should never have come home because you've done such a big misdeed that you have no right. Don't forget, he's been purified, he's a non-sinner again so he has pure thoughts. Then he crawls away from his father and tries to cover his nakedness with this tiny black cloak. He tries to huddle into a corner to say, 'I'm not really here' and 'I can't face what's going to happen inevitably in the next ten minutes,' that moment of coming back to the Father and saying, 'You were right and I was wrong.' That crawl on his knees towards the Father is fabulous, gosh, when he bangs his knees into the stage. Eddie used to bleed. He said he felt he didn't do a good performance of *Prodigal Son* unless there was blood in the end.

And then you fall forward and touch the feet. That's the part furthest away from the head, and you don't want to get *there*. The feet have no emotion of their own. And you slowly build it to the knees, to touching the hands, and to actually making the final crawl up his legs. And I've added certain things, like a symbolic foot-washing from the Bible, Mary Magdalene washing Jesus Christ's feet. That becomes a kiss of the left foot of the Father. It's all in the mind. It doesn't come across, I know, but it's important to think things like that and to feel them for yourself.

I've danced it with Danny, Vergie [Derman], and Vyvyan Lorrayne. The partner can make the center section very different according to how she plays it, whether she's blatantly sexual or very unsexual to start with and blatant at the end. But then, you come to the crawling at the end, and the feeling is the same. Yet there has to be spontaneity in every performance. That's what makes performances so interesting for the dancer and, hopefully, for the public as well. You don't really know completely what's going to happen 'til you get out there. Absolutely anything can happen in a performance.

There's a thought that I have sometimes which I have to put away from me. Over the years, people have said, "Oh, you must see Desmond Kelly in *Prodigal Son*. He's marvelous." So each time we come to re-do it, I think, 'People say I was so good last time. I'm going to be terrible this time, because I can't live up to what people think I should be.' But I can't let that thought dominate me; I have to throw it away, start again, and do it my own way each time, like I'm doing it for the first time.

But I'm very lucky. I've got John Auld, who plays the Father, who's assistant director of the company, and Peter Wright, and they both think *Prodigal Son* is a truly great ballet. And that's important;

that's helped me a lot. Each time I do it, I know one of them will be out front and will always come back to tell me his reaction. I build from that, and also, to a certain extent, from an audience response. But you have to be careful about that, because you play to so many different kinds of audience that if you take it as a gauge, you might go haywire. It's not a continuous thing, whereas Peter's reaction is.

While the ballet's going on, the audience reaction makes no difference at all. But at the end ... well, every dancer has an ego — otherwise they wouldn't be on the stage — and if the audience's reaction is poor, of course you feel a sense of failure that you haven't been able to win that audience over. But *Prodigal*'s such a basic story and such clear choreography that the sophistication of the audience doesn't make any difference. That's why it's such a great ballet. I think the more basic the people are, the better impression they have of it. Two or three years ago, we did *Prodigal Son* in the Athens Festival, and the reaction was incredible. People got up at the end and rushed down to the front of the stage to try and touch the cast, just to touch the bodies, because it was such a religious experience for them. I cried. It doesn't happen every day, that kind of thing. Wouldn't happen with an English audience, but the English audience does get carried away with that ballet now. When we first did it, people didn't think it was so good, but that's because we didn't do it so well. I think all the cast has grown with it.

I have coached *Prodigal*, and it doesn't make any difference to my own feelings or interpretation of the role. But giving class and teaching other dancers teaches you an incredible amount. Dancing actually becomes easier. Because you translate it into words for somebody else, those words go back into your own brain. They've been there subconsciously all the time, but not obviously. By telling other people, "For God's sake, use your head, use the rhythm," you do it yourself automatically. I've never been a great turner, but when I was recently showing what the steps were going to be in class, one boy said to me, "God, you turn well." I nearly passed out. It was only because I was doing what I wanted them to do. It was easy, obvious. Why didn't I think of that before? But coaching would only make a difference to my performance in a ballet that I didn't feel secure in. With *Prodigal*, I know exactly what I want to do and nothing other than Balanchine could influence that.

It's very exciting to discover that you're able to act. It's a lovely feeling when your director says to you, "You can act. You do that role very well," so much nicer than being told you turned or did entrechat six very well that evening. It's so much greater for somebody to say, "You moved me tonight."

Why is it that dancers love to act so much? Is it because we're so terrified of the steps we have to do? A ballet without a character is much more terrifying — I'm thinking specifically of *Etudes*. The first time I saw it, it was Toni Lander, John Gilpin, and Flemming Flindt, and it was just fabulous. I still think of it like that, all up in the air. And *I* had to try and attain *that* with nothing to hide behind, no personality. It was just going to be me in a white costume, doing what they did. I did then and still do have a preference for doing a role that I can . . . isn't it awful to say "hide behind"? I don't really mean that. I mean that a lot of actors feel that if they can immerse their own personality and get rid of it and have something else to put up in front, it's so much easier than being yourself on the stage. I do love that, completely building a new personality and character, from the beginning.

But as your personality develops, you carry a reaction to a certain emotion from one ballet to another without realizing you're doing it. As much as we say we put another character in front — 'That is Albrecht. It's not me at all' — there are certain basic things that go back all the way to your birth that must be you. You cannot 100 percent put another character in. Perhaps great actors can do that, but I can't.

You've asked me at the wrong time if there are roles I'd still like to dance, because at the moment my mind's taken up with being ballet master. I'm trying to force my ambition out of myself because I don't want to be hurt. I'm trying to decategorize myself out of the rat-race and concentrate entirely on the other thing. If I'm going to coach and teach somebody a role that I'm not going to do anymore, and if I'm still ambitious, that's going to hurt like hell. And I don't want to be hurt; I don't like being hurt. And also, besides my own feelings, I want to give as much to the person I'm coaching as possible, without holding anything back for myself.

What I did enjoy was being versatile. I enjoyed people telling me that I was versatile and that I could do anything I wanted. And I was very lucky in having people who wanted me to get on and do things. I've been lucky my whole life. I've always fallen on my feet. I appreciate all the things those people did for me. Julian Braunsweg at Festival Ballet was one of the people that really believed in me and gave me a lot of opportunity. Whenever anything came up for the next person, it was me. He always said, 'If you stay with me, I make you a star.' I used to laugh privately, but I hoped that he would make me a star.

Who do I dance for? God, I've never thought of that. For myself? That's not entirely true. For my job? That's not true. For money is not true. For the audience isn't true either, not entirely. I don't know. I dance for dance's sake. I dance for the ballet I'm doing that evening. If I'm going to do *Giselle,* I dance *for Giselle.* If I'm going to do *Prodigal,* I dance for the ballet, to make the ballet great, to make it happen for that audience that night. Is that an answer?

July 1979
London

Jean-Pierre Bonnefous

Jean-Pierre Bonnefous (b. Bourg-en-Bresse, France, 1943) received his early ballet training in the Paris Opéra Ballet School from the age of ten. He entered the Paris Opéra Ballet in 1957 and achieved prominence and the rank of étoile in 1964, with his creation of the title role in Maurice Béjart's La Damnation de Faust. *Outside the Opéra, Bonnefous appeared in* Swan Lake *and* Giselle *as a guest artist of the Bolshoi and Kirov Ballets, in Roland Petit's* Le Loup *and Rudolf Nureyev's* Sleeping Beauty *at La Scala, as Balanchine's Apollo in Berlin, and with the Frankfurt Ballet and the National Ballet of Canada. Having visited New York in 1968 and 1969 to perform with Claire Motte, also of the Paris Opéra Ballet, he settled there in 1970 when he joined the New York City Ballet as a principal. Since then, he has ventured into every corner of the company's repertory, from* Orpheus *to* Bugaku *and from* Liebeslieder Walzer *to* Diamonds, *dancing his first performance of the Phlegmatic variation of* The Four Temperaments *in 1975. He has originated several roles, most notably in Balanchine's [Stravinsky]* Violin Concerto *and in* Union Jack, *where he created the Costermonger pas de deux with his wife, Patricia McBride. Bonnefous left the New York City Ballet in 1980, but he continues to choreograph as he has done in America since 1976.*

Somewhere behind the façade of Jean-Pierre Bonnefous' face and body lay a series of intricate, interlocking processes, like the works of a Swiss watch, which produced his dancing. You could say the same of every dancer, but most of them show you only the dancing, the end deliberately divorced from its means. Bonnefous offered you both what he could do and a tantalizing sense of the intelligence powering the body that was doing it. He was simultaneously physical and metaphysical. As a result, he brought a mysterious dimension to The Four Temperaments — *and to every ballet I ever saw him dance — that captured the eye, the mind, and the imagination.*

I started dancing at ten years old in the Paris Opéra, and I was also an actor in three movies, at ten years old and then at twelve and thirteen. At one point, I really didn't know what to do between dance and acting. At fourteen, I was supposed to start on a play and I didn't know whether to do it or to wait, because in six months I had the chance to enter in the corps de ballet of the Paris Opéra. I had no idea what I wanted to do; I was really excited about both of them. So my parents went to see an Indian man, a Hindu, one who could see the future. He told them what he thought was right for me to do, and they decided for me. You see, from fourteen to maybe eighteen, there are no roles for an actor. You can't do anything; it's almost finished. So that helped the decision, but he also said very good things about what I would do in ballet. My mother asked — Father also — when I should leave the Opéra, at fifteen or sixteen or when. And the man said, "No, much later than that. When he will be at the maximum there, then he will be the one to decide." So he was very important.

And Pierre was very important, Pierre Reynal. He was one of the most important influences of my career. He is one of the best teachers for actors right now in Paris, and an actor himself. Much later I worked with him on two ballets, with a text for *Phèdre* and on *Giselle,* just to work on how direct the pantomime could be. He was not a mime, but he was an extraordinary man.

My first teacher when I was in Paris Opéra School was a great influence. Her name was Suzanne Lorcia. For years she was a marvelous principal dancer in the company before she began teaching. She was very powerful, very tall, and she used to do the barre with us. And she had a sense of theatre that she could teach; you could sense it with her right away. Then I had a crazy lady, [Jeannette] Gerodez, for four years. She was not very famous, but she knew how to teach the academic steps very strongly and exactly. That was very hard, and I sort of learned to be afraid of teachers and not to trust myself. Sometimes when a teacher is so strong, she can make you feel that you're not very good, and it doesn't work that well.

Something important is that at one point somebody came to Paris Opéra — his name is Lifar — who tried to change everything. And he did. But happily two persons kept what was good about the old school and the old ballets, kept the tradition that Paris was losing. If they had not been there, I think it would have just followed Lifar, and eventually most of Lifar's ballets became old-fashioned so it would have been a disaster. Albert Aveline was one of them, a very important teacher; he did some ballets also, and he had danced with Carlotta Zambelli. He was very small; they were very fast, very Italian, very fun. Those two, he and Zambelli, came to direct the School, so even when all Paris became followers of Lifar, at least they were there and the School remained strong.

At one point, Paris Opéra didn't have any ballets that really worked. Balanchine did ballets that are still good. Lifar did ballets that are not good anymore, and the dancers had the education of Lifar which they couldn't use. I was there when Lifar was there, so I saw how it was with him and I saw the transition. I have memories of crazy rehearsals with Lifar when everything was done with enthusiasm but there was not too much happening. He was an extraordinary personality; people would just follow him, and he knew how to get an extraordinary atmosphere of work. But his ballets . . . well, they worked very well at the time, for Paris, but they didn't last. When he left, in 1958 or '59, Aveline was still taking care of the School. Zambelli was about seventy-five, but I remember her still teaching class, by then outside of Paris Opéra.

If you were in the corps de ballet and you didn't like the teachers you had, you would go outside to take class. It was very common. I went up through five different grades in the company with an exam every year. That was pretty lousy, and it was so hard that it was ridiculous. One of the teachers was with me for the fourth and fifth grades; he advanced every time we would advance. I couldn't have survived for three years with that teacher, because I really hated falling asleep at the barre and only waking up when we went into the center. We did the same barre every day — all the teachers were like that. It was awful. When I was fifteen, sixteen, I knew that I was not bad, and there were so many things to try and to look at — I adored looking at the girls — and with that teacher I was always falling asleep. One day in rehearsal, it seemed I wouldn't have too much to do. It was like two hours that I had to myself. So I took a position and I decided I would try to stay for two hours in that position, and I did. I was part of the rehearsal, maybe an understudy or something, but nobody really took care of me so I did it. And I could have done it again, a few times. It's just a stupid story, but I think it shows a bit of something.

If you want to improve a school, or to give a better chance to youngsters, you figure always they should learn piano or jazz and so many things. But finally, what's most important is that they have one or two teachers that they really respect and admire and follow. Those teachers can show them things that they will never forget. If they go to other classes, they would learn how to count or how to read music — these are important things also — but not as important as somebody who really gives you something.

I had a marvelous teacher in Paris who really helped me, with the voice and with a stick; he used to make a lot of noise with the stick. He was so strong that his strength would help me to do it whether I was tired or not. Sometimes you need that. I worked with him for ten years, three or four times a week, alone for one or one and a half hours, no piano, just him and me. And I kept a lot of his classes — I wrote them down so I could read them back. That teacher was Gérard Mulys. In the first generation of excellent teachers for men in Paris Opéra was Gustave Ricaux, who formed a lot of male dancers, very good strong dancers. Mulys was a pupil of Ricaux and so was Raymond Franchetti, also a teacher of mine and right now one of the best teachers for male dancers in Paris. At that time, the most famous teacher for male dancers in Paris was Serge Peretti. There were the most extraordinary confrontations, competition, in his classes, and he gave wonderful combinations, so beautiful.

They were *all* very important to me. The classes were all very important, and what's so bad when you don't dance enough is that classes are more important than the performance. You are more important than the audience. You never know: should you dance for the audience or should you dance for yourself? I always figure that I should dance just for myself, and if it's good enough, the audience will see it anyway. And then I think that if I dance for the audience, I'm going to be very cheap — kick my legs and I don't know what — to get their attention, and it won't be the right thing. It's very hard to know how to decide all of that. When you take a lot of classes, finally the only way is just to dance for yourself, but then you are the same onstage as you are in the studio.

At Paris Opéra, I used to take two classes every day of one and a half hours — that's three hours. Then I had at least four hours of rehearsal — that's seven hours dancing, six times a week, and I would be dancing onstage only once or twice a week. That way, dancers have no sense of what it is to be onstage. You can't just learn that on the side. Older dancers or different friends would tell me, in the last years in Paris, "Take any concert, good or not good, bad stage, slippery stage, twelve persons in the audience, no lights, anything. Do it, because that's where you learn reality." Reality. The reality for a dancer is onstage, and the rest doesn't give him any sense of the reality. That experience would be one of the regrets in my whole career as a dancer — being thirty-six, I'm thinking about when I will stop. One of the reasons I left Paris was because I didn't dance enough. I was really trying, I was dancing everywhere, I was dancing a lot, the maximum, but I didn't dance enough really. And when I came here, finally I danced.

Nobody really knows here about the Paris Opéra. The repertoire was not so good. There were not enough good ballets and the dancers didn't dance enough. And what builds a good dancer is his repertoire and to dance a lot, a lot, a lot. I have memories of an American friend telling me that in America dancers would often go on tour and dance every day with one free day. I said, "What do you do with your free day?" "Oh, we wash our tights." I thought, 'Awful! What an awful life!' You see, I really had a completely different idea of a dancer's life then. Also, when you are a dancer in New York, I don't think you are as much a part of the whole social life of the city as when you are a Parisian. In New York you can just go in one direction, just dance, and that's plenty. It's the only way to improve. But in Paris it was very exciting to go out, to be involved with Paris as a city and be a part of the important people in Paris. I had to come here a few times to see the difference.

I was nineteen or twenty, just in the corps, when I danced in *Four Temperaments* at Paris Opéra. In fact, it was the first role I did. I was one of the couples who come at the beginning of the ballet, the third one, which is the most beautiful one. I didn't do Phlegmatic then, no, but I was also the understudy of Melancholic, and later I did the Sanguinic. What's important in *Four Ts* is how great the choreography is, how great the connection between the music, the choreography, and all the dancers — it's the same with *Violin Concerto, Donizetti [Variations]*. It's so interesting that all of that is coming from the same man. But what was more exciting was to be alone with a part on the stage, all alone, which I had never done before except for special galas. I was more amazed by that than to know who the man was behind any of it. And also, the partner I had, Martine Palmain, was very pretty. The two of us were very blond, long bodies, very young, and eager to do well. When Balanchine came, I think he was much more interested to look at her than at me. I remember how precise he was with Palmain, that he knew so well what he wanted. I was not chosen for that by Balanchine — Una Kai set it. And even when I came here, I asked him if he remembered it, and he wasn't sure. So I said, "You remember my partner? She was blonde," and he said, "Yes. I remember now." He has very good taste.

The first thing I had was that short role in *Four Temperaments*, a very beautiful role. And then one of the principal dancers at the Paris Opéra, Attilio Labis, did a very classical ballet, and I danced with him in that. That was my second chance. And then, where I really had something very important was with Béjart, *Damnation of Faust*. Then I went on doing a lot of Béjart and Roland Petit, and a lot of classics. As a first dancer, I had everything I wanted. Three principal dancers shared the roles so I could do a whole lot of different things, and I knew that if choreographers would come, most of the time they would try to work with me. One thing I wanted was to get more and more perfect in the classics. It was always very important to me to have that geometry of each step, which is so perfect, so beautiful. I think I was almost working too much in that direction. At that time, the young dancers were influenced by Erik Bruhn and Nureyev; we were also working for that purity, those pure lines. I was dying to learn that, and I was also dying to work with a choreographer, because I could feel the impulse of their movement and it was so much easier and more exciting to have a part in the creation.

Then there was a cultural exchange between France and Russia, and somebody from Moscow saw me dance. "Oh, we would like to have him," they said, "and Claire Motte. Maybe the two of them could dance." I was not afraid of anything, so I said, "Sure, fine, I'll go there." But I realized that I'd never danced *Giselle* and I'd never danced *Swan Lake*. When you are a principal dancer in Paris Opéra . . . maybe not anymore, but you used to have to wait for the older ones to dance first. I was a principal at twenty or twenty-one years old; at twenty-three, I danced various ballets, but my chance to do *Giselle* and *Swan Lake* would have come maybe two years later. So I went to the director of Paris Opéra and said, "I'm going to dance with the Bolshoi, so I really have to dance those ballets." They gave me one *Giselle* and one *Swan Lake* and then I went to the Bolshoi. That was my whole experience with those roles, and I never told. [Vladimir] Vasiliev was the one who showed me how they do the pantomime in the Moscow version. He was so nice; he told me, "We usually do this, but you do whatever you usually do in Paris Opéra." Of course I had only done it once, I barely even knew it, so I said, "Oh, no. Show me your version." When you do a job when you're so young, you can take all the chances. It's great not being afraid of anything.

It really went very well, and I still have friends from that time. I went back to Russia with Paris Opéra and then again with the New York City Ballet, and most of my friends in Russia couldn't understand my making the switch from one to the other. They would say things like, "You're not dancing *Giselle* any more? Not dancing *Swan Lake*? How can you live like this?" It would be hard for them to understand. Without Balanchine I would have stayed there, because I was really involved. At one point I wanted to go every year to Russia, to see my friends and take classes with them. By working less than two months in Leningrad, my dancing improved more than in one whole year in Paris.

I also started to choreograph at that time. I was more excited about dancing, but because I wanted to see new things or try different things, I started to do little things for television, choreographing for actors and dancers. It was nice, but I don't know what would have become of it. I guess it would have gone nowhere, because I am definitely sure, positive, that to be able to choreograph, to do something at least not too bad, I needed to see Balanchine. Now I say to myself, 'How would you deal with that problem?' and looking at Balanchine ballets, you sometimes can figure how he did it. I had a rehearsal today for a ballet I'm starting now. We rehearsed for one and a half hours and it was not very good; I got really depressed. I wanted to see something better than that, so I turned the Betamax on to watch a bit of one of his ballets, and it was extraordinary.

I think I would have stopped dancing at twenty-seven years old, because I was going nowhere by dancing everywhere the same ballets. I really wasn't interested in dancing the same old ballets over and over again. I had to know what was happening now. I was doing all those classical ballets which were so old, so long ago. I was satisfied with that part of ballet which I thought was almost finished and which I couldn't do any more with — I couldn't analyze, I couldn't improve, I couldn't get excited. One of the reasons for me to come to New York and work with Balanchine was because I started to be bored. I needed something new, new blood. I wanted to do things of our time.

The only way was with Béjart and Roland Petit. It was very exciting to work with a choreographer, an ideal situation. Béjart choreographs right in front of you; the music is on and he's doing the steps. He's not really preparing you — he's preparing the work with the music. He needs to do the movements himself to do the choreography, so you just have to imitate what he's doing. But it was done for you, for your body, so you could feel pretty special. You're a part of it, because if you can't do a step and by not being able to do it you do it another way, that other way catches the eye of the choreographer and it becomes the ballet. Béjart always had a lot of confidence in his dancers, but the patience of Balanchine was the thing that struck me the most when I started. He'd encourage you in a low tone, a low voice, not low but no tension — very, very calm. The tension would come from the steps, and no impulse was disturbed by the voice. So it was very different.

I danced *Apollo* for the first time in Berlin, then in Paris and in Copenhagen, but I've never danced it in New York. I didn't learn the role in Berlin; I learned it before, with John Taras in Paris. And then I had four days left before the last dress rehearsal, and I worked for those four days with Balanchine. John Taras showed me everything, but he was not the choreographer and he couldn't tell me, 'That was the first version and it didn't change' or 'I did that because . . .' Balanchine emphasized certain movements — it was absolutely incredible how forward we were going in one direction. In four days . . . I don't know what I learned, but it gave me the strength to go through ten more years in dancing. When you know that somebody like that exists somewhere, even if you're not working with him, it gives you a goal. It's necessary; you need to be amazed all the time, to be fresh, to be interested always. It was that, but it was also to learn movements. If somebody as important and as great as Balanchine asks you to do something, he must know. For example, I had learned to do rond de jambe with the push always from the leg, but to do it with Balanchine, the push was from the hip. That's something completely different. Most people would just say, 'Make it sort of classical,' but to see Balanchine do it, you understood the difference. Or he would say, 'It's an arabesque, but it doesn't go directly in the pure arabesque. It travels from the beginning' or 'Use the space better.' He also said to know a lot about the music. I had just piano, like everybody else, nothing to do with Paris Opéra — there was really very little music there — just on my own.

I was doing better than all right in Paris before I left. For two years I had a special contract with them. You see, the principal dancers have a contract all year long, but one dancer, just one, had the courage to ask for a guest artist contract. It was Yvette Chauviré. Nobody had done that before. And that's exactly what I needed, and because they needed me so much at that time, eventually they gave it to me. I had to do maybe twenty or thirty performances a year with them — that was the minimum — and then I could also go other places. After getting that contract, I remember I was supposed to dance with Carla Fracci in Boston, and the Paris Opéra changed their program and didn't tell me. They said, "Oh, by the way" — maybe it was one or two months before — "we have to change the program." It was a singer; the singers were always more important than the dancers. So they said, "Sorry. You can't do it." I had a big argument with the director, and I said, "I want to be freer than being a guest artist." Finally I couldn't stand the way I was working any more. Leaving was not an artistic decision really. It was a general decision, that I wanted to be free from the Paris Opéra. Maybe I could then have gone anywhere, but I came here just because of Balanchine.

It took me such a long time to adjust, a few years. I was so confused. In the beginning, I started to analyze the ballets of Balanchine the same way I would analyze *Swan Lake* — about steps, about directions, about exactly how it would feel — and tried to understand it. And it's not something so much to understand. It's just something to live. You live it, you live with it, and that's the best way to do it. I learned to enjoy ballets. Before, it was more like a duty, to respect the choreographer. Ballet — that's what was important to me, and the dedication of a dancer. I didn't think it should first be fun to do it; it was not supposed to be fun. There's something more important than having a good time. When I came here, Patricia and different dancers asked me, "Did you have fun doing it?" I said, "What is that? I tried to do my best, that's all. It has nothing to do with enjoying it." I thought I was doing the ballets right, I thought I was doing my best, but they didn't look right. I could feel that Balanchine wanted different things.

Apart from Balanchine and John Taras, one person who helped me to be patient was Lincoln Kirstein. And otherwise, the person who really helped me to understand, to learn ballets, was Pat. And dancing with different partners, rehearsing with Balanchine, made me aware mainly of where I was placing myself and where I was placing the music. I got very excited about it right away. The style was not so much a way of moving; it was more about the contact with the music, how you almost precede the music. You don't wait for the exact beat to arrive; you know it's going to come and you must precede it. It's like the way a conductor leads the orchestra. He's not going to make his movement exactly on the beat. He's going to make it a little bit before so they will play it at the right time. It's like that for the dancer. The whole movement has to be created just a little bit before the music is there, so the impact is at the maximum together. It's something that I thought I was doing, I thought I had that contact with the music, but I didn't.

I started, the first year, with *Swan Lake,* and I didn't like dancing it at all. It was the second act only, but I didn't come to do that and I was not very happy. What I really wanted was to be a part of the whole thing. I came not to be recognized, not to stand outside of the company, but to be a part of it. And not only to be a part, but to dance like everybody and to dance a lot, a little bit of everything. I've always wanted to dance everything — not dance each performance, but dance any kind of role. When Balanchine was telling me about Don Quixote, the old man with the beard, I said, "Oh, that will be exciting," and I did that. And I wanted also to do *Bugaku.* In fact, that's the only ballet I asked to dance, maybe the first or second year I was here, and he agreed right away. That ballet didn't seem so strange. I knew I could do it and it was closer to me or, let's say, closer to a Béjart ballet. It's very theatrical, and it has a way to give the character life which you could have learned outside of Balanchine ballets. So I felt very close with that. Balanchine would always decide the rest.

I only got into Phlegmatic in *Four Temperaments* not too long ago. It came back in the repertoire just three or four years ago. I felt it was a classic, and I attacked it like a classic. It's not only a classic but a very exact ballet, much more precise than *Violin Concerto* or *Symphony in Three Movements* which really have so much to do with the way you bring movement to them. *Four Ts* is so dry and so exact. The movement goes directly to a corner; you have to go there; it goes there; it's getting smaller. The possibilities for the movement are very small — it's right there. I don't think that each performance changes too much. *Bugaku, Violin Concerto,* things like that, each performance is very different, but there's just one way to do *Four Temperaments.*

It's like a photo or a sort of shadow, or something . . . Like a box, and you go to that thing. It's like two pieces of wood that go in towards each other until they meet in a corner, almost like a mold. It's hard to explain because it has so much to do with the music. The way to hear the music is almost to feel the music. You feel the whole ballet, you do it with the feeling, with the music, but you don't have many choices.

I don't know anything about painting, for example, and I'm reading now something on Picasso. At one point, he was trying to do less and less and less; it became like a skeleton of what he wanted to do. On the page you see that he did a little bit less and less. *Four Temperaments* is really like that. I spent my whole career doing steps, but finally the one thing to keep would be *Four Temperaments* — more than *Apollo,* more than *Violin Concerto* which I adore, more than so many things. That one is so naked, so bare. That's my favorite part of it, that I couldn't replace any movement of it. It's by doing those movements, exactly those, that I fulfill something, in me and in the music.

I don't even remember who taught it to me. Not Balanchine, not Arthur Mitchell . . . I don't remember. Isn't it funny? It's more like I feel that it came from another place. I did see Arthur dance it before I did, and I think that shaped what I wanted to do a little. It certainly did in *Agon.* I learned that from Arthur and I really liked the way he showed it; it was so jazzy and so much fun, so exciting. But *Four Ts* — I have no recollection of who taught it.

The most helpful way to begin on a Balanchine ballet, on this ballet, is with Balanchine. I worked with him before I danced *Four Ts,* and he was very specific. What was that unbelievable thing he did? It was very strange, almost impossible. It was a turn, just before the exit and in another place too. You stood flat on one foot and the other one was pointed and crossing at the ankle, with the toes just touching the floor. Keeping your feet like that, it was a complete turn without changing the position of the feet. Eventually everybody developed a preparation to do that turn, but Balanchine wanted it from a dead position, without preparation at all, with the body just straight and not twisting around to push. It gives something so unusual, so strange.

There's no character but the quality of the movement. It's going somewhere and it's so exact — it's that movement and not something else. There was never anymore explanation than that. When you think about something absolutely abstract, you have absolutely no idea of what it is but it still feels so full. That ballet is maybe the closest I came in my whole career to whatever abstract is. I don't even know if it's phlegmatic. I don't really know what phlegmatic is — it feels like laziness almost, in the body. But if you think too much about that, then it doesn't work because he wants it very, very tense. It's nothing of relaxation. It's all tense.

The problem of weight, for example — not the weight on the floor, but the body weight, just how much you weigh yourself — is very important. You feel much better in some ballets when you are very thin, and this ballet feels extraordinary when you are absolutely thin. I can remember doing it — I know it sounds pretentious, but anyway — like those Giacometti statues. It has to feel like that, which is strange because the movements are so full. They don't feel thin, they don't feel like a piece of metal, but dancing it feels like that. You think of taking off all the extra, planing it away, making less and less.

Technically it's not hard. I had things to do this morning and I didn't take class, but I could do it right now, technically. It would look awful and I would be very sore after, but I could do it. I would need maybe five minutes of concentration before, just for the balance maybe, but I could do it.

You know, I heard Margot Fonteyn's interview with Dick Cavett. She was saying that right after the war, she was doing so many *Swan Lake*s and *Giselle*s, and the steps in one at one point were so close to the steps in the other, that she would almost start to do the wrong ballet. For me, there is one place that is so close, not in *Four Ts*, but between *Bugaku* and *Agon*. It's just a connection of form, where the man is placed next to the woman in the pas de deux. Twice in *Bugaku* and once in *Agon*, he's almost on the floor and she's up above him. That feels the same, but it doesn't stay — it's just a moment. Otherwise, in any other Balanchine ballets, I never felt that I was close to that kind of confusion. Never. There's no connection at all. And that's also one of the most amazing things about Balanchine. He sets a ballet, and it will have nothing to do with the one before. He never repeats himself.

When you choreograph, you have to be careful of not using some type of formation that you like. By the end of the day, you discover three steps or three formations that you have made. Something came. You say, 'Where did that come from? It came so normally, naturally, to me.' And then you discover either it came from one of the ballets of Balanchine or Robbins, or it came from someplace else. It's amazing to see what kind of selection your memory, the body-memory, makes. It's the same when you dance. It brings you a feeling from I don't know where. You don't make any selection — it just happens.

I think that when Balanchine does a ballet, a part of it, maybe the largest part, is the kind of movement he wants to do anyway. But also I think he's influenced by the dancer himself. I remember being very, very close to the steps in *Violin Concerto*, because I think Balanchine took a part of it from what he could see the dancers doing. It would be pretentious to say it was coming from me, but it has something to do with it.

Four Ts has something to do with you in the feeling you bring to it. And you have that music, which makes you remember some deep things, or scars. All that walk when he arrives, all that music, is a lot of things that you remember. It's a long, long trip, that first diagonal, just walking and arriving. He goes forever and ever, which is very hard because it's only the beginning — it's awful if you miss it. For me, that feeling maybe came from *Giselle*. The reason I feel comfortable with that walk is because in *Giselle*, in the second act, he's walking when he enters, and I always tried to enter as if he's been walking for an hour. That really helps. He walks for a long, long time, and he eventually arrives onstage — and it's on a stage and Giselle is there. But it's almost like he doesn't even realize that he's arrived, like he didn't really try to turn left and right. He only arrived there because he was going there anyway, it was his place. I remember walking forever before that act of *Giselle*, trying to forget completely about jumping and warming up. People would see me and say, "My God, what's he doing?" I would walk in the wings at least for three or four minutes, and then arrive exactly at the right moment onto the stage. It's a completely different feeling from just walking on. The good days, when you feel ready for *Four Ts*, you have the feeling that you arrive from far away, and then you are there for a long time.

And when you enter in the second act of *Giselle*, it's not so much that you live that time as Albrecht. It's more that you arrive in that cemetery without trying ... and even more than that, you remember. That's what you do. It's not so much that the time is alive, but that it is real in your mind. The second act of *Giselle* is about memory. You see her because you see her in your mind; you remember how she was. When you come on in *Four Ts*, it's not like you're going to tell a story. You just remember. Remember that, remember that, remember and go there. All of that is not 'Hi,' waving, when you lift the arm. It's more, 'I remember I was doing that once. I was saying hello.' So it brings a delay when you reach out the arm, it delays the movement. You see, it can be so personal that it's incredible.

You dance alone, but you're aware also of all the sharp movements those four girls are doing. They're like a square around you, like four walls almost, which concentrates the attention even more strongly. Sometimes you need a better concentration and you can't find it without imagining something — not really a situation, just a concentration, like putting yourself in a . . . I don't know if it's a place or what. And for different personages, you support your strength with different centers. You'll see tension in the neck sometimes, or some people have it in the forehead or behind the eyes or in a knot in the stomach. It depends on the role. In *Bugaku*, for example, the tension of the neck was very important; the center felt absolutely in that rigid neck. The role becomes very easy to do when you put the center in the right place. I think actors also learn that.

The acting was very important to me. I go about a ballet like *Coppélia* as an actor, starting with trying to imagine a text, trying to make everything clear, trying to make a walk be true — which is almost impossible. I tried the walk forever for the old man, Don Quixote, and Balanchine got sort of mad. He said, "No, he's not quite so old." It was fun; I looked at the Gustave Doré drawings, and I adored working with the props. People would see me in the corridors every day wearing that long lance and the mask, and I rehearsed with them all the time because they're very important.

You approach comedy as you would anything else. It's just something fun, a funny story, and you have to bring that story to the stage. As soon as you enter, you are something else — every time you enter, in any role. I never felt I was only myself; I never felt it was enough to be myself onstage and bring nothing. I can't just come all alone. I have to get ready before. For example, if I work in front of the mirror — I'm thinking now about just before the Costermongers in *Union Jack* — and maybe it doesn't make any difference on the stage, but anyway — it takes a few minutes to get to the expression you want to do right away onstage. If you don't get ready, the expression will take two or three seconds to come out, and then it won't work. You need a few minutes to find it, and then you can see it in the mirror yourself. You try to persuade yourself of something, and you just look in your own eyes in the mirror and see if the face is changing a little bit or not. Once you are warmed up, you think about the situation and something in the face is doing it right away. On the stage, it will come on the face at once.

It seems that Balanchine's steps are so logical when they are on the right tempo of the music. When you try to remember the steps, you have to know also the exact tempo. If you do other ballets, of other choreographers, usually you have to remember what's coming next or maybe a logical way to do a movement. But for Balanchine it makes so much difference if you do the right tempo. The tempo was a big adjustment for me when I came, and the speed. I think Nureyev met Eddie Villella one day and said, 'Why are you dancing so fast?' That's the feeling you get when you are here first: 'Where are they going?' But it's what we think is necessary to be alive onstage when you become a Balanchine dancer.

Balanchine's the same in class; he teaches the same thing. He teaches you to be aware of what the human eye can catch. You know, I collect posters. Posters used to be full of things, and people had the time to look at them. But more and more the posters are simpler and simpler, and now people have just a few seconds to catch them, to catch what it means. I think it's the same with dance also. The audience sees so much, so many things every day, that you have to be absolutely fast and absolutely decisive. More than anybody else, Balanchine has that sense of what it is now to be a dancer, that sense about speed, about what *we* see every day, how *we* catch things. In the first six months that Balanchine was in New York, what he caught must have been incredible. If only we could have a repertoire of what he caught, of all that speed that he understood American bodies could do, the people could do, the dancers. To dance his ballets, I think you have to learn to be a part of New York.

Whether it's Stravinsky or anybody else, if the choreographer explains the music right, he opens the door for you. I don't feel it was something I had to understand on my own. The first time I heard *Violin Concerto*, I wondered what it was, but eventually I knew it so well that I knew exactly what was missing if the musicians would not play something. I never worried at all about understanding it. I always knew that Balanchine would explain to me what it was, and he did. I don't remember hearing any music that I really didn't like, or making myself like any music. But you see, I never felt that I was the one to choose the music; it was just something I would have to get used to. Of course it's different when I'm choreographing. When I choreograph I feel I'm serving the music, but I'm serving the choreographer when I dance.

To say what dancer is a musical dancer, I would just give names; I couldn't explain it. I would say Pat, I would say Fred Astaire. And so many more also, but those are the two to start with.

I'm very happy about what I did, coming here, but I never danced *Giselle* here or *Swan Lake* or *Sleeping Beauty*, and I regret sometimes that I never showed that part of what I could do. *Giselle* is the only one of those old classics that I miss. *Sleeping Beauty* for the music, which I adore, and *Giselle* for the role. *Swan Lake* I don't miss at all. *Nutcracker* pas de deux is my favorite Tchaikovsky music, but I do that here. And there are some Roland Petit ballets I would have wanted to dance here. One is *Notre-Dame de Paris*, which was really great, and the other, an old ballet, is *Le Loup*. Those I miss. If I'm thinking about the ballets that I would still wish to dance, they would be Balanchine ballets. One I would have loved to dance, and I think I would not have been bad in it, was *Square Dance*. And I never danced *Rubies* — that's great also. In Robbins, I would have adored to dance *Other Dances*. I guess that's all. Oh yes, *Prodigal Son*, sure. So in fact there are quite a few things.

I'm just trying to remember the best time I've had onstage. I think I have even a better time with a partner than alone because I really like the exchange, but it's even more rare than to have a good time alone. In real life it's the same: very often it's easier to have a good time alone, in a certain place or with a good book, when you enter in your own world. I learned partnering in Paris Opéra, from fourteen until twenty, in pas de deux class. I just remember starting — starting was hard. But partnering's also something you can do better and better. If certain dancers could dance until sixty years old, they would become better and better partners, through experience. I'm a better partner now than before, definitely.

You always have the feeling that you're trying to progress every time you dance. After teaching something like *Four Ts* to someone else, you feel that you're going ahead a little bit faster. That's all; it just helps you to progress faster, to see something you would have seen anyway but it might have taken longer.

For a long time, I thought it was cheap to dance for the audience; for years I didn't want to dance for them. I thought that if you dance for the audience, you start to do just the things they like. But since I'm in New York, I figure that you really dance more for the audience than for yourself. You're still there, but you dance for the imagination of the audience. I've realized that they are the reason you're there onstage. But I hardly feel like a dancer anymore, so it's hard to say. When I went on tour with Pat a few days ago, I was sitting in the audience trying to be much more aware of how they would react to the ballets, trying to listen more to them. Lately I think I'm listening more and more to the audience, as a choreographer and as a sort of director, no, an organizer of a company. But as a dancer I don't think it was like that. I don't think I was trying to be aware of what happened on the other side or reviews or anything like that. I think all those years I really danced for Balanchine.

December 1979
New York

Peter Martins

Peter Martins (b. Copenhagen, Denmark, 1946) first studied ballet with Stanley Williams and Hans Brenaa at the Royal Danish Ballet School, which he entered when he was eight. At eighteen, he graduated into the company and into featured roles in its Bournonville repertory and in modern ballets by Birgit Cullberg, Flemming Flindt, and Frank Schaufuss. Martins' association with the New York City Ballet began in 1967 when, shortly after making his debut in Balanchine's Apollo *in Copenhagen, he replaced Jacques d'Amboise in the role at the Edinburgh Festival. He made regular guest appearances as a principal with the New York City Ballet for the next several years, frequently partnering Suzanne Farrell with whom he still dances often, and joined the company permanently in 1970. His vast repertory extends from* Agon *to* Coppélia, *from* Dances at a Gathering *to* Fancy Free, *from* Afternoon of a Faun *to* Diamonds. *A sample of his created roles includes Balanchine's* [Stravinsky] Violin Concerto *(1972),* Duo Concertant *(1972),* Chaconne *(1976), and* Robert Schumann's "Davidsbündlertänze" *(1980), and Robbins'* In the Night *(1970),* Goldberg Variations *(1971), and* In G Major *(1975). In 1977 Martins choreographed* Calcium Light Night, *his first ballet and the first of many he has now contributed to the New York City Ballet repertory.*

Even seeing is not always believing. Can you believe that one dancer possesses a Praxitelean body, a flawless but never bloodless technique, a natural musicality, and a sense of humor? And that the same dancer is as striking in repose as he is stunning in motion? And that by spending his gifts lavishly, at every performance, he continually refines and replenishes them? It's all true, and Peter Martins has confirmed and reconfirmed it before my own eyes for the last ten years, but I still occasionally find it hard to believe. Apollo is a landmark ballet in his personal history as a dancer. Today it inspires him to a performance that is a landmark in his career, a distillation of all he knows instinctively and all he has so avidly, gloriously, learned.

*T*o start chronologically, I would say Erik Bruhn was probably the first influence. Not by anything he said to me or taught me, but simply by being what he was. That was plenty. Naturally, little boys and girls study and steal and wonder, and I did too. Erik Bruhn was our idol; this is what we all worked to become. I thought he was just God. I couldn't believe anybody could dance like that and look like that. He actually was my first teacher, for maybe two or three months when I was eight years old, but he made no impression then — I was too young. He began to make an impression on me when I began to understand what ballet was about. I can't imagine now, in retrospect, if I hadn't had Erik, if I hadn't had this picture of perfection, what direction I would have gone in. I'm sure I would have managed somehow anyway, but he seemed that important.

And then, he got out of the system and much more important was my teacher Stanley Williams. He was really the one who injected the ballet in my blood, because he treated me in a certain way. When you're twelve or fourteen, you're not so worried about what you're being taught. You're more concerned at that age about, Do you like the teacher? Do you respond well to the teacher? Does he respond to you? Stanley Williams seemed to have a terrific aura around him and an enormous respect for his pupils. There was no looking down upon people or condescending. That didn't exist. Immediately he made me feel that he was saying, 'This is a talent and I respect this talent.' Of course, then you love him and then you want to work. All this was unintentional on his part. That was the way he was, and the way he is to this day.

Apollo might have been the first Balanchine piece I ever did. If it wasn't the first, it might as well have been, because if I had done Bizet at that point, I didn't know it was Balanchine. It was just a ballet called *Symphony in C* — it could have been Petipa. There was no difference to me in those days. So dancing *Apollo* was really my introduction to Balanchine. I was very young and I had just been made principal. I think I saw part of Henning's performance once from the wings, when I was probably seventeen or eighteen, but I had never seen the whole ballet from out front.

But there was Henning Kronstam teaching it to me. It was one of his big roles in Denmark, and I remember him being very specific and very detailed about every little move. And I said to myself, 'This is not his ballet. He didn't choreograph it. How does he know all this?' Anyway, he taught it to me and I did it for a couple of performances, and I think I remember I got very good notices. The Danish critics said, 'This is what it should be.' I must say it felt like a glove. Not like a glove — it sounds too pretentious and clichéd — but it felt very natural. I felt somewhat at home.

Then a couple of weeks later, I was called over to Edinburgh to replace Jacques, and there Balanchine started working with me. And then it became completely different. I wouldn't say it became uncomfortable, but it began to really make sense to me. Balanchine explained to me, by showing, himself, the whole purpose. Each little movement had a purpose. What Henning had done was to teach me exactly what he'd been doing, which was fine, but he didn't explain in that sense. I didn't know exactly why, why you do this step, and Balanchine, without really too many words, just opened doors. All of a sudden, everything had a meaning. Nothing was there by accident. For example, at the end of the big solo, you do a double pirouette on your knee and you look up. Just before that, there's a place when you take little tiny tac-a-tac-a-tac steps. Henning hadn't said anything about it — not that he should have. This is not a criticism of him, but there's a difference in having a ballet taught to you by the choreographer. Balanchine said, "It's like fire, like you're dancing on hot coal. It should be very little, very quiet, just barely touching the floor." I did that, and all of a sudden it made sense. The movement became a different movement to me, and it felt right, more right. Every step was like that.

And you know what? Not so much by partnering Suzanne, but when I sat on the chair and watched her dance her solo, the way she danced it revealed a whole frame of mind and a whole attitude towards this ballet that I'd never seen before. I was fascinated by the way she did *Apollo*. It was absolutely glorious. All of a sudden it was not steps, even though she certainly did do the steps and they certainly were beautiful. But she never made me think she was aware of specific steps. She revealed a goddess, or a muse; she just danced, she just moved. Anna Laerkesen in Denmark, who was a fantastic dancer and danced Terpsichore wonderfully, didn't feel that. The more I grow up and the more I am around in this world, the more I think it's sad for people who do Balanchine ballets not to work with Balanchine, especially the good ones. Somebody like Anna Laerkesen could have benefited tremendously if she'd had one hour with him.

When I went to Edinburgh, I had no idea what I was getting into. They were looking for an Apollo all over Europe, and they ended up with me because nobody else was available. I was the last choice. But there I was, and I had gotten good notices. So I said to myself, 'Well, I'm sure I'll be fine except I have to show it now to the choreographer. I wonder what he will think.' Balanchine never said a word before the first performance. He just wanted to leave me alone. I don't know what his image of me was, if he even had one. My image of me was that I was a ready, prepared dancer, full and well-educated. Even though we all know we always get better, basically I thought I was as good as anybody else. I thought I was the result of the highest education in the land . . . in the world. I didn't know any better. I was now a principal dancer, a very talented dancer — I was good.

So Suzanne and I kind of adjusted versions. What Henning had taught me was a very correct version, which was a great help, but I realized immediately that for Balanchine it had altered over the years. Which fascinated me. Actually, the whole beginning of my relationship with Balanchine was that that fascinated me, the fact that he changed ballets if he felt like changing them, even if they were called masterpieces. He didn't care; he changed them, and I liked that. After my first performance, he completely redid everything. I was there for a week and I did five or six performances, and by the time I got home to Denmark, it was a whole new ballet for me. Even steps seemed different, and yet they were not. When I danced it again in Denmark, people couldn't recognize it.

I was thinking of going to America already, before I was even asked to go to Edinburgh. Just prior to my promotion in Denmark, I wanted to leave, not for New York City Ballet, not for American Ballet Theatre — as a matter of fact, it wasn't really clear to me which company was the most desirable. I just wanted to go to America, and it wasn't only balletic reasons. I thought America was an exciting country to go to when you're an ambitious young man and you want to get ahead. And even though I was a dancer — and I knew I was a dancer by then — I felt that America was the only place where I could be challenged tremendously. Denmark had always seemed like a Lilliput country. It's a wonderful country and I love it, but it's so tiny. You could count the ballet dancers; in all of Denmark, there were ninety, or maybe one hundred forty. That was it. And that meant, what, forty boys? I already had accomplished principal status, and I felt, 'All right, where do we go from here?'

The night I was called from Edinburgh, Stanley Williams was in Denmark on a visit and we were having dinner — by then, we had become friends. I said, "Stanley, they just promoted me to a principal, and they left an impression on me that when they promote somebody, they want to keep him." Naturally, because they invest in him, they want interest back. "So they want me to stay. However I want to go to America. What is this New York City Ballet you're working for? Do you think I can come over there?" And he said, "Well, I don't know. Balanchine's a very strange man. Maybe he'll take you, but I don't think you should expect a principal status. Maybe he'll take you as a soloist, or maybe even corps." And I remember saying, "I don't care. I get the feeling that in America it doesn't matter what you're called." In Denmark, you have ranks; the King makes you this or that. "It matters what you are, what you can do. If I get to the corps, I'm sure I will be promoted later on. Can you get me in?" And he said, "I'll try."

That was during the main course. And as true as it sounds, during the dessert Vera Volkova called and said, "Peter, John Taras is here and he's waiting at the theatre. Can you come and audition for him?" I said, "I'm not going to audition for anybody at eleven o'clock at night." And she said, "Please, just come over and talk with him." So I went, and the next morning, Stanley and I are on a plane to Edinburgh. It was such a coincidence, really so weird. After that week, of course, I didn't have to go to New York City Ballet. I had also had offers from the Stuttgart Ballet, the National Ballet of Canada, and the London Festival Ballet before all this. But I felt, 'No, America.' That one week in Edinburgh really decided me. Balanchine fascinated me — I think it's fair to say the man more than the ballet. All right, so he changed *Apollo* and it became more interesting, but it became more interesting because of him. Essentially, it was him. He gave me a fix.

I didn't keep working on it when I came here to the company — *he* did. Balanchine kept working on it. I discovered then how important *Apollo* was to him. He always rehearsed it, he always fussed with it, he always changed it a little bit, even according to his moods sometimes — at least it seemed that way to me. I said to myself, 'Didn't he tell me two weeks ago to do this? But now he wants this. Maybe I didn't do quite what he asked.' He was willing to play around with it, which made the ballet so interesting, and it never became stale.

Basically, I went through a period of adjustment mentally. I began to realize that the way I danced was not the only way to dance, especially when you had a repertoire like this that required you to do so many different things. When Balanchine put you in certain ballets, he simply expected you to be those ballets. And when he took you out of a classical, normal, Petipa-style ballet, like Bizet [*Symphony in C*], and put you in a Stravinsky something, *Agon*, he expected something else. If you did one the same way as the other, he took you out and put somebody else in who was better in it. That was difficult for me to understand, because you don't take somebody like me out. Once you get a role in Denmark, you have it, you own it. That's your role 'til you die, 'til you can't crawl anymore, unless you become pathetic. Roles here were switched, given up, taken away. My vanity was upset with it, and yet it made sense. 'Why not?' I said to myself. 'He's right. You should be able to do this style and that style on command.' And all those challenges that he put on dancers became essential to my interest in dance.

My Bournonville training helped simply because I had already been exposed to good choreography. It is good choreography, Bournonville, and it's difficult to dance his steps; sometimes they're very quick and very demanding. In a sense, when I had to do certain Balanchine ballets, I'd already done them. I had them in my system already. Some of them are so similar to some Bournonville ballets that it's frightening. But, more than Bournonville, Balanchine used the space. That's another thing that I became fascinated with about him. The stage in the Royal Theatre in Denmark is tiny in comparison to the huge stage at the New York State Theater — I had always been dancing on a stamp. And there was Balanchine moving his dancers across, diagonal, and around, even to every corner of the stage, and especially because I'm big, I loved it. But it was difficult to move, not only to jump up and do things fast, but also to cover space. The first time I saw Jacques dance, in *Nutcracker*, I couldn't believe that anybody could cover that much space in such a short time. Musically, it was incredible.

Then I saw Jacques in *Apollo*. It looked different, it was a different approach, everything was different from what I did, and I felt I didn't want to look at it too much. There were certain points I learned from him. If they made sense to me and appealed to me, I would say, 'Well, he's probably right. He knows. I'm going to do this too.' But on the whole, I felt there was no need for me to look at too many people.

As a rule, I prefer not to look at too much or do any reading. If you have to do *Romeo and Juliet* or *Hamlet*, you have to know what it's all about, and then you read about it. It's nice to know the story. But *Apollo* is a Greek myth, and what more do you need to know than this is a young god? You need to know he's the son of Leto? Fine, all right, so you know that. You look that up and you see a picture . . . But what pictures do you look at? Michelangelo's Apollo? Who do you look at? There's a wonderful story about Balanchine — he told it to me. After the première of *Apollo* in Paris, somebody said to him, "How could you make Apollo look like this, walking on his knees and all awkward? Apollo is a god. He doesn't look like that and he shouldn't do stuff like that." And Balanchine said, in response, "How do you know what Apollo looks like? Who knows?" So you can look at pictures of Lifar, and you say, 'Ah, this is what Lifar looked like.' But so what? As long as you know he's the god Apollo, he has the three Muses, he chooses, that's all you need to know. I personally always resent — not resent — but I try not to get too analytical, because the role can lose its spontaneity and its flavor.

The music is what you dig into, especially when you work with Balanchine, because that says a lot. I got a record of *Apollo* and I listened to it a lot, and I think several things were revealed to me by listening to the score. But you don't have to analyze story lines or meanings. With *Four Temperaments*, you might ask, 'What does this movement mean?' But the minute you hear the music, you know. You think, 'Ah, this is why he made that movement,' and often it's not because he's trying to tell a story.

Having not done *Apollo* for seven or eight years now in this company, I did it for the first time last night. And suddenly I felt that all these Stravinsky ballets I've done with Balanchine over the years became a great help. This is something I just discovered last night . . . or this very minute. All of a sudden, *Apollo* was different from the others, also a Stravinsky ballet but early Stravinsky, and easier in a way. Maybe also because I choreograph now, I really know what Balanchine means.

I don't mean to analyze and tell a story about *Apollo*. I'm sure Balanchine has a story in his mind, but I don't know and I don't really care to know what it is. I don't want to have him sit there and explain in terms of a story. I'd much rather discover it myself through the steps. What he wants to convey is so obvious and so clear in the steps. But where the ballet starts now, in the new version, Apollo is already — in *my* mind anyway — in command. He's not a child; he's a god. Therefore, you have no development of a character, which for some-body like me who's done it so much is maybe too bad. It's nice to do the little child and grow up and build the character to the end. But this is just as valid; you already are when the curtain goes up, and you remain the same person throughout. I thought I would miss the staircase, but I didn't. What happened last night made perfect sense. I'm not saying I prefer it or not; that's for an audience to judge. For me, this way also works, and if that's the way he wants to see it — speaking now as a starting choreographer myself — it's his privilege.

How does choreographing affect me as a dancer? Well, a dancer wants to do less, by nature. If you have a choreographer in a chair and a dancer standing, I think the dancer generally wants to do less initially, and the choreographer wants him to do more. As a dancer, I'm pretty lazy in a certain sense; whatever comes easy, I prefer. We all do — I don't think it's only me. Balanchine's most famous line of all is "Why save? What are you saving for? For when?" But we don't want to hurt or strain ourselves too much; that's very much a part of a dancer's approach. If a choreographer tells you to do something, you find an easy way to do it.

But the minute you go into the choreographer's chair, you want more. You want the dancer to give more than he can. Or normally does. Or normally wants to. You don't want him to jump higher or turn more, but to move quicker or sharper, right on the music, or change directions more abruptly so it becomes more surprising. When I started choreographing, I wanted that and I forgot that I was a dancer. If I have a rehearsal where I choreograph, I don't even know that I am a dancer until I finish. Then I have to rehearse as a dancer myself. And then I remember, 'I just choreographed, and I just beat the shit out of those poor dancers. Now here I am dancing, and I should do more myself.' Also, I don't like dancers in my ballets to goo it up. Therefore, not that I ever tended myself to goo up things, but I do even less now. So I think I've changed tremendously. How could I not? *Violin Concerto* was one of the first things that I discovered, 'Hey, you never really did this right, Peter.' Balanchine even commented himself. After I started choreographing, he said, "You understand much better now."

Something like *Apollo* is so simple, so rich in itself, that you don't have to add anything. It's all there. To me, the less you add, the stronger it becomes. Anything you add becomes an obstruction, gets in the way. There's no need to add — I hate to say, but I can't find better words — anything of your own. To say consciously 'I'm going to add something of me' is wrong. You just have to do it the way you are; that's why you were chosen to do it in the first place, because the choreographer sees the way you are. There's no need to do more than is required; the interpretation is already in the pure dance-design. That's again why I so much prefer Balanchine ballets over anybody else's, because they're pure dance-designs that don't need fuss.

There is a big difference between *Violin Concerto* and *Apollo*. The minute you start adding to *Apollo*, you would tend to add a story. Maybe not a story, but feelings and emotions. What else could you add? But there's no feeling or emotion or thought to add to *Violin Concerto*, so what you add is purely physical; maybe you do a jump differently. But also, when he choreographed *Violin*, he used my dancing. He said to me, "What can you do here? Do what you can do." So *Violin* is much more me than *Apollo*. I dance *Violin* the way *I* dance, and that's *why* I dance it. In *Apollo*, I'm doing somebody else.

I want you to see a child being born. He comes out of the bandages, he's born, and he screams. And he simply cannot stand up at all. The two maidens take his hands and teach him to play the lute.

Then there's a blackout, and the next thing you see is him starting out dancing. It's as if you're seeing ten or fifteen or two years roll by, just in the first variation, the 'birth' variation I call it. He's actually discovering his two legs, like a little animal, like a horse when it's just born. The solo is like the first time you see a little child walk. Progressively, he becomes more secure; the first step he cannot walk, the fifth step he all of a sudden can sense the solid ground with his feet. Essentially, the variation finishes as it begins, with him playing the lute. But there's a big difference. Now — not to over-analyze and not to interpret to the last detail — now there's a slight . . . not authority *per se*, but now he knows what he's doing. And as he does that, the three Muses come on. He plays the lute, and there they are. This is how I see it. It has never been explained, never been told, it's not written anywhere why he calls them, but you want to select the one for you. You want to select your Muse.

I wouldn't say you challenge them, but you play with them. That's a very difficult part of the ballet, because there you shouldn't be too mature already. Even though at the end of the variation you're not a little boy anymore, you're still playful with them. He pulls them after him, he takes two away, he takes one away, he plays. One is already selected in the choreography, when he splits the two from the one. Already there you get the idea of selection, but it's basically playfulness.

Now I want to see what they are offering. I give one symbol to each of them, and I essentially say, 'Dance for me. Show me what you have to offer.' Then I sit down, and the way I am sitting is . . . now I have authority. Without a doubt, the most difficult part of the ballet, to me, is when I sit there and watch the three variations, because you cannot act. You cannot sit and emote. Even though the first girl is playing all to me, I cannot pull away and I can't lean towards her. It's still a neoclassic, abstract ballet. And yet I cannot sit slumped. There has to be a certain presence and a certain awareness of what they're doing, yet without acting. And you cannot do it in your face at all. This is my view of it — I'm not talking for Balanchine; he never told me this. But you cannot show in your face dislike or happiness or pleasure or any emotion at all. You have to show everything in your neck, in your spine, and in your being. And you have to show very little, or else your sitting there becomes ridiculous. When you're dancing, then you are using your body, and the choreography expresses what you are supposed to express. But when you're sitting there and you have really nothing to do, that is the most difficult thing.

I do my solo right after, and now I am a man or a young god.

I'm not a boy anymore — now I know what I am doing. I have already selected Terpsichore and I am dancing for her, I suppose. That solo is very strong, very powerful, and very masculine in a sense. There isn't any more to it than the fact that I am now completely in charge, I have selected my Muse, and I dance.

It's a love pas de deux, like any other pas de deux. We're expressing our love for each other. It's not a difficult pas de deux at all. I wouldn't say any of *Apollo* is technically difficult. The plasticity of it, the shaping of it, is what's difficult. I mean, entrechat six or entrechat cinq or double pirouette turned in is not difficult, but it's difficult to make that look interesting. I've always found the most difficult part about *Apollo* is not to fall into the temptation to act the ballet. I have seen people do that, and it looks wrong. It's too much. I don't mean you can dance the steps without being there, and without believing that there's something behind them, but I don't think you should start acting in your face and putting in a character that you have analyzed beforehand. That'll ruin it all. That's why it is very difficult to talk about, also.

You know that his authority keeps growing, simply because the music progressively gets stronger and stronger until the very last moment when his father calls. After the clap, when he collapses on their hands, then his father or the god calls him from heaven — that's one trumpet note — and says, 'Come on, boy. Bring the girls.' And he does. He answers him: 'O.K., I'm coming' — that's another trumpet note — and he takes the girls and brings them up the mountain.

When we were all children, twelve, thirteen, fourteen, we learned music theory in Denmark, we learned to read music, and we learned to play the piano. But I don't know if it makes a difference now. I cannot play the piano today and I can hardly follow the score, because I didn't keep it up, so in essence I should say I did not have musical training. But there was always an awareness there, and I've always considered myself rather musical. Not necessarily meaning I dance musically — because that I don't know — but I understand music and I've always felt very close to it. There are some dancers who have been called musical, and I cannot bear their kind of musicality. I don't like it when people overphrase, when they play too much with the music. It's the worst; it's like overacting. I prefer it much stricter, much more limitation on the dancer in terms of the music. Of course you can phrase, you can be a little flexible, but it's so dangerous if you do too much. Then it becomes unmusical and it becomes disturbing to watch.

When I came here, Stravinsky was very difficult for me. I had never danced that music before and I found myself, for the first time in my life, counting. I don't count when I learn a ballet — I never have. I just listen to the music. But *Agon*, I think, was the first Stravinsky ballet I did, and I had to count. It was very difficult, but it was also a lot more interesting than to dance to the old masters like Tchaikovsky. There's a whole different dimension to Stravinsky's music, and also, many times it sounds different. When I do *Violin Concerto*, often the music sounds different to me — not only because they play it sometimes lousy — and I think it definitely affects me.

But I would say Balanchine's approach to music has affected me more in terms of myself as a choreographer than myself as a dancer. I have studied it: 'Why does he choreograph this section to this part of the music, and then break it up right there, when you would expect him to . . . ?' But I never really analyzed that when I danced.

People always ask me why I stay with Balanchine for so many years. It's not because I'm brainwashed — a lot of people think that, maybe not about me, but about dancers generally. For me, it has to do with a deep, rooted — again, cliché word — philosophy about dance, about what has always attracted me about dance. When I was a little boy, before I even met Balanchine, I always had ideas of what dance should be. I always thought that mediocrity and academic approaches, and the square way of dancing correctly, were totally boring and uninteresting. But I was dealing with people who had set ideas. Balanchine was the first man for me, and also the only man since, who had this incredibly sophisticated outlook towards what dance was all about. It was never just one thing in his mind. It could be anything. Look at the ballets. They're so much, and yet they're all basically the same, right? They're all a man versus a woman. Whether it's *Agon* or *Diamonds* or *Apollo*, it's always this enormous adoration for women. Well, I've always also adored women. Not meaning that I am a runaround, but a woman onstage is beautiful, and I've always thought that she was number one. Everything, choreographically speaking, is centered around her.

That's why I like partnering so much. I learned it, just like anything else. In Denmark, I was taught partnering for three years, fourteen to seventeen — a very basic, academic, ABC sense of partnering. And because I had an absolute inborn love for it — a much bigger love for partnering than for dancing — I very soon became very good at it, and I also extended it. I had a good teacher, Frank Schaufuss, but within two years I already surpassed him, in the sense of saying to myself, 'Now, wait a minute. What he's teaching me is all right, it's good, but it certainly is not very sophisticated. There is much more to partnering.' So I discovered ways for myself; I extended the technique. You hold a woman at the waist, yes, but there are many ways you can hold her. Do you hold her with two hands? With both paws clamped to her waist? When do you put your hands there? Before she starts? After she starts? Do you put one and then another? It depends a lot on the woman, but I'm talking now about style. This is what I mean by sophistication. Partnering has always looked academic to me, and I don't think it should.

Apollo may not be the best example of how much you change your performance with different girls, but even with *Apollo* you change. Maybe not to the point where most people can see the difference — I don't really know whether it's visible — but it changes for me depending on the girls because their approach and their physicality are different. Basically it's my viewpoint that changes. I react to Suzanne very differently as a man from the way I react to Patty [McBride] or to Heather [Watts], and that reaction is transferred to the stage. There is a different thought with each one, a different aura — and I'm not talking in terms of it being a girlfriend or not. That has nothing to do with it. Each is a different woman. She looks different, she behaves differently, her arm goes here instead of there, and you respond to all of that.

Nobody liked partnering in Denmark. All the boys hated it because they were standing behind the girl. I didn't think it was demeaning or uninteresting to stand behind. I never looked at myself as being *behind* the girl; I thought of myself being placed accordingly and presenting her. What I did was very important to her, not in terms of technique, but how I looked behind her and what I did to present her. Most men feel when they dance with a girl, 'This pas de deux is just passing time. Let's get it over with, and then comes my big solo.' I never thought that. Actually, I think the pas de deux is the seed, the seed of a fruit, and the variations are the other things.

I do like to dance by myself occasionally, but primarily I prefer to dance with a girl. I hate to dance in a group. I can't bear it. As soon as I have to be like somebody else, I always am *not* like somebody else — it has to do with confinement. The most difficult thing for me is to do the beginning of *Agon*, in the four boys. I do it, and I think I'm all right, but I always think about, 'Am I doing wrong? Am I kicking my leg too high? Am I kicking my leg too low?' I cannot do the same as other people, at the same time.

I'm perfectly happy not dancing the nineteenth-century classics. On such rare occasions do I get the urge. I'm asked occasionally to dance this one or that one, but the practicality of time makes it impossible. I do *Giselle* every once in a while, and I do *La Sylphide* which I think is more interesting. Well, I grew up with *La Sylphide*; from when I was eight years old, I stood and watched all the Jameses pass by, so maybe I'm not objective about it. I'm not saying it's a better ballet, but for me there's more to the role of James than to the role of Albrecht. It's a lot bigger bite to chew, both dancing-wise and character-wise. I do *Swan Lake* sometimes, but it bores me by now. Even though there's a big, beautiful white pas de deux in the second act, it doesn't interest me at all. It sets me back. I feel like I'm walking in museums, and you can only do that so much. I like to walk in the museums and look; every once in a while it's nice, but you don't want to do it every day.

How do I approach something with no story and no character? Like what? *Divertimento No. 15*? *Divert* is one of the most difficult ballets I've ever done in my life. Technically, number one, and number two, because it's absolute pure classicism in the sense that there are no hide-aways. This is exposé — you're exposed down to the nitty-gritties. You cannot go out there and act, and play . . . play anything. You just dance. In a sense it's very academic, and yet the choreography is not classroom steps by any means. And to go back to your question about how important is the music, this is one ballet where the music has a huge impact on me. I cannot help listening to this music, while I dance, before I go onstage too when I wait for my solo to begin, when all the other people dance their solos, when I do the pas de deux. The music is like paper-thin glass, and you're walking on it and you don't want to break it. Sometimes I feel too big in the ballet. It's silly, but I get the feeling that this ballet is crystal, and here I come in being a beer mug. It's so delicate and so crystal clear. It scared me stiff when I first had to do it.

Barocco reminds me a little bit of *Divertimento*. It also has a hell of a lot in it besides the steps, and there also the music has a huge impact on me. I walk out there, I do absolutely nothing — you're right, nothing of steps — and I feel that the more I do, the more misplaced I am. I should just be a ghost in that ballet. The man appears in the second movement, and the woman swims and floats through the air. You don't hear anything. When the pas de deux finishes and he disappears, it would be perfect if you said to yourself, 'Was there a boy here or not? I think there was a boy. I think I sensed a boy.' Not necessarily *saw* a boy, but *sensed* a boy. *Barocco* and *Divert* are the two most severe, in the sense that the music really sets the pace.

Now, I cannot think of anything more opposite to George Balanchine choreography, in terms of what is there already in a ballet, than Jerry Robbins choreography. Robbins is an interesting case. People always talk about them being so different, but working with them, you discover how different they really are. I haven't worked that much with Jerry, so I would not be the expert, but all these things I thought about Balanchine are practically the opposite with Jerry. Actually I only created one Robbins ballet, *Goldberg Variations* . . . oh, and *In G Major*. In *In G Major*, I was absolutely confined to what he wanted, to absolute specifics. He told me how he wanted me to phrase the music! I'm not talking about counts; I'm talking about phrasing I was required to do. Now, I'm not saying this is not right. This is a whole different approach. What it does to me, personally, is make me restricted. I feel I have a straitjacket on. Where do *I* come in? Not that I contribute so much to Balanchine's ballets, but already by the fact that I'm not being told, "Don't do . . . ," I'm not restricted. Not that I'm going to go out there and overtake, but it gives me at least the opportunity to think my way. The times Balanchine has confined me have been so rare I can hardly remember them. Every once in a while, he doesn't like what I do automatically and he tells me, but basically I have the freedom of choice.

Fancy Free killed me. *Fancy Free* murdered me, absolutely. It's a ballet that I've always liked. It was America to me, the part of America that I'd always loved. And the part of Jerry Robbins I'd always loved — and always admired and always wanted to do. I always thought that if I could only do *West Side Story*, I would give my life. So when I was called to *Fancy Free*, I was ecstatic. I thought, 'This is Jerry Robbins personified. Nobody but Jerry Robbins can do this, this well.' Then I went through a period of I can't remember how many months of pain. Here are three sailors coming to town who are going to have fun, right? Naturally, you cannot just have that general approach. You have to dwell on little specifics in the steps. But in order for the ballet to remain alive today, you have to give freedom to the sailors and be willing to alter a little bit, unless you specifically want it to become a period piece. And then you're going to look at it as a little novelty from then, and that's what I think becomes uninteresting. Again, Jerry's approach to his ballets versus Balanchine's approach to his is what makes the ballets look different. I didn't contribute anything to *Fancy Free* of my own simply because I was told not to. Of course, it's not my character or my ballet, and Jerry may disagree with me and say, 'But that's not true, Peter. I wanted you because you have this certain quality.' And yet, not only in terms of choreography but in everything, the closer I got to the original view of the part, which happens to be his own, the better. I felt that Jerry wouldn't give up the part to me. And then I saw him on a film and I don't blame him, because he was good. But that's not the point. The point is that this is now, forty years later, so let's get over it.

I feel that my way of dancing never appealed to Robbins. I'm taking a chance here; I assume this. There are several male dancers in the company that don't appeal to me at all. I certainly can't say they're not good, just that I would rather not use them in my choreography. But sometimes I can't avoid them, and this is the same with Jerry Robbins: How can he avoid me? So he prefers somebody else. Good for him. It's his prerogative. But I think he was never really interested in making dances for me. He did an excellent dance in *Goldberg* for me, and with that solo he gave me more freedom than he ever had before. Or since, funnily enough, and I was not even as good then as I am now in terms of being able to adjust to what he wanted. In his view, I'm probably better now, but he gave me more room then and I enjoyed it more. I like dancing it very much.

There are very few ballets I have not done in this repertoire, but I never did *Four Temperaments*. It was never discussed. I never asked for it, Balanchine never asked me to do any of the parts in it, and maybe it's better to leave it that way. Maybe there's a reason. But this is a ballet that I thought, 'Wow! I'd like to get into that.' And *Romeo and Juliet* has always interested me; it's also the only classic I haven't done. I'm beginning to say to myself, 'Well, maybe I'm getting a little old now,' but I still think I could do it and I'd like to, because the material is so wonderful. I don't look upon it like *Swan Lake*; this is Shakespeare, and it's a beautiful story, and if there has to be acting, wow, this is it. This is the sentimental part of me, or maybe the self-indulgent part of me, but I would really love to do it. I have been offered it several places, but it needs three or four weeks of rehearsal, so I'm probably never going to arrange it. I don't have the time. But it would be very interesting for me to do now.

I've always been very independent in my thoughts. I never really listen to anybody. That even goes for my teachers; in the beginning, I didn't listen to them. Maybe that was a mistake. I listened to one teacher, the one that captured my interest, Stanley Williams, but nobody else. Now I listen to Balanchine, to what he says and what he doesn't say. The things he refrains from saying and the things he eliminates are the things that I imagine. And naturally I listen to friends when they give me advice. Sometimes I certainly ought to take it, but most of the time I don't. Basically, I don't listen to anybody. I read all the critics, everything, as much as I can get my hands on. I go through it all, and it has no impact on me. I put it down. I forget it. I read it because I'm interested to hear what people think of me. I want to know 'He sucked' or 'He was terrific' or 'He gained weight' or 'He lost his pirouette' or whatever. I'm interested to see what people observe — it's like a pastime. After all, it is my life, and I'm not beyond vanity. I don't like to get a bad review, and I also don't like to get a good review when I've danced poorly. It's interesting to see who can judge, who can tell. I don't mean to challenge critics — maybe they'll now give me worse reviews — and I don't mean to say that I'm beyond criticism. I certainly am not. But I never cried inside or outside, visibly or not visibly, over a review, and I never got ecstatically happy over a review. It doesn't make a difference to me.

I'm dancing because I love it. I can't think of anything I love more, and it's nothing to do with the fact that I'm good at it. It had something to do with that in the beginning; I stayed with it when I was young because I was good at it. But now I'm staying with it because I love it, and I feel I really can do a lot. I think I can make my presence in the dance world, in the future, very important. I don't know if I will do great ballets one day, or if I will be a wonderful director, or even a good teacher. Honestly, I have no idea what my contribution will be, but I know that I can contribute something very important, much, much bigger than my dancing. I'm not talking about historically — I don't care about that. I care that I can inject a lot of life and energy and knowledge and thought into the next generation.

My own dancing is so strange. It's based upon so many weird things. I never liked to dance in front of an audience that much. I don't like people watching me — I never have. It's nice to dance in the studio; I'm all right there because there's only a few kids watching. It doesn't matter. But I am not comfortable having five thousand people watch me, even though I have an exhibitionistic part of me. I like my lover to look at me, not five thousand people I don't know. There's something always absurd about the fact that — I think of this often — people go in and they buy a ticket, for twenty bucks, and they sit in a chair, and they open a program, and they say, "Peter Martins." And the curtain goes up and there I am. And then, they sit and they look at me. They paid money to look at me. What an absurd thought. Right? No? What an absurd thought. But I'm also very down-to-earth, and I say, 'Well, they paid big bucks to see me do whatever I can do. I'm going to show them what I can do.' And then I show them as best I can. And I stop thinking about it any more, until the next time.

January 1980
New York

David Wall

David Wall (b. London, 1946) received his entire training at the Royal Ballet School, which he entered at the age of eight and left nine years later when he graduated into the Royal Ballet Touring Company. In 1966 he was promoted to principal at the uncommonly young age of twenty; when he transferred to the parent company at Covent Garden in 1969, he had already established a solid reputation as a danseur noble, as Margot Fonteyn's selecting him to partner her on several guest tours would indicate. Equally at home in the nineteenth-century classics — Giselle, Swan Lake, Sleeping Beauty, and Nutcracker — and in such abstract, twentieth-century classics as Symphonic Variations, Agon, and Song of the Earth, Wall has also showed a marked preference and a remarkable gift for dramatic roles. He danced the leads in de Valois' The Rake's Progress and MacMillan's The Invitation for the touring company, and in Balanchine's The Prodigal Son and Cranko's The Taming of the Shrew at Covent Garden. Following his 1970 debut as Romeo, he created Lescaut in MacMillan's Manon (1974) and Crown Prince Rudolf in his Mayerling (1978).

Time works on dancers like water on stone, smoothing and shaping them, slowly revealing their most characteristic features. If you frequently see someone dance, you won't notice any change in him at all until you look around one day and find that the dancer he used to be has disappeared. David Wall used to be a promising youngster standing at the end of a long line of Royal Ballet princes. Then, one by one, each of his predecessors vacated the throne. While I was watching Blair, Gable, Nureyev, MacLeary, and Dowell depart, over a period of years, Wall was emerging as the logical heir to their legacy. He quickly fulfilled his early promise as a danseur noble, but only with time have I discovered the dramatic depths, shadows, and myriad colors of his dancing. Today, as if suddenly for me, he has the maturity, authority, and unerring theatrical instincts to create a tempestuous, adolescent Romeo.

I wasn't really involved in the creation of *Romeo*, but I was around the excitement of what was happening and I was very close with Christopher Gable. I didn't see any of it in rehearsal, but I saw the first performances of it. Before I danced it, I'd seen all the interpretations of the other dancers — Anthony, Rudolf, and Christopher. Although at that stage I was very involved with the repertoire of the touring company, I used to come up for performances often. And I realized that it was a wonderful ballet and a wonderful opportunity for different interpretations.

But probably the first thing that brought me close to it was seeing it as a play. In fact, I must have seen the play many times before I saw the ballet. Funnily enough, about ten years ago I was speaking to Celia Johnson, who came to see the ballet for the first time. Since she had played Juliet, as an actress, I was very interested in her views of the transformation from live theatre to ballet, and she thought it almost worked better as a ballet. She said that somehow the feel was more complete throughout the work. Obviously, I don't know the details of the flaws she felt were in the play, but she was most impressed. I was really reckoning on her not actually approving.

My whole career has evolved alongside actors. A lot of my dearest friends are actors, and I've always been very close to theatre. It's sort of a give-and-take thing. My actor friends come and see ballet, and they know nothing about the technical side of it; they can just sit in the audience and enjoy it totally. And vice versa: I can see them working and be totally taken, on cloud nine. All I get when I watch people acting on the stage is what they're trying to put across. I don't know how they're doing it. Yet within that, one evolves a lot of ideas that one can incorporate into one's own work.

Probably the first person that really influenced me as a personality on the stage, and as a personality interpreting a role, was Paul Scofield. This was when I was fifteen, sixteen. I felt fantastic power, which I hadn't really felt with dancers because I was so involved with looking at their technical approach to things. The first actor I saw do Romeo was Ian Holm, who was very, very good. Physically he didn't come up to what I was expecting, but somehow he managed to get over that. And then another marvelous interpretation was John Hurt's in Coventry. And Tom Courtenay. And the Zeffirelli film I felt was a good landmark, though, funnily enough, I learned more about Mercutio and Tybalt in that production than I did about Romeo. But I can't count the number of interpretations I've seen.

I was taught the steps through dance notation, and of course I was in my first performance with Lynn [Seymour], which was an incredible help. It wasn't me doing Romeo: it was me and Lynn doing

Romeo and Juliet. That's what evolved naturally. I allowed my interpretation to be very much influenced by hers. We both knew Kenneth's ideal of what he wanted out of the performance, and we discussed it, but not to any great detail because we seemed to be on the same wavelength anyway. Kenneth didn't actually put me through the hoops, but whatever he saw in my interpretation he liked. There's such vast scope within the role. If one just got up and did the choreography, you'd find that the emotion evolves very much out of that. It's built-in. I don't think there's a way that one could do the Bedroom pas de deux and not put over some sort of feeling. You could do it with your head in a paper bag and people would still get the feel of it because of the way he's constructed the choreography.

I don't think I really started to develop in the role for some years. Well, not "for some years," but I dread to think of what my first performances were like. Having had a year's lay-off with an injury, it took me a long time to regain any form of confidence on the stage. I was feeling insecure and I hadn't really worked with Lynn a great deal, although I think both Lynn and I perform rather than actually dance. That was happening, but I wasn't particularly happy at the beginning performances because of not being on top form. I had something like four or five weeks, from the time we came back from our vacation until the opening night.

Another influence was working with Ahronovitch, a Russian conductor who came over and conducted a few performances about four or five years ago. He breathed fresh breath into the production because he really knew the score and the way Prokofiev wanted it. He helped enormously to make us understand what Prokofiev was meaning in the music, and he certainly influenced a lot of what I do on the stage now. He would see things, in the Madrigal for instance, and say, 'Well, that to me doesn't look right because the music's doing this. And Romeo wouldn't rush up to Juliet and suddenly kiss her hand, because it would put the fear of God into her.' He had a very good eye. Although he was a musician, he really looked at what was happening to the production. Of course, one's always governed by what the music is doing, but for two or three weeks before he did the first performance, he got into very detailed discussions about Prokofiev's notes. In fact, often they were slightly conflicting to what Kenneth's views were on it, so one had to pick and choose, weigh up. But that's what one does with everything.

I have a great love for music, but no musical training at all apart from what I learned at the Royal Ballet School. They gave us a very sure grounding in theory, but there wasn't really time to pursue an instrument as well as dance and do one's academic work.

Romeo's very difficult technically — it's very quick. I can understand Christopher doing those solos, and for him it was a natural process because he created the role. It brings out a lot of his speed and abilities as a dancer. He was the first person I saw do it, so he influenced my reading of it quite a lot, subconsciously probably more than consciously. But physically he's very different from me, so it was a bit of a struggle to put it onto my frame. There's hardly a moment in *Romeo* when you're not doing something, but since Kenneth choreographed it, he's choreographed two other ballets that are far more taxing. He really seems to put the boys through it. So now if you get to do Romeo, it's not a ride by any means, but after *Mayerling* and *Manon* it's not that bad. To a young dancer doing the role for the first time, the steps *are* difficult. But they become part of the whole thing, and the more one performs the ballet, the more natural they seem. One finds that the stumbling blocks are disappearing each time.

Most of the hard work is alleviated by the music, by the way the pas de deux are constructed, and the feel of the ballet. You usually find when you're on the stage that what leads you on to the next thing is the music. With *Mayerling*, a great deal of that third act . . . Sometimes I walk on and I don't quite know how I'm going to get through to the end, but Liszt somehow aids me, gets me through. And in *Romeo*, the lifts and all are not really isolated things. The pas de deux are very enjoyable parts of *Romeo*; I find those the highlights to dance.

Partnering's always come very naturally to me, probably through my early training in the touring company. When I joined, there was a shortage of sort of male principal dancers, so I found I was dancing with two or three girls a week. And consequently one had to evolve a very sure technique, and I think that by doing that at an early age, I began to enjoy the partnering very much.

And also, it's lovely to be working *with* somebody, as opposed to doing a solo where you're out there by yourself. It's lovely to be able to really communicate through movement, in a pas de deux. The *Mayerling* pas de deux are very exciting, because within their construction you know you can force the girl to do something that perhaps she wouldn't do — and vice versa. The same with *Romeo*, except that's slightly more romantic and lyrical, less force. In *Mayerling*, one can really go to town. I've always found anyway that if there's something I can react to onstage, or something I can encompass myself in, then I'm very much happier. The ballets that I really enjoy performing — like *Manon, Mayerling, Rake's Progress* — are usually the interpretive ballets where you have shrouded yourself in a cloak and put on a mask, and you're not being you. And I sort of get on another level of consciousness in a pas de deux, because it's two people becoming a unit and making something together.

With different partners, one basically rehearses the technique but then you try to make a unit. You discuss it and come around to some form of solution, but the main thing is to get across the story. And this story's about two young people in love, so that's what you're fighting for. Juliet's not going to be doing the Balcony pas de deux her way while Romeo's doing it his way — they're going to be doing the Balcony pas de deux their way.

I don't like stereotype performances. With some dancers, one can subtly change emphasis without even telling them, and they'll pick it up. It's just like being tuned-in. I found that very much with Lynn. Obviously there are risks of becoming staid in an interpretation, but I think in every partnership of caliber the people involved are consciously trying to get something more out of the performance every time they go out on the stage.

At the beginning, it's the unit of Benvolio, Mercutio, and Romeo which is very important, and I think it's valid to have three very different characters on the stage. Chums. Mercutio is the most aristocratic and wise of the three, an academic, a poet, like the tutor figure almost. Then you've got Benvolio, the studious bookworm, slightly withdrawn and gentle. And Romeo's really a rather confused character who, through his relationship with Juliet, suddenly finds that the confusion is disappearing. Whereas before he was sort of an adolescent youth, enjoying and loving life but not really having a specific direction, now, for once, he's got an aim in life. Romeo's a dreamer. He likes to listen to Mercutio's verse as opposed to creating it himself. I don't think he's a very boisterous character, but that's part of his charm. Look how attractive he is to women — I have such a fine relationship with the whores. That comes naturally to him; he doesn't have to work on it. I think he's just going along with his chums, an adolescent, very vibrant, but not totally together yet.

The feud is a matter of course, an inherent thing as opposed to being a cause for him. That's why I very much liked Mercutio's death in the Zeffirelli film. They weren't out to kill each other. The feud was there, for a generation before them, though of course they're continuing it and tantalizing each other with it. But then, suddenly, they start fighting, and Mercutio gets killed accidentally — as opposed to it being the O.K. Corral scene. You can't really take that element to the ballet unless you direct the whole thing differently.

Romeo is there at the ball because he wants to get another glimpse of Rosaline. They're just there for a lark, you know, 'There's a party down the road. Let's go and see for ourselves.' I don't think he's ever seen Juliet before, and he's intrigued by the way she's looking at him — as opposed to him looking at her. There's certainly what one would term a magical moment. It's like when you go into a party; you can look at people within a room and know the ones you have rapport with. And if you see a beautiful woman and feel you have rapport with her, then one tends to try to continue, on some line anyway. I try to make the reactions that I'm showing onstage natural reactions, and I try to relate them to normal circumstance.

I see her before the magical moment. I see her first, and the moment comes later. And the moment's really hers. I'm intrigued by the physical beauty of her, and when our eyes meet, I realize that perhaps she's intrigued by the physical as well. I think it's a very physical relationship, and I can't see, within the context of the ballet, that the relationship goes much beyond the physical. Because basically they don't have that much time, and you know how long it takes to build up a relationship other than physical — years and years. There's got to be one thing that starts it, the intriguing thing, and then from the physical, other things grow. I just don't think they have the opportunity to allow anything else to grow.

The solo? That's the peacock scene, that's the tantalizing, 'Shall I, shan't I? Dare I?' That's what Mercutio then continues when he plays with them and pushes them. That solo's pretty straightforward, the peacock syndrome.

Then they're all off eating, the rest of the cast, and Juliet comes on by herself — she's not very hungry. For him, then, that's a genuine attempt to say, 'I'm sorry for making a fool of myself in the ballroom. I didn't mean to. I didn't mean to make a scene. In fact, *this* is what I feel.' But he doesn't have to go as far as telling her. She comes on wondering about this character she's just met. And when he comes on and she attempts to go, he says, 'Please wait!' and then it starts from there. He does fall in love with her, yes, but infatuation is the main ploy, the main driving urge, right up until he sleeps with her. I mean, he had no idea that the physical side of it would even work, did he? They might have gone to bed with each other and found it was a total disaster, and then the story would be very much different.

Initially it's Juliet who instigates everything, and Romeo, in a way, is just taken along on the crest of the wave. But he does plan the Balcony scene. He doesn't actually say, 'I'll see you at the balcony at half past ten,' but I always try, before I leave the ballroom, just to confide in her that I'll see her again some time. Everybody around is doing a polonaise thing, and Romeo and Juliet just look at each other, and he slowly comes towards her. Mercutio tries to stop him,

Benvolio tries to stop him, but he's away with the beauty of this woman. Sometimes I touch her; sometimes I just keep looking at them but think to myself or try to convey something that will lead on into the Balcony. But I don't think Juliet's actually aware of it — she's not. She's mooning around on the balcony, and suddenly there's a shadow down there.

On that entrance, I don't think one's being conscious of the audience at all. I feel that moment very much. One's trying to live the moment for Juliet, so that slow walk to the center is very important. To me, it's a tentative moment, questioning whether to proceed or whether not. He's had this sleepless night after the party, he's got this woman on his mind . . . Sometimes I feel it's the moment where he's totally absorbed in her presence. Probably the audience doesn't get it, but there's a great deal of tension in my body when that moment happens. I don't think one could do it and not convey something to the person that's looking at you from the balcony. You don't just place yourself in the correct position without the feeling that goes with it. And then, the pas de deux is the apex — no, not the apex — it's the start of the emotional feelings they have towards one another. There has to be a newness about it, a freshness, and an excitement when one does it. Otherwise, I think it tends to fall flat. It has to be full of elation and exploration, which will then lead on to the next act.

Once the first act is over, one is slightly relieved. You've only got the first scene of Act II where you're dancing a lot; that's very taxing technically. Once you've got that over with you're not taxed, so it's quite nice to get that put behind you.

Also, there, it's hard to convey to the audience that there's been a change in the boy. Therefore, it's very important at the beginning of the first act to assert a different feeling within those surroundings. In the first market scene, that opens the ballet, I always try to be more boisterous and fun-loving. The entrance in the second act, which is in the same environment and everybody else is basically projecting the same as Act I, you have to really be very much into yourself, more thoughtful and pensive, wondering. That's quite hard actually, to make that work. You've got to be pensive, but you've got also to have an elation about your pensiveness — it's quite a hard balance to get. His circumstances have changed. He's realized something within himself that he hadn't ever felt before. I mean, if one asserts that he's whored around or he's not a virgin, you have to then assert in that scene that that's all now behind him. He's living and thinking something else, something new, something purer. Yes, I think he's not a virgin. A romantic virgin maybe, but not a horny virgin.

The happiness and excitement of what has happened make him

act the way he does with the Nurse, plus the help of his friends. It's so vital to be helped by your Mercutio and Benvolio. It really has to be a threesome, because probably his relationship with them is one of the stablest relationships he's experienced for security and friendship. There *is* a moment in the first act, during all the turmoil of the fight scene, when Romeo's mother comes on. I try very much in that terribly short space of time to somehow portray that he's very close to his mother and father, more to his mother. There's not much time to register it, but he has concern for his mother, with all that fighting going on. And his mother's constantly telling him to stop fighting, to cool it. And when the two families are on either side of the stage, I constantly try not to be too much part of Mercutio and Benvolio, but more mother, father, and Romeo, just for that brief moment. It's the only chance you've got to show that.

In this scene, the start of Act II, his quietness is something that should be a little bit new to them: 'What on earth's the matter with him? If he's in love, he usually tells us. He's not telling a thing!' He detaches himself slightly. He's probably said that he's in love so many times that they'd laugh him off the stage anyway.

I'll tell you what the letter says *some* nights. No, no, I won't — rude prop man. To me it says 'I'm madly in love with you and let's get married. This is where we're going to go.' It's the same letter that he shows to Friar Laurence, so Juliet has put it in writing. And probably that takes him aback, knocks him down even more. And confuses him probably; he hasn't had time to go into any details about what church and how many guests they're going to have. But no, he doesn't hesitate, because it's what he wants as well. I don't know whether one does hesitate in situations like that. You do nowadays, but obviously he's convinced by the time that happens.

As I did with Kenneth when I was doing *Mayerling*, Christopher and Lynn obviously discussed and motivated everything in *Romeo*. Then, when it gets handed down to other casts, one's having to find one's own motivations. In scenes like that, one hasn't discussed why, what's motivating him. You know it's set that way and you have to do it, and within that you find your own motivation. You fit yourself to it. And one does tend to change things a lot, change emphasis and ideas. Perhaps I might go and see Wayne [Eagling] do it next week and suddenly think, 'Oh, that's good.'

About the marriage. I think it was part of Romeo's upbringing to be devout. Historically, in that period they were all pretty devout. And rather than being a leader, he was easily led; if he was told to do something, he would probably do it. So his devotion was more something that was put upon him — it's a devotion of tradition — but there's no thought about getting a divorce next week or a five-week annulment or whatever. In fact, he hasn't thought about the consequences. He's the weaker of the two. It's Juliet who makes all the decisions and instigates every situation. They're probably, secretly, planning to abscond with each other.

The plans go slightly askew because the Prince of Verona has placed upon the village that anybody seen fighting or killing gets banished. So when Romeo kills Tybalt, he suddenly realizes that he's going to be banished — he can't stick around. Whereas last week they'd patch up their wounded and bury their dead and life would go on, that no longer can happen. Everybody goads him on to fight Tybalt in the beginning of that scene. It's not because of the banishment that he doesn't want to fight him. It's because it's his cousin-in-law . . . if that's possible. He's now part of the family, and Romeo's got a great deal of faith in human nature.

The way that fight and the killings evolved was what I found so great about the Zeffirelli production, the accidental death of Mercutio, as opposed to an out and out, cold-blooded in the back thrust. Tybalt didn't intend actually to kill him — it was an accident. And from there, Romeo was forced through conscience and his love for Mercutio. There's a marvelous moment in the ballet, before the fight starts, when there are five chords and Romeo is just standing, seething with anger, confused. Then the anger totally overcomes him, and he starts fighting. The relationship between Romeo and Mercutio is very, very strong. Mercutio to Romeo is his tutor, his father, his mentor — in a way, he's responsible for the way Romeo is as a person. To me, Mercutio is the most aristocratic and learned of them. He's the most experienced as far as women are concerned and in enjoying himself. There's a deep, sincere love between the two of them, and as soon as Mercutio dies, I think Romeo starts realizing what he's lost through Mercutio's death, which is what makes him kill Tybalt.

I do Mercutio, and I find it very valuable for my Romeo. When Anthony does Mercutio with me, and then I do Mercutio with Anthony, it helps both of us very much because we both know what is needed. And there are moments, certainly within the town scene, where you need people around, you need to have a motivation or you need help. It's the same with *Manon*: we both do the two roles in that. I just love to be onstage as part of somebody else's performance, as opposed to it all being sections, Mercutio's performance and Romeo's performance. I don't think that should exist. I think I'd feel the same if I were doing a peasant or a villager in *Romeo*. They're part of a whole. One talks about an individual interpretation; in a way, one should really be talking about the interpretation of the company, because that's vital to our individual interpretations.

In the bedroom, I don't think it's a pas de deux of loving. It's a pas de deux of trying to separate and not being able to. There's more anguish in it — one knows that rather than a unity at the end, there's going to be separation. That's what inspires the whole pas de deux. He goes to the window to leave and her strength stops him, but there's no conclusion. Nothing can be fulfilled by him staying except for a few more kisses. He has to go. That's what makes it so poignant. That's why there has to be urgency in everything that's done, as opposed to tranquillity and unison. She knows that Tybalt's died, but they're oblivious to the facts. It's the parting of the ways that is the motivation. And whereas Romeo has had sex before, it's something totally new to her. She's frightened probably, but she also wants . . . If she had been continuing on the same line, she'd have said, 'Right. Get up. Out!' But this added emotion thing of sexual unity has turned her mind, and that's why she's lusting for him not to go.

Once I leave, I usually try to watch. I think it's the greatest scene in the whole ballet, her going to Friar Laurence and trying to make the decision to take the potion. I just watch it; it keeps me going, and musically it's so wonderful. So then when I come on for the Tomb scene, I'm even more distraught.

The killing of Paris isn't a malicious attack. I feel it's almost self-defense. His one thought is to get to her and be with her, and there's Paris in the way with a dagger drawn. The quickest way is to stick his knife into him. It's an instinct: 'He won't stop, so I have to kill him.'

It's not difficult technically, that pas de deux with her body, but it's very difficult to keep a frenzy and an anxiety in it. He just wants to hold her and fondle her and be close to her. And because she's dead, he wants to kill himself with her, though at the end I do try to show apprehension. It's a big step, killing oneself. That's why I usually hold her hand when I take the potion. Only as a sort of contact, regardless of her being dead.

How would you react with a dead body? You can't just accept the audience's reaction, as you could then get away with doing very little. You must try it this way, that way. Through the process of elimination, I learned the technique of actually acting. I've never had an acting lesson in my life. The only way I can ever do it is to feel it. *Mayerling* was particularly difficult; every book I picked up gave me conflicting theories. In the end, the only thing that gave me a lead was that nobody was really in conflict about Rudolf's infancy and childhood, up to about fifteen years old. He wasn't really a bastard figure; he was totally lost since the age of eight when his tutor came into his room and fired a gun in an endeavor to make him into a man. So I based the rest on how I would feel starting with those horrendous facts, and I always felt enormous sympathy for him.

Early on in my professional life, I had a director who would allow me to make mistakes. John Field emphasized that as much as he wanted my technical ability to hold the performance up, on top of that one needed to have a craft of theatre. He introduced me to companies like the Royal Shakespeare; we used to go often to Stratford-on-Avon. And while I couldn't criticize any actor on his technical performance, I could criticize any artist on his ability to keep my attention and interest. I mean, I watched last night a master class that Jacqueline du Pré was giving, and it was stunning. Again, I don't know anything about the technicalities of playing a cello. I couldn't fault any of the girls that were playing, and it was pleasant listening. But as soon as she got hold of them and started impressing upon them what she was feeling about the music, feeding them ideas, then their playing became an alive thing as opposed to being just a physical thing. That's the only way that dancers can actually be creative, in their interpretation. That's what makes it theirs and not just a ballet.

Ballet is very much an art that has an aura about it of being totally detached from any form of life. And lots of people are quite content to go along and watch it and be fed. They get everything they want out of it by just liking the beauty of the actual movement and the unison with the music. I could never watch ballet like that and enjoy it 100 percent. One's job is to involve the audience in a set of circumstances, not just present them with those but involve them in terms of what they can understand — laughter, tears, sorrow. It makes them part of it.

I've always found one of the most valuable things about being on tour in the provinces, playing to basically uneducated-in-ballet audiences, is that you as an artist have to compensate. You have to work on being explicit about what you want them to be feeling. I don't want an audience ever to sit back and just look; I want their interest to be kept, their emotions to be stretched. There's nothing more wonderful than knowing you made somebody cry at *Giselle* or feel empty at the end of *Mayerling*. When I go and watch theatre or listen to a concert, I don't want to see a group of people going through the motions — I want to go through it with them, and therefore their interpretations have to reach out and grab me.

Certainly there's a difference between performing a ballet like

Mayerling and, say, *Symphonic Variations*. *Symphonic* can be danced impeccably and nobody's going to complain. But Sir Frederick always wants there to be a spirit to the performance apart from just the technique. It's such a balanced, perfect work that even at the worst, it's going to be a beautiful ballet. And given the right sort of lift and feel, it just transcends.

The same with lots of Glen Tetley's ballets, and the last thing you would probably think about with Tetley is interpretation. Glen, and Jerome Robbins as well, are very definite about the feel they want to movement. While you're working on the ballet, that is being built in as well. Jerry will work for hours to get the interpretation out of the steps through their musicality and emphasis, without you having to be conscious of interpreting them. One's not conscious of having to imprint one's own personality. That will probably happen anyway.

What I really feel is that lust for actually creating something. And I don't classify going on the stage and doing the steps as really creating anything. Rather than seeing any dancer and saying, 'Right. That's Anthony doing Albrecht,' I like to be able to watch Anthony and not see Anthony but see Albrecht.

Even with something like *Swan Lake*, which is a pretty fantastic fairy tale, I'm not content to see cardboard cut-outs. It's not enough to see a figure on the stage wearing the Prince's costume, doing all the steps, emoting. One has to bring a certain amount of realism to the character, which perhaps the audience can understand. It's not like watching the Queen Mother drive along a road waving her hand, because much of the time in *Swan Lake* the audience is seeing that prince figure at moments where he's by himself and where he's being himself. What you can do within the classics is bring out the emotions in a realistic way. You're not confined in the way you interpret it, as long as it's within the right style and period and the right sense.

Mime is all part of the same whole. Again, one is restricted by the convention; but you can't just do it, you've got to actually live it. Although one's using a pretty archaic technique to express it, it still has to be expressed with sincerity. Nowadays it's not used very much, but certainly with things like the first scene of *Giselle* . . . That's all mime, but if you see a sincere performer do it, you're not really conscious of how stupid it all is. In a way, ballet is like that throughout. When you think about any of the classics, they're all pretty stupid. There are wonderful moments of beauty and what not, and wonderful pyrotechnics, but you start pulling it down to the skeleton and you think, 'Christ, how could anybody actually think they could con an audience like that?' The only way it succeeds is if the sincerity's there within the performance and within the producer and director. That's what constantly makes these classics change and grow and work, and that's what makes the audience like them.

When you create a role, you're instigating the choices and motivating the plot. That's what's so marvelous about creating something with a scenario and characters that one can read about and learn about. You can have a definite idea about the way the said character would react, and when you go into the rehearsal room, that idea is in the back of your mind. If the choreographer asks you to do something, you do it in the style that you've already worked out. And if there are barriers, then you break it all down and remotivate it. If it's not going to work for the person it's being created for, then it's not going to work.

As dancers, our responsibility towards the choreographer is that one should arrive totally naked. They're like an artist mixing the paints, and you're just the paint. In whichever direction they want you to go, you go. If there is confusion or disagreement, it gets ironed out, remixed. But basically our job is to allow the choreographer the freedom to do with us what he wants, and not what we would like to think we want to do. The problems all choreographers have are the same; they just overcome them differently. It's totally different working with Fred Ashton and Glen Tetley. We always try to accommodate our techniques to whatever we're working on, but then the choreographers have to aid you to get out of yourself what they're wanting to see. One can't do it all by oneself. And it would be very boring if one could, because you wouldn't then be fulfilling anybody else's ideals.

I find it very interesting to coach anybody in the roles I know, and very rewarding. I've done it with some students, not on an official basis and not on entire roles but on solos, which I find slightly less interesting because one's only working on one dimension, the pyrotechnics. But you can still feed into them emphasis and phrasing and musicality, and just bring them out. With *Mayerling*, I helped teach Wayne and Stephen [Jefferies] what Kenneth had given to me, but in no way did I try to influence their actual performance. I've watched them and come back to say what I felt were weak parts or unfocused parts, because I know what Kenneth wanted the focus on.

The majority of dancers are terribly responsive to anybody's assistance. I've always been especially responsive to my actor friends who come and watch performances. They see me dance as I see them act, and they can pick out moments. I've always tried to make myself very conscious of their criticism. And of course criticism from one's colleagues is very valuable. Rudolf, Margot . . . All those people that come to watch are terribly generous with their knowledge and craftsmanship, and usually their criticism is very sincere. I find that all the great dancers, regardless of what company, what country, are always willing to help. When Marcia [Haydée] came to do *Taming of the Shrew* with us, there was no feeling of selfishness about 'the way I perform.' And if somebody is interested in knowing *my* feelings, my anxieties, or how I cope with certain situations, they've only got to ask and I'll be only too willing to let them know, as opposed to feeling it's an infringement on my privacy or that they're trying to outdo me.

I try not to read the critics. Well, dancers are very highly tuned machines. They know what's going on with their performances and their techniques. They don't necessarily have to be told by the critics. The critics have a very needful job, but if your double saut de basque is all askew one night, a critic writing it in a newspaper the next morning is not going to make the double saut de basque work. Of course, there are also numerous accidents onstage. One time, which is hysterical to look back on, we were in Cambridge. We had a lot of injuries in the company, and my work schedule was quite heavy. We did a matinée and evening performance of three ballets; one was *Les Sylphides*, the middle ballet was *Rake's Progress*, and the last ballet was the third act of *Sleeping Beauty* — and I did all three, in the matinée and the evening. Now, there's a lot of tension involved in *Rake's Progress*, especially with the arms. The last scene is in the Madhouse, and it's choreographed with a clenched fist like this, a lot of tension, and sort of maniac-type movement. Well, I got to the evening, did *Sylphides*, did *Rake's Progress*, and came on to do Aurora's Wedding pas de deux with Doreen [Wells]. We walked on from either side of the stage and as I gave her my hand, I got cramp in it. My whole arm and hand buckled up toward me, and there was nothing I could do about it. I was very worried because I had this folded-up hand — she just looked at me — and I turned my back to the audience and managed to straighten it out with the other hand. That was very funny.

Or a critic might put into print a moment of spontaneity that worked, and you read that. He says, 'The moment when Romeo saw Juliet, there were sparks flying, and the angle of the head was superb,' and all this business. You get to do Romeo the next week and you say, 'Oh, this is that moment that critic was talking about,' and you've lost it. The spontaneity was there, and he made you conscious of something you didn't want to know about — you wanted to do it. You know deep down if you've done something to your utmost and it's worked — the moments in performance are few and far between, I can assure you — so in the end you are your severest and harshest critic.

One usually finds one's performing in a rehearsal as well. You're performing for the choreographer if you're creating something, or if Fred takes a rehearsal of *Symphonic*, you're performing to him. Then, when you have an individual rehearsal, say for *Sleeping Beauty*, you're doing your solos to give yourself security to get on the stage and to know that you're going to be able to do them. In that way, you're working for yourself.

But I really dance for the audience, without a doubt. The people that are concerned with mounting a production are going to be in the audience anyway. I'm doing it for them, and I'm doing it for my granny. And I don't really think about it very much. I just get up and do it the way I do it. And if somebody doesn't like it, they're going to tell me. And if somebody does like it, they're going to tell me. And if nobody says anything, I'm still going to know.

October 1979
London

Merrill Ashley

Merrill Ashley (b. St. Paul, Minnesota, 1950) began to study ballet at the age of seven in weekly classes in Vermont. In 1963, after her second summer at the School of American Ballet, she moved to New York to continue her training at the School and also enrolled in the Professional Children's School. She joined the New York City Ballet in 1967, danced her first performance of the Sanguinic variation in The Four Temperaments *in 1975 while still a soloist, and was promoted to principal in 1977. Her repertory ranges from the purely classical* Divertimento No. 15 *and* Symphony in C *to the jazzy* Who Cares? *and from the meditative lyricism of* Dances at a Gathering *and* In the Night *to the spectacular virtuosity of* Square Dance *and* Tchaikovsky Piano Concerto No. 2. *She has created leading roles in Balanchine's* Ballo della Regina *(1978) and his* Ballade *(1980).*

George Balanchine once said, "You must know what you are doing because the dancers can tell if you know or you don't know. If you know, they will do whatever you say . . . If you say, 'Lift both your legs and stay in the air,' they will do it." Merrill Ashley is the proof — Merrill does it, whatever it is, whatever he wants. She is the ideal paradigm for today's New York City Ballet: young, fast, strong, cool. Secure in her prodigious technique, she defies gravity and reason nonchalantly, but her face betrays a delight in her own abilities that is contagious. Intoxicated by it, you begin to believe that dancing is simple, that anyone could do it, that you could do it yourself.

*F*rom very early, from I would say four or five, I was already very single-minded about dancing. I don't know if I was saying it to anybody, but I think I felt that way. I wanted to start, but I was in Minnesota at the time, and the school there said, 'No, you're too young. You can't take class here until you're eight.' My older sister was taking there — she was eight and I was five — and I'm sure my mother went to pick her up and I tagged along. It just looked like fun, what she was doing. I remember seeing them jumping over piles of coats in the middle of the room, you know, "Try and jump over the pile." 'Well,' I thought, *I'll* jump over the pile.'

Then my family moved to Vermont where there was no ballet school really, but there was some lady who came from out of town once a week to give class, and she turned out to be pretty good. Actually, I barely remember it. And there was a company in Minnesota that I must have gone to see, but I don't remember those performances either. But when we moved to Vermont, we would come to New York sometimes, whenever the Royal would come or Ballet Theatre. I have some old New York City Ballet programs too. There wasn't that much ballet in New York then, so I think my parents took whatever was available. We'd come for the weekend, we'd go to the ballet once or twice, and then we'd go home.

Once I started class, I think I decided I wanted to be a ballerina, but in what form I don't know. There was something about the whole thing that appealed to me. I don't know if I wanted to be in tutus or long dresses . . . I really don't remember *what* it was, but I was always very active and athletic and physically oriented, so it must have been the movement that attracted me, and that it was all so glamorous, and pretty costumes. I remember always being intrigued by the costumes. It just seemed sort of magical.

I'm trying to think who did what for me at the School. I went there first for three months, when I was twelve, and [Hélène] Dudin and [Antonina] Tumkovsky were the only two teachers I had. I couldn't understand either one of them, to be quite frank. I kept thinking, 'What are they saying?' And I had never really learned the names of positions — *croisé, effacé* — I didn't know any of that. First arabesque? What's that? I could do this or that, but I didn't know what it was. So apart from their English, what they were asking me to do didn't mean anything anyway. That confused me a little bit, and I was a little scared of their toughness. But on the other hand, I wanted to learn, and I was really trying to grasp what they were saying.

When I went to the School next, it was for summer course, and I had [Muriel] Stuart a lot. She was the first person who talked about placement, and that intrigued me: 'Oh, you mean you can think about this muscle and that muscle?' I had never had that before; I just did the steps and whatever happened, happened. So that intrigued me, and then Stanley [Williams] carried that further. For example, I couldn't turn at all. Could not do a double pirouette to save my life. Stanley worked hard on my turns, and it took him a long time, a *long* time, to help me with that. But I was really intrigued with his teaching.

I did so little performing in the School that I really didn't learn anything about it from the teachers. I did two Workshops, but being onstage was so foreign, the exposure was so brief, and I felt so much pressure just to do the steps right and 'don't fall down and don't get in anybody's way and stay in line' that somehow the real performing part of it escaped me. And I had all sorts of misconceptions. I remember Danilova saying something about, 'You have to play to everybody, to the Fourth Ring as well as to the Orchestra.' So I did the whole first Workshop looking up at the Fourth Ring — I never looked down once. You take these things in such a peculiar way. I took everything too literally, like 'You have to smile all the time.' So it's hard to learn to perform. You learn by doing it, but it takes a long time, and it's hard to see yourself the way you really appear to everybody else. I had to listen to other people and watch other people who everybody else seemed to feel performed well, thinking, 'Now, what do they do that makes them an interesting performer?' I kept watching everybody — no one in particular — and everybody's so different. Some things I saw them do I wasn't comfortable with, or I felt I was just imitating and I didn't want to do that either.

I always liked *Four Temperaments*, although we didn't do it very much. We did it right when I joined the company, and then it didn't go for a while. I remember watching Balanchine rehearse Marnee [Morris] in it when she was still doing Sanguinic, and that was at the old school on 82nd Street, so it had to be a long time ago. I was an understudy in the Melancholic section, as one of the four girls, and I did that once or twice. Once, one girl just didn't show up for performance so I volunteered, but I didn't know *what* I was doing. And then the ballet dropped out for a while, so I wasn't that familiar with it.

There certainly are roles that you look at and think, 'That would really appeal to me. I'd like to do that,' but I didn't know Sanguinic well enough to think that about it. And the little bit I remembered of it, I remembered as being very hard and having hard turns, which I didn't want to have to face. So I didn't expect to do it when it was revived. Marnee was still in the company; although she was not dancing all that much, I thought she'd probably do it. Actually, Marnee was out of favor and Suzanne [Farrell] had been back in the company not very long, so I thought she'd do it. And then I thought, 'Well, Marnee.' They told me to learn it, but as it was being revived, I felt they were just trying to cover everything, teach several people in all the roles. I felt like I was third on the list — which I was — and like 'I'm never going to do it unless they're all out.' Anyway, Marnee was the one called to teach it to me. I guess Suzanne knew it, but she had other things to do and Marnee didn't have much to do. And then, suddenly, the casting went up, and there it was. I had less than a week to get it into shape, and I just panicked. Help! I was really terrified of it.

I loved it, but there were certain steps I couldn't do. Well, there was one in the middle of the variation where Pat Wilde used to do gargouillade and land and emboîté and gargouillade. I just couldn't do it somehow, especially landing on my weak foot, my bad foot — I just couldn't land on the one foot. So Balanchine changed it to one rond de jambe and then like a split and land on two feet, and that's what I do now. I think that was the only thing that was changed. That was for my protection, yes, but also I just couldn't do the step. He's not that locked into steps. It's wonderful. The step itself doesn't mean anything to him. It's the general effect the step will make that matters, and he can always produce another one. He has a certain idea about how he wants it to look, but if you end up not being able to do it, he'll usually change it. Like with the gargouillade — he knew he just wanted something 'flash.' He changes things all the time. Sometimes they're things he hasn't liked for a long time, and maybe it happens to be the thing you're having trouble with. He'll say, 'Well, I always wanted to change that,' and because you're having trouble with it, it's a perfect excuse.

I'm trying to think when I rehearsed it with him. There must have been a complete rehearsal in the main rehearsal room during that week before I did it. He didn't have much to say; he seemed fairly pleased with it. There were one or two spots he picked on. One of them, everyone kept saying, "Nobody can do it. Nobody does it." And indeed, it is hard. How can I describe it? He wants you to step backwards on pointe, and then, without traveling at all, just put the heel down flat and fall out of it, fall back but not fall too much. It's very hard, especially the stepping on pointe backwards. You get so far over on your pointe that to control it coming down is very hard. Inevitably you travel, and he doesn't want you to. I think I come closer now. I finally decided, 'Well, I just won't put my foot so far over. I'll put it straight down and drop the heel,' and that seems to work fairly well.

The other thing I never could do the way he wanted was one entrance, and I don't think I can yet. I modify it a little bit to try and get more of the effect he'd asked for, but I still don't think it's right. You leave at one point completely, and the boy does his variation. Then Balanchine wants it flying, the entrance. He wants you in the air with one leg in front of you and your arms open, leaning back as if you were on pointe but falling off pointe. He wants you falling backwards and flying forwards through the air. But when I land from jumping like that, I feel like I'm going to rip every ligament in the landing leg — your weight's so far behind you. Well, I can't do it. I used to get to that open position only after I'd landed, and then I'd fall out of it. Now I try to get in that position — but more perpendicular — sooner, while I'm still in the air, and then somehow land.

Thinking back, there are some performances where I really feel joyful, especially towards the end. I think, 'God, this is such fun to do, and I'm so happy doing it,' and that's really what Sanguinic's about. I find myself smiling a lot, in spite of myself, but then I realize it's fine to smile in Sanguinic, so I don't stop. But there are other performances, maybe because of tempo or something, where I don't feel quite so . . . 'happy' I guess is the word. Or I feel a little more — 'odd' isn't really the right word either — a little more eccentric. I don't smile as much, and I somehow emphasize the angular parts of it more. If I were in one of the other movements, I might think about the title more, but I just think of Sanguinic as being bright and normal, not too anything. The others seem more extreme to me. It's almost as if Sanguinic is the . . . I hesitate to say 'normal' section, but it's much more straightforward than the others. And yet it has its eccentricities too.

The first thing to do with a role like this is to contrast the music and the steps, see how they fit together and whether you need to match the music or contrast it. Sometimes you have to add something to it; the step seems to be emphasizing something that's faint in the score, so you give it a little extra nudge. And then there are the few little things that Balanchine says, the steps he wants emphasized. The steps that seem most important to him frequently give me a clue as to what the role's about. As far as *Four Ts* went, at the time I first did it I hadn't seen him rehearse other people very much. But from watching him rehearse in general, I knew there were certain steps in other ballets that he would always correct. He would always want that step done a certain way, and then he'd let the individual do the other steps the way they felt inspired to do them. So when he focuses on a step, I start not only trying to do what he wants, but paying special attention. It's a little clue as to what the role is about. And it changes with time anyway, without my even knowing it or working at it. You just become a slightly different person as the years go by. Some steps get harder; sometimes, because of injuries, you can't do a certain step as full-out or as well as you'd like to. So you have to find something else to make up for that, and you begin to find new things that way. Or by dancing with different partners.

I've done Sanguinic with quite a few people: Tony Blum was the first, then Danny Duell, Sean Lavery, and Joe Duell. It can make a lot of difference. Some of them are stiffer, some are more flexible, and you have to mold yourself to that so it works as one piece. Certain steps we do side by side, and if one of us is very extreme and the other is not extreme at all, it doesn't quite work. It's funny: after I've said it's fairly straightforward, the corrections that I end up giving — suggestions, I should say — are usually to make things a little more extreme, that it's too straightforward or too classical or not angular. And the timing has to be right, and the accent of certain steps has to be musical. Sometimes with a partner it hasn't been, and that's one place I'm not willing to compromise. There are many places where there's a step on every count, almost as if you're stamping out the rhythm with your feet, and if you're not exactly even, the effect is lost. The music is even, and the steps seem to have been created to emphasize that particular rhythm. And if you don't emphasize it, you've lost the role.

I studied the piano for six or seven years, and though I haven't touched it for years, I think that somehow, somewhere, it helped a great deal. It makes you listen a little bit more closely. In Sanguinic, the music is everything. It sets the tone and it's a tremendous guide — which is always true in Balanchine's ballets, but I think in the modern ones even more than the classical ones. In classical ballet there does seem to be more of a defined relationship between the partners — it's more a man and a woman. In, oh, *Symphony in C,* he's there to make her look good, to present her. It can be something romantic like the second movement, or something more formal like the first movement, where there's no romance but there's a definite sense of 'lead you forward, take you back, guide you here, guide you there.' Those relationships can still exist in the modern ballets, but they're not as recognizable somehow. It's just something different.

I'm making generalizations that might not necessarily hold true. I mean, in *Agon* pas de deux there's a definite relationship. In Sanguinic, it's more the two of us doing steps side by side, whereas in *Agon* there's more actual partnering; he's really manipulating her. In Sanguinic, the biggest amount of partnering is the lifts — that's *all* there is — and I don't even see the man. I feel like I'm just riding around on top of the world, just floating. You're hardly even aware that there's somebody behind you, grabbing you and taking you there.

Sometimes when I watch it, and I suddenly see this pair of legs running, I think, 'Oh! Yeah. There's somebody there,' because when the lifts are done right, you just feel like a deer in slow motion. It's extraordinary when they're really done right. Fantastic. I don't know how it is for the man. They're really difficult to do well, and just exhausting for him because of the position. If he could straighten his arms it would be easier, but the hardest place to hold is right in front of you, with the bent arm. They just die.

A lot of partnering is experience; you just have to be partnered a lot. I did a lot of concerts with Jacques [d'Amboise], and he gave me a lot of clues: 'You can't take a partner's hand with a locked elbow,' for example. I'd be thinking, 'Support!' and tensing everything, and then there's no give-and-take. A partner can tell you, 'Just let me do the whole thing,' but you have to learn to relax and yet hold yourself in one piece. If your torso is weak and wobbly, it makes it very difficult for him. My tendency was to try and help my partner do everything — it still is, a little bit — and that actually makes it harder for him. If he's a good partner, he can fix it whether you're helping him or not. He has to work a little harder, but you can still feel comfortable. But if you're with a young partner, it might not be so true. You also have to learn to take off for lifts a bit differently with different partners, to give a little more time and show your preparations. Glissade has to be really clear, not just a little short movement, as a guide to them.

If you'd asked me a few years ago, I definitely would have said I'm more comfortable dancing alone. I probably still tend to be that way, but I'm in the middle of changing my mind. I don't really know why. Maybe I'm just relaxing more. Balanchine frequently says to me, "Don't look at your partner. Don't relate to your partner. Just let him do everything." Sometimes that seems completely right to me, because sometimes people get too involved in creating something other than what Balanchine intended. They create their own story and superimpose it, and suddenly the movement gets hidden and all you see is emotion. And yet other times, I miss relating to my partner. Some pieces of music are so romantic that you just stare in your partner's eyes — certain odd moments in *Diamonds*, for example.

Sure there's a difference between dancing those romantic ballets and the modern ones. I still haven't conquered *Emeralds*, so it's hard for me to talk about that one. I haven't yet done with it what I can or what I should. I feel I just have to forget the steps, try not even to care what my feet do. There aren't that many steps to begin with in *Emeralds*, so I try to concentrate on my upper body and on calming myself down. In a funny way, I almost hypnotize myself — I have too much energy, I want to *do* everything, and I can't just let it happen. I have to make that effort in lots of ballets. It's hard for me; it doesn't come naturally.

Swan Lake is another ballet that Balanchine keeps saying, "Don't act. Don't emote. Don't relate to your partner," and that's the one where I have the most trouble. The music sweeps over me, my impulse is to react — to emote, to do lots of everything — and he keeps saying, "No, it's too much. Do less." He doesn't want any acting at all, especially in the pas de deux. He just wants dance. He seems to concede, 'Of course, in the beginning you have to do a little something' — he'll allow that. But at the end of the ballet, when all the girls are racing around and I'm basically about to leave, he says, "Don't do anything. Just stand there." I went out front and watched Ghislaine [Thesmar] do it, and in many ways it's very dramatic and that stillness is so arresting. But the hardest thing for me to do is stand still. Maybe he sees this tendency in me to want to go overboard a bit too much, and he's trying to prevent it from happening. Maybe he feels it's dramatic enough as it is. Maybe he still feels it's too much, the way I do it. I think he has a different view of *Swan Lake* from almost anybody, and I'm not sure I understand yet what he wants. I'll find out one day. You know, *Swan Lake* was not one of those ballets I had dreamed of doing. In fact, when I was told to learn it, I wasn't excited about it; I dreaded it in a funny way. I was probably just terrified of it.

Actually . . . well, then there's *Who Cares?* Up until about the last two years, I would get hysterical, burst into tears, *sob*, just go out of my mind over *Who Cares?* I'd see it on the schedule and think, 'No. Please. I don't want to face it. I can't.' Because I really do have a complex about turning. In the middle of rehearsal, sometimes with Balanchine there, I would lose it completely — I was so embarrassed — and get myself into such a state that I couldn't think of it as anything fun. Now I just toss it off. I don't worry about it, and it works. I was making such a big thing out of it in rehearsal that I finally decided, 'Just forget about it. Rehearse it once — that's it — and go on.' That's the way I've done it ever since, and it feels better than ever. It's the only ballet I've done that not rehearsing seems to help. I think I could actually work on it now, check little things — not so much the steps, but head and arms — without making myself hysterical, because I've been able to do it well for long enough that I don't think I would lose confidence.

I still make problems for myself in other ballets, mainly the ones I haven't done a whole lot. Sometimes I have to struggle so much with the steps that there's not room to add anything else. It's not that I'm not suited to those ballets, but that they're just not perfectly me;

I haven't found my own version yet. I can get worked up in those rehearsals. It's funny — in general, I keep everything inside, but, boy, it builds up sometimes, and then Look out! Here comes Merrill! Clear the decks! I don't like it. I'd rather let the anger and frustration out a little bit at a time. It's not too attractive when it comes out all at once — the rehearsal pianists could tell you. Dancers don't know each other as well as the pianists know us.

Balanchine is really the one I turn to when I don't know what to do, and the one I really believe in. He has the most uncanny sense of what's right. When he says something, sometimes I think, 'What??' But then I think, 'How would what he suggested work?' or I watch somebody else in the role, and suddenly I see, 'He did it again. He's right.' By now I've gone through that so many times that I almost never stop to question. He can give you reasons for why you do it, which helps, and basically I'm doing *his* ballets. Other people can say, "You look awkward here" or "You didn't point your foot there," but as far as making the role what it is, Balanchine is the only one I rely on. When I joined the company, I was terrified of him, as well as being in awe of him. I'm still in awe of him, but I'm not terrified any more. That helps. I'm basically a shy person, and he, in many ways, is a shy person too, so sometimes it's hard to get the two of us going. But once we get started, it's fine.

When I was dancing with Jacques in those concerts, the thing he helped me with the most was understanding what Balanchine wanted. Sometimes he carried things a little bit further on his own — and some of the things he suggested I sort of rebelled against — but he believed a great deal in what Balanchine taught. Balanchine's not a man of many words, especially when you're young and afraid to talk to him, and very often he doesn't explain in really clear language. I mean, the language itself is clear, but he tells stories or uses some analogy, and it's not that simple. He makes you think for yourself. I needed somebody to pick it apart for me, to get me going in the right direction. I'd say, "Does he really mean 'Don't put your heels down'?" and Jacques might say, "Well, dear, *almost* put your heels down. It's to get this kind of plié and this look." Then it made sense and I could go ahead and work on it.

Those concerts gave me a lot of performing experience in difficult roles, too. I had very few solos in the company at the time; I was only in the corps. But on the concerts I was doing things like *Sylvia: Pas de Deux* and *Apollo*, both Terpsichore and Polyhymnia. I did *Diamonds*. I did *Who Cares?* — every single role in *Who Cares?* I did a lot, which was really valuable. And Jacques had things to say about performing — I'm not sure I agree with all of them now, but at least it was something to think about. You had somewhere to start. It's such a broad seed, performing. Where do you start? What do you eliminate? What are you aiming for?

I think going out front, not only watching other people but watching them from the front, is a tremendous learning tool. You're suddenly struck by so many things that you never see from backstage or in the classroom. There are always problem spots in any role. Somehow you don't know quite what to do; you feel you're not doing the right thing with it, you don't know why, and you don't know what direction to go in. Seeing other people, you can decide that you either want to go in their direction or in the opposite direction. Or their performance will just give you a completely new idea. And from the front, you see the choreography more as a whole. You're less involved in the actual steps and more aware of the total effect. That's one of the hardest things about doing brand-new works — you can't see them as a whole. Once he's finished, you know what you have to do, and you've seen the other people dancing so you sort of know what they do, but you don't know what happens when you're all dancing together. You don't know what the costumes really look like, or the scenery, or what the lighting is going to do. And it's very hard to figure out what aspects to emphasize, because you just haven't seen it. And you can't see it.

You contribute an awful lot when you create something. I'm basically speaking about Balanchine; I haven't really worked with Jerry [Robbins] when he's choreographing. Balanchine watches your body and sees where and how it's inclined to move, so that even without trying to do anything, you're doing it. We all have steps or ways of moving that feel most comfortable, and we tend to impose them on our dancing. Sometimes he lets you indulge in that, but even when he says you can't, there's still a lot of room. In *Ballade*, there was lots of room for me to create whatever relationship I wanted with . . . well, it started out being Sean. I found myself playing around with it; I certainly did not do the same thing in every rehearsal. Balanchine almost never sets arms, and when he does, they're usually quite specific and meant for a very special effect. So I played around with the arms, trying to get different effects. But I don't know what I do out there. I don't know what effects I make. I have my own funny ideas about it, but I don't know that they're right. And I'm sure there are lots of things I would change if I could just see myself.

It's really interesting to listen to comment, and almost more interesting to listen to comments of members of the audience who are not terribly knowledgeable. Especially for me, because I don't have to worry too much technically — it's the other side that's my weak area. People who aren't somehow overwhelmed with how good my technique is focus on other things, and they suddenly say the most perceptive things. When I first met my friend Kibbee, he'd only been going to the ballet for about two years, and he certainly didn't know anything about technique. Well, we went on vacation, we went somewhere out to dinner, and we were dancing. And he said, "You know, I've just watched you for the last minute, and you've had about a hundred different looks on your face. When you dance on the stage, you have two — and they're not particularly attractive, either one of them." Then he said, "I've been afraid to say anything. I know the steps you do are difficult, and you're working so hard at doing steps. But you really have to start using all the rest." Nobody had ever said that to me. Right at that time, everybody was telling me, 'Merrill, you're such a good dancer' and 'I don't know why you're not getting more' and 'It's just not fair, what's happening to you' and all that sort of stuff. And when he suddenly said that, I thought, 'Oh my God, they must all see it. Why hasn't somebody said it?'

Oh, he also said, "You look front all the time. You never stop looking at the audience." But that was one of the things that Jacques used to tell me all the time: 'Look front. Look front. Always look front.' I believed him — I always looked front. But Kibbee said, "It looks so odd. You have to look somewhere else." And he didn't know anything! It was just that, as a member of the audience, he found it peculiar. Those are the things that really affect a performance. They may be little things, but they make all the difference in the world, and people in the company don't ever hear about them. As dancers, we're too involved. I still find myself looking at feet and legs, and forgetting sometimes to look at the whole thing. People who don't know anything automatically look at the whole thing — they can't help but do that.

You can learn a lot from watching yourself on TV, but you can also be misled. It was interesting watching the filming of certain ballets, or even a section that I wasn't involved in, and then looking at the tapes immediately afterwards. You start out watching the real thing, live, and you see certain exciting moments and certain mistakes, a flaw in the partnering or 'Whoops! Didn't that turn look a little shaky?' And then you go to the film, and the botched spots don't look so bad — they're kind of hidden — and something else that you didn't notice at all is suddenly like a big sore thumb. The worst thing is that you lose the excitement, usually when the camera's at a distance. Things that were breathtaking in real life just become 'nice.' It's lost.

It's very hard to dance for the camera. First of all, it's hard to know when your performance is going to be. In the theatre, we build

up and build up, and then suddenly you're out there, you're performing, it's all done at once, and it's finished. And if you didn't like
it, well, better luck next time. With TV, you walk through it, you mark
it for the cameras, and then you mark it some more for the cameras,
and then you change a step or two because 'that didn't look too good
for the cameras.' And then you have a full-out rehearsal to make sure
the final everything is right. And *then* you do it. By which time, it still
feels like the rehearsal. You can't tell whether it's a performance or
not, and there's no continuity. You do your section and stop, and wait
some more. The best is when you can do it in long stretches, but
you're taking more risks that way, because if a step doesn't go well,
you either have to do the whole thing over again or be stuck with the
step that doesn't work. And believe me, by the time you've rehearsed
all that time . . . you care, but your body is so tired that you don't
care anymore. You would rather suffer with that shaky turn than go
back and do it again, because there's certainly no guarantee that the
second time through will be any better.

I kept feeling there were things I should be doing for television
that I shouldn't do on the stage, and vice versa. Or 'When is the close-
up coming?' You never know exactly where the camera is, which leaves
you a little bewildered as to what to do. There's no real way you can
know. *They* don't even know what angle they're going to use sometimes;
when they finally get into the editing, they decide.

The only thing that's missing in my repertoire is a dramatic,
acting role. Lovers in *Midsummer* [*Night's Dream*] is about the closest
I've come to any sort of real acting. I would love to do the Siren in
Prodigal Son — *love* to do it. Other than that, I have the terribly
romantic, lyrical roles, and the terribly technical allegro roles, and
everything in between. But I still have a list. I would love to do *Barocco*.
I would love to do all of *Rubies*; I've only done the pas de deux. I
would just love to try *Bugaku*. I might get into it and think, 'Oops!
It's not really for me,' but I've always been intrigued by it and loved
it, and I think it would be interesting. And *La Valse* I would like to
do. Those are the ones that pop into my mind.

It's funny that I still haven't done that many of Jerry's ballets.
He gives you a more specific idea of what was in *his* mind, what visions
he had. In *Dances*, it's 'Here you're walking through the woods and
looking at the trees. And here you're with your soldier who just came
back from the war, and you haven't seen him for a long time.' He
really gives you something specific to think about, so that you get the
right mood. With Jerry's things — and I've only done *Dances*, *Goldberg*,
and *In the Night* — I have to think less about the steps and try to work
out more of what's in his mind. Actually, the steps feel different; they

tend to be less concrete than with Balanchine. There's a lot of walking and melting from one step into another. It's not as clear-cut, and that's hard for me. And there's almost no pointe work. It's very odd. I'm much more comfortable on pointe. Because of certain injuries and arthritis in my bunions, it really hurts me to go on half-pointe. So one of the hardest things about Jerry's ballets for me is trying to dance on half-pointe. I end up saying, "Do you mind if I do this on pointe?" and he says, "You *want* to do it on pointe?" Most people are trying to get things off pointe, and it's just the opposite for me. It's funny.

I don't think I miss the classics. They're what I was exposed to most when I was young, but I've never felt an overwhelming urge to do them. If I were given the opportunity, I have a feeling I would get quite involved in them and enjoy doing them a lot, but now is not necessarily the time to do it. Physically, the time to do the repertoire that I'm doing now *is* now. Soon the speed will go, and all sorts of things will be harder and harder to do. *Square Dance* will probably be the first thing I'll feel has vanished. The real ability to do it the way I want to is going to go — it already is starting to be harder than it used to be. So I would rather concentrate on those ballets that I can do well now and won't be able to do nearly as well, say, in five years. The classics will always be there, and I might even be able to do them better if I wait longer. I'll be more experienced, more knowledgeable about performing in general, and I'll be able to make my first attempts at a much higher level than if I started now.

I'm trying to do several things at once when I dance — not one or the other. They're equal. I have to please myself. I have to be comfortable and like what I'm doing or there's no point to it, even if everybody else loves it. If I hate it, forget it. And yet, there are lots of things that I enjoy doing, or that come naturally, that aren't particularly attractive to watch, and I have to eliminate those. The audience is definitely a part of the equation. You have to take them into consideration and try to find a way of pleasing them that pleases yourself.

June 1980
New York

Index